Writing Games

Multicultural Case Studies of Academic Literacy Practices in Higher Education

Writing Games

Multicultural Case Studies of Academic Literacy Practices in Higher Education

Christine Pearson Casanave
Keio University

2002

LAWRENCE ERLBAUM ASSOCIATES, PUBLISHERS
Mahwah, New Jersey   London

Lawrence Erlbaum Associates, Inc., Publishers
10 Industrial Avenue
Mahwah, New Jersey 07430

Cover design by Kathryn Houghtaling Lacey

Library of Congress Cataloging-in-Publication Data

Casanave, Christine Pearson, 1944-
    Writing games: multicultural case studies of academic literacy practices in higher
education / Christine Pearson Casanave.
        p. cm.
    Includes bibliographical references and index.
    ISBN 0-8058-3530-X (cloth : alk. paper) – ISBN 0-8058-3531-8 (pbk. : alk. paper)
        1.   English language—Rhetoric—Study and teaching—Social aspects—Case studies. 2,
    English language—Study and teaching (Higher)—Foreign speakers—Case studies. 3.
    Academic writing—Study and teaching—Social aspects—Case studies. 4. Second language
    Acquisition—Case studies. 5. Multicultural education—Case studies. 6. Educational
    Games—Case studies. I. Title

    PE1404 .C35 2002
    808'.042'0711—dc21

                                                                                    2001055592

Books published by Lawrence Erlbaum Associates are printed on acid-free paper,
and their bindings are chosen for strength and durability.

Printed in the United States of America
10   9   8   7   6   5   4   3   2   1

Contents

Foreword

Paul Prior
Center for Writing Studies
University of Illinois at Urbana-Champaign

A central challenge for researchers looking at academic writing and socialization is to capture the relation between the situated personal, and very unsettled experiences of people doing academic work and the seemingly tidy, settled, quite ordered representations of that work that typically appear in books, journals, and other formal settings. Consider, for example, the following two texts:

Writing Games offers a broad and complex exploration of academic writing, disciplinary socialization, and identity work. Drawing especially on theories of practice (e.g., those of Bourdieu, Lave, Wenger, Ortner), Casanave links a series of qualitative case studies, some fairly longitudinal, to create a rich cross-sectional view of trajectories of participation in academic disciplines ranging from early undergraduate classes through professorial work. In an area of research still dominated by decontextualized analyses of texts and case studies focused on single classrooms or organized around the production of single texts, the developmental depth of Casanave's research is striking, as is her strong orientation to questions of diversity and power, to the stories of international students and scholars, women, and U.S. minorities. Casanave's case

It is a cool, cloudy June day. I am sitting at Café Kopi, waiting for Nora to finish her piano lesson, drinking from a large glass of the dark organic house coffee. I begin drafting thoughts for the foreword to Chris' book—a task I need to finish over the next week before the family leaves for 3 weeks of kayaking, hiking, and birding in northern Michigan. The loose pages of her 2-inch thick manuscript sit on the heavily scored wooden table. I am writing on one of the pages, at first blank except for the following inscription: "Foreword, Paul Prior (to be added)." As I write, I am flipping through the pages, reading marginal notes I wrote, looking at passages I underlined. And I am struggling with questions: What is a foreword supposed to accomplish? Am I supposed to sell the value of the book studies are less concerned with how people learn to make academic texts than how people struggle with writing and its contexts, and ultimately with how such writing makes people. *Writing Games* should be of great interest to students learning new games as well as to scholars already deeply involved in the varied overlapping fields interested in academic writing and socialization (e.g., Applied Linguistics, Writing Studies, English for Academic Purposes, Rhetoric, or Higher Education).

to potential buyers, position it in some scholarly frame, or both? Even trivially, I wonder, as I do when writing letters of recommendation, whether to refer to Chris as Chris, Christine, or Casanave? And I worry as well. Will I find a way to write this foreword that satisfies Chris and me? Looking at my watch, I see it's time to go. I gather the pages of the manuscript, cap my red pen, and drain the cup.

The text at left is conventional, author-evacuated, academic prose. The representational focus is on the content of the book and its intertextual relationships to other work in the field. "I" am absent from the text and the subjects of the sentences are objects like *Writing Games*, "Casanave," "Casanave's case studies," and "the developmental depth of Casanave's research." The practice theorists cited are all well known, located particularly in anthropology and balanced in gender. Interpersonally, there are few signs of my relationship to the author, who is named in the same manner as other figures in the text like Bourdieu. The text at right, on the other hand, is descriptive, narrative, autobiographical. It represents a time, a place, certain events. The content is hybrid, with the academic work of a foreword mixed in with the coffee I am drinking, the kind of table I am sitting at, and references to my daughter's piano lessons. "I" am the subject of almost every clause and *Writing Games* is less a reference to a book than to a messy physical object—loose pages, marked up in pen and pencil, lying on a wooden table in the coffee shop. I am not only represented as an academic struggling cognitively with an intellectual problem, but as a person experiencing emotions and juggling family schedules. Finally, the text on the right suggests some interpersonal context between Chris and me, although it doesn't point with any specificity to the 10 years or so of attending each other's conference sessions (at TESOL, CCCC, AERA, the 1996 Uni-versity of Hong Kong Conference on Knowledge and Discourse), to our meetings—sometimes over coffee or a meal, to periodic e-mail exchanges, or to our readings of each other's publications.

Together, these two very divergent representations are relevant to this foreword, not only because of their content, but because in this book Christine Pearson Casanave is working to bridge the many gaps between the two columns.

She is working to write a text that is oriented to, and grounded in, the field and its theories yet is also readable, personal, situated. She is working to produce an account of academic writing and life that acknowledges the value of disciplinary representations in building theory, but that also honors the situated practices and complexly laminated identities out of which such representations are forged. At the center of this effort is her organizing metaphor of games and a multivoiced approach to the writing.

Playing games with texts (cf. Austin, 1962) may not at first seem to capture our sense of the serious and sincere nature of disciplinarity. In Chapter 1 and throughout *Writing Games*, Chris develops the metaphor of academic writing games, making clear that it is intended to invoke neither some idyllic, idealized world of innocent fun nor a world of cynical scheming. Her notion of games draws on Ortner's (1996) accounts of gender identity formation as learning the rules of serious social games, echoes Wittgenstein's (1953) discussions of language games within forms of life, and links up with Bourdieu's (1990) notion that the mark of fluid sophisticated practice in a field is a "feel for the game" (p. 66). Of course, this metaphor also fits well with many students' and scholars' own descriptions of learning to play the games of the academy, being willing (or unwilling) to play along, and sometimes of changing the rules in midstream. In short, it is a serious and powerful metaphor here, as long as it is not read in limiting ways (like games as fun).

One way to read her metaphor is through the everyday prototype of games like chess. This reading highlights the interactive, dialogic nature of games and the idea that years of study and practice are needed for players to develop expertise. Within the rules of chess, there is also considerable room for innovation and personal style. However, we usually think of the rules of such games as fully explicit and fixed, characteristics that few academic games display. Therefore, another valuable prototype would be the games children play, where rules and roles are somewhat negotiable, settled in that gray space defined by power, tradition, liking, affiliation, desire, and interest, often on a thin edge between rigid ritualization and outright revolt ("I quit!"). Chris' accounts of academic writing and disciplinary socialization are not only accounts of learning to play games or of games played, but also very much accounts of games with some play (some degrees of freedom) within them. As you read the literature on academic writing that has emerged since the early 1980s, you can see that it is easy to produce either a top-down vision in which people appear to be automatons assimilated into some disciplinary discourse collective or an asocial, individualistic account of rhetorical free agents who seem to be making everything up as they go. A strength of the game metaphor as Chris deploys it is that it nicely skates the line between the sense of rules as determining the game and the sense of players as agents; It is an account that balances social structure and reflexive actors, very much in keeping, as Chris intends, with Giddens' (1984) notion of structuration.

The game metaphor (following Ortner) is also used here as a way into processes of identity formation, a perspective that might at first seem less familiar. However, what games people play can be linked to identity and social relations in two ways. First, games are themselves socially marked. We expect to find that people who play chess are different in some significant ways from people who play football from people whose game of choice is roulette. Second, we should expect that frequent playing of some game, football or poker, chess or charades, will come to shape a person's practices and personality. Chris' case studies in this book are very much concerned with questions of identity, with ways that particular writing games produce certain kinds of people, oriented to certain kinds of practices, affiliated with (or disaffiliated from) certain groups and institutions.

The many voices of *Writing Games* produce a rich, complex view of academic writing. It is important to note that, in addition to her research over the past decade on how people take up academic writing, Chris has also been a leading advocate of change in academic writing (see Casanave & Schecter, 1997), arguing for the value of personal narratives and accessible writing in demystifying the disciplinary. Chapter 6 focuses in part on the challenges writers face in taking up a different academic voice, especially on the vulnerabilities that can come with certain kinds of personal revelation. However, throughout *Writing Games*, Chris enacts her ideas on academic writing and knowledge making through the voices she presents as well as through the content. In her case studies, Chris weaves together voices from the literature and her own research, from participants and herself. The case studies are presented in very narrative and readable terms, with the actors, their thoughts, and their feelings foregrounded. Moreover, one of Chris' key case studies, the most longitudinal of all, is the autobiographical reflections on her own experiences and transitions from undergraduate to MA teacher-in-training, to PhD candidate to tenured professor in a Japanese university. Chris blends voices comfortably here, producing a text that is attuned with both disciplinary theories and the human experience of disciplines.

As the left column text in the first paragraph suggested, a central contribution of *Writing Games* is its developmental depth. Following Lave and Wenger (1991), we might imagine disciplinary practices as a kind of cone stretching from the very peripheral, shallow participation that happens, say, in elementary school and popular media representations of a field to the highest level of technical scholarship in that field. The cone then would be a space within which people traverse particular trajectories of participation and non-participation, take up and come to own certain practices (never all), and reject others—sometimes disengaging from the field. If you think of the cone as the growth of a person's knowledge and abilities, a trajectory might trace some path from the narrow tip of those early school encounters to the wide circle of full participation. However, if you think of the cone in terms of the number of people participating, the orientation would flip, with the narrow end marking the highest levels of disciplinary work. Of course, as Lave and Wenger's theory would suggest, it is best to think of this cone as a living organism, made up of the people and things operating within it, immersed in the currents of a sociohistoric sea, as an open, constantly changing, living system. *Writing Games* offers the most detailed and fullest views yet published of developmental trajectories in such open disciplinary systems and of the roles writing plays. And it offers these views in a form that is both theoretically rich and readable.

Writing Games succeeds in its goals. It demystifies much about the human experience of learning, writing, and life in the academy. At the same time, it expands the grounds for dialogic, practice-oriented accounts of academic writing and enculturation. It is a book that I greatly admire for all it has achieved.

REFERENCES

Austin, J. L. (1962). *How to do things with words.* Oxford, England: Oxford University Press.

Bourdieu, P. (1990). *The logic of practice* (R. Nice, Trans.). Stanford, CA: Stanford University Press.

Casanave, C. P., & Schecter, S. R. (Eds.). (1997). *On becoming a language educator: Personal essays on professional development.* Mahwah, NJ: Lawrence Erlbaum Assocites.

Giddens, A. (1984). *The constitution of society: Outline of a theory of structuration.* Berkeley, CA: University of California Press.

Ortner, S. B. (1996). *Making gender: The politics and erotics of culture.* Boston, MA: Beacon Press.

Lave, J., & Wenger, E. (1991). *Situated learning: Legitimate peripheral participation.* Cambridge, England: Cambridge University Press.

Wittgenstein, L. (1953). *Philosophical investigations.* (G.E.M. Anscombe, Trans.). Oxford, England: Basil Blackwell.

Preface

This book presents 10 years of my work in the field of academic literacy in higher education. It explores how writers from several different cultures learn to write in their academic settings, and how their writing practices interact with and contribute to their evolving identities, or positionings of themselves, as students and professionals in academic environments in higher education. Embedded in a theoretical framework of situated practice, the naturalistic case studies and literacy autobiographies include portrayals of undergraduate students and teachers, masters level students, doctoral students, young bilingual faculty, and established scholars, all of whom are struggling to understand their roles in ambiguously defined communities of academic writers. It is my hope that readers will find multiple ways to connect their own experiences with those of the writers portrayed in this book. It is also my hope that writing scholars will appreciate a book that pulls together published and previously unpublished case studies, which usually tend to be read as single instances of research, under a common interpretive lens.

The discussions of the studies I present in *Writing Games* reflect a situated and local rather than an abstracted view of academic writing. What abstract theorizing there is appears as one of the several frames in Chapter 1. This framework draws on the work of sociologists and anthropologists who have adopted different versions of a theory of practice to frame their work (e.g., Pierre Bourdieu, Anthony Giddens, Sherry Ortner, Jean Lave, Etienne Wenger). From the perspective of situated practice, the development of academic literacy and identity in university and professional life is seen as the acquisition of a set of local practices, embedded in a larger framework of social practice. Disciplinary enculturation and participation are thus conceptualized as experiences that are necessarily partial, diverse, conflicted, and fragmentary. This conceptualization contrasts with one in which academic writers are depicted as acquiring sets of fixed genre conventions and discipline-specific values. In the situated practice framework, people's writing lives are shown to be influenced by and interwoven with idiosyncratic personal and local factors that may or may not be anchored by more stable genre practices. The result is that writers' identities are always multiple yet incomplete, and their positions within their fields always in transition, as Roz Ivanič (1998) has found in her work on writing and identity. Because of the transitory and fragmented nature of the evolution of people's identities in academic settings, I portray writers in this book as seeking coherence and stability in the midst of complexity and uncertainty. This search for coherence involves activities that are not just cognitive, linguistic, and intellectual but also deeply social and political. Writers do not write in isolation but within networks of more and less powerfully situated colleagues and community members. They learn to forge alliances with those community members with whom they share values or whom they perceive will benefit them in some way and to resist when accommodating does not suit them. Both newcomers and oldtimers in academia shift roles and locations over time and across settings, with greater and lesser senses of agency and control.

In addition to the notion of practice, the other powerful concept used as an interpretive framework in *Writing Games* is captured by the metaphor of "serious games" (Ortner, 1996; Chapter 1). This metaphor suggests first that social life itself, including the social practice of writing in academic settings, is organized according to sets of rules, conventionalized practices, and strategies. Second, goal-oriented actors interact and shift identities and positions as they learn to participate in the multitude of structured social practices—the games—that make up our social life. Third, the players are constrained by game rules but retain agency and intention that allow them to play strategically, stretching the game rules, finding inconsistencies and loopholes, and interpreting ambiguities in ways both reinforce and change the game. In short, the game metaphor is designed to emphasize the point that the practice of academic writing is shaped but not dictated by rules and conventions, that writing games consist of the practice of playing not of the rules themselves, and that writers have choices about whether and how to play.

Writing Games has a multicultural focus in the sense that the people I portray are from a number of different cultures within and outside North America. Often the term *multicultural* is understood as "nonnative-English speaking" or as referring to nonmainstream ethnic diversity. However, my intention in this book is not to front the non-nativeness of any of the characters or to dwell on cultural, ethnic, or linguistic differences among them. Several key presumptions in the book are first that mainstream Whites[1] are necessarily included in the term multicultural; second that mainstream Whites (or any other cultural or ethnic group for that matter) cannot be considered a homogeneous group because of significant within-group differences; and third that in spite of obvious and serious imbalances and injustices, cultural, ethnic, linguistic, and social class diversity is increasingly common in English-medium college and university classrooms, in Internet communication, and in globally oriented professions. This diversity, though not the injustices, therefore needs to be treated as normal in the sense that we are discussing practices and issues that affect all students in similar ways, regardless of cultural background. Such is the case with learning to write in academic settings:

---

[1]I struggled with the use of the term *White* in this book, since in discussions of ethnic and cultural diversity it seems to be the one remaining term that refers to people by color. With some reluctance, I use the term as a default term, as do Robin Lakoff (2000) and many others to refer to Caucasian ethnic groups. I apologize to any readers who may be offended by my choice.

All students are thrown onto the same playing field and engage in many new practices and ways of thinking. Differences surface everywhere as students, teachers, and researchers learn to accommodate, to resist, and to shape practices. However, the significant differences have as much to do with factors such as experience with academic literacy, purpose, and access to mentoring and apprenticeship relationships as they do with the cultural, ethnic, and linguistic backgrounds of the players. A detailed discussion of the political, ethical, and gender issues in the study of academic writing is the subject of another book, which others are attending to (e.g., Benesch, 2001; Canagarajah, 1999; Kirsch, 1993; Norton, 2000; Pennycook, 1994).

Although this book is about writing and writers, it is not a linguistics book. It does not frame issues from a linguistic perspective and I do not analyze any writing linguistically. Rather, it is an interdisciplinary book that fits within naturalistic, case study, and narrative research in the fields of first and second language education and writing. Focusing on people rather than on experiments, numbers, and abstractions, it draws on concepts and methods from narrative inquiry, qualitative anthropology and sociology, and from case studies of academic literacy in the field of composition and rhetoric. The book also follows to some extent the postmodern tradition of multivocality. As author, I position myself as both insider and outsider and take on the different voices of each. Other voices that appear in the book are those of my case study participants, other authors, and their case study participants. My own case study participants come from different cultures and subcultures in the United States and Japan. They are portrayed as individual writers engaged in a broad array of writing practices rather than as representatives of any particular group. Readers are not expected to learn about culture-specific or genre-specific writing practices, in others words, but to come to appreciate the diverse and locally situated nature of academic writing and to ask questions about themselves and their own students and colleagues as writers.

The style of the book is accessible and reader friendly, eschewing highly technical insider language without dismissing complex issues. It includes my own persona as reflective actor and agent, and portrays participants as people with whom readers can connect and interact. Although I refer to much of the literature on academic literacy, I also discuss several important published case studies in more detail than is usually done in a traditional literature review. Along with my own research, these detailed summaries become part of the case studies of the book and help make writing experiences come alive. One of the purposes of the book is just this: to portray issues and actors in such a way that readers can relate them to issues and experiences in their own lives. The detailed presentation of a small number of individual studies helps achieve this purpose. A further characteristic of the style of the book is its questioning and inconclusive stance, designed to tweak the curiosities and imaginations of seasoned as well as novice academic writers. Questions are integrated into the prose itself instead of being presented in more didactic discussion sections, and consist of issues that are unresolved in the field and that promise no easy prescriptions or solutions. The questions lay out and probe a variety of scenarios that can be transposed and adapted to readers' own experiences.

In general, *Writing Games* is designed for people who wish to see issues in the development of academic literacy reflectively, from multiple perspectives, including their own, within a framework of situated practice. More specifically, it is intended for graduate students, teachers, and scholars of academic writing at the university level who are interested in learning more about their own and their students' and colleagues' writing experiences, and in exploring how those writing experiences contribute to changing professional identities over time. The book's concentration on specific, concrete cases will be especially valuable for students and practitioners in English for Academic Purposes (EAP), language teacher education, and rhetoric and composition studies. In particular, it provides graduate students and novice scholars in writing with a rich introduction to the literature and key issues in academic literacy in higher education. As such, the book is about them as well as for them.

As will become clear, my general stance is that some or many aspects of academic writing are difficult for most of us. I don't know how accurate my perception is, and am aware that a few of my own colleagues disagree with me. I know, therefore, that it is possible that those readers of this book who find academic writing to be a joyful and relatively unconflicted activity will not relate to my own anguish at writing and to the many stories of frustration and conflict presented in the following pages. If you are one of these fortunate people, then the experiences that I relate may help you understand what the rest of us go through. For those readers who share my love-hate relationship with academic writing, my message to you is that in spite of the difficulties, the effort is usually worthwhile. The writers in the case studies that I discuss in this book all had difficulties of one kind or another, yet most succeeded in their own ways. I continue writing in spite of many moments of doubt partly for the pleasure of seeing a creative task through to some kind of completion and partly for the way writing pushes me to continue studying, learning, and organizing my thinking. Stories of struggle, in other words, do not need to end in despair and failure. The struggle enriches and even contributes to the successes.

CHAPTER STRUCTURE AND CONTENTS

Writing Games has seven chapters. The first chapter lays out some conceptual issues and frames the subsequent chapters in several ways. Chapters 2 to 6 present studies of writers and writing teachers in higher education from the perspectives of undergraduates, masters students, doctoral students, novice faculty, and established faculty. Chapter 7 concludes the manuscript.

Each of Chapters 2 to 6 is divided into several sections that differ in style and purpose. These sections can be read separately or as part of the whole chapter. The first part consists of a personal introduction in which I recount some of my own experiences with writing as an undergraduate, graduate student, and professional. I reflect on issues that have puzzled and intrigued me over the years and that motivated my reading and research in academic literacy. My main purpose in beginning in this unconventionally personal way is to encourage readers to approach the issues in the book from an equally personal perspective. The book is not full of information to be absorbed but of experiences to be reflected upon. Readers' involvement with the themes in the book will deepen as they see themselves and their own practices in its pages.

The second section in each chapter introduces key issues from the field of academic literacy by reviewing some relevant literature including case studies. This fairly traditional literature review provides graduate students in particular with an introduction to what scholars of academic literacy have been interested in in recent years. This review is followed by a less conventional approach to the literature—a more detailed summary of several well-known published case studies and literacy autobiographies of academic writers. The more detailed summaries convey the experiences of actual writers, and it is this kind of detail that I wish to highlight in this book.

The third section of each chapter presents my own research. This work consists of naturalistic case-study type research in which I look at a small number of people and their writing practices within one setting. One of my goals is to present opportunities for readers to relate the issues and practices I discuss to their own writing lives, not to make general statements about writing or writers. The final section consists of Chapter Reflections. The content of each of the chapters is summarized next.

In Chapter 1 I discuss several key concepts that form the foundation for the ways the case studies in this book are conceptualized and interpreted, first from a common sense perspective, and then from a more theoretical perspective. In my common sense introduction the first concept is that of academic writing seen metaphorically as a game. The second is the concept of transitions, the main thrust of the argument being that personal and professional transitions of many kinds constitute an inevitable aspect of the writing life in academe. A third concept is that of identity in academic settings. These "common sense" notions provide the basic rationale for why I wrote the book. In the following section, I present an accessible theoretical framework based on the notions of situated practice, identity, and disciplinary enculturation. The framework of practice includes the following: a broad theoretical view of practice; a view of practice as situated learning; and a genre-based perspective on the practice of writing. This section is followed by a theoretical discussion of identity. I review here a small body of work that emphasizes the multiple, changing, and contested aspects of identity.

One of my purposes is to find a way to talk about the longing for coherence of identity and practice (a topic to which I return in the conclusion), since the postmodern view of the fragmented self contradicts the desires of people for stability and coherence in their lives. This section also includes a discussion of the concept of disciplinary enculturation, its necessary redefinition as a fluid and fuzzy, rather than unambiguously definable notion, and the place of texts in the enculturation experience. Because a piece of writing in some sense represents a self that is put forward for public scrutiny, the issues of identity and disciplinary enculturation intertwine. In the final two sections of Chapter 1 I review the assumptions that I began the project with and describe the methodologies I used to carry out the case studies.

Chapter 2 focuses on academic writing in undergraduate settings. I review several well known case studies of undergraduate students and then present my own study of two teachers of an undergraduate academic writing class in a Japanese university. The research adds to the debate about whether a "community of practice" (Wenger, 1998) can be established in such a setting and about how to help students prepare for the transition from EAP (English for Academic Purposes) classes to classes in various disciplines. A basic question in this chapter asks to what extent the academic literacy practices of undergraduates represent a game of survival in a fragmented environment or an introduction to the serious academic games that characterize different disciplines.

In Chapter 3 I summarize several case studies of students learning to write in academic settings at the masters level. I then introduce five masters degree students in TESOL (Teaching English to Speakers of Other Languages) from my own research. These students were trying to figure out how to play the writing games in their MA program as they learned to write for different professors, and who they were becoming as a result of the interaction between the demands of their program and their personal goals. The students faced a variety of practices and professional values in their courses and needed to sort out the messages implied in their writing practices in the process of developing their own professional identities. One of my questions about these students was whether the academic literacy practices they learned in a short 12- to 18-month program could contribute to their evolving identities as professionals in language education or whether in situ practice in the workplace would be needed to help them step into the profession.

I introduce the research in Chapter 4 with some well known studies of the academic enculturation of doctoral students. The chapter continues with my own case study of a first year doctoral student in sociology, "Virginia," and her response to "indoctrination" courses in two core theory courses. Though the courses required recipe-like writing games, Virginia and her classmates began shaping their academic identities in a variety of directions, through accommodation, resistance, and acknowledged game playing rather than through the classic notion of enculturation. This chapter raises questions about the purposes and practices of doctoral programs and about what might be considered successful cases of disciplinary enculturation.

Chapter 5 focuses on the academic writing experiences of young bilingual faculty. It begins with the summaries of the published literacy autobiographies of two bilingual academics, who reflect on the writing games they needed to play in their second languages as they established themselves in their careers. It continues with my case study of two young bilingual academics in their first academic positions at a Japanese university. These Japanese-born scholars, educated in PhD programs in the United States with certain sets of values associated with writing and publishing, were struggling to establish themselves in two academic cultures, one in Japan and the other in North America. They faced daily decisions about who they wanted to become, how to divide their time between writing in English and in Japanese, and what kinds of writings to prepare for the different audiences within and outside Japan. A key question in this chapter concerns how multilingual academics learn to play the serious game of constructing and maintaining multiple professional identities and how they forge allegiances and alliances in their academic literacy practices.

Chapter 6 focuses on the efforts of established academics to bend some of the conventional game rules of academic discourse and to write in ways that are both more personal and more openly multivocalic and reflective. I discuss Victor Villanueva's mixed-genre literacy autobiography, *Bootstraps* (1993), then turn to an experience I had as a coeditor of a book of personal scholarly narratives and to the author–editor relationship between me and several authors who were having difficulty letting go of their familiar academic discourse conventions. We all had trouble constructing a coherent and convincing personal narrative about our own professional identities. The negotiations we undertook and the views of the authors as to where the difficulties lay highlight both how important and how challenging it is for established scholars in language education to expand the range of styles and voices in which they write (i.e., to learn to play new games). Questions raised in this chapter deal with the relationship between status and risk taking in academic writing and with the nature of the author-editor relationship.

The main purpose of Chapter 7 is to reflect on the case studies and to suggest that academic writing games can be characterized as "efforts after coherence" within social, political, and discoursal playing fields. In seeking coherence of identity and practice, writers, teachers, and researchers create and impose order from the complexity and uncertainty that surrounds them and at the same time, paradoxically pursue complexity as part of the academic writing game. I emphasize that academic writing involves the serious game of making choices and constructing selves, not of finding and representing truth. In this chapter as well as throughout the book readers are urged to look closely and reflectively at their own past and present writing experiences and at the teaching and learning of writing in their professional lives. They are encouraged to consider these practices as creative "efforts after coherence" in the face of otherwise intolerable complexity.

ACKNOWLEDGMENTS

No piece of writing of this scope comes into being without a great deal of participation of others, directly and indirectly. Many case study participants contributed time, talk, and feedback to me throughout my various research activities. Without them there would be no book. Colleagues and friends helped me think, rephrase, cut, and focus. Other colleagues and friends doled out encouragement when my energies flagged. Special thanks go to my friend and colleague Yasuko Kanno, who read and commented on much of the manuscript and who has thus seen my writing at its worst and still urged me to go forward, and to Paul Prior, whose work is reflected throughout this book and whose ideas and encouragement have inspired me for the last decade. Others on my list of important people to thank include David Shea, who has shared ideas with me over the years and helped me develop my thinking about academic writing; Naomi Silverman at Lawrence Erlbaum Associates, who believed in me and this project from start to finish and thus helped bring it to life; and Charles Bazerman, Diane Belcher, Paul Kei Matsuda, and Trudy Smoke, whose valuable critical commentary and insightful suggestions on the original prospectus and on the later draft manuscript have helped shaped this book from its earliest stages. If I have not lived up to their expectations the blame lies entirely with me. For other kinds of help of the more tedious kind I thank Carry Miller, Kyla Stinnett, Hideyuki Kubo, and Sondra Guideman. For their generous support of my research activities since 1990 I am deeply indebted to Keio University in Fujisawa, Japan.

I dedicate this book to my father, Gordon Francis Pearson, who doesn't have a clue what it's about but who loves me anyway.

—Christine Pearson Casanave

1

Games and Frames:
When Writing Is More Than Writing

In this chapter I introduce the key ideas in this book: that academic writing is a game-like social and political as well as discoursal practice that takes places within communities of practice, and that writers' practices and identities in academic settings change over time. I frame the studies in this book in two ways. First, I present a "common sense" frame. I begin with a common sense view because this is where my own interests and insights began, and because I believe that I am not alone in having experienced and thought about academic writing from the perspective of one deeply engaged in the day-to-day practices of it. I then stand back and look at some of the same issues more theoretically, framing them in the voices of others. A third kind of frame grows out of these two, and forms my underlying assumptions about academic literacy practices—assumptions with which I began and continue my work in academic literacy, and assumptions that I continue to refine and revise. I conclude this introductory chapter with some thoughts on case study methodology and with a description of my own methods and procedures.

A WORD ON FRAMES .

I seek ways to frame the issues discussed in this book that encompass the local and situated aspects of the different projects I have been involved in over the years. Written as a simple sentence like this, the project of framing sounds eminently sensible and not particularly daunting. However, I often find the task of framing difficult, partly because there is so much to choose from. Frames of many different kinds and styles can help explain the same phenomena. It is also the case that in my work I have always been more caught up in the details of local practices than in the explanatory functions of broader frameworks. But I recall in my early college days as an art student that sometimes a frame made all the difference in how I saw and understood the details.

In the field of art, in order to set off an artwork so as to see it in one way and not another, I can choose a fancy gilt frame with multiple layers of matt, a simple aluminum or wood frame with a single matt, or a uniframe that barely encloses a picture at key points on all four sides—just enough so that the picture can be tied in the back and hung from the wall. One frame is not necessarily wrong and another right, though one may be esthetically more pleasing than another, or highlight one aspect of a print and not another. In discussing frames for my case studies in academic literacy, I need to recognize that similar criteria apply: There is no right or wrong; some frames will be esthetically more pleasing than others; some will highlight these, and not those, aspects of what I am observing. And I do not need to be committed to framing a print, or my research, in just one way. I can experiment with one frame today, and if I am not pleased with it tomorrow, or next year, change it for another. I can also, as I do in this first chapter, think about several kinds of frames simultaneously. I do not need to fear experimenting or succumb to the dreaded academic phobia, Fear of Framing. So onward.

Perhaps because of my interest in local practices and in specific people I have found myself most attracted to discussions of academic literacy that assume that learning to write is as much a localized social and political as a cognitive activity, and that it is above all an *activity*, a way of doing and being in particular social settings, a specialized form of practice. Like the social oriented theorists, I see the practice of writing, in other words, as involving much more than learning to put thoughts to paper or screen, although I myself felt consumed by this challenge when I was in graduate school. At that time I did not see clearly and could not express well in words the many other aspects of writing as a social practice that influence what writers can say, who they can say it to, how they can say it, and how it reflects who they are or how they wish to be seen. By "can" I don't mean just "ability." I refer to what writers in academic settings are allowed to say within various webs of convention, power, and expertise (i.e., within the "rules of the game") and to how they conform to, resist, and construct identity-shaping practices. Several common sense and theoretical perspectives help tie these practices together. In the discussions that follow, therefore, I experiment with frames for the case studies in this book that help me understand the local as well as the broader aspects of academic writing as social practice, ones within which concepts like "game," "transitions," "identity," and "disciplinary enculturation" can comfortably fit.

COMMON SENSE BEGINNINGS

Why the Game Metaphor?

For many years I have seen and heard the word "game" used in reference to what it is like to learn to write in the university. The word is also used quite casually in articles on composition and rhetoric, and by a number of people I have interviewed as part of my research over the years. It seems to depict people's sense that academic writing consists of rule- and strategy-based practices, done in interaction with others for some kind of personal and professional gain, and that it is learned through repeated practice rather than just from a guidebook of how to play. I recall in particular a young man from the United States, in his first year of a doctoral program that I was observing, using the word "game" to depict his decision to go along with a particular way of doing sociology at his university. He had determined to finish the program as quickly as he could, without causing himself major philosophical and methodological stumbling blocks. "I'll play their game for a while," he told me, suggesting that he remained, at the end of his first year at any rate, noncommittal about whether he wished to assimilate the foundational beliefs and values of his professors' world views, or just plain get through the program and on to the rest of his life.

There are no doubt dozens of other ways I could characterize academic writing, but I chose to use the metaphor of a game in this project, since this one has been reappearing in my thinking about academic writing over many years. Let me go over some of my "common sense" thinking on this metaphor, with the understanding that I intend the metaphor to function only as a conceptual tool, not to be taken too literally as an analogy or as a sign of cynicism. (See the discussion of Ortner, 1996, below.)

At first glance, the game metaphor may seem to trivialize the very serious topic of academic writing. Games are usually fun, not life-controlling or threatening, and they tend to be associated with play and not work.[1] Most of us do not view our academic lives as a game in this playful sense (although I think our professional and personal lives might be better off if we did). As most of us know first hand, the academic writing that students, teachers, and researchers do can affect course grades, graduation, hiring, promotion, tenure, and reputation. However, I think a number of common

---

[1] I do not discuss here the negative connotation given to "games" such as that in Eric Berne's popular 1960s tome on transactional analysis, even though the idea of strategic behavior is comparable. Berne's use of "game" as strategic manipulations that people use in relationships—"an ongoing series of complementary ulterior transactions progressing to a well-defined, predictable outcome" (Berne, 1964, p. 48) may fit better in my context than the idea of game as entertainment. Both, however, miss the point that I wish to make about the seriousness and inevitability of games in structured social situations.

sense aspects of the notion of game fit the serious dimensions of our way-too-serious academic writing practices.

Games, for instance, are played according to rules, conventions, and strategies (see the discussion of Anne Freadman's [1994] work on genre below)—a handy way to envision what we do as academic writers. There are various ways to compete in different kinds of games, and relatively clear-cut ways to determine winners and losers, often through systems of judges and referees and scorekeepers. Players can choose from rather solitary games, or can play in teams and groups. In some games it may be possible to invent and modify rules, whereas in others it is necessary to follow externally imposed rules, with whatever flexibility that may be needed to fit within those strict guidelines. In all cases, including the case of academic writing, a range of rules and conventions guides the players, and helps them decide whether to follow or flout the rules, or indeed whether to play at all.

Games differ in the extent to which the outcomes are determined by chance or by skill, or as may more often be the case, by an interweaving of both. A player may carefully orchestrate the steps and stages of a game in strategic and insightful ways, then be undone by a mistake caused by a bad night's sleep, a competitor who cheats, a mistake made by a referee, or a flukish missed opportunity. Players who win one round may explicably or inexplicably lose another, but as long as they keep playing, the tournament will continue. Few players, in other words, win or lose all the time. Knowing how to do both gracefully, knowing when to stay in the game or to drop out altogether, knowing that there is this choice, characterize the insightful and savvy player.

Players who are new to a game usually don't play very well. Depending on the difficulty and complexity of the game, novice players may require months or years to advance to expert status. They need to practice, observe, imitate, and rehearse until they internalize or embody the rules so that the rules no longer require their conscious attention. Recall Michael Polanyi's (1966/1983) discussions of tacit knowledge, how this knowledge is part of one's body—an "indwelling." "When we make a thing [a tool, in his example, but also a game?] function as the proximal term of tacit knowing, we incorporate it in our body—or extend our body to include it—so that we come to dwell in it" (p. 16). Players who wish to become experts need also to acquire a deeper, perhaps more conscious knowledge of the rules (if they believe that this kind of metacognitive understanding will help boost their performance). As Polanyi said, "The formal rules of prosody may deepen our understanding of so delicate a thing as a poem" (p. 20).

Where novice players are serious and willing amateurs or budding professionals by choice, uncoerced by murky and malignant internal and external forces (greed, desire for fame rather than the desire to excel, pressure from institutions and authority figures who do not have the best interests of players in mind), the practice, though effortful and burdensome perhaps, can be undertaken with enjoyment, energy, and purpose. Players who enter a game unwillingly, or when they don't understand or agree with the rules, when they do not or cannot practice enough, when other players or referees wear them out by undermining their efforts, suffer all the torments of anyone asked to perform complex tasks without sufficient information, experience, sense of purpose, or support. In both my teaching and my writing I have experienced, and observed others experiencing, both the joys and the tortures of playing academic writing games.

Another aspect of this initial common sense characterization of the game metaphor for this book on academic writing concerns the variability in players' commitment to the game, as suggested in the preceding paragraph. Some players take the game very seriously, letting it consume their lives even at the expense of other important things in life (such as real play), whereas others do not play with enough effort or attention to allow themselves to progress in any meaningful way. Trainers and coaches and teachers thus agonize over what to do with a half-hearted player, who, for personal or external reasons cannot drop out or chooses not to. Insightful players themselves, feeling trapped at either end of this extreme, may agonize similarly. Quite a serious game indeed.

A reviewer of something I wrote once took issue with my description of academic writing as a "writing game," probably because I had not fully explained the serious side of this metaphor. This reviewer claimed that he or she took the activities and mission of academic writing as a professional quite seriously, and actively and willingly subscribed to the values reflected in the field's writing. Many of us do so, if not with whole-hearted internal conviction at least partially, with varying degrees of instrumental as well as integrative motivation. But the issue of whether one takes an instrumental view of academic writing or believes that writers do or must incorporate a field's practices and values internally does not detract from the game metaphor. In both cases, people must play some serious games. Moreover, the metaphor seems particularly apt if we are trying to represent how novices or transitioning professionals experience unfamiliar literacy practices, such as the acquisition of specialist genres that form part of the practices of rhetorical communities.

Finally, the notion of games is easily conceptualized as a plural phenomenon, allowing me to refer throughout this book to a multiplicity of games involving a wide range of formal and informal discoursal and social conventions. Most academic writers, I presume, are probably playing several kinds of academic writing games at the same time. Whether we are students or scholars, most of us have experienced what it is like to: second-guess what a teacher, reviewer, or editor expects on a paper; select appropriate literature for a literature review and then find language that is polite yet authoritative for discussing the works of others; shape one's reading, writing, and thinking so they fit within the fuzzy boundaries of a scholarly community and use the formal conventions of structure and lexicon that suit that community; read a colleague's or student's work in order to assist the writer in moving a piece of writing forward according to a balance of personal goals and academic convention; react with consternation at oppressive discourse conventions such that we seek ways to resist; learn to contribute to rather than just observe and absorb academic "conversations." All of these I consider to be examples of the many serious academic writing games in postsecondary educational settings.

To conclude this section, I do not wish to suggest that all academic writers themselves consciously play at behaving like assimilated or contrarian members of a community or themselves hold a gamelike view of their behaviors. Novice academic writers, for instance, may or may not benefit from seeing their enculturation experiences as game-like. I believe, however, that such a view might help them see the strategic, convention-based nature of writing and thus to appreciate their own agency in choosing how to play. It might additionally help speed up students' active involvement in their own learning processes and their own perception that many choices are available to writers. It could help them escape the sense that they are constrained by one mythical kind of academic discourse, and it could also help them become aware of the time required to learn to play well. On the other hand, without some rather sophisticated perspective taking, it might convey to novices the impression that the rules and conventions of the game leave little room for choice, flexibility, and change, or that writing practices involve trappings rather than identities, stances, and values. I hope that teachers, students, and scholars of writing, should they choose to see their own writing through the lens of the game metaphor, adopt the belief that writing offers them choices and potential empowerment as they learn how to participate skillfully and flexibly in academic writing games.

Transitions

I guess I first got interested in the transitions that people make during university life when I was in the middle of a PhD program as an older student. Well, "older" is relative, I suppose—many of my colleagues at the particular school of education that I was attending were in their 30s and 40s. At any rate, it struck me about half way through my program that many of the people I knew entered PhD programs with one sense of who they were and what they wanted (some with much clearer ideas than others) and left with a different view. I wondered what it was that went on in the ensuing years that prompted this transformation. Given that our lives were characterized by literate activities day and night (we read, we wrote, we learned symbols and acronyms, we read some more, we studied and made tables and graphs, we wrote even more, endlessly . . .), I postulated some connection between these activities and people's evolving, transforming identities. As is the case when people learn any kind of game, they do not begin with the identity of an expert player. They gain expertise through long hours (years?) of practice with the tools and rules of the game in the company of experts.

Luckily for me, I was evolving my own identity in the presences of Arthur Applebee and Judith Langer at that time, and Arthur, on learning of my curiosities, passed on to me a paper he and Judith were reviewing as editors of the journal *Research in the Teaching of English*—Lucille McCarthy's study of an undergraduate learning to write in several different courses, "A Stranger in Strange Lands . . ." (McCarthy, 1987). This paper led me to others, including another key study, still cited often, Ann Herrington's study of the ways of writing and thinking in two chemical engineering classes (Herrington, 1985). Judith and Arthur themselves were working on *How Writing Shapes Thinking* (Langer & Applebee, 1987). These works, and my ongoing curiosity about what was happening to me and my colleagues, led to my own study of disciplinary socialization. When I graduated, I recognized that my identity too had changed in interesting ways. I had entered with a strong sense of self as an ESL teacher and left not knowing who I was or where I belonged. So much for the traditional notion of disciplinary enculturation. I reflect more on this experience later in the chapter and in Chapter 4. (My transition turned out to be for the better, in retrospect, although I have not known since then what to put on a business card.)

Nearly 10 years later, I was interviewing, as part of another leg of this research, a woman who was a visiting international student in the MATESOL program at the Monterey Institute of International Studies in California. (I'll talk more about her in Chap. 3.) I gave her my interview guidelines for that day's interview, which was to deal with what it was like for her to write for different professors in this program. We did talk about that, but she also eagerly told me of a revelation she had had the day before about herself: She had suddenly become aware of how much she had changed since entering the program in Monterey. A teacher with many years of experience, she had been exchanging e-mail with a well-known American professor with whom she was working on her MA and who had helped set up an American university program in her home country of Armenia. Her e-mail to him that day, she jubilantly proclaimed, suddenly felt like it had a professional ring to it. Not just the language she was using, she clarified, but also the concepts she was using to talk about her MA research project plans. This is an example of some of the transitions I explore in my case studies of people writing in academic settings.

Another aspect of the notion of transitions has been piquing my curiosity in the last several years, during my work with undergraduate students in Japan (see Chapter 2). A couple of years ago, a colleague and I decided that our students (some of whom were near native speakers of English having spent formative years in an English-speaking country) needed a course that would help them make the transition from a Japanese undergraduate university to an English medium graduate school. An increasing number of our students, it seemed to us, were applying for masters programs in North America and England, yet there was nothing in our general "intensive English program" that would help these students understand what was facing them in terms of the amount and kinds of reading and writing they would be doing. I had been writing letters of recommendation for some of these students, praising their English language proficiency, but not really knowing whether these students could handle the workloads or the synthetic, analytic, and critical reading and writing skills that I myself had suffered greatly to learn in the course of my own graduate reading and writing practices. Even mother-tongue English speakers struggle with these literacy games. To be fair to these students, we reasoned, we needed to provide some assistance that eased them toward this transition. The transition, in other words, was one that the students had not yet experienced but that the designers and teachers of this course had experienced themselves and were imagining for the students. As a colleague and I became more involved with several of the teachers of this course as part of a research project, we realized that transitions in practices intertwined with transitions in identities.

Two other kinds of transitions captured my imagination in recent years, both involving writing. One concerned the ways that young bilingual faculty on my Japanese university campus—people with graduate degrees from North American universities—negotiated the transition from their university life of writing for and with an English-medium research faculty (advisors, professors, colleagues) to a two-pronged writing life in the Japanese university (see Chap. 5). In their new jobs, they felt pressured to write in Japanese and participate in Japanese academic societies, yet were deeply enmeshed in ongoing conference, writing, and research projects in the medium of English. What kinds of identities had these faculty formed during their graduate studies, and how were those identities changed or changing as they learned to participate in academic literacy games in the Japanese setting? How were some of the more established bilingual professors managing this two-pronged life?

The other perspective on transitions struck me during a 5-year editing project with a colleague. In this project we sought out well-established educators in fields of first language, second language, and bilingual education, and asked them to document a career-evolving event or events in their lives—to relate how people and happenings helped them shape who they were becoming in their professional lives (see Chap. 6). The phenomena we were asking people to reflect on were themselves transitional sorts of life experiences. However, another aspect of the transition was motivated by the very writing of the essays, which we requested be written in a personal and narrative form, eschewing jargon, esoteric theorizing, and the voices of others (i.e., literature reviews and concomitant citation practices). We were not requesting simplistic narratives of "how I became a famous person," but deeply reflective and personal explorations of unresolved issues in the lives of the authors. We asked for the authority of the pieces to emerge out of the voices of each author without overt reference to a professional life full of the familiar supporting voices of mentors and literatures. We asked authors, in other words, to write in what was for many of them an unconventional academic style about things they had not written about before in public. We asked them, I now see in retrospect, to break or bend some of the rules of conventional academic discourse. Little did we realize how difficult it would be for some of us (I include myself here) to shift our discourse from our familiar "academic" stances and tones to a more reflective, personal positioning of ourselves within academe. This game was unfamiliar to many of us.

In short, I believe that changes and transitions of many kinds figure as basic to people's experiences with academic writing over time. I don't know fully how to characterize these transitions yet. Nevertheless, I see change all around me, as well as great resistance to change, in the academic literacy practices of students, teachers, and professional academic writers. People seek stability, yet must change in order to learn and grow—an uncomfortable and paradoxical inevitability.

Identity

The constructs of transitions and identity intertwine so thoroughly that they cannot be separated except artificially for purposes of discussion, which is what I continue to do in this section. I must admit up front that I discuss the notion of identity with some trepidation, even though I've said often in the work that I do that I am more interested in the relationship between writing and professional or academic identity than I am in microanalyzing linguistic aspects of academic texts. This means I must harbor some sense of what I mean by *identity*—a complex, slippery, vague, and even misleading term. In its common usage it is probably too abstract and too imprecise to serve me well, and I do not have the background in psychology to discuss it from that disciplinary perspective. Further complicating my discussion of identity is the view from the postmodernist camp that I am outdated and misguided in my attraction to the term. I recall once at a conference chatting with a woman at lunch about the term. She informed me in the firmest possible way that I would not be able to use the term *identity* in a way that the academic community would accept in this postmodern era, and that I must, instead, use a term like *poststructural subject* and talk about *subject positioning* rather than the development of identity. After lunch, Roz Ivanič, who had been sitting across from us, told me that she herself was just finishing a book in which the word "identity" appeared in the title, and as a key concept in her own studies of academic writing (Ivanič, 1998). She claimed she had used the term purposely throughout her work because it was so commonly (if intuitively) understood, and because she wished to reach a broad audience of people without putting off those who don't take to postmodern jargon. I resonated with this line of thinking, and thus chose to use the word "identity" in my own work, alongside notions of subjectivity and positioning. In the discussion that follows, I offer some common sense views of identity that help explain the interests that motivated the research that I describe in this book. I wrestle with a more theoretical discussion of identity below, "in the voices of others," but refer interested readers to (Ivanič's (1994, 1998) more thorough discussion of this construct and how it figures in discussions of writers and writing.

At one level, I see identity as tied up with language in the form of labels, and with actions, in the form of what people feel they can do and say in different rhetorical situations. For example, in some settings, I label myself a teacher. But if someone asks me what I consider a teacher to be and do, I can construe an additional cluster of labels with which to identify myself: facilitator, manager, evaluator, mentor, disciplinarian, nurturer, proofreader and editor, grammarian, resource person. . . . Within one setting, according to what I am doing and with whom, I may use or be referred to by one or more of these labels, all under the umbrella term "teacher." A common sense view of labels, then, includes those that people apply to themselves (internal labels), and those that other people apply to them (external labels). These internal and external labels mutually construct each other in many cases and clash in others. The fact that people can apply so many different labels (and layers of labels) to themselves and others demonstrates that identities are never unitary, but always multiple, even if they describe more or less marginal and core aspects of selves. It also demonstrates that identities in great part are a matter of perceptions of self and others rather than objective and stable constructs.

In my discussions with doctoral students in sociology (Casanave, 1990, 1995b; Chap. 4) and with several bilingual academics in Japan (Chap. 5), I was interested in how people's labels for themselves changed over time within the academic settings in which they were studying and working. One man in the sociology program, early in his first year of doctoral studies, labeled himself a "graduate student." By the middle of his second year, he was ready to add (not substitute) the label "novice sociologist." One of the bilingual academics in Japan that I got to know was still working on his dissertation proposal in communication from an American university during the first year of his 3-year research and teaching contract at our university. He still saw himself as a graduate student in that first year, and spoke once of enjoying "recovering his identity" as a graduate student during a long academic break where he had the chance to work on his proposal. He described how he loved the uninterrupted time during which he could surround himself with books and papers, as he had done during his graduate studies in the United States. By the time he was in the third year of his contract at the Japanese university, however, his view of himself had changed, although his dissertation was still not finished. Having seen his first publications in print, presented at several international conferences, and secured a permanent position for the following year at another Japanese university, he had begun to see himself as a budding professional academic, one who was evolving an identity as a specialist in Japan on simulation and gaming.

My own labels for myself have changed over the years, suggesting that my multiple identities are in flux, an observation that helped generate my curiosity about professional identity. To be frank, I was far more comfortable in the 1970s when I saw myself rather unambiguously as an ESL specialist. Then I went to graduate school at Stanford's School of Education for doctoral work where there was no ESL subspecialty nor even one called applied linguistics. I knew that UCLA, where I had also applied, had a much stronger, much more clearly defined reputation in the applied linguistics/ TESOL (Teachers of English to Speakers of Other Languages) world, and sensed at the time that I may have been making a mistake to head north (from my hometown in Monterey, California) rather than south.

But I had been charmed by Stanford's beauty, welcomed by a couple of people I knew there, and was delighted to be close enough to home to be able to escape to Monterey every weekend. In my second year there, I was awarded a teaching fellowship in the ESL program for foreign graduate students, so thus kept up with ESL-like practices, and maintained the identity of an ESL instructor during my teaching and office hours. But my well-carved out ESL identity began eroding at the edges the more coursework I took in education, linguistics, psychology, sociology, and anthropology, until I realized that the issues I was interested in cut across disciplinary boundaries, and pertained not at all exclusively to the ESL world. I left Stanford some years later unclear as to how to label myself in my professional life, even though my work was still connected with second language education.

In recent years, my confusion has continued, heightened by the sense of misplacement I feel in my work and at all the conferences I attend in composition, TESOL, and education, while still feeling strong links to each. I don't believe that others consider me a professionally confused persona in the particular dramas we are all living and the particular academic games we are playing (although I would have to consult with them about this, probably over a drink). They do not see me as a lost soul seeking a place in academia to call home. I put on my (serious) act while teaching, presenting at conferences, and constructing pieces of writing, so that in these arenas I can project an air of authority and a voice that attests to a certain amount of experience. It helps that my hair is graying. This act is sometimes so much a part of me that it is no longer accurate to call it an act, so perhaps I am no more at a loss for professional identity than are those around me. In fact, as more personal narratives get into print and as I talk to more people about my sense of not belonging, I find that many share my sense of residing "on the margins" (Edelsky, 1997). I wonder how many of us have trouble labeling our professional identities, seeing these identities as coherent and unfragmented. I wonder, too, whether the coherent identity is most often a perception that others have of us because we play the game well, behaving and practicing in ways that fit a certain label. I think it is the doing that counts and that constructs the label.

The people that I discuss in this book, from the literature and from my own work, were all doing things with writing that helped them to develop identities as competent students, evolving novices, or experts in academic fields, and to position them within a variety of fuzzily defined fields and subfields. For instance, in Japan, what we were trying to teach undergraduate Japanese students in a course on Academic Reading and Writing was a set of behaviors involving interactions with texts and people that were typical of practices they might encounter in English-medium universities. Although perhaps the goals were unspoken, I believe that we hoped our students who studied abroad someday might thus be labeled "business student," "sociology student," or "East Asian Studies student," and not just "foreign student," or "ESL student." The latter two labels suggest an identity of one not yet competent in English, let alone in the text-based practices of academic communities.

At the graduate level, some of the MA and doctoral students I have spoken with over the years entered their graduate programs seeing themselves not just as graduate students, but also as teachers or prospective teachers. In the course of learning the writing practices of their academic settings, some came to see themselves as researchers, or as teacher-researchers because they were gaining competence in a new set of text-based practices. The bilingual academics that I got to know in Japan used writing practices to help shape their professional identities both within and outside Japan. They maintained and expanded text-related practices with networks of readers, co-authors, and colleagues with whom they discussed and prepared work that was designed eventually to end up in print. They used these practices, with the written products as the showcased self, to help find their way into multiple academic communities, and even to help shape those communities. The established academics in language education that I worked with for several years in the production of an edited book were trying to shift their writing practices from conventional academic discourse to discourse that was more personal, literary, and narrative in style yet that still found outlet in academic publications. This shift involved their exposing to the public a nontraditional academic identity, one characterized less by authority and certainty than by change, uncertainty, self-doubt, and growth. Constructing essays for the book involved, in a sense, unlearning many of the textual practices we had all come to feel were appropriate and natural to our professional identities. (It helped that this shift has already taken place in some field such as composition studies. See the review of studies in Chap. 6.)

In short, I see all these people's identities, including mine, as in a state of flux, and as inextricably linked to writing-related practices that I metaphorically refer to in this book as game-like. All of us constantly assess who we are talking to in particular settings in our writing, which helps determine what can be said and how it can be said. All are making choices, or struggling to learn to do so, about what kinds of topics, teaching, and research interests to pursue and draw on for our writing practices. Some are clear about how they are, or want to be, seen ("I am/want to be known as a ___"), and others are less sure. Still, I believe that many of us perceive that our academic writing practices centrally influence our evolving identities in our academic settings.

I am tempted to conclude my framing activity with this common sense perspective. But others have such interesting things to say about some of the same issues. Their views, plus my common sense perspective, have helped construct my assumptions about academic literacy games (laid out later in this chapter) and guide my research projects over the years.

FRAMING IN THE VOICES OF OTHERS

The common sense framework of the issues underlying the case studies in this book provides a comfortable way into a complex set of topics that can also be framed in other ways. In this section, I frame the issues of practice, identity, and disciplinary enculturation in the voices of people whose histories, experiences, and central concerns differ greatly from mine. Their voices differ too, and as I have drafted and redrafted this chapter I have not found a way of blending these voices with my own in ways that entirely satisfy me. I'll keep trying in future work.

Of the many possible frames that I could discuss through the voices of others, I explore some that allow me to conceptualize writing games as a type of broader situated social practice as expressed in Etienne Wenger's (1998) work on communities of practice and in Sherry Ortner's (1996) theory of situated practice. Ortner, whose work builds partly on that of social theorists Pierre Bourdieu and Anthony Giddens, relies heavily on a game metaphor. Her ideas have helped me construct the game metaphor used in this book. Within a theory of practice I see identity in academic settings as constructed in part through the socially situated practice of writing (Ivanič, 1998), and disciplinary enculturation as centrally involving textual practices that help construct academic identities.

Perspectives on Situated Practice in the Voices of Others

I have found in my work on academic literacy and in my own participation in academic literacy practices over the years that university academic life is an inherently interesting part of social life and in some ways can be seen as a microcosm of the broader social world. It consists of complex social and political structures, it brings newcomers into the fold through a variety of caretaking and apprenticeship practices, and it perpetuates and revises itself over time. I adopt Wenger's (1998) conceptualization of practice as "... doing, but not just doing in and of itself. It is doing in a historical and social context that gives structure and meaning to what we do. In this sense, practice is always social practice" (p. 47). Wenger continues:

> Such a concept of practice includes both the explicit and the tacit. It includes what is said and what is left unsaid; what is represented and what is assumed. It includes the language, tools, documents, images, symbols, well-defined roles, specified criteria, codified procedures, regulations, and contracts that various practices make explicit for a variety of purposes. But it also includes all the implicit relations, tacit conventions, subtle cues, untold rules of thumb, recognizable intuitions, specific perceptions, well-tuned sensitivities, embodied understandings, underlying assumptions, and shared world views. (p. 47)

Wenger's perspective is satisfying in that it can be applied easily to concrete cases of practice, including in academic settings.

Feminist anthropologist Sherry Ortner's work is similarly tied to concrete cases and is similarly satisfying for its emphasis on practice as situated in the realities of people's lives. Although she builds her theory of practice to some extent on the work of other well-known theorists of practice, such as Pierre Bourdieu (1977a, 1977b, 1991) and Anthony Giddens (Cassell, 1993; Giddens, 1979, 1991), she finds that neither grounds his work in the concrete details of everyday, observed experience. When I read both of these theorists, I was interested in Bourdieu's ideas about routinized and embodied[2] behavior patterns and about language as a key aspect of symbolic power within social life, and in Giddens's views about how the routines of social practices are reproduced over time and space. But like Ortner, I missed the connection of these ideas to the details of actual experience. Instead Bourdieu and Giddens draw on general observations and anecdotes for their examples rather than empirical data from the lives of particular individuals.

I was irritated by the position of Bourdieu, for instance, who, in attempting to escape the objectivist–subjectivist dichotomy, insists on a "break with immediate experience" as a way to ensure that the analyst does not reduce people's knowledge of the world to personal, practical experience (Thompson, in Bourdieu, 1991, p. 11). Giddens (1979, 1991) seems more interested in individual experience and in an analysis of the social world that grants individuals autonomy and agency. But like Bourdieu, he wants to understand the patterned and recursive behaviors of people in a complex world, where local and global factors reflexively construct each other. A detailed observation and description of the lives of real people is not needed in the work of either scholar, as it was not in Goffman's extraordinary body of work (e.g., Goffman, 1959, 1974, 1981). First-hand accounts in this work could have provided vivid descriptions of social practices in the flesh and thus highlighted the diversity and unpredictability of individual experience. Scrutinizing routines and patterns helps me understand the regularities I might observe, but I am equally interested in the irregularities and discrepancies—the local and individual details of lived experience that do not readily fit the broader patterns. Ortner provides such details in her work.

I also share with Ortner the critique of Bourdieu's and Giddens's attempts to account for change in existing social practices rather than just their reproduction. Both Bourdieu and Giddens portray change as depressingly difficult to effect by people who—in their words—lack resources, capital, legitimacy, and hence power. This difficulty is particularly evident in Bourdieu's work; Giddens pays somewhat more attention to agency and intentionality. Both make room for change, in a theoretical sense, noting that social practices are not governed by fixed and formal rules, but by informal rules that are susceptible to modification at any point. Still, it is the people with resources (Giddens) and with the symbolic capital of authority and prestige (Bourdieu) whose voices and practices effect change.

---

[2]My use of the term *embodied* throughout this book reflects the idea, compatible with Bourdieu's use of the term *habitus* and Wenger's (1998) use of the term *embodied*, that knowledge and practices over time become routinized such that they are experienced as inseparable from one's body. Embodiment, in other words, refers to a felt sense, rather than to an intellectual perception, of knowledge. See, e.g., the edited collection by Selzer and Crowley (1999), *Rhetorical Bodies*, for a more specialized view within composition studies.

In academic settings men more often than women have these resources, not necessarily by virtue of their superior knowledge or ability, but by their superior control of the rules of the game and their greater interest in and commitment to competitive struggles. But in my studies of academic literacy, many of the people I came to know were women, not by any design of the studies, but by chance. As feminist literature has documented, women find it especially difficult to get their voices heard and to have those voices regarded as authoritative. Donna Haraway (1988) and Sandra Harding (1986), for example, in their feminist perspectives on science, treat this problem in some depth. After many years of competitive struggle on the field of science studies (as Bourdieu might put it), both these scholars have managed to develop authoritative and "legitimate" voices in their pursuit of nonpatriarchal, multicultural, multivocalic approaches to science. Chris Weedon (1997) and Patti Lather (1991), too, authoritatively represent the subaltern, women in particular, in their work on feminist poststructuralist theory, as does Gesa Kirsch (1993) in her study of the writing lives of academic women. I wish both Giddens and Bourdieu had paid more attention to this struggle of diverse peoples including women and nondominant men to be heard, to position themselves in ways that allow them to garner respect, expertise, and agency.

Ortner (1996) addressed some of these questions in her own theory of practice, which is more sensitive to the details of lived experience and to the challenges that traditionally powerless people face as they seek ways to escape oppression. Although she appreciates efforts by Giddens, Bourdieu, and others to construct a theory of practice, she herself wishes to understand how notions of situated and constructed practice fit real people in real time and how resistance and negotiation on the part of the dominated contribute to social change (she cites the work of Marshall Sahlins as more satisfactory in this respect). Existing theories of practice, she notes, treat as marginal a number of areas that she wishes to consider central:

- the multiple and contested forms of power and resistance
- the many kinds and degrees of agency
- the many perspectives on identity, viewed as issues of race, class, ethnicity, and gender
- the ways that a concept of structure can more adequately account for change (p. 3)

Ortner recognizes that people are not totally free agents, that their lives are to some extent constructed, governed, and constrained by social, cultural, and political factors. But she does not grant too much influence to constructivist positions, and indeed wishes to do away altogether with the particular dualist fight between constructivist and individualist perspectives, or at least to realize that it is not necessary to make a choice between the two (p. 11).

These framing perspectives on situated practice offered primarily in the voices of Wenger and Ortner will resurface in direct and indirect ways throughout this book. But perhaps even more salient as a frame in this book is the game metaphor, particularly as it is conceptualized by Ortner as part of her theory of practice.

Ortner's Game Metaphor. Ortner's (1996) game metaphor helped provide the theoretical frame for the "writing games" metaphor that I adopt in this book. For Ortner, life itself is a serious game and an inherently social one. She understands the common sense association between the term *game* and a connotation of play or lightness—a connotation she wishes to avoid. In talking about the social practices of actors (agents, subjects, individuals), she therefore adopts the qualified term *serious games* to refer to the "motivated, organized, and socially complex ways of going about life in particular times and places . . ." (Ortner, p. 12). She lists the following aspects of social life that parallel games in some basic ways, and that recall the theatrical and performance metaphors in the work of Erving Goffman. These characteristics apply as well to academic settings:

- Social life is culturally organized in terms of defining categories of actors, rules, goals, etc.
- Social life consists of "webs of relationship and interaction between multiple, shiftingly interrelated subject positions" in which "none are autonomous agents."
- Still, agency exists in that "actors play with skill, intention, wit, knowledge, intelligence." (p. 12)

Because the stakes are high, having outcomes that concern positions of power and status, people play the many social games around them with great seriousness.

In her own work on Sherpa nunneries and Sherpa mountaineering, Ortner (1996) has been interested in how subalterns, women primarily but including nondominant men, find loopholes, slippages, and points of disjunction in dominant social structures, and strategically negotiate, resist, and transform those structures so as to improve their lives. The people in her work find that they are simultaneously constrained by certain "game rules" and liberated by the many choices offered by the disjunctions in the multiplicity of serious games (colonial, racial, gender . . .) they encounter. In general, Ortner finds that the game metaphor helps her fashion a theory of practice that suits her work better than does the practice-oriented theory of scholars like Giddens and Bourdieu, which is less centrally concerned with changes in social practice that will benefit dominated minorities. She reasons that using the game perspective opens up the following possibilities for a theory of practice that is friendlier to the subaltern than existing theories:

- The game perspective retains an active intentional subject, without resorting to the unsatisfactory (and discredited, thanks to the postmodernists) notion of free agency and free will. Agents and structures mutually determine each other in the sense that players are construed by the game but simultaneously stretch the game in the act of playing.
- The game perspective allows the researcher to focus on relations of power and authority, since a game is always some kind of contest even if only with the self.
- The game perspective breaks the loop of unchanging reproduction of social structures and practices without giving up the notion of structure. At particular moments, as well as across time, a multiplicity of games will be enacted, all of which are characterized by only partial, not total, hegemony. (p. 20)

Ortner's game metaphor thus illuminates how people in concrete settings, including academic ones, contest for power, find themselves included and excluded, and use intentionality and agency to skillfully and strategically play and "stretch" (i.e., change) the game (see Freadman's [1994] use of the game metaphor in writing, discussed below). All these activities occur within a social life that is organized in terms of defining categories, rules, goals, and webs of relationship and interaction (p. 12).

In sum, unlike Bourdieu and Giddens, Ortner insists that her framework of practice be grounded in concrete cases and that the subaltern have agency. This insistence and her skillful use of the game metaphor[3] all suit my own leanings. Interestingly, Ortner's commitment, and mine, to concrete cases may seem to go against traditional notions of "objectivity," a notion that requires distance from historical particulars. However, the objectivity–subjectivity dichotomy is done away with by the idea of "partial perspectives," which Haraway (1988) claims is all that is available to us anyway. Haraway wants to honor multiple and local knowledges without giving up accounts of a real world, and hence asserts that a feminist science does not need traditional conceptualizations of objectivity: "Feminist objectivity means *situated knowledges*" (italics in original) (p. 581). Haraway's persuasive argument for adopting a partial perspective, and her insistence that we remain committed to a "real" world (as well as to the idea of historical con-

---

[3]See also Bourdieu's (1991, pp. 179–183) clever use of a game metaphor to discuss the maneuverings of political groups.

tingency) further support my belief in the importance of looking at concrete cases of situated literacy practices in academic settings and help protect me from feeling put off or intimidated by the totalizing tendencies of grander social theories.

Academic Writing as a Game-Like Situated Social Practice. The view of writing as situated social practice represents a radical shift away from the stalled-out programs that conceptualized writing as a cognitive problem-solving endeavor, where researchers were trying to model through flow charts and computer simulations the mental processes that people used as they engaged in writing activities (e.g., Flower & Hayes, 1981). This approach tended to neglect crucial social factors that now seem inseparable from the practice of writing (Barton, Hamilton, & Ivanič, 2000; Baynham, 1995; Flower, 1994; Gee, 1990; Kress, 1993; MacDonald, 1994; Miller, 1984; Street, 1995). The view of writing as a situated social practice also represents a shift away from a characterization of genre as consisting primarily of conventionalized textual formalisms to one in which textual patterns and regularities are considered to be aspects of broader social and rhetorical practices. This shift parallels the one in sociolinguistics, where otherwise quantitative studies of linguistic variation in speech communities have been enriched by including local and situated ethnographic perspectives (Eckert, 2000).

Perhaps the social turn in studies of writing was triggered by Carolyn Miller (1984), who turned a few heads by writing what became a seminal piece on genre. In that piece, revised slightly for its appearance in an edited volume on rhetoric (Freedman & Medway, 1994), Miller described genre not as a form, but as typified, or recurrent, rhetorical and social action. Unlike the concept of uniqueness, the concept of recurrence depends entirely on social factors—the intersubjective agreement (read: construction) by people of what it is that recurs. As did Alfred Schutz (1970) in his sociological theory of typification, Miller (1994a) claims that "what recurs is not a material situation (a real, objective, factual event) but our construal of a type" (p. 29), and that this act of construction occurs in response to a social motive ("exigence" p. 30). In a more recent article in which she rethinks her original piece on genre, Miller (1994b) laments specifically the typical first year college writing program in which genre tends not to be treated as social action. Rather, the typical college writing program "turns what should be a practical art of achieving social ends into a productive art of making texts that fit certain formal requirements" (p. 67). But because homogeneity and harmony are not the defining characteristics of a rhetorical community, textual formalities represent a deeper social practice. It is the centripetal forces of genre—those forces that provide a sense of sameness and recurrence such as narrative—that prevent the rhetorical community from flying apart in a centrifugal display of disunity and diversity (Miller, 1994b, p. 74). Following Ortner (1996) at the broader social level and Freadman (1994) at the level of writing, I use the metaphor of games to help characterize these diverse yet patterned relationships and practices in academic settings where writing is a central activity.

In beginning her discussion of the game metaphor to describe her view of genre, Anne Freadman (1994) points out that at its simplest, the metaphor suggests that facility with a genre involves writers learning the rules of the game, understanding what roles the participants can play, and then practicing the skills until they can play correctly. As Freadman says, this view implies that a text is the output of a set of rules, where some speech-like action is done with words (Austin, 1967; Searle, 1978; Wittgenstein, 1953) according to those rules. She calls this a "recipe theory" of genre (p. 46), and notes its inadequacies in accounting for the many recalcitrant examples in the textual world.

A better use of the game metaphor, Freadman points out, looks at the rules that distinguish one game from another, such as the game of tennis from the game of chess, not as rules that lead to a product but as rules for how to play. In tennis, we can think of the game as the giving and receiving of tennis balls, but this view places no particular value on the shots in tennis. A tennis shot, says Freadman, takes on value by what it enables, and what it prevents, for each player. A return, for example, takes its particular shape depending on the skill of the server and the skill of the receiver. Without this "uptake," which is determined by particular interactions between players, there is no game. In other words, a game consists not of its rules per se, but of the practice of its rules, including the ceremony of the game—activities surrounding the actual game (warm-up, opening and closing rituals, ways of keeping track of scores, and so on).

Freadman takes issue with the idea that a text is "in" a genre, or that a genre is "in" a text (that the features of texts and genres are describable in terms of each other), preferring instead in her game analogy to require that a genre consist of at least two texts, in some kind of dialogical interaction. Her examples include: a theoretical debate; a brief and report; a play and audience response; and an essay question, the essay, and its feedback (p. 48). Such a view accords with Bakhtin's (1981) notion of the dialogically situated nature of utterances, and with Bazerman's (1994b) descriptions of "systems of genres" in complex texts, which are characterized by multiple actions and effects. In his analysis of patents, for example, Bazerman (1994b) notes that a patent consists not of a single-genre document, but of a legal activity, "in essence, a complex web of interrelated genres where each participant makes a recognizable act or move in some recognizable genre, which then may be followed by a certain range of appropriate generic responses by others" (pp. 96–97). Such relationships help define writing games.

Another potentially useful concept discussed by Freadman in her genre-as-game analogy is that of place. Place constitutes genre, she claims, not formal linguistic features. Form, rather, is determined by a text's place and function within ceremonies (p. 60), *"once the 'receiver' is positioned in the right game"* (p. 63, italics in original). Learning to write, therefore,

> ... is learning to appropriate and occupy a place in relation to other texts, learning to ensure that the other chap will play the appropriate game with you, and learning to secure a useful uptake: The rules for playing, the rules of play, and the tricks of the trade. (pp. 63–64)

John Swales (1990), too, in his discussions of genre, points out the game-like nature of people's participation in discourse communities when he notes that people who participate in specialized communities do not necessarily assimilate the community's values. For a variety of reasons (an obvious one being if one is a novice who is either transitioning into an unfamiliar community or who is participating in one or more communities primarily for instrumental reasons), people may take on roles and behaviors that help them achieve their purposes, without necessarily taking on the identity of a believer. He notes that there is "enough pretense, deception and face-work around to suggest that the acting out of roles is not that uncommon," and that in academic settings, students who take courses in a variety of disciplines seem to survive without "developing multiple personalities" (p. 30). Regardless of whether academic writers take on the identities of full-fledged members, the value of the game metaphor is that it can help us understand the strategic and negotiated nature of literacy practices in the academy and thereby help us understand more about who we are and how we define and position ourselves in academic settings.

Perspectives on Identity in the Voices of Others

The term *identity* can be used in many more senses than I can possibly review in this book. I am restricting my uses to the common sense one discussed earlier in the chapter and to its use in discussions of how the self is positioned within communities of practice and within communities of academic writers in particular. In the studies I review and report on in this book, I was regularly struck by the extent to which people in academic settings develop identities as academic writers in a social and political as well as linguistic environment. In such an environment, or community of practice in Wenger's (1998) terms, people's identities are shaped by a variety of factors, including fundamentally how we participate in a community's practices and reposition ourselves from the role of newcomer on the sidelines of a game to the accomplished player's more central place. Within a community, identities are also shaped by labels and credentials that both reflect and construct who we are (Bourdieu, 1991). Most pertinent to the case studies in this book, when people write something for public consumption in academic settings (even if just for one teacher), they represent themselves in their writing—they construct what Ivanič (1994, 1998) calls a discoursal identity. These views on identity will help us see how freshmen in college, for instance, participate in disciplinary communities in one way and professors who conduct and write about research participate in those same communities in a very different way. Their specific communities of practice, the labels and credentials affixed to them, and the representations of themselves in their writings all differ greatly, with the result that their identities vary widely within the same general setting.

Wenger's Identity Construction in Communities of Practice. Etienne Wenger (1998) and Jean Lave (1996, 1997) studied how people's identities evolve as they participate in and learn from the practices of their communities. In Lave's (1996) work on situated learning, identity is intimately connected with learning in the sense that within communities of practice, learners (including teachers) are "becoming kinds of persons" as they change how they participate in the community's practices and as they engage in "identity-making life projects" (p. 157). Hence, "identity, knowing, and social membership entail one another" (Lave & Wenger, 1991, p. 53).

In Wenger's (1998) later work, the author devotes a major portion of his book to an elaborated discussion of identity using concrete examples from his study of insurance claims processors. He calls identity a "negotiated experience" in which we "define who we are by the way we experience our selves through participation as well as by the ways we and others reify our selves" (p. 149). The key aspects of identity in Wenger's formulation include the following:

- Identity as community membership, in which people define who they are by what they find familiar and unfamiliar;
- Identity as a learning trajectory, in which people define themselves by past experiences and future possibilities;
- Identity as a nexus of multimembership, in which people reconcile their many forms of membership into a coherent conceptualization of self;
- Identity as a relationship between local and global ways of belonging to communities of practice. (p. 149)

Identities are not fixed, in other words, but constantly being reconstructed and negotiated through different practices and modes of belonging. For my purposes in academic settings, I view people's identities as continually in the process of being constructed as the members of academic communities learn to engage in different sets of practices and envision themselves on different possible trajectories. Students, teachers, and researchers all come to an academic setting with a history, with a more or less well-defined sense of where they want to go, and with opportunities to engage in practices that define them as members of the school community and perhaps also as emergent or expert members of a disciplinary or rhetorical community.

As Wenger reminds us, and as is obvious in the many studies of academic literacy that I review in this book, the processes of developing an identity as someone who belongs to a community of practice may be filled with tension, conflict, and abuses of power. Newcomers inevitably feel the foreignness of unfamiliar practices, the unwieldiness of new forms and tools of communication, and relationships with more experienced participants that are not necessarily harmonious. Freshman writers, new graduate students, and novice faculty members alike need to figure out how to participate competently in their academic subcommunities (to become skillful and strategic players) and to see themselves and these communities in relation to a broader academic enterprise. Identity construction and learning to belong go hand and hand, in other words, and both take time and effort and may never be complete.

In sum, the identity-transforming phenomenon of learning in Lave's situated activity theory and Wenger's communities of practice perspective does not involve learners' internalizing transmitted knowledge (Reddy, 1979) as much as it does their "increasing participation in communities of practice" (Lave & Wenger, 1991, p. 49). Within communities of practice of many kinds, learners' roles and identities thus evolve over time as members change their patterns of participation. Both the communities of practice and the people themselves, "masters" and "apprentices," are transformed in the process.

Labels and Credentials. In institutions of higher education, people are identified greatly by how they participate in the practices of the academic community. But they are also identified in part by the labels and credentials attached to them. These signify that they have undergone the routines that are expected of title holders: An "A" or a "D" student, a holder of an MA degree, and an associate professor are all seen to be certain kinds of people. Bourdieu (1991) is interested in the ways that identity is constructed through such linguistic and ritualized processes in which identity comes about only when people recognize it as legitimate (cf. Lave and Wenger's, 1991, notion of "legitimate peripheral participation"). People "possess power in proportion to their symbolic capital, i.e., in proportion to the recognition they receive from a group" (Bourdieu, 1991, p. 106). Labels and credentials help construct this legitimacy.

Bourdieu (1991) refers here to the "theory effect" (cf. Giddens's [1991] notion of reflexivity)—the way that the expressions of a theory both describe something and, by its expression, bring about the construct or phenomenon being described (p. 133). A person's identity is constructed in similar ways, suggesting the power of labels and naming that usually accompany credentialing rites. Others have investigated this phenomenon in concrete cases, noting the power of labels to create that which they describe: McCarthy (1991) and McCarthy and Gerring (1994) discuss the influence of categories and labels of mental illnesses in the standard manual from the American Psychiatric Association in constructing the diseases they describe; Ravotas and Berkenkotter (1998; Berkenkotter & Ravotas, 1997) document how a patient's descriptions of herself get translated into the language of the same manual; and McDermott (1993) and Mehan (1993) demonstrate the power of labels to construct the identities of children in schools, often to the detriment of the children. In educational settings where credentialing procedures obtain, notes Bourdieu, the same labels and "formally defined criteria" that help construct identity also create the mechanisms by which inequalities are constructed and sustained (Bourdieu, 1991, p. 24). Those without credentials that are recognized as legitimate are unable to construct identities that may in fact match their abilities and goals. They remain outsiders.

The Construction of Academic Identities. In academic settings as elsewhere, labels, credentials, and behaviors need to match for identities to be convincing to self and others. However, both first and second language writers at all levels in academic communities face the difficulty of figuring out what to do and who they are amidst multiple and conflicting practices, as the studies that I review in this book show. A student who is categorized as a freshman faces one set of expectations, and one who is labeled a graduate student faces others.

It is not that academic institutions consciously set out to subvert the efforts of students and new faculty to construct coherent academic identities. In the case of expectations for writing practices for students, for example, institutional and teacher-produced guidelines often abound. The expectations as written out, however, may not be transparently obvious to students, nor are the guidelines for writing themselves necessarily coherent or consistent (Lea & Street, 1999). Learning the game rules and constructing identities as participants in the game seem to involve the uncomfortable process of actual trial and error practice and of gradually garnering awareness of patterns across conflicting behaviors and practices from more expert participants, whose own knowledge may remain largely tacit. In all cases of identity construction in academic settings, identity is shaped in general by power relations among game players and more specifically by the discoursal constructions of self in the writing that people do.

In the case of the second language academic community, some theorists have described it as a heterogeneous community where struggle and contestation are inevitable as people position and reposition themselves within networks of unequal power (Cummins, 1996; Ivanič & Camps, 2001; McKay & Wong; 1996; Norton, 1997, 2000; Peirce, 1995). Within such communities, learners' social identities shift in accordance with their investment (Norton, 2000; Peirce, 1995) in the language they are learning. However, these points apply not only to the second language community, but to the so-called first language community as well. Roz Ivanič's (1998) study of eight mature undergraduate students brings alive this heterogeneity within a predominantly mainstream group of students (two were African-American) and focuses on issues of identity that arose as the students made choices about how to position themselves in their academic communities via the essays they wrote for their college classes. "Writing does not just convey information," she reminds us; "it also conveys something about the writer" (Ivanič, 1994, p. 3). Her theorizing about and case studies of identity construction by writers in academic settings help frame my own studies and demonstrate vividly how "writing is more than writing."

Ivanič's theoretical conceptualization of academic identity was influenced by sociologists Giddens and Goffman and by sociolinguists Halliday (e.g., 1978), Fairclough (e.g., 1992), and Gee (1990) among others, all of whom are especially interested in social interaction and social positioning of self with networks of power and influence in society. Ivanič's particular interests draw her to the sociopolitical aspects of identity in academic settings as seen in the ways that writing and identity intersect. She expresses this connection as follows:

> Writing is an act of identity in which people align themselves with socioculturally shaped possibilities for self-hood, playing their part in reproducing or challenging dominant practices and discourses, and the values, belief and interests which they embody. (p. 32)

Always embedded in a sociopolitical context, a relationship explored earlier by Clark and Ivanič (1997) and later by Ivanič and Camps (2001) in a study of L2 writers, the act of writing itself requires that writers negotiate a discoursal self amidst a wide array of choices about who to align themselves with. Hence there is no such thing as "impersonal writing" (Ivanič, 1998, p. 32). Moreover, writers bring many selves to the task of writing, including an autobiographical self built from life histories, a discoursal self that is purposely constructed a particular way for a particular piece of writing, and a self as author—someone who can speak with authority with varying degrees of confidence. The multiplicity of contexts, of selves, and of practices that surround the activity of writing in academic settings leads Ivanič to insist that we must speak of literacies, not literacy—that there is no single thing called "literacy" that people acquire or exhibit.

Ivanič's view of identities and literacies as multiple allow her to escape the notion of an all-powerful discourse community that molds student writers into clones of full-fledged members. Instead, as she found in the cases of the eight students she worked with, academic literacies develop on a playing field that is characterized by tension and conflict and by ongoing struggle between the academic institution and its members. Students bring "multiple practices and possibilities for self-hood" to academic institutions (Ivanič, 1998, p. 106) and position themselves in relation to institutional discourses in a variety of ways (Hirvela & Belcher, 2001; Ivanič & Camps, 2001), making challenges to the status quo almost inevitable.

The perspectives on identity that I have reviewed blend nicely to help me see writers' identities in ways that neither essentialize them nor suggest they are blindly shaped by disciplinary socialization experiences. Writers bring personal histories to every writing task; they necessarily learn by active choice or by default that the acts and products of writing position them within sociopolitical networks in academic communities and are associated with various labels and credentials; and they learn that the discoursal selves they construct in particular pieces of writing will be seen by readers in particular ways whether that self feels authentic to the writer or not. In accordance with this complex conceptualization of academic identity, I embrace in this book the belief that diversity, contestation, and change characterize all people in educational settings, and that people's efforts to make sense of all this complexity will be evident somehow in their stories about themselves and in their writing.

Practice, Identity, and Disciplinary Enculturation

To conclude this discussion of framing in the voices of others, I turn to ways that the concepts of practice and identity help characterize what has been called *disciplinary enculturation*. The term captures some of the richness and complexity of what it means to learn how to participate in the specialized activities of people who live and work in academic settings and who hold (or behave as though they hold) certain values and beliefs about what knowledge is and does. As the previous discussion of practice and identity predicts, a concept like disciplinary enculturation helps clarify why people might feel like outsiders or strangers (McCarthy, 1987) when they begin university work at undergraduate and graduate levels, and why later they feel at home in their departments and subfields.

The term *disciplinary enculturation* implies that something like a "disciplinary community" or "rhetorical community" exists into which people become enculturated. The community metaphor is a powerful conceptualizer that can help frame how people interpret their own and others' experiences as they learn how to participate in specialized activities in academic or other settings (Swales, 1990; Wenger, 1998). It implies there are insiders and outsiders, people who either belong or don't belong to particular communities. However, the term *disciplinary enculturation* doesn't convey the partiality and layered complexity of the enculturation experience. Wenger's (1998) notion of communities of practice helps complexify this particular reification. In particular, Wenger counters the myth that at the beginning of an enculturation process people do not share the values and practices of a particular community and that later, through the process of enculturation, they do, in quite unambiguous and uncomplicated ways. Wenger documents and theorizes about the complexity of the process in ways that support the discoveries I made through my own experiences and learned about from the people whose stories appear in this book. When I use the term *enculturation* in this book, therefore, I intend it to refer to an experience that is ongoing, layered, and necessarily always incomplete.

The term *community* deceives too, as Miller (1994b) has noted, with its implications of clear physical boundaries and of a physically contiguous group of like-minded people. But if we resist the temptation to reify the *community* metaphor, and see a community instead as characterized by shared values and practices (Swales, 1990) that can function over distances via writing and electronic media, then the metaphor retains its usefulness. Seen in this broader, less physically constraining way, we can understand the many ways that people belong to and identify with some communities and not with others, and the partiality of most of these senses of belonging. Further, once practicing as insiders, people may not even be aware of the many factors that distinguish them from outsiders. Their knowledge becomes tacit, felt, embodied.

Disciplinary enculturation, then, can be seen as a process in which novice community members learn to engage in a community's practices and hence to participate in ways that redefine their identities. Texts and people's relationships with texts and with other people who are producers and users of texts lie at the heart of the process. Some years ago, Thomas Kuhn (1970), Stephen Toulmin (1972), and Clifford Geertz (1983) described disciplinary communities and enculturation in ways that highlight the centrality of texts and of the social, political, and technical practices surrounding their production. Like Wenger (1998), these earlier scholars also saw practice, repertoires of techniques and tools, and multigenerational relationships as central to the construction and perpetuation of scientific communities.

More recently, Paul Prior (1998) documented at length the social nature of disciplinary communities and enculturation. Disciplinary communities and enculturation processes are about people and their activities rather than about forms, rules, and abstractions as some structuralist approaches suggest. In the sociohistoric view that he adopts, he sees enculturation instead as an unstable, multivocalic social process in which clear divisions cannot be drawn between members and nonmembers and between expert and novice practices. Following Lave and Wenger (1991), he characterizes activity in a disciplinary community as complex relationships and practices among people (Prior, 1998, p. 21). Activity as a social construct then becomes a core unit of analysis in studies of disciplinary communities and enculturation (Engestrom, 1993; Russell, 1995, 1997). However, in disciplinarity, "much of the work of alignment is centered around texts, around the literate activities of reading and writing" (Prior, 1998, p. 27). Prior described the centrality of textual practices in disciplinary enculturation as follows:

> This literate activity is central to disciplinary enculturation, providing opportunity spaces for (re)socialization of discursive practices, for foregrounding representations of disciplinarity, and for negotiating trajectories of participation in communities of practice. (p. 32)

The earlier views of enculturation are not inimical to this social and textual view; they are just incomplete. After all, when Toulmin and Kuhn were writing about enculturation and practices in scientific communities, the fascinating landmark social studies of the differences between how scientists actually work and how they represent their work in texts had not yet been written (e.g., Gilbert & Mulkay, 1984; Knorr-Cetina, 1981; Latour & Woolgar, 1986). Neither Toulmin nor Kuhn fully appreciated how messy, partial, and political the process of enculturation was. What they did appreciate, and what is implicit in later studies of disciplinary enculturation, is the fact that in order to demonstrate their grasp of a discipline's knowledge and practices, novices need to display their knowledge publicly. Unexpressed, intuitive knowledge does not count. One of the main ways that all participants in a disciplinary community demonstrate their "legitimacy" (Bourdieu, 1991; Lave & Wenger, 1991) is thus through the texts they write. Written texts embody a disciplinary group's (or subgroup's as is more often the case) intellectual traditions, practices, and values and thus link writers' identities to particular groups.

In sum, the concepts of practice, identity, and enculturation into disciplinary or rhetorical communities intertwine in fluid yet inextricable ways. In academic settings in higher education, texts lie at the heart of this intermingling. First, because the texts that have been chosen for use in an educational setting are discrete products that have been created through practice by the community's elders and sanctioned by the local and global community, they appear to represent a field's authoritative wisdom—its legitimated end products of knowledge-building research activities. Second, texts reflect attitudes toward and beliefs about knowledge by virtue of the ways that knowledge is represented, even if no explicit theoretical stance is taken in the document. In this sense, to produce a discipline-specific text is to identify with an intellectual and epistemological tradition whether or not one intends to or is aware of such a commitment. Third, as end products of the inherently messy and often serendipitous as well as conventionally constrained activities of researching and composing, texts construct and transform reality into the discrete entities we call knowledge. Such order is not found in the laboratory or in the field, but is created in the act of producing a public, discipline-specific document. Finally, through the practices surrounding the production of texts, participants in academic community practices shape, change, and represent their own identities as community members. Over time writers in academic settings learn the social, political, and rhetorical games of how to orchestrate written texts so that realities and identities are constructed from the imperfections and complexities of school tasks, research activities, and conceptual explorations. This book examines how writers learn these games and how their changing practices influence how they see themselves and their shifting positions within their academic communities.

ASSUMPTIONS: THE END OF THE BEGINNING

I cannot identify all the sources of my assumptions and beliefs about academic literacy practices. Some can be traced to my own experiences (hence the importance of including bits of personal history in this book), some to readings I have done over the years such as those represented above "in the voices of others" and mulled over during long walks and discussed with interested colleagues, and some to the ideas expressed by colleagues themselves, who also developed their own assumptions within webs of multiple influences. Bakhtin (1981, 1986) would no doubt inform me that the heteroglossic development of my beliefs was not only normal, but inevitable.

First, like many linguists and writing specialists, I believe that writing is (pardon the expression) an unnatural act. People need to be taught to write in ways they do not need to be taught in order to speak, the arbitrariness of the sounds and shapes of speech being extended one level further to arbitrary visual signs and symbols of sounds and meanings. Not only is writing in general unnatural, writing in schools is a specialized kind of writing favoring some ways of representing meaning and not others. The How-to-Write-in-School game is one that everyone in school settings needs to learn, whether they are starting from scratch or whether they have a head start in understanding the dominant written discourses of whatever culture they belong to.

Second, I assume that the acquisition of school-based literacy practices happens both interactively and incompletely. A practice like that of writing and reading cannot possibly develop from the one-way transmission of knowledge of how to write from expert to novice. Students may learn *about* writing in this way, but they will not learn to write until they themselves write and discover whether their writing successfully communicates something (to others or to themselves as readers). However, writers of any age or level of expertise never develop complete control over their ideas and their language—their knowledge of the practice of writing can in principle continue evolving indefinitely even if such development comes to a halt for one reason or another. Moreover, as a linear representation of nonlinear ideas, writing necessarily represents only incompletely the ideas and identities of individual writers, which are both too complex and multidimensional to be reconstructed fully into lines of visual symbols.

Third, I assume that people who write in academic communities do so from a wide range of starting places, purposes, and interests. The diversity makes the job of teaching (teaching anything, not just writing) challenging, since no matter how teachers may try, individual students will inevitably end up in different places, achieving course objectives in their own ways, for their own purposes, and to the extent that their own talents, understandings, and interests allow. In university-level academic writing games, this diversity means that no disciplinary canon, if such a thing exists, will ever be acquired in its entirety by even the most accomplished of developing writers. Writers in disciplines therefore contribute to change and novelty within their specialties even if they don't intend to do so, if for no other reason than lockstep disciplinary socialization is impossible to achieve.

Fourth, I assume that academic writing includes many kinds of text-based literate behaviors, including reading and talking, hence my use of the terms academic writing and academic literacy practices interchangeably. However, I also assume that academic literacy practices are more than text-based; they are also deeply social and political. I am in good company here (see, e.g., Barton, Hamilton, & Ivanič, 2000; Baynham, 1995; Benesch, 2001; Canagarajah, 2001; Clark & Ivanič, 1997; Gee, 1990; Kress, 1993; Luke, de Castell, & Luke, 1989; Street, 1995). People in schools (not just students) write in social settings in conditions where hierarchies of power influence how and what they write.

Finally, I assume that my knowledge as a researcher and my ability to convey my ideas in writing in a publication such as this one are both incomplete and biased for at least two reasons. One is that I cannot escape my own background experiences, interests, and motivations. They will color all I do, from my choice of research topics to my interpretations of what I see and hear in my research activities. The second reason is that whatever I learn from others about their writing experiences is not only colored by my own biases and interests; it is also necessarily partial and biased knowledge from their perspectives. I end up knowing my informants incompletely no matter how deeply I try to probe and no matter how many angles I try to view them from. I then add to my incomplete and faulty knowledge the fact that any research report that I write up necessarily selects only a small portion of data to display that I hope will convince readers, and myself, that I have made accurate and trustworthy observations and interpretations. The good news in this potentially bleak picture is that all writers and researchers are in the same partially constructed boat, including those following paradigms of the so-called objective or scientific type.

Taken together, my assumptions express my sense that I will never be able to comprehend fully the complexity of academic writing games or the diversity of writers. Such completeness and accuracy are therefore not my goals in writing about writing practices. Instead, I hope my assumptions relay the excitement and challenge of studying a practice as diverse and complex as is writing in general and of exploring the vagaries of writing at the university level in particular. Part of the excitement comes from realizing that it is useless for me to seek fixed answers or to try to convey the sense that there is a fixed body of knowledge to be learned about writing practices. The other part of the challenge comes from my conviction that scholarship about writing practices is about people as much as it is about texts and that one of my responsibilities is to talk about people who write in a way that resonates with readers who write.

CASE STUDY METHODOLOGY

In this book I explore facets of academic identities and practices in transition by means of case studies and literacy autobiographies (a kind of self case study?). A case study is a detailed examination of one setting or of a limited number of people in one setting over a period of time that is long enough for the people to get to know each other as more than distanced and disinterested researcher and observed subject. As described by Strauss (1987), case studies cover a temporal span, and involve just one social unit, in my case, a person rather than an organization. Traditional scientific gauges of worthiness, such as generalizability and validity are misapplied to case studies and other qualitative inquiry, which need to be evaluated by other means (Donmoyer, 1990; Eisner & Peshkin, 1990) such as credibility and relevance.

Case studies are becoming increasingly powerful research methods in fields like education (Donmoyer, 1990) and language learning (Nunan,1992), appreciated for their in-depth observations of one site, one individual, or one group. In addition to close observation by researchers, one of the main data gathering techniques is interviews in which people narrate events and life stories to researchers who function as interested listeners. Narration, in fact, lies at the core of the case study (Newkirk, 1992). But researchers themselves are storytellers, as has been pointed out by many scholars (Brodkey, 1987; Conle, 1997, 1999; Connelly & Clandinin, 1990; Newkirk, 1992). Although there are different kinds of case studies and case histories (Bogdan & Biklen, 1982; Strauss, 1987), mine are about people, including myself as both the teller of other people's stories and of my own. I wish to include myself rather openly as a character in this book, because the stories of the roles that academic writing plays in my life are as much mine as they are my informants'. As is the case with perhaps most research, mine began with questions and curiosities that unsettled me during graduate school, a time when I saw my professional identity being both shaped and undone by the serious games I was learning to play in my particular settings.

Case studies are rarely brought together and discussed under one conceptual umbrella. More work of the sort that contextualizes and synthesizes case studies is needed in the literature on academic and professional writing, and in *Writing Games* I contribute to this effort. Some of the case studies I present in the book are summaries of studies done by other scholars. These particular studies are ones that detail in more or less effective ways the experiences of writers in academic settings. The ones most pertinent to my own work are those that track the writers' transitions, usually from the uncomfortable state of being a novice to the more familiar one of having learned the ropes.

The other case studies are my own—ones that formed parts of several different projects over a 10-year period beginning with my dissertation work in the late 1980s. While I have not included case study analyses directly from my dissertation in this book—the analyses and discussions were all done after 1990 when I moved to Japan—the data for the story of Virginia, a first year student in a doctoral program in sociology, come from this earlier period (Chap. 4). Other case study data come from several studies I did from my base at Keio University in Japan (Chaps. 2 and 5) and from a project with masters students in second and foreign language education in Monterey, California while on a sabbatical leave (Chap. 3). In all these studies, I interviewed a small number of volunteer informants—students, teachers, and faculty members—multiple times, and got to know many of them quite well as friends and colleagues. I interviewed most people from a set of written guidelines I had prepared (see Appendices), but expected our talk to develop in natural rather than constrained ways. After the first few interviews, I tended to let issues that had come up feed into the themes of subsequent interviews. As such, I was never absolutely sure where one of these conversations would lead, nor where the entire series of conversations would end up. I was mainly interested in listening to what people had to say about themselves, about their writing and their writing practices and attitudes, and in watching them discover things about themselves as writers along the way. This self-discovery that often results from in-depth open interviews—the learning that happens as people listen to themselves put feelings and experiences into words—contributed both to the clarity and complexity with which people I interviewed view key issues in their lives. Although I did not systematically analyze writing or program documents, we often talked with pieces of writing in front of us—course syllabi, assignment descriptions, drafts or final versions of papers that I had copies of. I was interested in how particular pieces of writing developed from assignment guidelines, templates, models, or professional requirements and in writers' interactions with and responses to feedback from teachers, peers, and editors. I taped and transcribed all interviews.

I also attended and took detailed field notes in three or more sessions of selected undergraduate and masters classes of some of the case study participants, and most sessions of three first year core classes in theory and methods of a small cohort of doctoral students in sociology. In the cases of the young bilingual faculty in Japan, I interviewed them multiple times over a 2-year period, following written guidelines, and often discussing pieces of written work in their offices on campus or in mine. However, I did not visit any classes they were teaching, nor did we talk much about their teaching, which seemed to occupy a separate niche in their academic lives.

As is normal for studies using narrative inquiry (Clandinin & Connelly, 1994, 2000; Connelly & Clandinin, 1990) and grounded theory (Strauss & Corbin, 1990), I did not begin with a system of categories that I imposed on my experiences. It was inevitable of course that I began all of my studies with concerns that stemmed from my own experiences and interests, and to deny this fact would be dishonest. Moreover, it was also inevitable that over time I began to perceive issues that people talked to me about as clustering in certain ways and not in others, and that my discussions, no matter how I try to adhere to the stories themselves, will reflect these clusterings. My interpretations, therefore, are my stories of the stories of others. I have no interest at the moment in other analytical games such as model building and theory construction, although I hope I have come to understand concrete events in terms of larger social practices with the help of several of the compelling theoretical constructs that I discussed earlier.

To be honest, I do not really care for the term *case studies* to describe what I am doing even though the term is now common in qualitative research in education. The term strikes me as too clinical and too impersonal. I want to interact with, analyze, and depict real people, not cases, and to impart an embodied sense of their selves in the stories I construct. At one point, I wondered if, in contrast to the case study approach, I should be adopting and adapting Sarah Lawrence-Lightfoot's technique of "portraiture" to help me depict the people I got to know (Lawrence-Lightfoot & Davis, 1997). Portraiture, as described and exemplified by Lawrence-Lightfoot and Davis felt like what I wanted to do. It uses methods from ethnography, case study, and narrative inquiry; it pays acute attention to detail; it allows for literary and esthetic dimensions to complement complex empirical phenomena; and it brings readers into settings and into people's lives in richly detailed and humanistic ways.

But I would be cheating somewhat if I now looked back on my many years of interview projects and relabeled them (for this is what it would be—a relabeling) portraits. They did not start out as projects in portraiture in the way Lawrence-Lightfoot and Davis mean. I did not keep the particular kinds of detailed notes on my observations and experiences that are requisite tools of portraiture. I did not view my interactions with people at the time as an esthetic experience, and did not "paint" pictures of people, settings, and experiences the way a portraitist might. But in some ways I wish I had.

Instead of Lawrence-Lightfoot style portraits, I have written what I guess must be called case studies. I hope they are neither dry nor "objective," but full of real people, including myself, and all our ups and downs, incompleteness, unpredictability, and quests for meaningfulness. I hope my own biases come through, as well as my own sense of wondering what games there are still to learn and my own lack of certainty about how things are and what they mean. One of the traditional games of academic discourse is to mask confusion and uncertainty with the authoritative voice of the researcher, who has seen, understood, and therefore concluded. I cannot play that game very well any longer though I'm sure that I tried for many years. The irony is that in expressing my uncertainties more openly, I feel more honest, hence more confident, hence (perhaps) more authoritative. In giving up the conventional game, I am indebted to Lawrence-Lightfoot and Davis (1997), to other authors who have found alternative ways of writing about people in the social sciences (e.g., Eisner, in Saks, 1996; Eisner, 1997; Ellis & Bochner, 1996; Neumann & Peterson, 1997; Trimmer, 1997), and to the wonderfully quirky, personal, and literary styles of several well-established anthropologists for helping me recognize the range of possible portrayals increasingly available to academic writers (e.g., Clifford Geertz, 1983, 1988, 1995; Dorinne Kondo, 1990; Mike Rose, 1989, 1995; Renato Rosaldo, 1989/1993; John Van Maanen, 1988; Harry Wolcott, 1990, 1994). I am not in that league, and it is often said that only the recognized stars in a field can push at the boundaries of academic discourse. However, part of my own transitions as a writer within academic settings, part of the game that I am playing at the boundaries of several rhetorical communities and at the center of none, inspires me to keep pushing at these boundaries in small ways. After all, those of us who do not feel like privileged insiders to any clearly defined community of scholars do not have to worry about being thrown out.

2

The Beginnings of Change:
Learning and Teaching Undergraduate
Academic Literacy Games

CLUELESS

Every now and then I am reminded of how wretchedly difficult my first writing experience was in college. I didn't know how to play any of the academic writing games, not the textual ones or the social and political ones, nor did I imagine the existence of the latter at the time. I had to write a 5-page paper on some topic in ancient thought and history about which I clearly knew little and in which I had no interest. I sat up all night (I am not a night person) in an armchair in our dorm study room, pulling out sentences and phrases so slowly and painfully that I thought I would never finish. The night seemed endless. I turned in the paper, such as it was, at 7:55 A.M. the next morning, 5 minutes before it was due, and got a C– as I recall. Luckily my imperfect memory has saved me from a lifetime of recurring nightmares about this experience, but even without the details, the sensations still haunt me.

It's not that I was ever a bad writer. In fact, I occasionally got high praise from junior high and high school teachers for my writing (Miss Wilson, my 8th-grade English teacher, had written in my year-end autograph book: "I hope English will be your forte," but she would not tell me what 'forte' meant). I also passed a college writing test that exempted me from any English courses. But that first college writing experience shriveled all confidence I might have had, or might have nourished, in my undergraduate academic persona. I saw it as clear evidence that I correctly had chosen to be an art major, that I was not focused or bright enough to succeed in classes requiring extensive reading and writing on bookish topics. That I had passed the school's writing test was little consolation, and indeed this fact was buried so deeply in my memory that it did not find its way into the first draft of this chapter. I wonder how many undergraduates, including those in the privileged White[1] middle and upper class, struggle with their early college writing experiences this way, and later find they can, with some confidence, consider themselves writers. I wonder, too, how much of the struggle has to do with lack of practice, or with lack of knowledge of a writing topic, with simple lack of interest in the assigned tasks, or with lack of mentoring. I was the none-too-proud possessor of all four of these lacks.

Learning to write in academic settings is about change in ways of thinking, using language, and envisioning the self. I see that now, but then I think I saw it as a matter of survival. I have queried some of the very bright undergraduate students at my Japanese university about their attitudes toward writing, and some of them echoed my sentiments of decades ago: We just want to survive, to turn in (not learn from) this report, to pass the class, to put it behind us. One student who had been raised in the United States told me that she had tried in her first semester to write "real" papers, but had quickly learned a different game. "Nobody writes real papers," she said, "because there's just no time." She continued by describing how students pulled things from the Internet and from books and pasted them together, without revision, since the teachers never gave feedback or returned the papers anyway. These students no doubt experienced change, but I am guessing that the changes concerned developing better survival strategies.

I don't know if I changed much during my undergraduate years as a result of writing. I have no memory of developing a sense of identity as an academic writer until I began graduate studies some years later. But of course then I was choosing what to study with a much greater sense of awareness, interest, and focus. Could this transformation have happened earlier? Or is there something about being an undergraduate—a novice at writing and at almost everything else as well, a self-conscious postadolescent who fantasizes about social life and not about Roman history, a partially formed personality that doesn't know what it really wants or why it is writing—that makes writing such a torturous tooth-pulling blood-sweating task? Or was it just me?

I escaped my undergraduate years as quickly as I could, repressing most memories of classes except those held in the art studios. What remained of those times were social and artistic, not intellectual, lessons. Now, after teaching writing in undergraduate and graduate settings in Japan for some years, I am astounded at how easy it is for me to be on the other side of the

---

[1]See my comment on this term in a footnote in the Preface.

torture chamber, at how rarely I recall my own past pain, and at how hard it is to know what is really going on inside the minds of the kids who sit in my classes. How many of my own students have gone through the all-night agony I went through, and this in a foreign language? Among the bilingual students, how many of them write as fluently and confidently as some of their drafts suggest they do? And why am I making the undergraduates write, anyway, if in their other classes they just need to survive, to turn in unrevised reports in Japanese, and where their writing techniques are unabashedly electronically plagiarized? I don't know the answers to these questions, but my experience and reading of the literature as well as my research and teaching convince me that writing at the undergraduate level is just plain hard partly because every undergraduate writer needs to reinvent the writing wheel for him- or herself. In particular, the case studies I have read and conducted have made me reevaluate my expectations for undergraduate writers and for myself as a writing teacher. They have also made me ask more pointed questions about my novice writing students' needs and goals, and the extent to which these arise and evolve from them as individuals and from influences outside the classroom, or in interaction with me and others in the context of specific practices in particular classes. When I was an undergraduate I certainly did not know what I wanted as a writer, and indeed had no sense of myself as a writer until many years later. But like other writing teachers, I persist in wanting my students to achieve in a semester what it took me a decade to learn, even though many of my students may never have to write again in the ways I'm asking them to write. No wonder I'm sometimes confused and frustrated.

PUBLISHED STUDIES

Before looking more closely at some published case studies, I want to review some of the issues that have been explored in undergraduate writing, particularly in the second language education "EAP" (English for Academic Purposes) literature. Although this chapter concerns undergraduate education, many of the issues I review here apply also to graduate level EAP courses and their influence on students' academic enculturation (Chap. 3). Scholars in EAP seek ways to help a multicultural, multiclass population of students make the transition into English-medium universities and to link issues these students face with broader issues of literacy across the curriculum that all students confront (Matsuda, 1998; Zamel 1995, 1996). Many of these studies have tried to figure out specifically what game rules, strategies, and practices students need to learn in order to write successfully in their academic classes. The findings show that disciplinary discourse practices cannot be characterized in any unambiguous sense, thus making it difficult for EAP teachers to know what to teach. Those studies that presume a relatively unified discourse community into which students need to be integrated by adopting known sets of discourse or genre practices can be critiqued for not addressing the actual diversity and possibilities for agency in disciplinary discourse practices (e.g., Bartholomae, 1985; Berkenkotter, Huckin, & Ackerman, 1988; Bhatia, 1993; Walvoord & McCarthy, 1990).

Nevertheless, perhaps because it is their livelihood, many writing teachers, materials developers, and researchers advocate explicit teaching of some kind, believing that some aspects of what students learn in a writing class can be transferred to discipline-specific content classes or become part of novice academic writers' permanent repertoires of knowledge and strategies. This belief exists in spite of ongoing debates about the value of explicit instruction and awareness in areas of language education such as form-focused grammar instruction in second language acquisition (e.g., Ferris, 1999; Truscott, 1996, 1998, 1999) and genre instruction in writing (Freedman, 1993a, 1993b; Williams & Colomb, 1993). We also have not resolved the question about what the content of EAP writing courses should be: language, genre, subject matter content, ideological and political issues, critical thinking tasks, or some combination (see, e.g., discussions on genre in Bhatia, 1993; Freedman & Medway, 1994; and Swales, 1990; on critical thinking in ESL by Atkinson, 1997 and Pally, 1997; on content by Gosden, 2000 and Parkinson, 2000; and on ideological, cultural, and pragmatic issues by Allison, 1996; Atkinson, 1997, 1999; Benesch, 1993, 1996, 2001; Ramanathan & Atkinson, 1999; and Santos, 1992).

In an early piece by Ruth Spack (1988), the message was that writing teachers should leave the discipline-specific aspects of writing to the teachers in the disciplines. Her point at that time that we hear echoed in different forms in later work by other scholars was that students need to be "immersed in the subject matter" by attending lectures and seminars, reading, discussing, and observing professional writers (p. 40). "English teachers cannot and should not be held responsible for teaching writing in the disciplines," she said then. Rather, they should teach general inquiry strategies and rhetorical principles, helping students to learn to evaluate and synthesize data and reading sources (p. 40). Another second language researcher who has studied the demands that academic literacy makes on students is Pat Currie (1993). In her study of a social science class, she identified the following potentially generalizable skills in the class writing assignments: finding and recording information, using a concept to find and report observational details, using a concept to analyze data, classifying according to a concept, comparing and contrasting, determining causal relationships, resolving an issue, and speculating (p. 107).

However, in another study by Currie (1998), such skills were not explicitly highlighted by the professor in a content class. In that study, Currie followed "Diana," a native speaker of Cantonese, throughout a one-semester undergraduate course in Management and Organizational Behavior at a Canadian university. Although Diana did have language and reading problems in spite of a high TOEFL (590), she faced even greater difficulties understanding the ways of reasoning and problem solving that her writing tasks required. In interviews with the professor of this class, Currie learned that the professor was not able to articulate explicit guidelines for writing and reasoning tasks because much of this conceptual knowledge was tacit, and deeply embedded in social practices within his field (see also Leki, 1995b).

Another potentially teachable and generalizable aspect of academic writing in Western cultural settings is awareness of plagiarism. The less pejorative notion of textual borrowing has been identified as a survival strategy for both first and second language students in academic settings who often need to write from their readings (Campbell, 1990). Indeed, Currie (1998) found that Diana eventually resorted to extensive "textual borrowing" because she was so distressed by her low grades in her weekly writing assignments. Her copying went undiscovered by the teaching assistant who read her papers, and her grades indeed went up. Can students in EAP classes be taught the serious game of textual borrowing, including how to recognize and avoid plagiarism, then apply this knowledge to their content classes? Deckert (1993) for one hopes so, since his first year students at a Hong Kong university seemed to have little concrete sense of what it was or why it might be considered a serious problem. Pennycook (1996) was not surprised at this, given what he learned about the complex history of the culture-loaded notion of plagiarism and the inconsistent uses of the words of others by published scholars in the West (see also Scollon, 1995). Discussions about textual borrowing as a cultural practice continue, with questions about how and what to teach undergraduate students unresolved. One thing we can do is to help both undergraduates and graduates understand that citation conventions are not just formalisms but one of the many serious game-like social practices within particular academic communities. We are learning more about these practices through fascinating sociolinguistic analyses of how and why the authors of research articles cite the words of others (Hyland, 1999; Paul, 2000). However, the findings have as yet had little impact on undergraduate academic writing courses, which tend to focus on the formal aspects of citation and oversimplified sanctions against copying. The social and political game rules and strategies are perhaps too complex to be taught explicitly and unambiguously and may more appropriately find their way into graduate level writing texts (Swales & Feak, 1994, 2000).

Ilona Leki (1995b) is not sanguine either about what explicit aspects of academic writing within specific disciplines might be taught by EAP teachers. One of her questions, reflected in the discussion above, concerns the ability of writing teachers to teach genre-specific writing, given that so many disciplinary differences exist and that so much of what disciplinary insiders know is tacit, lying out of reach even of the probing questions of researchers. It is not reasonable, Leki (1995b) claims, to expect "those who do not participate as conversation partners in a discourse . . . to teach the explicit, let alone implicit, rules of that conversation to others" (pp. 236–237). For this reason, Bhatia (1993) and genre specialists in Australia and North America (see Cope & Kalantzis, 1993, Hyon, 1996, and the introduction to Freedman & Medway, 1994) suggest that special purpose English courses (ESP) follow a genre-based approach in which broad similarities of structure and function of writing across disciplines be taught.

In a related but somewhat different approach, Ann Johns (1988) claimed that "generalized English skills, usable in any academic class" (p. 55) could be taught in special purpose writing classes. However, on closer examination of how skills such as summarizing and research paper writing were used in specific fields, she found more differences than similarities among disciplines (p. 55), as did Paul Prior (1998) in his studies of graduate level writing. Johns (1998) partially solved this problem by trying to "train students to become ethnographers in the academic culture," to discover for themselves what knowledge and skills were required in the specific academic communities they were involved in (p. 57). In later work Johns (1990, 1995) continued espousing an ethnographic approach to academic enculturation, recommending that students already enrolled in academic courses be trained to become aware of the social and textual conventions in their classes. Pat Currie (1999) experimented with this approach in two of her undergraduate EAP classes in Canada by asking the students to observe specific practices within their content classes and to report their findings in a "journalog." Alan Hirvela (1997) similarly recommended that students learn about literacy activities in their own disciplines and compile a portfolio of their findings. His study concerned graduate students but applies to undergraduates as well. In short, a partial solution to the dilemma of writing teachers trying to assist students with their disciplinary enculturation has been for teachers to set up tasks that ask students to discover the game strategies in their fields.

Even though my discussion has focused on specialized EAP courses, which tend to be offered only to nonnative speakers of English, mother-tongue English speaking undergraduates are thought to need special help with writing, too. This help is expected to take place in their freshman composition classes in the typical North American university setting. In this context, just as in the undergraduate EAP class, the purposes and value of general academic writing instruction for native English speaking college freshmen have been questioned by a number of authors, such as those in Petraglia (1995) and debated by L1 scholars such as Bartholomae (1995) and Elbow (1995, 1999a). Although a detailed review of the issues from an L1 perspective is beyond my goal in this chapter, I want to point out that it is increasingly difficult to use an L1–L2 dichotomy in discussions of under-graduate academic writing, where students of all kinds often find them-selves in the same freshman composition or remedial writing classes (Matsuda, 1998; Silva, Leki, & Carson, 1997). As will be clear from the case studies described below, the diversity of academic writing games in under-graduate settings raises challenges for all teachers of writing who wish to coach students effectively, not just for those teaching so-called nonnative English speakers.

Case studies, whether of students whose mother tongue is English or some other language, complicate the picture. What they show us is that even if we do consult disciplinary experts on college campuses and exam-ine actual successful samples of reading and writing assignments from stu-dents' classes, each teacher and each student differ greatly and interact in ungeneralizable ways with context-bound academic literacy activities. The picture is further complicated when we consider the many students who are not yet taking classes in their disciplines—full time students in EAP or ESL classes—or those who are studying in undergraduate programs in non-English-medium universities (see the case study of David and Yasuko, be-low). It is not clear, under conditions of such diversity, local exigence, and complexity, how to encourage students' engagement in specialized aca-demic literacy practices (Bazerman, 1995). Nor is it clear whether to urge students to take a pragmatic, accommodationist approach (assuming we know what we are accommodating to), a culturally appropriate approach (assuming we know what is culturally appropriate), or a critical resistant approach (assuming we know what to resist and question; e.g., Allison, 1996; Atkinson, 1997; Benesch, 1996; Canagarajah, 2001; Elbow, 1999b; Rama-nathan & Atkinson, 1999; Santos, 1992). It may be that none of these ap-proaches reflects the realities in many undergraduate students' lives. As Leki's (1999b) case study of Polish undergraduate student Jan showed and that some of the case studies I discuss below show in less extreme ways, the name of the undergraduate writing game may be Survival Strategies. Jan shocks readers with his wily and even illegal ways to get through the sometimes senseless writings and exams in his undergraduate years. Situa-tions like Jan's cause Leki to ask whether writing is "overrated" in under-graduate education (Leki, 1999a).

There are not a great many case studies in print about college students and college writing teachers. One reason may be that case studies generally take more time than other kinds of studies such as surveys, cross-sectional sampling, or quasi-experimental studies. Most teachers who also do re-search do not have the luxury of much research time in their busy lives or the money to fund long-term studies. Sternglass (1997) talked about this problem in the introduction to her 6-year study of undergraduate writing development. Another reason for the paucity of case studies may be that qualitative studies, especially those including narratives and stories (Clandinin & Connelly, 1991; Connelly & Clandinin, 1990), are not accepted in some quarters as "scientific" enough (Herndl & Nahrwold, 2000; Miller, Nelson, & Moore, 1998). As a result, scholars in "fuzzy" fields, especially if those scholars are not yet well-established, may hesitate to take chances with research that does not follow a traditional model (Bridwell-Bowles, 1992, 1995). Still, the big questions in studies of academic reading and writing seem to be shared by most people interested in L1 and L2 literacy practices: Why is it difficult for different kinds of students to learn to read and write in college? What kinds of literacy activities do students and their teachers actually practice in different disciplines? How do students' academic literacies and identities change over time? What factors contribute to changes? Case studies can help answer these questions. A disturbing aspect of case studies, however, is that we probably end up learning more than we want to: The case study invariably immerses the scholar in so much detail and so much complexity that the basic questions simply can't be answered unambiguously. Once someone becomes a real person in a study she can no longer be an abstract subject, simplified and tidied up in the interest of objectivity and generalizability.

Let me turn now to some of the influential case studies of L1 and L2 undergraduate writers. My mention of two of these studies, those of Sternglass (1997) and Ivanič (1998), is reluctantly brief, since their participants were older, mature undergraduates and I wish to focus on studies of younger students, similar in age and experience to those that the teachers in my own case study worked with.

Sternglass' and Ivanič's Case Studies

Marilyn Sternglass' (1997) study is billed as a true longitudinal study encompassing 6 years of interaction with nine students at City University of New York. The students who stayed with her for the duration of the study were primarily African American and Latino, with one Asian, and one White (all Sternglass' terms) as well. Students' personal lives, such as family relationships, work obligations, and gender identity influenced many aspects of their writing including their developing ability to integrate personal knowledge and interests with academic writing tasks. This ability to integrate aspects of their personal identities into their writing helped push some of the students toward greater control of their academic writing. Unlike Chiseri-Strater's (1991) Nick and Anna (below), we do not see them as silenced in their academic writing, but as liberated, through their own efforts and through some powerful mentoring efforts by concerned teachers. Moreover, Sternglass' study covered many years in her participants' lives as undergraduates. It is the longitudinal portrayal, Sternglass claims, that allows us to see the changes in students' academic literacies and identities and to recognize the fundamental need for students to interact with interested and engaged teachers over time. Their identities as competent players in academic writing game practices evolve over time, in other words, as they engage with more competent players (Wenger, 1998).

Roz Ivanič's (1998) shorter term case study of the academic literacy experiences of eight mature (over age 25) undergraduate students—her "co-researchers"—deals primarily with what she refers to as the discoursal construction of identity in academic writing. She does not want to view academic enculturation a students' passive acquisition of dominant discourses. Instead she sees it as an experience involving tension and struggle between people and institutions in which students have opportunities to resist, take advantage of slippages in the system, and bring about change (Ortner, 1996).

Ivanič's (1998) study focused on linguistic text analyses and students' discussions about their linguistic choices. Although she interviewed eight students about the construction of one major academic essay, her detailed case study of "Rachel" shows how complex the discoursal construction of identity is. Rachel, a social worker student, wrote a paper on a "Family Case Study," attempting to blend disciplinary, course-specific, and personal voices. The tensions she experienced and choices she made highlight the many possible identities available to student writers within particular disciplines, departments, and courses and in interaction with specific people such as tutors (British usage) and teachers. Ivanič emphasizes that Rachel's identities as evidenced in her essay were multiple, complex, and partial and that Rachel was not able to position herself confidently as a contributor to knowledge in her field rather than as a student:

> Rachel was caught in a web of sincerity and deception as she attempted to take on social roles and to portray qualities which were valued by her different readers and, whenever possible, to be true to herself. This process was complicated by the fact that Rachel was not a very adept writer: she had difficulty in playing these games and, sadly, even more difficulty in challenging the conventions and presenting herself as she ideally would like to appear. (p. 168)

In both Ivanič's and Sternglass' studies we see students doing much more than learning a set of formal game rules. Instead, we see them learning to participate in game-like practices, sorting through and blending different values, behaviors, and beliefs that they hold and that the institutions they write for seem to espouse. From positions on the periphery and the margins (Wenger, 1998) they forged identities through their writing that were inevitably multivocalic and riddled with conflict and inconsistencies but that could potentially contribute richly to their own knowledge-construction.

Both Sternglass and Ivanič provide numerous examples of students' writing; Sternglass incorporates examples into her discussion of research issues, and Ivanič does detailed linguistic analyses. The amount and kind of focus on actual writing differentiates the case studies discussed below as well as my own, as does the extent of researchers' focus on teachers or students. Sternglass and Ivanič, like the authors of most case studies in language education, focus on students including the studies of Anna and Nick (Chiseri-Strater, 1991), Dave (McCarthy, 1987), and Yuko (Spack, 1997a) discussed below. My own case study in this chapter focuses on two teachers of undergraduate EAP writing, with students playing background roles.

Anna and Nick

Elizabeth Chiseri-Strater (1991) revised her dissertation into a smooth-flowing ethnographic study of two mother-tongue English speaking undergraduate college students, Anna and Nick, over two semesters. In this case study, the author is fundamentally interested in the two students as individuals. She paints a broad portrait of them in their college lives during this school year, drawing on journals, dialogue in and out of class, observation, and the students' notes and papers to document their responses to a variety of reading and writing activities. Chiseri-Strater captures some of the real-life drama of the students' lives: Nick, a prolific and expressive doodler, with his earring and torn jeans, combative and resistant in one class, cooperative in another; Anna the dancer, Anna the artist, and Anna the writer. Each of these very different undergraduate students was faced with the challenge so common in undergraduate education, that of learning to survive the demands of many different writing games across a diverse curriculum.

Both Anna and Nick seemed to thrive in a Prose Writing class taught by the same teacher, Donna. Donna set up a writing community that allowed for "students' exploration of personal and intellectual literacy development" (p. 1). Students read essays and stories, wrote response journals and a final paper, discussed and collaborated in groups, and participated in several different feedback arrangements (group, individual conference, journal writing) that ensured their personal involvement in the literacy activities. The processes of talk, reading, writing, and discipline-specific thinking all supported students' learning (p. 12).

These literacy-related practices were valued differently in other classes that Anna and Nick took. Anna revealed herself to be an artistic young woman who doubted her academic competence, yet rebelled against the formal ways of learning in her art history classes. She talked to Chiseri-Strater about the "tension in her academic life between fields that require distance, detachment, and objectivity and those that welcome intimacy, engagement and subjectivity" (p. 56). In the art history class that Chiseri-Strater visited, Anna was not able, for the most part, to connect the polished lecture and slide shows or the dense readings to her own interests, partly because the teacher had set up no classroom practices to promote feedback and engagement. Whatever connections Anna made by the end of the semester she managed on her own.

As for Nick, Chiseri-Strater describes him as a bored and troubled young man who had changed majors several times and who rebelled against the idea of leading a "normal" life after graduation that would be characterized by "a profession, a wife, and a dog named Spot" (p. 96). He persisted in playing relatively nonserious academic roles and games in his junior and senior years and in distancing his personal life from his academic literacy practices. "School is what I *do*," he said, "Not what I *am*" (p. 97). Still, in Donna's Prose Writing class, he was confident, articulate, and expressive, dominating many of the class discussions. He wrote long response journals, in two voices—one formal and one personal—that demonstrated he had potential to push himself to think and write and rewrite in more complex and challenging ways, a goal that his teacher urged him to pursue in revisions. Nick, however, resisted all suggestions, revised none of his work, and continued to avoid difficult topics. The one real change that Nick saw in his writing in this class was a new appreciation for his audience, which now consisted of peers and a responsive teacher in addition to himself, no doubt as a result of the interactive practices that Donna involved the students in.

The game practices in Nick's class on Political Thought were interactive, too, but not in the egalitarian and narrative style of the Prose Writing class. In the Political Thought class the professor exhibited the persona of an expert and an authority, challenging students to debate and argue and to compete with his own authoritative views. Intimidated at first, as were the other students, Nick believed that the game in this class required that he come up with interpretations in his papers that matched those of his professor (p. 128). Unable until the final paper to connect his personal interests and his flair for expressive writing to the work in this class, Nick claimed to have "lost his tolerance for the formality of political science writing" (p. 131). The final paper, however, was opened up to different styles including the personal after Chiseri-Strater suggested to the professor that he encourage alternate forms of writing. This freedom allowed Nick to write in journal form and to express his view that education had limited rather than expanded his growth by channeling his ideas into narrow categories (p. 138). Chiseri-Strater concludes her portrait of Nick with the comment that he liked himself better in the Prose Writing class, where he played a cooperative, collaborative game than in the Political Thought class, where he took on the identity of an intimidated combatant.

Chiseri-Strater brings alive the issues of what it means to behave in literate ways in college, demonstrating how the students' personal lives interact with more traditional literate activities, how "literacy codes and conventions"—part of what I refer to as writing games—differ from one undergraduate class to another, and how little nourishment these two young people received from the academy. Nick and Anna, struggling with issues of relationships, intimacy, job fears, gender stereotypes, and identity as they tried to get through class assignments, simply did not respond to the sometimes hierarchical and competitive game practices in the academy in ways that contributed to their personal and intellectual development. As Wenger (1998) might put it, their academic identities were defined as much by their nonparticipation as by their participation. Not wishing to generalize from these two case studies, Chiseri-Strater tells us that the portrayals can help educators recognize the multiple ways that students enact literate behaviors, and the complexity of the development of their identities within academic settings.

Dave

As Chiseri-Strater's (1991) study of Nick and Anna showed, a student does not need to be a second language speaker or a member of an oppressed minority to find the academy a strange place. "Dave," the college student that Lucille McCarthy (1987) described as a "stranger in strange lands," is another nonminority student who probably led a college life similar to that of many undergraduate students in North American colleges. This life consisted of traveling from one "land" (i.e., discipline) to another during his first 2 years as he went about fulfilling the undergraduate requirements at his college. As was the case for Jan in Leki's (1999b) study, the game for him involved figuring out what his teachers expected from him in each course's writing assignments. In general, as a newcomer to academia, he faced an academic challenge in which each course and each teacher introduced a field and a way of writing that was new to him.

Dave, according to McCarthy, was typical of students at his college in that he was young (18) when the study began, had comparable SAT scores and high school grades, lived not far from the school, and was White. Dave told McCarthy that he was a "hands-on" person who did not particularly care for reading and writing, although he believed that "writing was a tool he needed" (McCarthy, 1987, p. 238). By the time the study ended when Dave was a junior, he had been working as a lab technician in a local hospital for about a year, work that he enjoyed greatly and that did not involve any reading or writing.

McCarthy documented Dave's writing experiences in three different classes over three semesters: a freshman composition class, a sophomore poetry class, and a sophomore cell biology class. She visited the freshman composition class once a week for 9 weeks, collected all the class documents from the composition and the poetry classes, and interviewed all the professors once or twice. She conversed often with Dave and two of his friends, and interviewed them at least once a month during the poetry and biology semesters, taping and transcribing the longer interviews. McCarthy collected several protocols—audiotaped and transcribed think-aloud sessions during writing—from Dave as he wrote one draft of several papers in each class. From these she categorized what she called the "writer's conscious concerns" (p. 241). She also analyzed the papers that resulted and the teachers' written responses according to Grice's (1975) Cooperative Principle.

We do not know from this article the details of all of Dave's writing assignments for each of the three classes, but we do know that he wrote a series of short papers in each one. In his freshman composition class, the paper that McCarthy looked at was a discussion of the wrongs of abortion. In the poetry class, Dave had to analyze the "true meaning" of one poem. In the cell biology class, he had to write a review of a published scientific journal article. From the think-aloud protocols, McCarthy learned something about what Dave believed each of these writing games was about. Dave understood that his composition teacher was interested in coherence—how ideas tied together—and seemed to care little for content. Dave found this concept valuable. In the poetry class, the teacher asked students to follow strictly a specific form for quoting poetry, and conveyed the impression that there was one correct interpretation that their analyses were to aim for, a task that Dave found meaningless. In the biology class, the teacher required that the students' reviews follow the standard organization of a scientific article and that students incorporate the language and concepts of the article into their summaries, a task he found useful when considering his future in a scientific field. It is little wonder that an inexperienced writer like Dave could not see commonalities across the diversity of game practices he was exposed to. Even though all three papers required similar skills of summarizing, analyzing, and of organizing, and all three papers were "informational" texts written for the teacher-as-examiner, Dave believed that each writing assignment asked for totally different things.

What stands out in this early study in light of much later work on the social and political aspects of academic literacy practices is that Dave was doing more than learning to write different kinds of texts. He also needed to negotiate his way through very different role relationships between teacher and students in each class, showing that it is difficult to generalize about the function of the key players in academic writing games. In the composition class, the teacher portrayed herself as a writer herself, working alongside students, who themselves worked together. In the biology class, the teacher played the role of expert and professional, a mentor who was helping students learn to do what scientists do (he told McCarthy that "it often comes as a rude shock to the students that the way biologists survive in the field is by writing" [p. 257]). In the poetry class, the teacher seemed to play the role of a distant all-knowing insider with little interest in bringing students onto his playing field. Dave, then, might be seen as playing the roles of collaborator in the freshman composition class, of newcomer to a discipline in the biology class, and of outsider in the poetry class. On each of these playing fields the rules differed in Dave's view and his participation and his academic identities differed accordingly.

As an undergraduate learning how to write in his academic setting, Dave thus seemed to be pulled in widely different directions, socially, intellectually, and textually, the rules of the game apparently differing widely in each specific context. It is possible that in this conflicted environment he may have begun to see himself as a writer, thanks to his composition class, and as a legitimate newcomer to a professional field, thanks to his cell biology class. But in his junior year the transition that he talked about was that of having learned the strategic game of survival. In recounting advice he would give new freshmen about writing in college he told McCarthy that "first you've got to figure out what your teachers want. And then you've got to give it to them if you're gonna get the grade" (p. 233). McCarthy (1987) realized that teachers concerned with the development of students' academic literacy may not like Dave's answer, but she insists that it reflects Dave's sensitivity to the social (and political?) realities of learning academic writing games in college:

> Successful students are those who can, in their interactions with teachers during the semester, determine what constitutes appropriate texts in each classroom. ... They can then produce such a text. Students who cannot do this, for whatever reason—cultural, intellectual, motivational—are those who fail, deemed incompetent communicators in that particular setting. They are unable to follow what Britton calls the "rules of the game" in each class (1975, p. 76). As students go from one classroom to another they play a wide range of games, the rules for which, Britton points out, include many conventions and presuppositions that are not explicitly articulated. (pp. 233–234)

In short, the diversity of settings and the often unstated game rules in an undergraduate context, combined with students' lack of identity as writers and their often uncertain purposes and interests make the task of learning to write seem even more difficult than it is in graduate and professional settings. It is no wonder that many of us floundered back then, myself included. This floundering seems normal in its inevitability. If so, it is astounding that so many young people, including students whose mother tongue is not English, manage to survive their undergraduate writing games as well as they do.

Yuko

In all of these case studies, we see how centrally important the situated local literacy practices were (Barton, Hamilton, & Ivanič, 2000), in contrast to general skills students might have learned in special preparation classes. We also see the beginnings of changes in identity as the students described by the authors found their way into their majors and found ways to survive—to meet their professors' expectations, with or without good mentoring. In the few case studies of second language learners in the academy, we see examples of strategies that novice readers and writers not yet familiar with English academic discourse develop to survive on unfamiliar academic playing fields. Ruth Spack's (1997a) study of "Yuko" is just such a study.

Spack's study of Yuko is a richly detailed longitudinal narrative, covering Yuko's experiences in nine undergraduate courses over 3 years and documenting Yuko's beliefs and interpretations of her experiences in relation to her education in Japan. Yuko came from a small town in Japan, some distance from Tokyo. In her childhood she learned to read before starting school, and later left home to board at a competitive high school in Tokyo where she learned the Tokyo dialect. During her school years in Japan she studied the books authorized by the Ministry of Education but did little other reading. She also recalled doing no writing except some 1-page "reaction papers" in a literature class. As for English, she studied the required 6 years in Japan, according to the grammar-translation methods used there, spent a year as an exchange student in a U.S. high school, studied several nights a week in her junior and senior years at a U.S.–British sponsored English school, and spent 10 weeks in a summer English program in England. These experiences, plus a great deal of extra preparation, Yuko believed, helped her score so well on the TOEFL (640).

Spack undertook this study when Yuko, at that time a freshman, begged to be let into one of Spack's ESL composition classes at her East coast university in spite of demonstrated proficiency on the standardized test of English. Yuko was one of those students whose high TOEFL score did not give her confidence that she could survive her first semester at the U.S. university where Spack was teaching. In halting speech, Yuko told Spack that in Japan she had not learned what she needed to learn in order to compete in a U.S. university, such as essay writing and efficient reading. Her many cross-cultural comparisons show that she believed that the games of academic writing differed in Japan and the United States. In her view, acquiring and memorizing information were needed to succeed in the Japanese educational context, and creativity and originality of opinion were needed in the U.S. context. She also seemed convinced that her silence in class, ingrained in her from her many years in the Japanese system, was holding her back. Pulled in conflicting directions, she was "attracted to what she perceived to be the 'American style' because, in the American way, 'I can have my own point of view,' " yet felt unable to participate actively and "superficially" in her classes as she thought many Americans did (p. 16).

At first Spack became curious about Yuko's literacy experiences in Japan and how those would compare to her experiences in her freshman college classes. But within a few weeks, Yuko was asking Spack for specific help with one class in International Relations that she was having trouble with. Spack decided to interview Yuko over the first year, to collect materials from the International Relations class, and to observe and take notes on Yuko in Spack's own English classes. Continuing the data collection into Yuko's third year, Spack held interviews and conversations with Yuko about her reading and writing experiences, observed Yuko in Spack's English class, and collected documents from Yuko's other classes and drafts of Yuko's papers.

We learn from Spack's study that perhaps the hardest aspect of Yuko's student life in her first year was what Yuko herself called her lack of background knowledge and vocabulary. In her first International Relations class, she simply could not understand the readings in her textbook. Spack provided us with an excerpt from the book which suggested that the fault was not entirely Yuko's. Still, when her professor then asked the students to write an "original," "aggressive" paper applying course materials to a choice of topics, she gave up and dropped the course, not having developed at this point any survival game strategies. In her second semester, she had a similar experience in a Philosophy of Religion course, finding she "didn't have a clue" what the readings were about. Having dropped two courses, she went home for the summer, wondering whether to change majors.

However, Yuko's experiences in Spack's English courses during that same difficult first year seemed to be those of another person. Although Yuko did not recognize fully the changes that Spack saw, she did in fact become a more fluent and fearless writer, and took on (in Spack's eyes) the identity of a person who could defend herself in class when challenged intellectually by classmates during debates and write clearly and coherently. Yuko did not yet see herself in these terms.

At home in Japan that summer, Yuko read novels in English. She came back for her second year refreshed, determined not to give up, more confident in her reading ability, and armed with new game strategies. For example, she told Spack that she had stopped worrying about not being able to understand every word of every reading, was avoiding difficult readings when she had a choice of topics, and read differently according to the kind of text and to the treatment that text was given in her classes. She also learned to choose paper topics to which she could apply some of her background knowledge of Asia, and she learned as well to string together passages of text, with page numbers given, taken from her sources. The teaching assistants and teachers who read her papers, and even Spack herself at first, did not notice the extent of Yuko's "textual borrowing." Yuko remained torn about these papers, believing that her job was to come up with original ideas and phrasings throughout her papers as well as in introductions and conclusions. She was surprised that the "Japanese style" of textual borrowing and repeating information that she had hoped to leave behind actually worked to improve her grades (p. 32; cf. Currie's [1998] Diana). However, she was still convinced at the end of the second year that "there was a Japanese way of writing and an American way of writing, the former being a repetition of the ideas contained in a reading and the latter being an original opinion provided by the (student) writer" (p. 39). Spack saw that Yuko was amply rewarded for repeating ideas from her readings, and recognized that student writers in the United States face the same dilemma—that of trying to write from sources and to be original at the same time. For her part, Yuko saw her confidence increase as she began to get As and Bs in her classes, a result, she believed, of "practice," of consulting with professors and TAs, and of learning to selectively ignore what she did not know (pp. 38–39). Yuko retook the International Relations course that she had dropped her first year, as well as a sociology course where the professor guided students to a deeper understanding of the material through reading response journals and systematic assignments. In her third year, Yuko continued taking more control of the reading and writing activities in ways that suited her abilities and interests and that integrated her own knowledge with what she was learning.

In the conclusion of her article, Spack describes some of the changes that Yuko went through in her freshman, sophomore, and junior years. For example, she describes Yuko's early model of reading this way:

- Good students grasp meaning the first time they read.
- Good students understand every word of every reading assignment.
- Good students read everything assigned.
- Good students read everything on schedule. (p. 45)

Yuko gradually began to dispel these myths as she learned to read strategically and purposefully (see Haas's [1994] case study of Eliza, an undergraduate student learning to read biology texts), and to recognize that "American writing" was not original in the way she had believed at first. Writers, she learned, drew on other sources all the time. Critical thinking was based on what writers understood from published authorities.

Yuko believed, according to Spack, that she had learned to read and write in an "American style," and that she had finally overcome her "Japanese style." Not having access to data on Yuko from Japan, Spack wisely refrains from commenting on the accuracy of Yuko's belief. What she does tell us is that Yuko's perception of her educational background in Japan influenced her approach to and her theorizing about the development of her academic literacy in the United States (p. 47) and that her background knowledge of Japanese culture became important in helping her develop topics for writing. Yuko, in other words, did not give up her Japanese identity, nor did she fully take on the identity of her mythical American student, but perhaps she discovered new aspects of her self, integrated them with the old, and played one off against the other. With time and maturity and with greater understanding of the complexity of academic environments and practices, she also lost some of her idealism. More realistic by the end of her third year, she had learned through situated practice in a wide variety of very different courses how to read and write strategically in ways that ensured her survival in a competitive foreign language academic environment. In the end, Yuko learned how to play the different writing games in her academic setting in her own way and crafted a complex academic identity that matched no stereotypes (even her own) of passive Japanese learners who supposedly depend on rote memorization for their success (see Kubota [1997, 1999] for critiques of these stereotypes). She was beginning to reconcile, in other words, her different forms of membership, what Wenger (1998) calls "multimembership," into a coherent and complexly negotiated identity that did not require that she give up any aspects of her past self. As part of her survival games strategies, she was learning instead to reinterpret her role and location of herself within the undergraduate community.

The Beginning of Change: Situated Survival?

The diverse and complex academic literacy games that the undergraduates in these case studies were learning required that the students develop survival strategies in multiple local contexts rather than expertise as academic writers in focused disciplinary communities. Students who might have been able to identify themselves as successful academic writers based on their early experiences in some classes (e.g., Sternglass' students in their composition classes, Yuko in her ESL classes, Dave in his biology and composition classes) apparently did not recognize these successes as ones that could influence their literacy activities or their academic identities in other settings. Rather, they saw them as isolated responses to particular teachers and assignments. They did not see the undergraduate setting as part of a larger enterprise in which embedded communities of practice might have shared goals and practices (Wenger, 1998).

Of course they may have had trouble seeing the commonalities in academic literacy games across the broad spectrum of classes they took because there weren't many. Indeed, research has revealed many disciplinary differences in academic writing, but equally importantly many differences according to particular teaching–learning situations. The key to the students' survival in academic settings thus involved their ability to figure out what was expected in each class—strategic social and interpretive skills rather than just formal academic writing skills. Moreover, as Brown, Collins, and Duguid (1989) pointed out some time ago, because much school learning takes places without immersing students in "authentic activity" in disciplinary domains, students are "asked to use the tools of a discipline without being able to adopt its culture" (p. 33). The systemic constraints of undergraduate education, with its brief forays into multiple disciplines and their concomitant literacy practices, make it unlikely that many students will come to identify with one or more of these disciplinary subcultures or will come to see coherence in the larger educational enterprise.

Although it is not clear that the undergraduate students I discussed in these case studies came to see themselves as participants in a community of academic writers or as experts within the academy rather than as just survivors, their evolving identities as survivors on a wide range of academic playing fields will stand them in good stead. They developed a sense of what kinds of games were played, who some of the key players were, and what strategies they needed to employ to—literally—get the grade. With or without a local academic village (Geertz, 1983) in which to situate themselves, they had learned that academic writing games involve more than learning sets of formal game rules, and this lesson is foundational to the development of academic literacy.

CASE STUDY: COMMUNITIES OF PRACTICE? GAME STRATEGIES IN TWO TEACHERS' EAP CLASSES IN A JAPANESE UNIVERSITY

In this section I wrestle with the question of what a "communities of practice" (Lave, 1996; Lave & Wenger, 1991; Wenger, 1998) EAP classroom might look like in an undergraduate English-as-a-foreign language setting and explore what kinds of game strategies might be practiced in such a setting. Given issues that have been raised in the literature discussed earlier, can such a framework be rationalized? What kinds of practices, identities, and transitions do teachers envision for their undergraduate EAP students, and what is it that students believe they are learning and practicing? In particular I hoped to learn what the two teachers I studied believed the most important aspects of academic writing were and how they introduced students to them in a brief one-semester course. Moreover, as proponents of versions of a "communities of practice" framework in our own teaching, all three of us wondered how such communities of practice could be enacted in a structurally constrained EAP foreign language setting in ways that would help students become participants in academic conversations (Casanave & Kanno, 1998) and help them begin to see themselves as writers with something to say. We could not send them out to become "ethnographers" of English-language academic literacy practices on our own university campus (Currie, 1999; Hirvela, 1997; Johns, 1990, 1995) because nearly all work was done in Japanese. Nevertheless, by the end of the study, I knew I would be able to present the study as a success story, one that demonstrated what was possible given hard work and engagement with challenging tasks (Bazerman, 1995; Leki, 1995a), in spite of my unresolved questions about academic literacy games.

Two Teachers, Two Communities of Practice

Background to the Study

In the spring of 1997, one of the teachers (Yasuko) and I undertook a semester-long research project on our Japanese university campus to find out what the attitudes and practices were of five teachers of a newly established Academic Reading and Writing course for our undergraduates. The course was originally conceived by me and the second teacher (David) as a step in helping prepare our junior and senior students for future graduate work in English-medium universities. Many of our undergraduate students are advanced users of English, and some of these and other students as well dream of one day studying abroad (meaning outside Japan). Much to our surprise, in spite of a course description emphasizing graduate preparation and a course enrollment limited to 15, more than 100 students tried to enter the first two sections taught by David that were opened the semester before this study was undertaken. Clearly many of the students wanted more than a narrowly defined course in graduate preparation; they wanted more academic English as well, or perhaps just more English, regardless of their plans for future study. We opened more sections the next semester.

Yasuko and I worked together to help set up the multiple sections of the course. The other teachers of the new sections requested some guidance about what and how to teach this course, so we provided a broadly defined template of the course on Academic Reading and Writing that David had written, one that emphasized that we hoped to prepare students for critical reading and writing that they might need in graduate school and that students should design their own writing projects (see Appendix A). All the teachers had the freedom to redesign the course in whatever way they saw fit, with the proviso that we wanted students to have a hands-on writing experience with topics chosen by them and not just to learn *about* writing. For the study, Yasuko and I observed five sections and took detailed field notes three times (beginning, middle, and end of the semester), interviewing the teachers after each observation, transcribing those interview tapes, and collecting class syllabuses and handouts. We also distributed a questionnaire in Japanese two times (beginning and end of the semester) to all students (about 140) asking them about their reasons for taking the class, their paper topics, and their responses to the class (see Appendix B). Students responded in Japanese or English, as they wished; I had the Japanese responses from David's and Yasuko's students translated to English by two Japanese assistants. We did not collect student papers since our project was not focusing on text analysis. For my part of this project, I observed and interviewed David and Yasuko. Because I knew David and Yasuko quite well, our conversations about academic literacy didn't stop when the tape recorder went off, so some of my "data" and my interpretations slide off the field note and transcript pages and into the fuzzy realm of remembered lunches, dinners, and phone and e-mail chats. I also taped an interview with five of Yasuko's students mid-semester in English, and kept copies of the first month of e-mail conversations among David's students and between them and him. I used the questionnaire information to compile a general profile of students from that semester and to learn more about the goals and responses to the class of David's and Yasuko's students in particular.

We began the project with questions that the three of us continued to explore throughout the semester about what we should be doing in an undergraduate academic literacy course in a foreign language setting, our responses becoming more complex with the accumulation of experience in our particular setting. I believe that similar questions can be asked of any course that aims to help prepare undergraduate writers for more advanced academic work. Here are some that underlay our project and that I continue to wrestle with: To what extent were these classes about teaching and learning aspects of the English language or about teaching and learning some of the social and political values and practices associated with writing in academic settings? Does the argument that students need to get a head start in possible future graduate work in English-medium settings make sense, given our belief in the situated learning framework and in the preeminent role of our own *in situ* academic enculturation? A head start in what? Does the apprenticeship metaphor work here, where EAP teachers are seen as mentors and expert models for novice practitioners, or does this metaphor work better at graduate levels (see Chaps. 3 and 4)? In what ways can the foreign language EAP classes of the two teachers I observed, David and Yasuko, be considered "communities of practice"? As "coaches" of academic writing games, how did David and Yasuko seem to understand and practice various academic writing games in their respective sections? In the discussion that follows, I first introduce David and Yasuko and their classes, then touch on some of these questions through a discussion of some of the classroom game strategies that David and Yasuko seemed to feel were relevant to their young students' development of academic literacy. I also bring in some of their students' views, in particular as documented in their open-ended responses in Japanese and English to questionnaires. The games were played in quite different ways in the two classes; some of the differences can be attributed to the two teachers' own experiences with academic literacy practices in their graduate school enculturation and in their current writing activities.

David

By the time I interviewed and observed David as part of the larger research project on our campus about academic writing, I had known him for almost 6 years. A colleague of mine and I had interviewed him for a 3-year position in 1992, for which he was hired. We both liked his sense of humor and his energy in addition to his CV. Tall and athletic, sandy hair beginning to thin, David was in his mid-thirties at the time. He had traces of a southern U.S. accent that made a nice addition to the collection of Englishes in our program. When he arrived on our campus David was just finishing his dissertation in language education from a university in Georgia. I didn't think he could finish in a year and work full time, but he did. Since that time he had taught, read, presented, and written in areas such as foreign language education, cross-cultural pragmatics, and intercultural communication.

Fluent in Japanese, married to a Japanese, and the father of two young "doubles" (he refused to refer to his children as "half Japanese and half American"), he had special interests and experience in Japan that made him a particularly committed teacher. He saw and resisted the constraints and limitations imposed by aspects of the Japanese educational system and worked hard to help talented young students see a larger academic world. At the same time, he understood and respected other aspects of the Japanese culture and educational system, and so seemed to me to feel pushed and pulled by conflicting understandings and goals. On our campus, David was particularly committed to helping high English proficiency students develop academic literacy. He had taught many conversationally fluent, seemingly bilingual English students in his undergraduate classes and believed these students could develop their full potential as bilinguals if they could become as literate in English as they were fluent in conversation. Moreover, some of these students wished to join graduate programs in English-medium universities, and one way to help prepare them was to introduce them to North American practices of academic reading and writing that he was familiar with. He was instrumental in designing the original template for the reading and writing course, three semesters before our project took place—a course that because of institutional constraints was limited to one semester. At the time we worked together on this template we both knew that a one-semester course could barely scratch the surface of what students needed: lots of writing and reading practice, in-depth discussions, and designing and carrying out their own writing projects. What we didn't talk about explicitly at the time were the harsh realities of academic enculturation, where learning to participate in the many kinds of academic practices seems to take place through immersion in academic settings, in sometimes highly politicized interactions with different professors and colleagues, over many years. We were familiar with these realities from our own graduate educations.

David had taken a number of courses in his own graduate program that dealt with literacy issues, and had been teaching aspects of academic literacy for a number of years. He himself was reading and writing whenever his tight schedule permitted, in Japanese (a lecture series course he was teaching) as well as in English. He wrote papers for conferences at least once a year, and whenever we talked, had several papers in the hopper waiting to be revised for publication. Talk about his research and writing was punctuated with acerbic though humorous comments about his heavy schedule, lack of time, and the dilemma of how to balance all of his obligations. David mentioned in his first interview that he felt he was not reading and writing enough, but that the manuscript reviews he did for academic journals and the masters thesis advising he did for an American university in Tokyo helped him understand what students needed in an academic reading and writing class. In other interviews he talked about designing his class activities and responses from "intuition." His high energy, intensity, and perfectionist tendencies kept him in a state of uncertainty throughout the semester, but also ensured that he did everything possible to conduct what he and students could assess as a successful class—one that resulted in students' production of a "good paper" and in everyone's sense of accomplishment. From my observations and interviews, I got a sense of what David thought the academic writing game was all about, and of what aspects of the practice he intuitively, as well as overtly, believed undergraduates needed to know in order to begin participating.

Yasuko

I first met Yasuko when she came to our campus for an interview for a position in our English section. A native Japanese, she was still finishing up the last details of her PhD program in Canada where she had specialized in bilingual education and qualitative research methods. I remember sitting at a lunch table with her and several other colleagues and being struck by how tiny she was. I felt clumsy, large, and bulky next to her. She seemed half my height and weight, and I wondered where she was able to find clothes that fit her. The second surprise was how articulate and firm she was in her discourse with us, in her slightly British-accented English. I wondered at the time where all this confidence had come from in someone so young and tiny when I, at 20 years her senior, was still experiencing unsettling ups and downs in professional identity and in my relationship with the academic world. Was it an act, the kind we all perform when we are on stage in the serious game of the job interview? Or did she really have a comfortable sense already of who she was? Or, a third possibility, had she just not yet been burned by any of the political games in academia that tend to sap one's enthusiasm for the job? At any rate, I was taken with her freshness, her commitment to continuing her research, and her excitement, tempered with questions and inexperience, about teaching undergraduates. I sensed that the students would respond to her with enthusiasm, which they did.

At the time I observed her classes as part of our project she had been teaching English at our university in her first full time job for about a year. She was teaching the Academic Reading and Writing course for the second time, two sections of it, plus regular required freshman and sophomore English classes. Throughout the semester in which I observed and interviewed her, she was doing her own academic reading and writing in addition to teaching her regular English classes, including "freewriting" that she did with her students and on her own, work on a paper from her dissertation for future publication, and reading in the areas of academic literacy, cultural readjustment, and Japanese minority children. She had had no formal training in the teaching of writing, although she had once taken an EAP-like course which she claimed had helped her understand what would be expected of her in her PhD program. Before arriving on our campus, as was the case for David, she had been immersed in nonstop reading and writing experiences for the 6 or so years of her doctoral work. As had David, Yasuko mentioned throughout the semester in which I observed her that her previous and current academic literacy experiences at the graduate level greatly influenced her class practices and reflected aspects of her own academic enculturation that she felt were important.

The Students and the Course

On our campus, an old private university, students came from all over Japan, many entering through the grueling entrance exam process (see Brown & Yamashita, 1995; Frost, 1991) and some through Admissions Office processes involving special applications and interviews. Quite a few students were "returnees"—students who had spent several years in foreign countries where their businessmen fathers were stationed. All students were required to take a foreign language in their freshman and sophomore years, and could take some of the few elective language courses once their language requirement was fulfilled.

From the questionnaire data gathered from all of the students (136 responded to the first one) at the beginning of the semester (Appendix B), we learned that most were sophomores (about 61%) and about 25% were juniors, even though the course was intended for juniors and seniors. Seventy percent were women, and more than half had lived abroad for 1 year or more. Over 80% had learned something about writing in Japanese in their past schooling, and more than 50% had studied some kind of writing in English. About half of the students said they would seek full-time jobs after graduating, and about one third said they would pursue graduate study abroad. Most students claimed they liked to write or at least felt neutral about it (83% for Japanese, 75% for English). Moreover, many of the students said they read books and magazines outside of class in Japanese (88%) and just over half claimed to do so in English (52%). These last two sets of figures say something important about the students who chose to take the Academic Reading and Writing course—most enjoyed and practiced reading and writing in both their first and second languages.

In the open-ended responses to the first questionnaire, students explained why they had decided to take the course and described what their goals were. David's and Yasuko's students, for the most part, stated that they hoped to maintain or "brush up" their English. About one third of their students said they needed academic English because they wished to study abroad some day or that they needed English for their future jobs. These figures accord with the general profile of the whole group. Specifically they said they hoped to learn aspects of basic writing skills, learn how to write good "high level" academic reports and papers, and to learn to express their ideas clearly and fluently. Some students, particularly those in David's very high level class, expressed a desire to learn specific techniques of writing, such as how to structure papers, how to collect reference materials, and how to write their opinions persuasively and logically. (Several of David's students had taken his class before and were aware of what they would be doing this particular semester.) In general, however, the students' personal goals for the class were quite general.

David and Yasuko taught two sections each, roughly considered the two highest levels. In the sections that I observed, one for each teacher, there were 15 students in David's class and 6 students, all women, in Yasuko's class. Yasuko's class included as well one student from the newly opened graduate school on our campus. The classes met once a week for 90 minutes for 14 weeks. Except for the few students in David's class who had taken this same class before, none of the students had had a class in the development of academic literacy in English, and none had worked for a full semester on a major single-authored paper on a topic of their own choice in English or in Japanese even though some of them had done quite a bit of writing in freshman and sophomore English courses. In both David's and

Yasuko's classes, most of the students had very high TOEFL scores, in the mid-500 to low 600 range, and some had spent more time living outside Japan than inside. These were "returnee" students, children of businessmen who had been stationed abroad by their Japanese companies and who had grown up bilingually. However, in some cases their English development had come to a halt in junior high school when they returned to Japan in order to enter the competitive race for entrance into a prestigious university. As Cummins (1981) and others have noted, fluency in oral conversation may be unrelated to competence in the text-related proficiencies required by people who need to read and write in the academy. Some students themselves were aware of and wished to close this gap.

The challenge facing David and Yasuko, and other teachers including me (I had taught a section the previous semester), was where to start, and what to do in just one short semester of 13 or 14 class meetings. It seemed to all of us that students needed so much. We ourselves had learned to write in academic settings over many years, and most of that in graduate school. The one thing David and Yasuko and I did agree on was that we wanted to consider the undergraduate students in the classes to be inexperienced academic writers rather than just students lacking proficiency in English. All of us, after all, had once been novice academic writers and David and I could recall developmental experiences even in our native languages that made us squirm with discomfort. (Yasuko on the other hand continually surprised me by her love of writing.) We agreed, too, that we wanted students to "own" their topics, and to have ongoing support and interaction with teacher and peers as they struggled through their first writing experiences in these academically oriented classes. And as Bazerman (1995) advised, we wanted them to feel motivated enough to work very hard. To these ends, David had his students read and respond orally and in writing to academic journal articles and write a paper supported by at least five published sources. Yasuko had her students read and respond orally and in writing to nonfiction stories written by people who had done fieldwork, and then do their own ethnographic-style fieldwork project about which they were to write their own nonfiction story and give a class presentation. Amidst these broadly similar goals, what specific practices did these two teachers set up for their students? After briefly describing the setting for the two classes, I group my observations under several categories that I label "game strategies."

The Setting

To my eye, our campus is not conducive to encouraging student motivation, study, and interaction. It was built on farm and forest land, opened in 1990, and was hailed as Japan's new innovative computer campus. It strikes me as gray and cold, built as it is of concrete slabs and a lot of glass. The landscaping in part makes up for the coldness; there are more trees and expanses of lawn than one usually sees at universities in the wider Tokyo area, and there is even a duck pond where an occasional snowy egret visits. On a rare clear day we can see Mt. Fuji from the fourth floors of the classroom buildings. But there are few places for the more than 4,000 students to sit, chat, study, and concentrate. The only outside seating consists of 10 card-table sized tables with a few metal chairs around each just outside the cafeteria and bookstore area. Weather permitting, some students sit on lawns. There are no dormitories, no general student center, and few quiet spaces in the media center–library, which is often crowded with noisy groups of students chatting behind a computer monitor or at one of the library study tables. Other than the rare empty classrooms, there are no other places for students to collaborate and study together. The classrooms themselves are square or rectangular gray concrete and glass rooms with bare walls, crowded with desk-chairs or heavy two-person tables with the teacher lectern or podium up front and close to the black or white board. Unless a teacher decides to take the noisy step of moving chairs and tables, all students face front in the regular 35–60 person rooms. Except for the smallest of the seminar rooms, chalk dust covered equipment abounds—large television monitor, VCR, OHP, tape system under the hinged desk top, and some with full computer-projecting systems.

David's and Yasuko's classrooms were designed to accommodate about 35 students. Like the design of the rest of the campus, the physical setting communicated that teaching and learning happens by transmission within classroom walls, from teachers-knowers to listening students, not around seminar tables or in lounges, cafes, and student centers. It did not convey the sense, in other words, that communication, engagement, and collaborative practice were central to the educational process. David and Yasuko, within these physical constraints, did what they could to create an atmosphere of engaged practice, warmth, and support for students, often leaving the front podium, rearranging seating, and joining student discussion groups. The "game strategies" they practiced in each of their classrooms differed in emphasis, but appeared in some form in both classes. I discuss six of these strategies below.

Game Strategy 1: Interact With Texts and With Others About Texts

David and Yasuko hoped that their students would begin to see texts as entities with which they needed to interact constructively and about which they routinely interacted with peers and teachers. They both wanted students to read extensively, respond to what they read in writing and in discussion with them and peers, and to begin to see themselves as participants in conversations with authors and with each other about authors. The students in David's and Yasuko's classes had not conceptualized their relationships with texts in this way before. How did these two teachers set up games practices that might encourage students' changing relationship with texts? Reading response journals, discussion, and teacher feedback helped instigate this change.

Reading Response Journals and Follow-Up Discussion. Both David and Yasuko asked students to read one or more common articles, write responses in a journal, and discuss their responses later in small group and whole class discussions. David also had his students read, respond to, and discuss articles each had found through an extensive literature search on an individual paper topic. David and Yasuko participated in discussions, sometimes as listeners, sometimes as commentators on the subject matter, and sometimes as guides to help students construct deeper, more critical and questioning responses, particularly in the case of a common reading article that they themselves knew well.

In my first observation very early in the semester, David was helping students learn the serious game of how to respond to academic articles in writing and in talk and to interact with him and with each other in their discussions of readings, activities that he himself had learned to do in graduate school and that he was actively pursuing in his own current work. He had set up a small-group activity with reading response journals designed to get students interacting with each other through the texts they had read. He explained to them why this response activity was helpful. "It gives writers a sense that there are readers," he told the students, "that people are listening." At the end of class, in which the students had sat in their groups reading each others' journals and chatting quietly, he reminded them once again about the conversational nature of this academic activity: "These journals," he reiterated, "should be a conversation," not just between teacher and student but "sideways" too, between and among student readers and writers.

In revealing where this goal had come from, and his sense of how it could be achieved, David said, "It came from my experience. It came from what I think is useful. Where else could it come from?" (Interview 1, 4/22/97). He clarified that this experience included not only his academic experiences in and out of graduate school, but also "peer advice and social interaction," his experience with Japanese schools, and his own theoretical orientations toward learning that he had developed through his own reading and study:

> The idea about reading and responding to a journal [article] was in part from my own theoretical interpretation about acquiring literacy, or acquiring language, through interaction, and by actually using the language. . . . I mean the

practice develops out of that theory or theoretical interpretation. (Interview 1, 4/22/97)

Sometimes it was difficult to get students to direct their reading responses to each other rather than just to the teacher. In my first observation of Yasuko at the beginning of the semester, she had asked her small group of women students to talk about the nonfiction readings they had chosen from her reserve list—a collection of well-written narratives she had put on reserve that were models of good nonfiction storytelling. She had chosen readings that she herself had found especially engaging and hoped that students, too, would become caught up in the stories about autistics, a male prostitute, or a well-known singing group, and find themselves getting to know the characters as well as the textual structure of the stories themselves. Her instructions to her small group of women students on this day were to talk about what they had read and about how they felt about what they had read. Her goal was to have students interact with each other about these readings, not just with her, and to respond to the descriptions and dilemmas of the characters and to the authors' manner of telling their stories.

The students did not yet know each other well, but I was struck in this early class by how hesitant and teacher-oriented this small group of advanced English-speaking young women seemed to be. The talk tended to be directed at Yasuko in the beginning of this activity, more like an informal presentation than interaction among group members. Like most students, these young women were more familiar with a transmission model of education where information from a text was to be displayed back to a teacher, not used as a basis for interaction with classmates or with the text itself. Students had written in their response journals on their chosen readings, so referred to their papers as they talked, but the first young woman to speak about her Oliver Sacks article on autism made eye contact only with Yasuko. Before the second student began to talk, Yasuko stood up suddenly and commented that students should be talking to each other. She then moved out of the circle and back to a seat behind a large teacher's desk. Just after the student began talking, again maintaining eye contact only with her, Yasuko quietly left the room. The speaker continued talking, looking down at her paper and now making eye contact primarily with the student who was sitting directly across from her. When Yasuko returned a few minutes later, the speaker continued without a break while two other women in the group nodded and backchanneled occasionally. Yasuko, at the teacher's desk, kept her gaze down at her own notebook of freewriting, flipping a page from time to time. Several other students talked about the articles they had read, fielding a few questions, and managing to interact with each other rather than with Yasuko, whose generally lowered eye gaze did not invite interaction with her.

However, Yasuko did participate actively in response to a pair of students who had both read the same article—the second of two Oliver Sacks stories that were on reserve, this one on the effects of L-Dopa, the theme of the film "Awakenings." Both women spoke from a handout, which the other students followed as they spoke. Yasuko once asked, "So what can we learn from this?" In the discussion that followed, Yasuko was trying to get students to link the two texts by Sacks, to compare their structures, and to help them learn more about Sacks as a person and an author with extra information she was able to provide them. The discussion picked up. The students seemed curious about Sacks and wanted to know what was in the "rest of his book" and about "why he didn't insist anything, about what we should do." Yasuko filled these gaps as best she could in the limited time, trying to shape the author into a real person with whom students could communicate. The class laughed when Yasuko told them that Sacks "really likes footnotes" (some had complained about this characteristic of his writing) and that some of his articles devoted up to half a page to them. Yasuko talked about Sacks in the way she might talk about a colleague she knew, as someone with whom she had interacted over time through the many essays of his she had read. Students were getting a sense from this discussion that it was possible to relate to the authors they read as people with whom they could interact and that a serious expectation of academic literacy games was that readers interact with authors in just this way.

In this early class activity, I did not observe Yasuko explaining to students how to communicate about the texts they had read, how to interact with the texts themselves through their journals (a required writing activity), or how to communicate with each other about texts. Yasuko chose instead to arrange the activity so that students would not be able to communicate in the traditional unidirectional way with her or just receive information transmitted from her, but would be forced to talk to each other. She also modeled how becoming familiar with an author's body of work could allow readers to see authors as people with a coherent agenda that could be discussed from the perspectives of their different writings. In particular in her descriptions of "inside information" on author Sacks, she showed students (did not teach them) that for her reading meant getting to know authors, becoming familiar with their quirks and personal styles, and finding in them tricks of the trade to apply to her own writing. I had the feeling as observer that the students had not practiced these kinds of interactions before, with texts, and with each other about texts, and that in their "presentations" and discussions they could not yet relate to the authors as people with or about whom they might have a conversation. They were just beginning to practice this interaction game, and in some cases did this through the back door: By mid-semester, I saw that Yasuko had begun to acquaint students with the interactive aspects of academic reading and writing by modeling a way of relating to reading and writing that she had acquired in graduate school and that was evident in how she herself talked about texts and their authors.

Feedback and Response. Part of the practice of interacting with and about texts, for both teachers, involved extensive teacher involvement through written and oral feedback, both on reading response journals and on student papers. These activities conveyed the sense that oral and written interaction with texts of all kinds was a normal practice that had less to do with grading and evaluation than with what David called the practice of "engaged discussion" between novice and more experienced academic writers.

For his part, David responded in depth in writing to students' reading response journals and to their paper drafts, modeling in sometimes excruciating detail his belief in the role of an involved listener in the development of academic literacy. This was one of his ways of "talking to" individual students. He felt particularly strongly about the mentor role of a teacher, noting that ongoing teacher–student interaction was essential for helping students produce a good paper—his main goal in this class. "The teacher has responsibility," he said. "A teacher's part of this whole construction. We're part of the conversation, and if we don't respond enough to the students, or motivate them, encourage them enough so they can produce a good paper, then we haven't really done enough work ourselves" (Interview 1, 4/22/97). In explaining his commitment to teacher involvement in the revision process, for example, he drew on his own experiences with publishing and the value for him of feedback and response from reviewers:

> And then the activity of writing the paper, the revision so necessary, that's not just theoretical. I've seen how students' papers have just changed after revision. And producing a paper—the one big journal article that I've had came out of intense negotiation with—back and forth with the editor. And any papers that I've had published have always been out of that revision process. The activities are doing what it takes to get a good paper published, my experience, what other people go through, this is in Lave and Wenger's—I mean this is actually the practice instead of the theory about it. Actually doing it. (Interview 1, 4/22/97)

Later in the semester David also provided numerous opportunities for students to read each other's paper drafts and respond with questions (especially of clarification) and suggestions. During these sessions he would circulate around the room, visiting each group as listener and commentator. Additionally, David and his students interacted by e-mail throughout the semester, although those interactions dealt primarily with formal and practical matters such as searching for journal articles and developing appropriate descriptors for an Internet search. For her part, Yasuko often met with students individually to discuss issues and ideas related to their field-work project. These practices, along with David's and Yasuko's extensive written commentary on journals and drafts, demonstrated for students the social and inquiry-oriented nature of the academic writing game and the role of readers and listeners as active participants in the construction and interpretation of ideas.

Game Strategy 2: Blend Voices

Another common practice that novice academic writers wrestle with is that of learning the serious game of merging the voices of published authorities with their own—to rely on others' voices and at the same time to stamp their written work with what Spack's (1997a) Yuko believed was creativity and originality. This challenge of merging voices loomed large for David's students, who were required to use at least five references with proper APA documentation to help support their arguments in their papers but who were not allowed to copy more than a few consecutive words from their sources without citing them. Yasuko's students, who wrote from a fieldwork experience, did not need to learn the citation game at this time.

In the mid-semester class observation, I watched David set up an activity whereby students were to figure out how two authors of published papers they had collected were interacting. An exercise in how to merge voices—students' and those of two authors, David asked students in small groups to "compare and contrast" the two articles they had read by trying to put the key information from both authors into one sentence. As each student summed the ideas from two authors, the other students were to listen closely, make notes that would allow them to paraphrase what each speaker had said, and ask appropriate questions, especially to clarify meaning.

Students had never tried to merge the voices of two authors before, nor to blend those voices with their own writing without the kind of textual borrowing that Westerners call plagiarism (Deckert, 1993; Pennycook, 1996). In this compare–contrast activity, and in students' papers, as reported by David, students found their first experience with multivocality extremely difficult. This conforms with my own experiences with undergraduate writers. In my mid-semester class observation, I watched David's students working together in small groups and was not sure whether they grasped how to carry out the practice that David had set up. At the end of the class, two of the students presented their multivocalic summaries to the whole class, pulling expressions from their readings and sounding authoritative. However, as one student said after presenting her brief but confident-sounding commentary on her two authors, "I didn't know what I was talking about." Kenny, the student who "didn't know what she was talking about," may have just been going through the motions of knowing how to play this particular game, but she and the other students had at the very least experienced their first tries at showing how authors "converse" and how they as novice writers could interact with these interacting authors.

At the same time, the students were encouraged to blend David's editorial voice with theirs without needing to acknowledge him as a source, a different game strategy altogether. In a final interview at the end of the semester, David talked about inter- and intratextual interaction, and the blending of voices. He noted that in his own editing of students' drafts, he did not consider students' use of his own words to be plagiarism:

> So that my comments to students when I gave them editorially on their rough drafts were designed in that way, so that I would instead of trying to correct students' writing, I see it as rephrasing, adopting their point of view and talking in their voice, and they can use my words to pick them up and incorporate into their own writing. That's a theoretical notion of what I'm trying to do in interacting with students, responding to their writing and helping them to coconstruct a paper. (Interview 3, 7/18/97)

For David, the major issue was not plagiarism. "The major issue," he said in the final interview, "is in terms of dialogicality, or heteroglossia, multivocality." A copied argument, he explained, was unevaluated and underdeveloped, and therefore needed to be rephrased and explained in students' own words—which themselves were a paradoxical blending of theirs and his—as well as paraphrased and cited from sources. David wanted students to own their topics and papers, yet believed theoretically and in practice in the necessity, the inevitability, of the multivocality of academic discourse. He had no intention of resolving this paradox one way or the other. As he did in his own writing, students needed to learn to wrestle with this paradox themselves with their new awareness that in academic writing games in English, writers tried to distinguish between words they owned and words they borrowed from others (Pennycook, 1996).

In Yasuko's class, the task of blending voices differed in that students' main writing project was not a library research paper but an experiential "ethnography," involving fieldwork observations and interviews that students then needed to craft into a well-told story. The voices that needed to be blended were those of people they had met, with their own voices as storytellers. Yasuko told me that she purposely did not ask students to consult library resources for this project because she did not want to deal with the problem of plagiarism and because one of her primary goals was to help students learn to tell a good nonfiction story from their own experiences and interactions with particular people in a particular setting. Such a story might, however, include direct quotes from her informants. The project, in other words, was set up so that the voices of others that found their way into students' work formed a natural part of the narratives that students constructed. Yasuko provided a handout to students on how to include these voices in their stories. I found it interesting that she did not consider this type of writing to be "academic," as is evident in the following quote from our mid-semester interview:

> We talked about citations a bit, although I don't focus too much on citations and APA style. Actually I don't focus on APA style at all because I don't think of this [project] as academic—academic reading and writing. Um, but then I thought you know if they want to quote their participants' own words, it would be useful to know how to cite people's words. So I prepared a little handout on that, and talked about that. (Interview 2, 6/10/97)

The only exercise in blending textual voices was in the first part of the semester in which students read and responded to nonfiction articles, described under Game Strategy 1. Moreover, unlike in David's class, Yasuko's students were not required to turn in drafts of their papers, but about a third did. In those cases, Yasuko provided extensive comments but without actually editing students' words. In all other cases, the first full draft that Yasuko saw was the final one. Yasuko's own voice, therefore, did not appear in students' papers in the way it did in David's. (See Game Strategy 3.)

Game Strategy 3: Own Your Research Experiences and Tell a Good Story From Them

A goal in both David's and Yasuko's classes was for students to pursue a topic of their own choice that had been developed and narrowed in discussion with teacher and peers. This they did. But because Yasuko's students did a fieldwork project in the second half of the semester, Yasuko felt they would be able to own their topics in ways that would be difficult to achieve with a library paper. The fieldwork, she explained in our last interview, was what gave students something to talk about, and was something uniquely owned by them. She talked in the mid-semester interview about some of these projects, which turned out to capture her own interest as well as that of classmates:

> Ok one woman is doing a study on a tea ceremony. [Yasuko describes the process briefly.] Another person is really interested in the interface between human beings and gadgets. And for that she is observing physically disabled people using computers. (...) And actually that's turning out to be really quite interesting. Because she's actually talking to one disabled person who communicates with her on e-mail, that way, because he actually cannot talk, or he has a hard time talking. But you know he uses the computer to talk with her. (...) And ah oh, what else are they do—oh another girl is observing a law firm. (Interview 2, 6/10/97)

Students then began to construct their stories in the form of informal class presentations soon after they had begun their fieldwork. Yasuko also provided instruction in how to structure a good story, including an exercise in which students analyzed the story structure of the readings they had done in the first part of the semester, and how to write a coherent paragraph (see Game Strategy 6). In the presentations of their final papers, a session that I observed, the students told structured stories about these real settings and people, using a variety of visuals that added another personal touch, such as their own Power Point displays and video clips.

By virtue of the fact that each of the students' fieldwork experiences was unique and incapable of being checked as one might check students' cited sources, students owned their projects in ways that differed from David's students. The sense that students had come to own their experiences and their tales of them was evident to me in the last class in which the students were giving their final presentations. Their stories, uniquely theirs, captured the attention of their peers, teacher, and me in ways that summaries and analyses of previously told stories could not.

Game Strategy 4: Speak With Authority

The practices that novice readers and writers engage in influence how they identify themselves within their academic settings and the authority with which they learn to express their knowledge and their identities. As we have seen from Chiseri-Strater's (1991) study of Anna and Nick, there is no guarantee that students will come to see themselves as academic writers in the way that more mature students might (Ivanič, 1998; Sternglass, 1997). On the other hand, from my own studies of journal writing I found that students can indeed come to see themselves as writers and thinkers in a university setting even without writing conventional academic papers (Casanave, 1992b, 1995a). In both David's and Yasuko's classes, in different ways, this was one of the goals that the two teachers had for their students. David and Yasuko wanted their students to begin to see themselves as writers who had something to say and who were aware that someone (peers, teachers) was reading and responding.

David saw this partly as an issue of voice. As I mentioned in a previous section, David felt that the students needed to learn to do more than just report on an article. In the mid-semester interview after the class in which he had asked students to merge the main ideas in two of their reading articles he said:

> The big issue is the authorial voice. They're finding articles, and they're pursuing a topic, so with five articles in less than ten weeks, I think topic development is great. The question is, you know, do they, in the words of a student who came to me after class today, do they know what they think. And the

question is, are they able to handle all of this, and to merge it, and to pull it together. Are they able to deal with it. . . . I see that as issues of voice and interpretation. (Interview 2, 5/27/97)

In asking students to do this kind of exercise in merging voices, David hoped to help students develop their own voices by helping them learn to be critical readers:

It's built on something that last semester and the semester before that I noticed, that the students in developing their authorial voice that they need to be able to evaluate. That puts them in a position that lets them judge the advantages disadvantages, good points weak points. It's strengthening their voice in a sense. (Interview 2, 5/27/97)

Students learn to mimic an authorial voice as part of the writing games they become familiar with in college. Bartholomae (1985) discussed this aspect of learning academic literacies, as did Ivanič (1998) in her study of adult undergraduate writers, all of whom took on different voices that distanced them from or identified them with voices in the academy. In Penrose and Geisler's (1994) case study comparison of authorial voice in a freshman and PhD level writers in philosophy, the novice freshman writer seemed to believe that an authorial voice was one that presented "facts" as gleaned from her sources. However, she had only a minimal sense of how the voices in her sources were speaking to each other, and no sense of her own role in this conversation. In my study, however, David seemed concerned with helping students develop confidence in themselves as writers who actually could speak with some authority. After all, they had researched their own topics in areas in which David himself and classmates as well were not necessarily authorities. Nevertheless, knowing how long the practice of learning to speak authoritatively takes to develop when young writers are relying on published sources (the "real" authorities, some students believe, by virtue of having claims in print), David felt he had barely scratched the surface of this practice with his students. He and his own students (as expressed in their final questionnaire) both knew that one semester provides too little time for inexperienced writers to take on authoritative roles as participants in academic conversations.

Yasuko's students, on the other hand, in their final presentations and papers spoke with the authority of "researchers" who owned their knowledge and experiential resources. No one else in the class, neither peers nor teacher, were experts on their topics, nor could expertise be accrued from published sources. Yasuko had helped her students find a formal structure for their stories, but the stories themselves were told by the students with the authority of writers who have first-hand knowledge. In our last interview, Yasuko described at length some of the presentations from her other class that I had not witnessed, indicating how much she and classmates had learned from each one. It seemed to me, in other words, that David's more formal academic exercise of writing from sources helped students own their topics and develop an authoritative voice (a textual phenomenon?), whereas Yasuko's project helped students develop authoritative personae (a social role?). As we know from work by Ivanič (1994, 1998), a writer's identity, which I believe includes both voice and persona, is constructed by and represented in texts, a most serious game indeed. (See Ivanič, 1994, for a discussion of Goffman's terms for the different ways identity can be represented in texts.)

Game Strategy 5: Learn to Love Writing (or at Least to Become Fluent)

Becoming a fluent, nonhesitant writer is a goal that some of us continue to carry with us into our gray-haired years even if we have given up hope of ever being able to say we love writing. Like me, David often struggled with his own writing even though he seems to me to be a fluent and accomplished writer in English and a budding academic writer in Japanese. Like most academic writers, he ties his writing practices closely to his reading practices. The two kinds of fluency go together. From his perspective, then, he sympathized with students greatly and understood how much reading and writing his class entailed. In his interviews he did not talk about helping students learn to love writing. Nevertheless, the weekly reading response journals and multiple paper drafts that he required ensured that students who completed the course would develop fluency they had not had before. In their final questionnaires, some students commented on how valuable the regular and extensive reading and writing activities had been.

Yasuko, on the other hand, hoped her students would learn to love writing, to become close observers of a setting and of the people in it, and to tell a good story, all intertwined aspects of qualitative research that she had learned in her PhD program. She wanted them, in other words, to come to see themselves as writers and as storytellers. In addition to the fieldwork experience, she also asked students to write often and write a lot in class, following the practice of freewriting that she herself benefitted from and paralleling in some ways the practice of regular journal writing that some of them had done in freshman and sophomore English classes. She also wanted her students to see her as a practicing writer. In one class early in the semester that I observed, she asked students to write nonstop for 10 minutes, as she herself wrote in her own journal, a Peter Elbow (1973) practice. As I both watched and participated, I marveled at the amount of writing that these Japanese students were producing in English and noted that some of them, as well as Yasuko herself, wrote faster than I did.

Yasuko explained that her goals for her writing class came very strongly from her own experience, not so much from being taught, but "by doing it" (Lave & Wenger, 1991), an experience she tried to replicate with her own students that semester. Believing that "you improve if you write a lot," she had asked her students to do what she herself had been asked to do in graduate school, where she had developed her own identity as an academic writer:

> I learned that from personal experience, mostly in grad school, when I was writing a PhD dissertation. Because I was— Oh because when I first went to Canada, I took a course, I think it was Merrill Swain's course on applied linguistics or something. And part of the requirement was that every week there was a talk by someone, and you had to read an article on reserve by that person, and you either have to write a summary of it, or write a critique of it. And so every week, you are supposed to write say two pages, three pages. And that was really really hard when I first went there. And maybe that was a three-day project for me? But then towards the end, after six years, I could probably sit down in an afternoon and do it. Because I had written so much by then. (Interview 1, 4/28/97)

At the end of that semester, she spoke about whether she felt her goals for her class had been achieved, goals that paralleled her own goals for her research and writing. She said that her goal of getting students interested in the process of writing came through in the final papers, an ambition that was close to her heart, as she had expressed in our first interview:

> I guess the reason why that's so important to me is because that's really what I learned to do in the course of my PhD. And that's really changed my life, my professional life, and my personal life too, in that now— I mean I used to follow the last minute shot, last minute writing pattern, too. But then after learning to do journal writing and writing narrative way, I learned to integrate writing into my life, and my life is so much richer for it? . . . So I guess I'd like my students to have that experience too. (Interview 1, 4/28/97)

Yasuko believed that her students had begun to see themselves as writers who could communicate their "owned" knowledge and experiences to an interested audience in an academic setting. In their final questionnaires, her students, like David's, commented on the value to them of the extensive opportunities for writing, reading, and discussion. I don't know if her students learned to love writing more than they might already have, but they learned not to dread it, and they learned that by practicing it regularly it did get easier. These are essential game strategies for academic writers.

Game Strategy 6: Make the Paper Look Right

Much has been written about the role of genre conventions and rhetorical structure in academic writing, and arguments persist about whether we should teach students to conform to or resist formal conventions (see comments in the previous section). In different ways, Yasuko and David both taught students some formal features of academic writing that they expected to see in the final papers, partly for reasons of convention and partly for reasons of readability (requiring coherence of paragraphs, transitions between them, and so on).

David, for one, provided students with a great deal of detailed information about rules and computer commands for formatting text and for citing and referencing in the very first class I visited, spending a full 10 minutes on these details. He insisted that students follow APA citing and referencing style, for example, and labored at length with examples on overhead transparency, handouts, and board to point out the dozens of details that he himself now used automatically (see Bazerman, 1987; Lynch & McGrath, 1993). David's focus on form as well as content from an early stage in the writing project communicated to me and to students a sense of his own values about the professional look of a paper, and about the need for formatting conventions to be practiced repeatedly (game-practice style) until they become second nature. The drafts of his own papers that I had seen in the past had all followed APA formatting conventions, those that he was teaching his students. Attention to these formal requirements at the earliest stages of writing, a much disparaged activity by some "process-oriented" scholars, might be thought of as attention to some of the sociolinguistically appropriate language game conventions that writers use when they communicate via academic texts.

In Yasuko's more formal teaching, to prepare students for structural analyses of some of the narratives they had read and to help them structure their own narratives later, Yasuko talked about technical aspects of nonfiction story writing (paragraph writing, topic sentences, the characteristics of a good story). Unlike David, she had explicit lessons on paragraph writing and did structural analyses of the published readings but presented almost nothing on how to cite sources from readings. In interviews she talked about how important she felt it was for students to learn to write a well-structured paragraph and was continually amazed at how difficult this task—now second nature for her—was for students.

In their editorial comments on students' drafts as well as in class activities, both David and Yasuko included comments that communicated to students the need to make their papers look right, although the formal features they emphasized differed. Neither teacher waited until the last stages of students' project write-ups to have students practice certain formal features of their writing, as so-called process approaches have suggested, but worked on them at different points throughout the semester, including in David's case from the very beginning.

Neither Yasuko nor David discussed their teaching in terms of strategies and games. However, as I reflected on my experiences in their classrooms and on my discussions with them, the game analogy helped me to conceptualize what I saw and learned as structured, interactive, rule-governed practices. It also helped me understand that novice writers in undergraduate settings require a great deal of practice in the company of more expert players in order to learn to participate in such literate activities.

Students' Perspectives

The students in David's and Yasuko's classes struggled with a variety of academic game practices that these two teachers had set up. The students found David's class, in which reading and responding to academic journal articles formed a foundational practice in students' construction of their own papers, particularly difficult. In informal written evaluations that David asked students to write, they commented on specific difficulties: how difficult the reading and responding was, how limited their vocabulary, and how faulty their grammar. But these students and others also wrote that they felt they were learning how to think critically, that learning how to write in the way David was instructing them was essential for being able to communicate in a world where English was the dominant language of business and the Internet, and that the class was difficult but important. In the final questionnaire (Appendix B) David's students said that by far the most difficult task in his class was finding appropriate journal articles, a literature search task that required that some of them travel to other university libraries. Several students commented on how difficult it was to blend voices: "[The most difficult thing was] combining all 5 or more articles and my opinion into one essay" and "Bringing the paper together at the end." For this last student, "Gathering the information was not at all difficult, but trying to mesh all the ideas together at the end" was. Looking back over the whole semester, students in both classes commented that classes were very hard work, but worth the effort.

The benefits, from the students' perspectives, were many. Five students from Yasuko's classes whom I interviewed at the end of the semester spoke little of the traditional student concerns in school (i.e., grades) but seemed much more absorbed in the new interactive practices and ways of thinking that they were learning. In both classes, a majority of students commented in the final questionnaire on how valuable the small class discussions had been and many noted the value of regular reading and informal presentations. A student in David's class wrote that he or she had become consciously aware of readers, and another noted the value of learning how to avoid plagiarism and how to use references to back an opinion. One of Yasuko's students said that in this class it was possible to learn "formal writing," and "how to present ideas in a coherent and intellectual way."

Quite a few students in both classes commented in the final questionnaire on the value of feedback and critical comments from teacher and peers. For example, as e-mail records from the interactions among David's students show, the students were consulting each other and David about various aspects of their projects, from descriptors needed to search for literature on their topics to technical and formal questions. Regular teacher and peer interaction occurred routinely in small group peer discussions and written commentary from the two teachers on journals and drafts. Yasuko's students as well shared fieldwork experiences and problems not just with Yasuko but also with each other. Lave and Wenger (1991) point out that in apprentice-type relationships it is quite typical that "apprentices learn mostly in relation with other apprentices" (p. 93).

A final question on the semester-end questionnaire asked students to give advice to a friend who might be thinking about taking the course. Nearly all students in David's class commented on how much work the class was, and only those motivated students willing to "stick to it" should take the class, such as those determined to study abroad. Unlike some of the expectations they expressed in the first questionnaire, some students noted that this was not a general English course: "If you just want to brush up your English, don't take it." A student in Yasuko's class said, "If you really want to learn something and think hard, I recommend this class," and one in David's class said "There is no other class that makes you think deeply."

In short, these students did not appear to view their classes in the same way they viewed their other undergraduate classes or other foreign language classes. Yes, they were being graded and yes, they had to turn in a final paper (called "reports" in their other classes), but they could not cut and paste at the last minute. In interaction with each other and with their teachers, they had to involve themselves in reading, discussing, and writing activities, and in Yasuko's case in fieldwork, throughout the semester in order to achieve the final goal. Although David and Yasuko set up different academic literacy practices in their respective sections, both seemed to me to have established what could be called a mini-community of practice in which all students were participating in one sense or another as novice academic writers. The games they were learning involved far more than textbook exercises in grammar and writing. This finding parallels that by Freedman, Adam, and Smart (1994), who found that even "wearing suits to class" did not turn school writing into professional writing, but that the simulation activities in they observed in a third-year financial analysis class did differ in important ways from more traditional class activities.

Communities of Practice in These Undergraduate EAP classes?

David and Yasuko, looking mainly to their own backgrounds in and current experiences with academic writing for guidance, had tried to figure out what their students needed and to create a community of practice in academic writing in English in a foreign language setting—a challenge by any stretch of the imagination. They hoped that the students would come to view themselves as participants in this classroom community of practice where writing and reading activities helped shape participants' identities. David hoped his students would develop an authorial stance—a sense of self as author—and knew this was particularly challenging for undergraduates (Ivanič, 1998; Penrose & Geisler, 1994). His goal was similar to that of the teacher in Stuart Greene's (1995) case study of the development of authorship in the practices of two students in a beginning college writing class. By authorship Greene means what David intended: "the critical thinking skills that students use in their efforts to contribute knowledge to a scholarly conversation, knowledge that is not necessarily found in source texts but is nonetheless carefully linked to the texts they read"—an interpretive not a reporting activity (p. 187). David's students, as well as one of the two students in Greene's study, found this activity extremely difficult. It is thus questionable to what extent students' identities and participation practices can change in just one semester, which was all that David and Yasuko had, particularly in a foreign language setting. David sensed the beginnings of change, as did Yasuko with her students, who had learned to own and narrate a nonfiction story based on their fieldwork experiences.

However, using a "communities of practice" metaphor for interpreting David's and Yasuko's classes is complicated by the fact that Lave and Wenger (1991; Wenger, 1998) do not consider a school to be a site where learning usually happens in the ways they conceptualize in their work in apprentice-style or organizational settings. In school settings, they point out, learning is usually viewed as internalization—in a cerebral sense—of bodies of knowledge as a result of students' being taught. They, on the other hand, are more interested in how learning happens inevitably as a result of learners' changing patterns of participation in the practices of specialized communities. This kind of learning, they note, results in ongoing changes of identity as newcomers become increasingly involved in the community's practices, including "new forms of membership and ownership of meaning" (Wenger, 1998, p. 219). Lave emphasizes that "learning is ubiquitous in ongoing activity, though often unrecognized as such" (Lave, 1993, p. 5). In a physics class, however, it is often not the community of physicists that students are learning to participate in, but the community of "schooled adults" except perhaps later at the graduate level (pp. 99–100). In this sense, students learn how to "do school" (Scribner & Cole, 1981)—learn how (as Mc-

Carthy's [1987] Dave concluded) to give teachers what they want and how to play the game well enough to get themselves through the system. In this view of school, students and teachers have clearly distinguished identities and participation practices.

In the communities of practice metaphor, however, learning happens and identities are constructed through ongoing participation by all members in specialized practices. In this view, teachers and students cannot be neatly divided. As Lave (1996) points out, "the social-cultural categories that divide teachers from learners in schools mystify the crucial ways in which learning is fundamental to all participation and all participants in social practice" (p. 157). Wenger (1998) emphasizes that cross-generational encounters are essential features of communities of learning and that all participants are involved and changed. The question that arises in school settings is what activities take place in particular local settings and what it is that students, and indeed teachers, learn by participating in them.

In David's and Yasuko's Academic Reading and Writing classes, it is clear that students were not participating in authentic, domain-specific academic literacy practices in apprentice relationships with their teachers (Brown, Collins, & Duguid, 1989). They might have done so if they had been involved as research assistants or coauthors on work that David and Yasuko were currently engaged in themselves. As do some graduate students, they could have done literature searches for a common teacher-directed project, read and written summaries of what they found, constructed reference lists, or helped analyze data (see my discussion of Prior's [1995, 1998] case study of Moira in Chap. 4). Perhaps such activities distinguish graduates from undergraduates. Still, the students in both David's and Yasuko's classes were certainly not just absorbing bodies of codified knowledge or learning only the formal mechanics of writing, and in neither class were tests of any kind used to evaluate their learning. Rather, students had to actually engage in the practices used by academics in both English-medium and Japanese settings in order to fulfill the class goals. The students' participation was indeed peripheral, but it was participation nonetheless. Following Lave and Wenger (1991) and Rogoff (1990), Freedman and Adam (1996, 2000) distinguished between "guided participation," which involves conscious attention to teaching and learning and "attenuated authentic participation," which does not. This distinction might be applied here. As described by Rogoff (1990) in the case of children's learning from caretakers and extended to the case of adults by Freedman and Adam, students can be viewed as guided by David and Yasuko into new practices in a conscious effort at scaffolding (Wood, Bruner, & Ross, 1976) in students' zone of proximal development (Vygotsky, 1978, 1986).

In terms of the game strategy metaphor, David and Yasuko helped their students learn games strategies that focused, in Wenger's (1998) terms, on both participation and reification in communities of practice. The students engaged in techniques of participation through their reading response journals and their interactions with peers and teacher, and through the academic practices of literature searches and fieldwork. They also learned some of the academic games that revolve around the academy's reifications—its genre conventions and documentation styles such as citation practices, its guidelines for interview and fieldwork research, its ways of using language, and its tools such as libraries, databases, and web sources. These game strategies were meaningfully connected to planned lessons because they linked the students to their individual projects. Moreover, game strategies such as the systems of interactive oral and written discussion, feedback, and response allowed students to interact cross-generationally with David and Yasuko, who as practicing academics were adults who "'represent their communities of practice in educational settings" (Wenger, 1998 p. 276). These teachers were not just textbook teachers of writing. They themselves were academic writers. In short, the students were learning writing game strategies that encouraged them to view their academic literacy activities as a form of negotiated engagement with expert community members and with the repertoire of tools, artifacts, and language that typify academic literacy practices. Although it is not clear from this short study how the teachers' identities or practices may have shifted, I believe that the one-semester experience contributed to the beginnings of a shift in the students' views of themselves as emerging participants in academic practices. As owners of their individual projects, for one, they were able to practice agency as writers and to recognize as well that their authority as writers was tied partly to the academic writing game of incorporating fieldwork experiences and voices from published sources into their own texts. At the very least, the students' awareness of practices of writing had changed, and with those changes they were beginning to learn new games, characterized by new sets of rules and values that involved reading, talking, listening, inquiring, and observing as integral practices to the sociopolitical practice of academic writing. And all of this, to my surprise, in a foreign language setting.

CHAPTER REFLECTIONS

As Wenger (1998) points out, "when we come in contact with new practices, we venture into unfamiliar territory and don't know how to participate competently" (p. 153). The case studies in this chapter show that undergraduate students who are learning to participate in academic literacy practices indeed venture into unfamiliar territory. Those of us interested in academic writing and disciplinary enculturation want to learn more about specifically what undergraduates find unfamiliar, why, and how to help them make easier transitions onto the academic playing field.

What is it that novice undergraduate readers and writers need to learn about texts and text-related practices beyond the widespread belief by undergraduates that they are primarily sources of information to be learned and then displayed back to teachers as another kind of text? If we follow Lave's and Wenger's work, a key sign of undergraduates' developing expertise in academic literacy games is their changing relationship to the texts they read and write. Their relationship to texts becomes more complex and layered, involving more aspects of themselves and of the people around them. All novice academic readers and writers, in other words, must learn to treat their readings and writings as media through which they are interacting with authors, professors, peers, and gatekeepers and to recognize the paradox of ownership and multivocality in their own writing. Such a view implies further that they need to learn to view themselves as communicators and builders as well as displayers of knowledge, taking on what Ivanič (1998) calls a contributor role, not just a student role.

In enacting more complex roles and in expanding their view of academic writing to include reading and discussion as inseparable from it, undergraduate students are faced with the possibility that their academic identities will evolve in even more fragmented ways than the already fragmented undergraduate curriculum predicts. This may be what happened to Anna and Nick (Chiseri-Strater, 1991), Dave (McCarthy, 1987), and Yuko (Spack, 1997a) in the first year of her program. Following Giddens (1991) and others (Linde, 1993; Polkinghorne, 1991; Wenger, 1998), I surmise that a major challenge for novice academic writers is to figure out how to survive what may be an inevitable period of relative incoherence as they face a wide array of writing games that differ greatly in their local peculiarities. Because it takes time to construct a coherent identity as an academic writer and, as Ortner (1996, p. 12) notes, to learn to play the game with "skill, intention, wit, knowledge, [and] intelligence," the primary challenge for teachers may be to help students survive within the bounds of academic playing fields (Leki, 1999b), and then to become aware that academic literacy games eventually consist of more than games of survival. It is not clear how much of a head start in constructing academic identities students can get in short-term EAP classes like David's and Yasuko's, or whether time and immersion (as in the case of Spack's [1997a] Yuko) and time and maturity (Ivanič, 1998; Sternglass, 1997) suffice. My observations of David and Yasuko convince me not to give up on the idea of EAP classes in foreign language settings. Something happened in both classes that worked: I saw motivation, hard work, engagement with texts, peers and mentors interacting, ownership, shifting identities and growing awareness, and a great deal of instruction in English that served larger purposes than language teaching. In these classes, the writing game definitely involved more than writing.

In this chapter I have discussed a number of undergraduate writing experiences from the perspectives of students and teachers that took place in different academic settings, not with the intention of generalizing about them, but of establishing a variety of connecting points, some of which I hope will resonate with readers' own experiences. The specific experiences of each of the students and teachers I discussed in this chapter cannot be replicated nor will they resonate in their entirety. However, each case can be reflected upon in terms of the serious games that were being learned, transitions that were or were not happening, and identities that were beginning to be constructed. All undergraduates (all newcomers to a community of practice) need to learn to figure out what to do and what their roles will be, as do newcomers to the teaching of academic literacy. Similarly, those who remain on the playing field will inevitably experience change of one kind or another as what was strange becomes more familiar, as they build background knowledge and skills, or as they resist and reject aspects of their academic literacy practices. Identities, always multiple, interacting, and often conflicting, and involving teachers as well as students, will take on some new facets, perhaps as strategic survivor as in the cases of Yuko and Dave, as sometime rebel and resister as in the cases of Anna and Nick, or as champions and mentors for newcomers of a practice in which they themselves are still developing expertise as in the cases of David and Yasuko.

What strikes me about all these cases is the asymmetry between the ways that teachers seem to perceive their worlds—full of complexity, detail, and purposeful rhetorical practices—and the confusion yet relative lack of complexity in students' perceptions. Certainly David and Yasuko could not easily put aside their post-PhD-level perceptions of what academic literacy is all about even though they were working with young undergraduates who could not at first perceive what the issues were or why they were important. I think that in some sense teachers of EAP want students to quickly become like us, to think and write in ways that have taken us years to learn how to do. Our lessons, our expectations are based on our own immersion experiences and our own drawn out learning of the serious academic literacy games we encounter, and these cannot be duplicated with students. After all, when faced with a new game, none of us can perceive its rules. We can certainly help students write papers that resemble the academic writing of more mature writers and that in some ways (as the case studies show) begin to initiate changes in practices and personae, particularly if as teachers we are practicing academics who are playing our own linguistic, social, and political academic writing games. However, the undergraduate students' sense of investment in their academic literacy practices probably cannot match the sense of investment or coherence that their teachers feel. This may be inevitable. There is probably not enough time or singularity of purpose, partly because of the fragmented nature of undergraduate education and partly because many undergraduates simply don't know what they want to do or who they want to be. Within their tentative beginnings, however, undergraduate students need to find a way to make some order out of the diversity of academic literacy games they are engaged in if only to survive. Perhaps a deeper sense of investment and coherence comes only later. I am reminded of composition scholar Min-Zhan Lu (1987), who came to understand the various writing conflicts and personae that she struggled with during her school years in China only much later, after time, experience, and reflection.

ACKNOWLEDGMENTS

Special thanks to Yasuko Kanno and David Shea for participating in the research reported in the third section of this chapter, and for their insightful comments on earlier drafts of the chapter.

3

Stepping Into the Profession: Writing Games in Masters Programs

FROM OBSERVER TO PARTICIPANT

There are no doubt countless reasons why individuals decide to pursue advanced study at the masters degree level, including pure love of study or desire to postpone entry into the work world. Nevertheless, I am guessing that for most people, the decision represents a life and career choice to become a person with a field-specific identity who wishes to practice particular activities in professions that can be identified by name (teaching, engineering, business and so forth). With some specialized knowledge and expertise, plus the certificate that promises something to the public beyond general competence, the holders of masters degrees possess more symbolic capital than nondegree holders (Bourdieu, 1977a, 1991). This symbolic capital can then be used as public proof that degree holders have a certain amount of authority in a field, that they therefore deserved to be listened to, and that they can be trusted to practice their trade in ways appreciated and shared by other practitioners.

In my field, which I would label broadly as second language education, many people return to school after some years of teaching, knowing now what they want and don't want. This situation is probably similar in other social science and business fields. Years of work experience may in fact provide masters degree students with more real, as opposed to symbolic, knowledge and expertise than could ever be provided in a 1 or 2 year program of study. In my case, after chancing into the ESL field as did so many people in my age group, I had been teaching and studying part-time for a number of years before being told that a full-time job would be available to me only if I completed my masters degree. I had been puttering away at the degree one or two courses at a time as part of a tuition-free package for full-time staff at my school (I managed the small bookstore and copy-mail service in addition to teaching part-time). By this time, I knew that I wanted to enter this field as a full-time professional, and the masters degree was the ticket for my journey as well as a symbol of my new authority. So I read, took classes, and wrote a lot of papers, none of which I recall much about. The first paper I recall writing in my field was not a school paper, but my first publication—a three-page article in one of the field's newsletters, written several years after I completed my degree. At about the same time, I presented my first conference paper (and was told afterwards by a colleague in the audience that I should have smiled more, a tough challenge when one is terrified). My real sense of increased authority, in other words, came with participation in the field, not only as teacher-with-MA, but as one who interacted in the field's public forums—its conferences and journals. The MA may have been one of the factors that gave me the incentive and confidence to join those public interactions.

My case was probably atypical, however. I stretched out my MA studies over several years, gaining teaching experience and a sense of professional identity at the same time. Most masters degree students plunge in full-time for 1 or 2 years, then seek or return to work with their new status as certified practitioner. In more recent years, post-PhD, I began to wonder how much enculturation could really take place in a masters degree program and what a program's writing requirements, especially in the second language field, reflected about that program's expectations and values and how those writing practices and values helped students reimagine their identities. If an embodied sense of identity comes mainly through participation in a field's practices (Lave & Wenger, 1991; Wenger, 1998), what can a school-centered academic or professional program offer beyond an introduction to some of the field's issues, arguments, and techniques and beyond the granting of a certificate that bestows a modicum of authority on the recipient to join the field's practices? If much graduate student writing is mimetic (Campbell, 1997), at what point do students take on a more contributory and authoritative role? Is it possible, in the short duration of a masters program, that students come to view themselves and the practices in their fields in new ways? How do the school-based practices in masters programs, in particular the writing and writing-related activities, help students make the transition from unauthorized to authorized participant in a community's shared practices? How similar and different are the writing games in MA programs and in the professions that follow?

PUBLISHED STUDIES

Published case studies of academic enculturation at the masters level are sparse. As the last chapter indicated, many scholars of academic literacy focus their work on undergraduates, the true novices in college and university settings. Studies of masters level students, however, should be revealing as to how the transition from novice to expert begins to take place, in the sense that masters students are positioned precariously between the status of novice and specialist (Ivanič & Camps, 2001; Reynolds, 1994). Second language students are positioned as well between cultures and languages (Fox, 1994). A number of studies comparing the writing practices of undergraduates as they move into professions can shed light on the practices that begin to reshape identities as students undergo these significant transitions. These studies show that writing practices in professional settings, with their multiple, embedded, and overlapping discourse communities, can strike novice professionals as very unlike the writing practices they are familiar with from school settings (Beaufort, 1997). They show further that novice writers in professional settings, like Doheny-Farina's (1989) adult woman learning to write in an internship program in a family planning clinic, tend not to appreciate the extent to which professional writing practices are socially enacted.

In the field of engineering, for example, Dorothy Winsor (1996, 1999) followed four engineering students through their undergraduate program and into the workplace. The writing they did in the academic context helped the students learn to manage technical information but did not help them see knowledge in their field as rhetorically constructed. As newcomers in the workplace, on the other hand, they learned to appreciate the social and political aspects of writing by being immersed in very different sets of practices. In particular, in the workplace setting they began to see how the writing in their engineering firm developed consensually among peers, supervisors, subordinates, and customers. In another study of fourth year engineering students involved in simulated and authentic projects, Deanna Dannels (2000) found that local academic exigencies dominated students' concerns even when products were being designed for real customers. For the students, the bottom line was to get a good grade. Interestingly, even though the students' bottom line concerns were situated firmly on the academic playing field, their conceptions of customer needs and relationships were more sophisticated than the academic materials (textbook, handouts) they were required to use. This finding suggested to Dannels that academic programs that intend to move students into professions should be more challenging, reflective, and authentically professional than this one was. Students' discourse and practices, Dannels points out, "illustrate the contradictions between the activity systems of the workplace and the classroom, as well as the power of the situated, local academic context" (p. 27).

Major differences in the nature of writing and role relationships between academic and workplace settings were also found by Chris Anson and Lee Forsberg (1990) in their case study of six English and journalism seniors in a professional internship program. The students held full-time positions for 10 to 15 weeks in local agencies in which writing was a main part of their jobs. The authors found that the students went through three stages in their transitional experiences: unrealistic expectations, disorientation, and finally transition and accommodation. Each of the students' experiences differed greatly in the details associated with each local context, but in all cases the students needed to find new ways to learn that were unlike those in their familiar academic environment. This need to find new ways to learn once students step into a profession is exactly what Aviva Freedman and Christine Adam (1996) concluded from their comparison of fourth year students doing simulated professional writing in an academic setting and graduate students doing workplace writing in an MA internship program. The MA students found that their academic learning strategies that stemmed from explicit assignments and evaluation criteria did not serve them well in their much more vaguely defined internship writing tasks, where supervisors tended to expect the students to take more responsibility for their writing than did teachers. In the workplace they needed to find new ways to learn since the purposes, genres, role relationships of key players, and systems of evaluation differed so greatly from what they were familiar with. Other studies of workplace and university writing confirm these differences (Freedman & Adam, 2000; Freedman, Adam, & Smart, 1994).

Within the MA context itself, which constitutes its own kind of situated learning environment, it is not clear whether students unambiguously find themselves stepping into a profession in the course of their studies. One nicely done study of MA students' discourse socialization in a TESOL program looks at the complex and conflicted enculturation process within the graduate program, focusing on students' experiences in two oral presentation classes (Morita, 2000). The author found in this longitudinal study that both native and nonnative English speakers struggled with similar issues as they learned to read and respond critically and present their ideas orally, but implications beyond the graduate context and into the professional realm were sparse. Some studies are too limited in duration and focus to address this question, such as Ulla Connor and Melinda Kramer's (1995) case study of five business management students. In that study, the authors tracked how five first-year masters students in a business management program, two Americans and three foreign students, carried out a single reading–writing task—a business case analysis—in one of their classes. They focus their conclusions on the international students, but their results suggest that the problems some of the students had situating themselves in the literate practice of a business management community depended less on native- or nonnative-speaker status than on students' familiarity with these practices from previous experience. Even this finding cannot be supported with the data presented in this study, since the background information of each student is sketchy. Also, as is the case with much other work on academic writing, this study focuses greatly on cognitive issues and textual analyses—how the students read a text and what the features are of the subsequent written products—in spite of mention in the introduction of the importance of "social constructionist" accounts of literate activity. Potentially rich areas to investigate, such as writers' previous experience, the complexity of the nontextual aspects of the task, differences in personal interests and motivation, and cultural assumptions about the roles of writers—not just writing—within graduate school and workplace settings are hinted at but not developed. The hints give us the impression that learning to participate in the literate activities of the business management community involves far more than learning the linguistic skills of reading and writing specialized texts.

Nevertheless, as Dannels (2000) noted, students' concerns about grades in the academic setting tend to take precedence over their concern for learning how to participate in a professional community's literate activities. This concern makes it difficult for researchers to detect whether and how students see themselves as stepping into professions in their MA programs. Students may simply not see their MA studies in primarily professional terms, but in pragmatic terms of survival: Without fulfilling their academic goals, they probably will not be moving on into a profession. A profound conflict in masters level programs arises when program goals focus on and try to simulate or practice authentic literacy activities as did the business program in which Connor and Kramer (1995) did their case study, and student goals focus on activities needed to be done to assure passing grades.

But in addition to the impossibility of escaping fully the academic goals and systems of evaluation, even students who are not preoccupied with grades differ in the extent to which they can take advantage of the professional aspects of an MA program. For example, some of Paul Prior's (1998) case studies of MA and PhD students in a Language Research class, particularly those of international MA students "Mai" (from Taiwan) and "Teresa" (from Spain), show that students proceeding through the same academic program take different trajectories in spite of the same "situated practice" environment. They participated in and learned from their academic game practices in very different ways. For her part, Mai participated more in the role of a novice, displaying rather than engaging with ideas, whereas Teresa participated more deeply, forging alliances with people, issues, and literature in her disciplinary community. For reasons not fully explored in this case study, Mai worked in relative isolation from both human and textual resources. Teresa, on the other hand, surrounded herself and actively engaged with both. In a very real sense, they both contributed to the construction of their situated practice environments, providing evidence that expertise develops not as a one-way transmission from a community of specialists to novices but interactively. The contexts for practice, in other words, did not exist for Mai and Teresa apart from their own involvements in them.

This variation in contextually situated involvement was also found in Suresh Canagarajah's (2001) case study of "Viji," a university English teacher in Sri Lanka. Viji, who was working for a graduate teaching certificate, took the time and effort to actively use material and human resources around her for her dissertation, the religious topic which she was personally committed to. Other students took a more individualistic and pragmatic approach, wishing to fulfill a requirement rather than explore a topic of personal importance. Also unlike other students, Viji resisted some of the expected academic conventions in her writing, negotiating for herself a hybrid voice of some power. In another study, Ivanič and Camps (2001) explored in some depth the textual aspects of how graduate L2 students in a British university negotiate a voice and position themselves in their writing.

These studies all address aspects of the questions I raised at the end of the first section of this chapter. I look now in more detail at two case studies of masters degree students who were trying to figure out the writing games in their academic contexts. One small study of unsuccessful academic enculturation coincidentally was published about a student at the same campus on which I conducted the research reported in the third section of this chapter and where I received my own MA. In this study, Melanie Schneider and Naomi Fujishima (1995) attempted to learn why a Chinese masters student was not able to fulfill the expectations his teachers and school had for him. In the second case study I return to the work of Prior (1998) to review his study of "Lilah," an MA student in an American Studies seminar.

Zhang

We know from Schneider and Fujishima (1995) that Zhang was a 30-year old student from Taipei whose older brother had obtained a masters degree in International Policy Studies from this same school, a small professional graduate school in Monterey, California (see the more detailed description in the next section). Zhang completed a bachelors degree in agricultural economics in Taiwan and had then spent 2 years in military service. In 1990 he applied for admission to a 2-year degree program in International Public Administration at the Monterey school and was only provisionally admitted because of a low TOEFL score (480). The school felt that the success of his older brother some years earlier indicated that Zhang would eventually succeed too. Zhang was required to take 16 weeks of intensive ESL instruction before beginning his regular graduate course load in the fall of 1990, and at the end of this period had raised his TOEFL score by about 50 points to 537, an impressive gain but still below the 550 recommended for masters level study at this school.

Zhang continued to take three English Studies courses in the fall, and in his eagerness to get through his masters program quickly and against the advice of teachers, he signed up for four additional courses in his Policy Studies program for a total of 18 credits. The results were predictable: a GPA below the required 3.0 minimum. In the second semester, although he cut back the number of courses he took, he was not able to raise his GPA to 3.0 and was informed by the Academic Dean that he would not be able to continue in his degree program. The Dean attributed Zhang's problems to "language," and to the fact that he did not seem to be as strong in math as his older brother had been. Indeed Zhang's lowest grades were in his English Studies courses—mostly Cs. Had these grades not been factored into his GPA he would have just earned a 3.0 since most of his grades in his major were Bs. The Dean claimed to be looking ahead and predicted Zhang would not succeed, that he would probably not learn the language games in his English courses and that this predicted failure would influence how successfully he learned the game rules in his Policy Studies program. This kind of unfortunate discrepancy was also noted by Johns (1991), who did a case study of "Luc," a young Vietnamese undergraduate student in biochemistry. This student had an A− in his major and was ready to graduate but he could not pass his freshman English competency exam.

In this study, we get only brief glimpses of Zhang primarily through the eyes of three of his teachers in English classes (including Fujishima) but also through journal entries written by Zhang for one of these classes. His teachers described him as a hard worker but as one who did not participate in the academic culture at the Institute beyond attending classes. He lived with other family members and left campus each day as soon as classes were over, leading one teacher to speculate that Zhang had little interest in American culture. His interests in the school, his training, and the language, she believed, were "very utilitarian" and "pragmatic" (p. 13). Even his in-class participation seemed out of tune to the "social realities" of the class, as one teacher put it, suggesting that he was not able to interpret the negative ways that other students reacted to him (his tendency to speak out, his difficulty articulating his ideas). The one sample of his writing from an English class that is included in this study shows that at the surface level his English is ungrammatical and unidiomatic, but the sample does not reveal anything about his ability to handle the writing he had to do in his Policy Studies program. Both as a game player in the larger sense and as a writer of texts, Zhang did not seem to be fitting in.

In Zhang's Writing Workshop classes, taken in two consecutive semesters, class activities were linked to the academic reading and writing that Zhang did in his program. Zhang revealed in one Workshop class that he read his graduate textbooks slowly and inefficiently. In a section taught by Fujishima he brought drafts of papers from his Policy Studies program to the Writing Workshop, where sessions were devoted to correcting the many word and sentence level problems. In the reflective journals for the Writing Workshop students were supposed to focus on broader aspects of writing in their other classes. The teachers learned from Zhang's journal that he seemed to have "insurmountable problems" narrowing a topic and organizing his ideas in a principled way (p. 17). We learn that Zhang was apparently not applying any of the very basic and well-practiced strategies for listening, reading, and writing he had learned in his English classes even though he was able to articulate what he needed to do in his journals: "I think it is not only to narrow my researches, but also to narrow my ideas and my writing content. And depending on my information, I should have an outline and method to organize my idea and writing content." He then asks himself "why I cannot improve my academic writing skills?" (p. 18). Schneider read this entry and "found herself vacillating between admiration for his ability to pinpoint his writing problems and frustration at his difficulties in writing intelligibly for different academic audiences" (p. 18). One of his Policy Studies professors expressed a similar confusion: Zhang was a student who worked hard but who had problems with English and who "got bogged down in detail," missing the overall analytical framework of a paper he had written (p. 18). Schneider and Fujishima (1995) concluded that Zhang, in spite of his anxiety and desire to do well, did not seem able to respond flexibly when faced with critiques of his work beyond his determination to "work harder" (p. 19). In particular, the longer paper assignments and readings seemed to bring him to a standstill. He was not able to apply his strategic knowledge and did not appear to have a classmate or group with whom he could share academic literacy problems outside his reliance on the Writing Workshop teachers. He seemed to know a few rules of the game, in other words, but not to be able to enact them or to participate with others in a community of learners. He also did not perceive the demands being placed on him as part of a serious academic game that was as much social as linguistic. The fact that his Writing Workshop focused on language problems no doubt contributed to Zhang's concern with fairly narrow linguistic and organizational aspects of academic writing.

Schneider and Fujishima's speculations from their study of Zhang, however, contribute to our understanding of the complex intertwinings of language issues with other factors (social, motivational, political) in the academic enculturation process. Zhang's most serious problems, in other words, apparently did not result only from an inability to write or understand spoken English (students with lower TOEFL scores had succeeded) but from factors such as sociolinguistic competence, motivation for studying, and strategies for learning (Schneider & Fujishima, 1995, p. 8). The authors also ask whether Zhang's case had been judged prematurely. I would add my own question to the case of Zhang about the extent to which he was supported by faculty in his program, not just in the Writing Workshop, in his academic literacy practices. Without good mentoring in a graduate program including rich cross-generational interactions (Wenger, 1998), students of all kinds may not learn to participate in academic literacy games even peripherally (Belcher, 1994; Casanave, 1992a; Chap. 4, this volume). We don't know the answer to this question from this study, but there is no evidence given from Zhang's journals that his Policy Studies faculty contributed to the development of his academic literacy practices or to his identity as a participant in their community of practice. As teachers, we are left with the question of where the responsibility for Zhang's failure lies, and as researchers with the question of what the role of EAP writing teachers is in helping international students in particular learn to participate in the game-like practices in their MA programs and eventually step into their professions.

Lilah

The complexity of academic literacy practices in graduate schools is addressed in much of Paul Prior's work in which one of the goals is, as is mine in this book, to move from "analysis of writing (texts and transcription) in discourse communities to analysis of literate activity and disciplinarity in laminated functional systems (situated and typified)" (Prior, 1997, p. 292). Prior employs numerous figures of speech (such as "laminated activity" from Goffman, 1981, and "legitimate peripheral participation" from Lave and Wenger, 1991) to make his point that discourse communities are not unified abstract fields in which experts participate in literate practices in generically prescribed ways. They are better characterized as functional systems—heterogeneous networks of relationships among people, practices, artifacts, institutions, and communities (Prior, 1998, p. 31). People participate in these functional systems in multiple ways simultaneously such that looking at just one aspect or activity (e.g., drafting and revising behaviors) will tell us little about how newcomers find their way into the system or what it means to participate. For Prior, studies of graduate education and writing, redefined from a sociohistoric, functional perspective, lend themselves particularly well to helping scholars understand the nature and activities of disciplines:

> Graduate education is one key link in disciplinary networks, a site of intense disciplinary enculturation (i.e., the continuing production of full participants

and the discipline itself as well as the integration or marginalization of relative newcomers). In graduate education, writing is a central domain of action, providing opportunity spaces for (re)socialization of discursive practices, representing a central medium for displays of disciplinarity, and mediating the (re)production of disciplinary communities of practice. (Prior, 1997, p. 277)

However, as Prior's later case studies show, the role of writing in the enculturation process cannot be explained by simply examining whether graduate students represent and carry out a writing assignment according to a professor's expectations. Instead, graduate level writing games are far more complex, involving factors outside the immediate classroom and stemming from multiple identities and relationships in writers' lives. These complexities became particularly obvious as Prior observed graduate seminars (Prior, 1991), which he described as an especially "laminated and dynamic activity setting" (Prior, 1998, p. 252). It is in such a setting that Prior situates his case study of "Lilah," a first year masters student in American Studies (Prior, 1997, 1998).

The American Studies seminar in which Lilah and 17 other students were enrolled was the last course in a three-quarter sequence of field research offered in students' first year of their graduate program. All students but two were native speakers of English. Their task as set up by the professor (Kohl) was to pursue an area of interest they had developed in the previous classes and to tie their interest to the local community, where they would do their fieldwork. At the end of the semester students had to turn in an outline for a larger work, a discussion of about five pages, and an annotated bibliography (Prior, 1997, p. 285). Lilah was the one student in the class who kept a log for Prior, so we know her through some of her entries rather than just through descriptions provided by Prior. We know she is interested in Chicano ethnicity, for example, but know little about her own ethnicity (which she describes vaguely as including German and "Bohemian" ancestors [Prior, 1998, p. 254]), age, background, or previous writing experience. The log, however, along with interviews, reveals that as a participant in the literacy activities of Kohl's seminar and of two other seminars in which she wrote papers for different professors on a similar topic, Lilah connected and blended issues from past and present classes, from home and personal experience, and from reflections on aspects of her project from inside and outside the classroom setting. Prior (1998) noted that the trajectories portrayed in Lilah's log "achieve [...] coherence through the continuity of her own biography and through central topics, especially ethnicity and course work" (p. 255).

Prior traced just one of these trajectories in Lilah's log and in interviews with her through the production of the paper for Kohl on the topic of Cinco de Mayo and of different versions of that paper for two other seminars. Prior found a theme of Mexican food (symbolized by "the taco") in multiple layers of Lilah's thinking and literate practice. She asked questions about it as a symbol of ethnicity in interviews with local community activists, she described a Mexican dinner she and her husband had as well as the neighborhood in which the restaurant was located, and she recounted the local history of the Cinco de Mayo festival foregrounding and challenging the taco as a symbol. She wove these threads into one kind of paper for Kohl, closely aligning her work to Kohl's representation of the task and allowing herself some playfulness with the taco symbol, and into other kinds of papers using a "more serious historical discourse" for two other professors (Prior, 1997, p. 290). In each paper, Lilah presented not just her issues but herself differently, as accommodating in one and challenging and "contrary" in another (p. 291). Lilah explained that her different approaches stemmed from her responses to the different personalities of each professor—professors who motivated her and at least one (Kohl) who did not. She perceived that different academic writing games were called for, in part because the players and her interactions with them differed, and responded accordingly.

Prior (1998) concluded his case study by noting the "multiple alignments" and "multiple identities" within the "heterogeneity of situated activity" (p. 261). His dense prose, complex descriptions of textual and nontextual influences on Lilah's writing, and multiple methodologies do not make for easy reading. However, it is this portrayal of complexity of what it means for an individual to step into the profession at the masters level that constitutes Prior's crucially important contribution to the work on academic literacy. Above all, his work reminds us that the writing games in particular graduate programs are not just textual, but personal and political as well (Clark & Ivanič, 1997; Ivanič, 1994, 1998; Margolis & Romero, 1998).

In the next section, I discuss my own case study of MA students learning to participate in the literate practices of the second and foreign language education field.

CASE STUDY: FIVE MASTERS STUDENTS STEP INTO THE SECOND LANGUAGE EDUCATION PROFESSION[1]

Many of the MA students in applied linguistics that I am familiar with want to teach, want to teach better, and want to understand how people learn a foreign language so that they can adjust their teaching accordingly. These students consider their MA a terminal degree. A few find they have had re-

---

[1]With the permission of all the faculty and student participants in this case study, I use their real names.

search chips implanted in their brains during their MA experiences and eventually enter PhD programs. Perhaps the most general statement I can make about the MA students I have worked with is that none of them knew the extent to which their lives in their MA programs would be defined by writing.

In the case study of five MA students I conducted during a sabbatical leave at the small institute in California where I had gotten my own MA, I wished to reimmerse myself in a familiar MA environment within my own field in order to look closely at students' experiences with and attitudes toward writing and to discover any changes over time in how the students viewed themselves and their field. With no responsibilities for teaching or evaluating these students, and with a primary focus on them rather than on their professors, I was able to concentrate on the perspectives of five very different students and to learn something about the centrifugal diversity and complexity within what seemed on the surface to be a tightly structured centripetally oriented MA program in educational linguistics. In the midst of this diversity, the writing games in this program required that students develop social and political strategies as well as learn several varieties of linguistic game rules and conventions.

The Setting

Monterey, California is an unlikely location for a highly specialized, increasingly well-known professional school. The setting for some of John Steinbeck's most memorable novels, it began as the Spanish capital of California in the mid-1800s, flourished as a fishing village until the canneries closed in the mid-1900s, and then became one of the tourist havens on the picturesque Monterey Peninsula. More recently it has become known for its several schools that focus on language study.

The Monterey Institute of International Studies ("MIIS" or "the Institute"), formerly the Monterey Institute of Foreign Studies, began in 1955 as a small private language school occupying the old Monterey Library. Known early for its intensive summer language programs taught by native speaking faculty, it grew over the years into a center for second and foreign language education, translation–interpretation, and international business and policy studies, offering some bachelors but primarily masters degrees. By the mid 1990s, the Institute had expanded to include buildings located over several blocks near the small downtown area and a student population of approximately 750. Always international in orientation and in population, the Institute hosts students and faculty from all over the world. During my research year on this campus, I often sat at a picnic table under the single large oak and redwood trees on the outdoor patio listening to people of all colors speaking Japanese, Chinese, French, Spanish, German, and Russian, and occasionally some familiar English.

The MA Program in TESOL/MATFL
at the Monterey Institute of International Studies

The Monterey Institute of International Studies (MIIS) Masters in Teaching English to Speakers of Other Languages (MATESOL) and in Teaching Foreign Language (MATFL) is a packed three-semester program in the Graduate School of Language and Educational Linguistics that runs year-round (including a summer session), with classes held mainly on weekdays. For local working teachers from the Defense Language Institute (the military language school "up the hill" from the Institute) who wish to pursue masters degrees on a part-time basis, some classes are scheduled in the late afternoons or evenings. Many students, however, come from around the United States or from abroad, and devote themselves to full-time studies. The program can handle up to 40 new students, although in some previous semesters the enrollment was lower than this. The primary faculty at the time of my study were eight full-time mid-career PhD holders, many of whom write and publish extensively and participate regularly in domestic and international conferences and other professional activities.

The preponderance of faculty who are very active professionally and the program decision not to rely heavily on part-timers contribute to the professional flavor of the MATESOL/MATFL program. In a 1998 large format brochure describing "the nature of the graduate program" in the Graduate School of Language and Educational Linguistics, two of the potential conflicts that students need to balance are mentioned—the conflict between teaching and research and between personal and professional goals. "Every good teacher is both a facilitator of language learning and a classroom researcher," the brochure states (p. 3). And in another paragraph: "Each program [TESOL and TFL] has a small and personal flavor in which faculty enthusiasm for the field is conveyed to students, and student involvement in turn motivates faculty members. Students and faculty frequently present joint papers at conferences and publish co-authored studies" (p. 3). The curriculum itself adds another clue as to the character of the program: Of the 37 required credits, most are required courses in applied linguistics, just 4 involve observation and practice, and only 4 are open electives. An exit mechanism in place since the early 1990s consists of a program portfolio and an oral conference with two faculty who have evaluated the portfolio. From this published information we get the sense that this program is not just preparing teachers, but that it is preparing people for a life of participation in a variety of professional activities, including participation in the field's knowledge-building and disseminating practices.

The MIIS Case Study Students

To locate students for the case study project, I contacted one of the professors I knew and asked if I could visit one of her classes to explain my project briefly and request volunteers. After the class, quite a few students approached me and offered to participate. With these volunteers and one other woman from Japan who had been suggested by one of the MA students, a total of six students, coincidentally all women, formed the case study cohort. Three of the women were from Japan, two were White middle class Americans, and one was an experienced teacher from Armenia. One of the Japanese women returned to Japan before we completed all of our interviews so is not included here. With a core of only five volunteers, I cannot be certain that these women represented anything typical about the MATESOL/MATFL student population. I can say that this population is characterized by more women than men and by its balance of international students, many of whom are from Japan, young White Americans, many of whom are on scholarships or who get loans, and older students from a variety of countries who were employed full time at the Defense Language Institute. Diversity of background, nationality, and purpose may have been the most typical characteristic of the student population, so the diversity of the case study participants was in that sense typical. I include in the descriptions below some background on the case study students' past writing experiences, information that adds a sense of how prepared they were for the academic writing in their MA program.

Kazuko

Kazuko was a young Japanese woman in her early 20s who had entered the MATFL program directly after completing her undergraduate degree in Japan. Her goal was to become a Japanese teacher, possibly in the United States. She was one of the few students in the program who had not taught before. She wore her hair long and straight, the way we used to in the 1960s, and smiled in a quiet and friendly way during our meetings, and in general seemed genuinely excited about being in graduate school in the United States in the company of not only native English speakers, some of whom were interested in Japan and Japanese, but also of many other students from Japan. Shortly after we met, she proudly and somewhat fearfully announced that she had gotten her first car, ever, a bright red sports car sold to her by its former owner, a friend and roommate. She also took on an American boyfriend, one who had a special interest in Japan and the Japanese language. During her time in the Monterey program, she began tutoring Japanese in the Institute's Custom Language Program. She also tutored me in conversational Japanese for several months.

As a young child in Japan, Kazuko says she hated writing. In elementary school, the children were not given clear instructions, but were instead told "just write." Later she was given some strict rules to follow for structure and punctuation and found writing a little easier as a result. She was never comfortable, however, with writing that was supposed to be "creative." As an undergraduate, Kazuko was an exchange student at a midwestern university in the United States, where she took an "English 100" course. She found it strange that her teacher there wanted students to submit all the stages of their writing—outlines and drafts as well as final papers. The final output, she claimed, is what should be graded. She said that at the Monterey Institute she and many of her friends felt that too much emphasis was put on writing. "Sometimes more practical things are needed," she explained.

Natsuko

From the first meeting with Natsuko, a young Japanese woman in her mid-20s, I was impressed with her intense, no-nonsense approach to my case study project and to her own work. Determined to complete the full MATESOL program within a year (a feat accomplished by very few native English speakers, let alone native Japanese), she had honed her work style to the point where every minute of the day, and much of the evening, was filled. She was known throughout the program, by faculty and by other students, as one of the best in the program and was admired as one who was computer literate. Small and pretty, she sometimes showed up at our interviews looking but not acting tired. During her year at the Institute, in addition to her studies she tutored Japanese in the Custom Language Service program and taught ESL in and helped administer one of the Institute's special ESL programs. She also tutored me occasionally in Japanese. Her plan was to return to Japan to teach English, a goal somewhat complicated by her steady relationship with a German boyfriend.

Natsuko enjoyed writing and did a lot of it from an early age. Throughout elementary and junior high schools she got awards for the expressive writing she did in Japanese in response to her fiction reading. In junior high she started to read nonfiction and her writing style began to change as a result of instruction in a more factual style and of models from her reading. In high school, her Japanese class continued to be her favorite, but she was surprised that her award-winning writing seemed less highly valued there. At the university, where she majored in American literature, she got a part-time job as a journalist for a Japanese magazine for junior high school students, a job that took her to different high schools for visits and interviews with principals and students. After reading many sample articles provided by the company, and having her first few pieces edited, she began to produce pieces that were published without editorial changes.

Perhaps Natsuko's most important academic writing experiences before coming to Monterey took place in her junior and senior years when she took classes and wrote papers in American literature, poetry, and history, in English and Japanese. She had two professors, one American and one Japanese woman who was educated in the United States. It was these teachers who taught her how to write. They told her that her writing was very "ambiguous," and tried to make her conscious of her writing style. Her Japanese professor was the one who told her "state the point directly at first, then restate it at the end." During her junior year, she wrote "all the time, a journal for each class, twice a week" for her American professor, who gave her feedback on content rather than grammar. In particular during her senior year, this professor was very explicit in her instructions, assisting Natsuko in producing a 30-page thesis in English. Natsuko's first attempts at drafting some pages of her thesis were rejected *in toto* by this professor, who claimed she had only summarized rather than made an argument. Natsuko says she went home and cried, feeling "overturned completely," given her long history of successful writing. With time, careful explanation by her professor, and self-discovery, she survived and flourished, later finishing her MA program at Monterey in record time as a star performer.

Karine

Karine was not officially enrolled at MIIS for the full MA program, but was there for a year by special arrangement with an American university program based in her home country of Armenia. She would be finishing her MA there, and continuing to teach and administer in her university's English program. Olive-skinned, with dark eyes and hair, she had a short but solid build as well as a firm aura about her that contrasted with the petiteness of Natsuko and the insecurity and youth of Kazuko. A much more experienced teacher than most other students in the program, she radiated an intensity in her discussions with me about writing that suggested to me not only a deep interest in writing but also a sense of urgency about her limited time in Monterey and a deeply emotional relationship with her field. Her interests ranged from article usage in her written English to philosophical stances on education. Trilingual in Armenian, Russian, and English, she had studied Russian during her school years in the Soviet regime, and had majored in English at the university, where the languages of instruction were Armenian and English. Of all the students I interviewed for my project, she was having the most trouble finding an "academic voice" that matched what some of her professors expected from her, partly because she did not wish to stifle totally her emotional and philosophical side.

Karine had been instructed in Russian from a very young age. In the eighth grade students were taught an explicit, rather conventional format for writing: introduction, body, and conclusion. She mentioned that many of these early writings were "dicto-comps," which I understood to be stories that were told then reproduced. She also read literature and wrote essays from these books, infusing her writings, as did other students, with Soviet ideology. She was good at language and literature, but resisted one of her teacher's attempts to get her to continue studies in Russian philology. In college she wrote a final project in English, but did not recall needing to follow any explicit conventions for citing or referencing works. She received feedback on grammar, vocabulary, and syntax, but not on the structure or style of academic writing. She commented that her secondary school Russian literature program had been more "academic" than her university English studies. Once at the Institute in Monterey, she found that she was not prepared for the kind of academic writing that she was expected to do.

Kirsten

Kirsten struck me as a bright and unpretentious white American woman, a casual dresser, and good-humored friend to her classmates. She radiated a sense of confidence and of security with her identity and her career goals. She had just returned from several years teaching in Japan when we met. Her husband was Japanese, and she herself was quite proficient in Japanese. Her projects in the TESOL program at MIIS reflected these interests and experiences. She told me that she had always liked writing, had done a lot of it, and rarely found it uncomfortably difficult. She expressed a confidence with her writing that most of the other students I got to know did not. Competent and self-taught with computers, she had a school job as a computer assistant, helping design and maintain websites and organizing two writing and computer literacy workshops for students. After graduating, she planned to join her husband in another part of California where he would be employed and to look for a job there teaching English. She was considered by some of the faculty that I spoke with to be one of the strongest students in the program.

Like Natsuko, Kirsten had always done well in reading and writing and had always enjoyed it and received praise for it from a very young age. In elementary school and junior high she was taught "formal schemata" for writing, and learned about thesis statements and paragraphing. However, at several points in our interviews she commented on how much she has always hated revising. This antipathy may have caused her some problems with her interdisciplinary BA thesis in Japanese studies. She did a "huge project" that involved keeping a journal and incorporating parts of the journal into the final piece as well as creating a performance art piece on Noh-like masks. The project also required that she write a literature review, which she found difficult. The writing was critiqued by her professor for "going off the topic." Once enrolled in the Institute's MA program, Kirsten's awareness of her writing changed, and for the first time she realized that she had to gear her writing to a real audience that had certain expectations of what they would and would not be reading. She continued to enjoy many kinds of writing she did in her program, but developed a much more complex understanding of what writing was than she had held previously.

Kyla

Kyla, young and inexperienced with just a year of teaching at a conversation school in Japan, looked like the stereotypical Californian—blue eyes, shaggy blond hair, sleeveless shirt, bermuda shorts, and sandals in spite of the cool, foggy Monterey summer. She seemed nervous in our first interviews, though part of this may have been her normal way of interacting with people whom she did not know well. She smiled throughout our first talks, racing through her comments to the point where I was sure that it would be difficult to transcribe her tapes (it was, according to the assistant who was charged with the onerous task). She talked about her efforts to become a clearer, more effective speaker with the help of the Toastmasters program, in which she was currently enrolled. She had majored in French and history as an undergraduate at the University of California, Berkeley. In her TESOL program, which she was combining with a certificate in language program administration, she used her experience from Japan as material for papers, having spent a year there teaching and having had little success studying Japanese herself. Of the four students who were on campus for the full duration of my study, she was the only one who had one more semester to complete before graduating.

In high school, Kyla was taught the classic five-paragraph essay, a topic of debate at her high school. In her stressful senior year she wrote a thesis on Virginia Woolf. Her perfectionist tendencies added to her stress, and prevented her from looking at an overall theme in her writing. Instead, she paid more attention to details, "stringing details together" to construct her texts. Later in college she had a number of classes in history and French that required that she write papers. She received no explicit instruction in how to write these papers, but had to teach herself to write. One strategy was to seek help from professors themselves during office hours or even on the phone beforehand to get specific advice on form, or afterwards for feedback on graded work. She found her senior thesis in history especially hard in that she had to find and combine sources, then interpret what she had found. At the Institute, Kyla continued writing a lot, both in and out of class: e-mail, personal journals, and school papers, enjoying in particular the academic papers that encouraged students to add a personal element (language autobiography, response journals). She continued her practice of seeking help from professors.

I interviewed these five women individually seven times from the end of the spring semester 1998 through the end of the fall semester, December, 1998. In the case of Karine, we held our seventh interview in the middle of July. We met on campus, often outdoors in a common patio area or in a comfortable lobby area of one of the buildings. I took extensive notes during these interviews, and recorded them as well for later transcription by an assistant. Each interview lasted approximately 45 minutes. (See Appendix C for Interview Questions.) The students also allowed me to copy many of their papers that had been marked by various professors. We talked about some of these during our interviews. I met informally with some of the students' professors and visited a number of classes but did no formal interviews with them.

The Professors, Their Classes, and Their Assignments

In order to contextualize the experiences of the masters students described above, and to help me understand what they were expected to do, think, write, and become, I visited four different classes, three required for the masters degree and one elective. My discussion focuses mainly on the required classes. I did not attend every session—time away from Monterey prevented this. I sat in on three sessions of the three required classes, collected handouts, and took extensive field notes during each visit.

What struck me after my visits and what came through in the interviews with the students was the diversity of professional styles and demands of the teachers on the one hand and the high level of expectations of and support from them with regard to students' academic literacy practices on the other. This high level of involvement of the teachers with their students' evolving literacy practices seemed radically different from the picture painted by Schneider and Fujishima (1995) about Zhang and his MA program in the same school. Unlike other studies of academic literacy practices in MA programs, in other words, my study can be told as a success story, a story of a program that encouraged students to engage actively in a wide variety of literacy practices and provided the support needed to help students find their way into this particular community of practice.

The Professors. In this MA program, the professors all taught several of the many required courses in addition to occasional electives. The required classes that I visited several times were: Educational Research Methods, typically taken early in the program, taught by Jean; Applied Linguistics Research, taken at the end, also taught by Jean; and Portfolio Seminar, taken in the final semester as students were preparing their final exit portfolios, the section I observed being taught by John. (All students called the professors by their first names, a custom I follow in this study.)

As was her mode of dress, Jean's style of teaching both Educational Research Methods and Applied Linguistics Research was simple, straightforward, systematic. In each class I visited, she distributed an abundance of handouts on different colors of paper. She punctuated her instruction with humorous comments and personal anecdotes designed to make the new students in particular feel comfortable and encouraged in a class that might intimidate them with its introduction to statistics in applied linguistics. The professor who taught the Portfolio Seminar, John, had helped design and revise the elaborate portfolio system over the past 6 years. He looked younger than he was—had a boyish look about him—and radiated a quiet blend of precision, seriousness, and good humor. He was known by both students and colleagues as a "stickler for details" and a "walking APA Manual," and was deferred to by all on matters of style and form in students' portfolio materials. A nonstop worker, he spent many late evenings in his office reading student papers, reviewing manuscripts for publishers, and working on his own writing. By all accounts Jean and John were located on the stricter end of the continuum of teacher styles in the program. The other end was occupied by two professors in the "touchy-feely" camp whom I had heard about but whose classes I did not visit as part of my project. Jean and John were active professionally, writing and participating in conferences.

The Classes and Assignments. Jean's Educational Research Methods class met twice a week for two hours each session. My case study participants had already taken this class, so I did not know any of the 22 students in it. Students in her class were learning to understand, evaluate, and use basic statistical procedures used in some kinds of language research. Students were evaluated by means of a critical summary of a study, a midterm and final examination, and a written research proposal. This research proposal was to be structured in a conventional way: abstract, introduction, method, subjects, materials, procedures, analysis, results, and discussion. The second research class taught by Jean, Applied Linguistics Research, met once a week for 3 hours. Two of my case study participants were in this class, Kirsten and Natsuko. The class required that students plan, carry out, and write up a research project according to their interests and to some of the research techniques they had been learning. In the classes that I observed, the students were learning to discuss and evaluate different kinds of data from readings and samples of interview and survey data and later in the semester were peer-editing each other's drafts of their own research projects.

The Portfolio Seminar taught by John that I observed was offered in students' final semester of the MA. It aimed at helping students bring together everything they had done in the program in a way that followed explicit Portfolio Guidelines so as to help students succeed on this all-important program exit mechanism. The Guidelines (a long and detailed document distributed as a packet at the beginning of the program) specified four major sections for the final portfolio, some with multiple subsections: (1) a position paper, (2) two revised works and literature in the field (in the form of a bibliography and summaries), (3) personal writing and professional products and materials, and (4) critiques (personal, peer, faculty). Each subsection was to be preceded by a cover note. The final portfolio was evaluated by two professors (the students never knew which two until they received feedback for revision) who then met with each student in a final oral hearing.

In John's Portfolio Seminar, the main piece of new writing was the position paper, perhaps the students' most important piece of writing in the program. In this paper students were to lay out a personal and rationalized pedagogical philosophy about language, learning, and teaching. It needed to be personal, but at the same time supported by integrated knowledge from the different strands of the program, evidence of familiarity with published authorities in each of the strands, and attention to the practical implications of theoretical issues. Color-coded handouts abounded in John's class. An early handout mentioned balancing a "personal imprint vs. playing the game." In other handouts related to the development of the position paper and in the class activities that I observed, a great deal of emphasis was placed on being able to name many of the authorities in the field, on following conventions for writing in applied linguistics, and on attending to details that apply to good writing in general (such as avoiding unclear referents).

Three of the case study participants in my study were taking the Portfolio Seminar in the fall (two sections offered, taught by different professors) and trying to finish up all requirements for the MA during my data collection period (Kazuko, Natsuko, Kirsten). Kazuko and Kirsten were both enrolled in John's section and Natsuko in another section. Kyla would begin her seminar in the spring. (Karine, as I mentioned earlier, returned to Armenia to finish her MA there.) During the fall semester when this class was offered, students in their third semester of the program talked of little else. Albatross-like, the portfolio requirement followed them everywhere and was now inescapable. Time was short and the task seemed overwhelming to some of them.

The classes that I described in this section represent just a portion of the classroom experiences and projects that the students in the MA program undertook. In other classes they learned about language teaching methods and materials, designed curricula and language tests, studied language structure, sociolinguistics, and second language acquisition, observed classes, and did practice teaching at one of the local schools. In most classes there was a great deal of small group discussion as well as teacher-fronted activities. The professors on this campus expected students to go on to contribute to the profession by being not only exemplary teachers but also by engaging in professional activities such as research and presentation, hence the relatively heavy emphasis on research courses and the minimal focus on practice teaching. According to one student who talked to me about this expectation, some students, particularly those without much teaching experience, disliked the emphasis on theory and research in this program and found one or two of the professors extreme in their demand that students live up to "professional standards." Nevertheless, she said, students benefitted from the diversity of faculty and of approaches in this program. Others, like Kirsten, joined this MA program because of its reputation for professionalism.

Amidst this diversity of classes, projects, writing tasks, and professors' personalities and demands, an equally diverse group of students had to find ways to make sense of the different academic literacy games they encountered in this program. It is to the students' perspectives that I now turn.

Students' Perspectives on Their MA Academic Literacy Practices

In the course of their MA program most students take at least one class from each of the full-time professors. From experience, and early in their program from hearsay, students become well-acquainted with the range of personalities, teaching styles, and demands of different professors and with the kinds of activities and projects each was likely to require. One of the social and political game challenges for the students was to work with or around the diversity and to avoid clashes with some of the more powerful personalities among the faculty who also had some clashes of values and practices among themselves. Related to this challenge was that of making writing, teaching, and research projects fit their own interests as well as meet the professors' expectations. This MA community was small—a small program on a small campus in a small town—and the full-time students could not avoid interacting with most of their diverse faculty. Students liked, respected, revered, feared, disliked, tolerated, and emulated their different professors, according to students' own personalities, expectations, and individual experiences with them.

Where there was broad agreement among all the students I got to know was in their strongly voiced opinions about the central role that writing played in the program. The writing itself took many forms in addition to the standard research paper, and the professors differed in how explicitly they laid out their assignments and then provided feedback. In the sections of my case study that follow, I look at the students' perceptions of the different genres of academic writing and their purposes, at their responses to different assignments, and at their experiences with different kinds of feedback. These aspects of the program communicated messages about values, norms, and writing practices that were important to particular professors and by extension to the field of language education. I conclude the case study with the students' perceptions of changes in their writing and in their professional identities.

The Pervasiveness of Writing and the Diversity of Writing Types. All of the students that I worked with in the MA program at Monterey had been in the program for nearly two semesters by the time we began the project. With this experience behind them, all emphasized that writing was the key to success in the program. There seemed to be no challenge to this view, nor even differences in the strength of their opinions. Kyla said that writing was "very important—everything we turn in is writing." Kirsten, a confident and comfortable writer, added three more "verys." She continued:

> There's no way you can go through this program without being able to write, not just write, but write in the way that professors here expect you to, as in a kind of academic writing, you have to know how to present ideas and support your argument and write with a certain level of detachedness. Not say, well, I think that such and such, you have to say it like you're not there. (Kirsten, Interview 1)

Natsuko, a strong writer in the program, noted that because the program did not rely on examinations, writing was "the main source for professors to evaluate our performance." She told me that "the first priority to success in this program is good writing skills." Kazuko commented that she had had only "two big exams" in her program and that everything else was "papers, papers, papers."

When I asked them what they understood by the term *academic writing*, the five women described it in a number of different ways. Karine said that academic writing was characterized by a "certain register" that employed specialized vocabulary ("jargonese") and a literary or educational standard. Kazuko mentioned these features too. Another characteristic for Karine was stance: "Every piece of academic writing in my today's understanding presupposes my position in regard to what I am writing." Finally, Karine noted that there were formal requirements, which she disliked greatly, having to do with formatting, citations, and reference lists. Kirsten, who had always written rather naturally and intuitively, noticed a change in her view of academic writing since becoming a "TESOL person," primarily in her awareness of audience. "I think about academic writing now in terms of how I would explain to someone who doesn't have the same kind of background that I do," she said. Natsuko had an interesting perspective on Japanese and English academic writing, one that echoes Hinds' (1987) views on reader and writer responsibility:

> Japanese academic writing, from what I understand, is pretty factual. Like, it must contain a lot of information, the details, and must use higher register, terminology, and it should be very logical and convincing, but at the same time, you don't need to explain everything. The burden was more on the reader, not the writer, to leave the room for the reader to imagine. And my understanding of academic writing in English, or in the U.S. is very, very consistent and coherent structured paper. And every time I like to mention somebody's work, I have to have accurate citations. (Natsuko, Interview 1)

The characteristics of academic writing that Kyla mentioned were that "you have to give credit," and take a position and support it in a structured way. Like Natsuko, she was especially impressed with the need to cite sources so often. Even though she had done a lot of writing in her undergraduate days, she said she "hadn't seen citations done this way before I got here, with like 300 names after each sentence. I've never seen that much explanation for what should seem really clear." Interestingly, in Kyla's experience writing for particular professors whose published examples she followed, she learned that stories, anecdotes, metaphors, and use of first person help enliven academic writing. Unlike Kirsten's view that academic writing should be "detached," she said, "It seems like here all academic writing can be personal."

In sum, the students described the game rules for writing as ones in which the author takes and defends a position, writes for an audience, relies on sources and cites them accurately, uses specialized terminology and formal register, and structures the writing in clear ways. The students differed somewhat in their beliefs about the extent to which academic writing could include "personal" elements, differences that their professors no doubt expressed as well. It also became clear that the students' drafting and revising activities could not be disentangled from the writing-related practices that allowed each piece of writing to come into being: reading the literature in the field, talking and working with peers and professors, observing classes and practice teaching, attending closely to handouts that described writing projects and procedures, listening to and asking questions of professors during class sessions, working statistics problems, learning how to use the computer to do graphs and tables, and studying examples of previously produced student papers. The term *academic writing*, therefore, must be understood in this larger sense, not only in this case study but throughout this book.

Genres of Writing in the MA Program. What kinds of writing are students required to do in MA programs? The simple answer is that they do academic writing that consists of conventional essays (introduction–body–

conclusion, with clear thesis and supporting evidence), summaries and critiques, or library- or data-based research papers. Genre studies of writing, however, have complicated our understanding by looking at the features of different kinds of research articles (Berkenkotter & Huckin, 1995; Hyland, 1996a, 1996b; Posteguillo, 1999; Swales, 1990), grant proposals (Connor, 2000; Myers, 1985), conference proposals (Berkenkotter & Huckin, 1995) and a variety of other genres associated with professional writing in the disciplines (Hyland, 2000; Swales & Feak, 2000). At the graduate level, Prior (1998) has examined writing related to masters and doctoral theses and to seminar papers, but without focusing on genre diversity within a single graduate program.

Johns (1997) points out that although genres have "shared names," the meaning of a name like "research paper" in academic settings may not be clear (p. 23). Johns believes, therefore, that one place to begin to understand what kinds of writing students do is with the naming game. Wenger (1998, p. 162) reminds us that labels and categories do not capture the complexity of lived experience, which is at the heart of both practice and identity. Still, in this case they provide clues as to how the five students in my study conceptualized their MA writing practices.

I therefore asked the case study participants to name and describe the different kinds of writing they had been required to produce so far (the first two of three or four semesters) and then to discuss what they saw as the purposes of the different types of writing. Each student, with little hesitation, named 10 to 12 types of writing they had done, only a few of which conformed to what studies and textbooks on academic literacy refer to as research papers (e.g., Swales & Feak, 1994). I combined the students' descriptions and came up with the following list of 16 types of writing, each of which required a different form and style and achieved a different purpose according to the writing samples I collected and to the students' descriptions of each type. Some overlap in labels no doubt has occurred:

Annotated bibliography

Case study

Critique (reaction papers, critical summaries, reviews of tests and textbooks)

Curriculum design

Language autobiography

Lesson plan

Library research and focus paper ("literature review"?)

Needs analysis

Observation and experience notes and narratives

Peer response

Personal/reflective journal

Position paper

Reading response journal

Research paper (with results, statistical analysis)

Research proposal

Test development and analysis

Not one of the students, regardless of mother tongue or previous experience, had been prepared for this diversity of genres in previous academic work or in preparatory writing courses. In addition to writing that required the standard introduction–body–conclusion they wrote narratives, test items, statistical tables and graphs, language exercises, reference lists and bibliographies, lists, and personal reflections, including some authentic writing for schools in the local community, such as needs analyses, curriculum designs, and lesson plans for their own practice teaching. By the time I interviewed them, they had all been in the program for some time and were able to talk about what they saw as the purposes of the many different kinds of writing they had to do.

Karine, for one, speaking in ways that were sometimes hard for me to interpret clearly, commented on a "qualitative change in my academic vision" as a result of the many different kinds of writing she was doing. She saw their general purpose as helping students see where a "narrow point fits into the whole field" and understand that "knowing theoretically is not knowing practically." Karine also saw strong connections between her reading and her writing, and between them and her ability to think. All the writing projects, she said, contributed to her "ability to think academically" in a field where academic writing was "absolutely different from other writing."

Kirsten spoke about the practical value of specific pieces of writing. The position paper, for example, would help her develop what she believed and "to have it concrete so I can answer interview questions when I go to get a job," and help her make principled rather than random decisions about her teaching. Other pieces of writing also had practical purposes, such as curriculum and lesson plans and the development of tests: "These are all professional tools and these are the things I'm actually gonna have to do in my daily life as a teacher." Kazuko spoke as well about the practical purpose of her test development and test review assignments. She said that "as teachers, we should know of widely developed, widely used tests, of that language. So we have to be able to critically review these tests, so we can recommend that to students. I think it's a necessary project as a teacher," she concluded.

Journals, on the other hand, were not seen in such practical terms, but as Kirsten put it had multiple purposes: They helped further her thinking about a topic, they allowed the professor to "track whether we read stuff or not," and they enabled an interaction to be set up between a professor and individual students. Research papers, too, had multiple purposes. Kirsten explained that they "socialize us into the discourse community of professional language teachers." Part of this socialization involved looking critically at published research. Kyla noted that writing a critical review not only helped students develop familiarity with the language and the field; it also enabled her to realize that "just because it's published it's not necessarily that solid, which is pretty shocking." Natsuko expressed a more personal and individual purpose for what she called "library research papers." These helped students educate themselves and, like the position paper, increased students' awareness of their own stances on issues:

> I think it is consciousness-raising by writing a paper, since we have to take a stance, it's a good opportunity for me to reflect, okay, how do I feel to this issues, what's my opinion on this issue? Writing requires a lot of reflection and conscious-raising process. (Natsuko, Interview 2)

Kyla, like Natsuko, also noted that self-reflection was a "key in this program," and that several kinds of writing encouraged reflection. She commented in particular about the purpose of writing a language autobiography, having it read by other students, and having to read those of other students:

> Well, for each [type of writing] there seems to be a direct reason for doing it, like the language autobiography was to get you to think about how you learned a language and then by having read other people's, because we were required to read five of them to see how different people's approach is. That was pretty revealing. Wow, some people managed to learn a language by never opening a grammar book, where, I'm studying the subjunctive and . . . I just didn't know, well, I knew you could do it, but just to see how many different ways there are is help for a teacher to know the different styles. (Kyla, Interview 2)

Each of the students perceived and could talk in some detail about many types and purposes of writing they had been required to do in their MA program. With few exceptions, such as the library research paper or essay, they had not produced these kinds of writings before. The students from Japan and Armenia, in this regard, were not disadvantaged relative to the mother-tongue English speakers. Their disadvantage resided primarily in their less facile control of surface features of the language and the extra time to have papers checked by friends. The point is that all the students were producing genres that were new for them, and all students found them purposeful. In the two next sections, I describe some of the ways that students figured out what to do from assignment instructions beforehand and from feedback after the fact.

Messages From the Task Descriptions. The students in this project said that the Institute did not provide any kind of routine writing instruction or guidelines when they entered the program. The trick for first semester students in particular, in the absence of a master game plan, was to figure out what to do in the first writing assignments before they had gotten their first feedback and before they knew the idiosyncracies of each of the professors they would be writing for. In some cases they could begin to do this from assignments that explicitly laid out a professor's expectations, but not all assignments were so detailed.

The students attributed the amount of detail or vagueness of assignment descriptions to particular professors rather than to particular classes. This or that professor, they explained, always gives very detailed systematic instructions whereas another doesn't explain much at all about what to do. The students who did not enjoy writing, such as Kazuko, relied heavily on handouts that specified the game rules for projects and write-ups in great detail, appreciating the exact requirements of form, treatment of topic, and other constraints. In contrast, the students said that they had little sense of what to do in response to a briefly and vaguely worded assignment especially at the beginning of their program. Here are several examples, first of a minimally articulated assignment, then of a slightly more detailed one, and finally of an explicit set of guidelines. Some of these are from classes I did not visit; they were provided to me by the students.

In an elective class on language teaching technology, the initial handout was described as a "Needs Analysis." It had a section labeled "Goals and Plans" in which students were asked what project or research they wanted to carry out. Projects then evolved from students' initial expression of interest and the specifics were discussed in class and negotiated with the professor. There were no handouts describing step-by-step procedures, formal requirements, or nonnegotiable aspects of the content or form of the projects.

From a class on second language acquisition, on the other hand, a term project was described in the following more detailed but still brief terms that still left room for variety and negotiation. The description was followed by a list of suggested topics:

> The term project is a student-initiated research endeavor that aims to examine a particular aspect of second language acquisition and learning. It could be a data-based research project which investigates empirical data obtained from learners (error analysis, progress report, case study, observational study, etc.). It could also be a library-based research paper which synthesizes

and evaluates current SLA research *in order to reach an informed opinion or stance on a particular issue* [italics the professor's]. The assignment provides an opportunity for students to explore a topic of interest in SLA and pursue it in some detail. Depending on the nature of the project, it can be done jointly if conditions necessitate such a joint venture. I will leave the format open, but would like to approve it before the project is undertaken. Any academically oriented paper as a final product should not exceed 20 pages, including references. If you have any questions about the analytical procedure or format you use, feel free to talk with me.

In a third example, from a class on testing, the following very detailed assignment for doing a "test review" was given to students (reproduced with permission of the teacher). The boldface type is the professor's:

1. **Choose a language test** that has been commercially developed (i.e., it is published for profit, such as the BSM) or is widely used (i.e., it has a broad impact on language teaching, such as the TOEFL, or has widely influenced language testing research, such as the DLPT). It should be a test in the language of your degree. (3 more lines of details)

2. **Gather information about the test** (from the publisher, from published research articles, from teachers who have used it, etc.). This information should include a summary of the history of the test and a sample test (if available) or at least sample items; test development information on its reliability, validity, and item analyses; pricing information and order forms; administration manuals and/or manuals for test score users. (2 more lines of details)

3. **Administer the test** and/or talk to teachers who have used it, and/or students who have taken it. Try to get a feel for how it works: whether it is face valid, whether the information it yields is worth the effort, whether it is "user friendly," whether the instructions are clear, etc.

4. **Examine the scoring system**. Determine how scores are derived and reported, what guidance for interpreting scores is provided to user agencies, what test security measures are used, etc. Decide if it is a norm-referenced or a criterion-referenced test, and whether it provides usable diagnostic information. Explain the scoring system and any problems that it may present. If any ratings are involved, provide rater-reliability data.

5. **Analyze the test** using Wesche's four components as well as Bachman's framework on page 119. In addition, you should incorporate any relevant constructs discussed in our seminar in your analysis of this test.

6. **Prepare a written review**, which is well-documented, well-organized and thorough (eight to ten pages per person, typed and double-spaced). The due date for the final written report is listed on the course syllabus. The re-

port should include accurate citations of appropriate references. Appendices may be added, which do not count in the page limit.

The assignment for the research proposal project in Jean's Educational Research Methods class (and the expected structure of the actual research project write-up in Applied Linguistics Research) was described in great detail, too. The proposal project was divided into numbered paragraphs, each describing the sections of the proposal: (1) Abstract, (2) Introduction (including review of the literature and statement of purpose), (3) Method (including subjects, materials, and procedures), (4) Analysis, and (5) Discussion. Each section description referred students to appropriate pages in their textbook in addition to providing descriptive guidelines.

John's handouts from his Portfolio Seminar included 50 pages of detailed instructions and advice: worksheets and checklists for each of the sections of the portfolio, ground rules, portfolio inventory, portfolio selection criteria, organizational hints, portfolio caveats, sample outlines for the position paper, and a $1^{1}/_{2}$ page handout entitled "General Recommendations for Position Paper Manuscript Preparation."

These are just a few examples of the many writing assignments that students told me about in their MA program. Each one reflected different messages, based on the personal proclivities of each professor, about the game rules in the field and about the roles of students in contributing (or not) to the content and form of a project. In some classes where assignments were open, students participated as contributors to knowledge in the field, helping educate each other and furthering the professor's own knowledge in some cases. The loosely structured assignments in classes like this allowed for a great deal of personal choice, growth, and reflection. In classes where assignments were more tightly laid out, norms in the field were more well-defined, such as in the shape of a research paper, in the statistical procedures used for test reviews, and in the expectation that a participant in the second and foreign language education community hold a clear and well-justified stance on the field's key issues. Students like Kazuko who were new to the field and who disliked writing appreciated the great detail and step-by-step approach taken by some of the professors and the other students as well noted that they knew exactly what was expected in such assignments. Their roles as students were clear in these cases. In other classes they were expected to participate more as contributors and to figure out on their own and in interaction with classmates and professor what their contribution could be.

Feedback and the Sociopolitical Game of Writing for Different Professors. The MA students that I got to know reveled in the moments of undivided attention from their professors that was provided by written feedback on individual papers. They developed a sense of themselves as evolving professionals by the kinds of comments they received. Not all feedback worked this way of course. When feedback was minimal or seemed rubber-stamped and generic the students claimed to learn very little about themselves or their writing.

The students told me that a particular professor's style of responding seemed consistent across classes, papers, and students: Those who responded minimally (there were not many) did so regularly; those who commented at length did so regularly. Similarly, those who tended to mark small errors (typos, grammar, punctuation) did so for all students, not just the international students, and those who refrained from making surface comments needed to be persuaded to do so even for international students like Karine and Kazuko who wanted all of their small mistakes corrected. When I asked her why she thought the faculty responded in such different ways, Kazuko told me she believed it was because of "personality, or maybe experience differences." But personality, she said, "is the biggest thing, how you specific, how you organize, how you easy-going, how you open to different styles and stuff." Kazuko's view matched those of other students who, like her, could correlate teachers' personal styles of teaching and interacting with the kinds of feedback they gave. The laid-back easy going professors tended to write more comments that praised than criticized. The very demanding teachers reversed this balance.

When I asked the five women what they thought the purpose of feedback was several of them said that it was different for each professor but that ultimately the feedback would help them revise papers for their portfolio. Kirsten explained that for those professors who require two drafts, the feedback is aimed at revision. Natsuko spoke at length about the purposes of feedback, stressing the differences among professors as well as the importance of feedback for the final portfolio project:

> In general, written feedback from professors aims at students' further improvement in their writing, in terms of logical development, and argument, organization, and ambiguity of the point in that paper. Written feedback is rather work as facilitator for the future writing of that student. Personally, so far, I've written several papers and have gotten feedback, but the length and the amount of the feedback varies from professor to professor, so greatly. For example, for one professor might give me just a short written feedback which might be related to my grammatical mistakes and misspelling only. On the other hand, one professor may give me a lot of written feedback related to my content of the paper, or the argument. And I believe the written feedback- Of course pointing out grammatical mistakes and correcting misspellings is helpful, certainly. But at the same time, what I'd like to see is their suggestions about how my papers, to improve my papers for the future development. The students in TESOL in this program have portfolio in the last semester, which

contains the revision of the previous papers that they wrote. In that time, I'm sure the written feedback from the professors would be a great help to revise these papers. (Natsuko, Interview 3)

At this same interview, with a specific paper in her hand that had very few marks on it she said, "But then when I look at, for example, this paper, I don't think I can revise it very well, because I don't know what was wrong and what was very good about my paper."

Kyla mentioned another purpose, one in which she expressed her sense of agency in monitoring how the professors were reading her work and in learning to see herself through their eyes. She wanted to know what they thought about her ideas, to get evidence that they had "actually read it" and had an interest in what she wrote about. "That's the main purpose," she continued, "just to oh, what did they think of this, was I completely off track, try to situate myself." Her self-assessment, in other words, developed in interaction with the views of her professors about specific pieces of work and specific ideas in those works. Their feedback helped her "situate herself" in relation to them and by extension in relation to the field.

Kazuko speculated about what she thought might be a cultural difference in how professors gave feedback. One of her past professors at MIIS had been "Asian," a fact she guesses might have caused him to give much more negative feedback than did other professors. (This professor, visiting for a year before my study began and not available for interviews, is not intended to represent a stereotype from my perspective.) She liked positive feedback, she said, finding that it gave her a "reward" by encouraging her. "I realized there are a lot of positive feedbacks here. The grade might not be that great, but the feedback is usually positive somehow." She continued, not concerned about her generalization:

Except [X]. He's Asian, and Asian professors, I believe they tend to give negative feedback so that they believe that students can improve their papers by making negative feedback. And I'm used to that kind of feedback, so I was kind of surprised to having positive feedback here in the States. . . . But negative feedback has to have more detail, what was wrong. It shouldn't just say "disorganized," for instance. I don't know why he thinks so. If the negative feedback is detailed and shows me which way to go, I think it will help. (Kazuko, Interview 3)

In spite of a few cases in which a professor gave little feedback of any kind, most of the papers that students shared with me had marks of some kind on every page, from corrections of spacing and punctuation to brief or lengthy marginal and end comments. Even the mother-tongue English speakers had mechanical errors corrected by some professors. The point of the surface feedback, however, did not strike me as being directed at language acquisition but at disciplinary enculturation. The game rules expressed by the professors who marked in such detail seemed to be that "your work needs to look professional if you want to graduate from this program" (also expressed to me by one of the faculty members as well as by students) and "you need to understand the conventions of how people in our field communicate." From those professors who, in the students' view, cared little about details of form and language, a quite different game rule seemed to be "we are interested in your ideas and want you to explore them to the fullest. If you don't have time to do everything, be creative and reflective and get your ideas expressed so you can learn about yourself." Indeed, students told me that they paid much less attention to mechanics such as the details of APA formatting when they wrote for certain professors, not worrying at all about them until time came to revise papers for the final portfolio. Several students suggested to me that the faculty in these two "camps" espoused different sets of values and practices, but that both contributed to their understanding of themselves in relation to an amorphously defined second language education field. We appreciate the diversity, they told me.

The point I wish to make here is that professors' feedback on graduate students' work, like advice from a good coach to a new player, can serve the powerful function of assisting students' movement into a particular community's professional practices but that very different kinds of feedback send messages to students that look contradictory. The contradictory nature of messages in feedback reflects a social and political reality of the academic playing field. The local community, being populated as it always is by people who differ greatly in terms of personality, expectations, and power, represents a social and political entity, not just a linguistic one, even though the field and its practices are defined through writing. The feedback, in other words, from the earliest stages of the students' immersion in the local academic literacy practices, helps students deal with the social and political realities of academic writing games, which as they discover in this program involve for the most part meeting the expectations of particular and sometimes very different professors. A specific example from the work of one student conveys a sense of what it was like to write for different professors in this program.

The Gamut of Feedback to Karine. Let me turn briefly to some examples of feedback to Karine and to her responses to that feedback. As I have already mentioned, feedback was viewed by a number of the students as a dialogue between the professors and them. The dialogic interaction was inherent to all the genre games in the MA program, a characteristic noted by Freadman (1994) in her game analogy of genres (see Chap. 1). Looking at some interactions between Karine and her professors we can note that the style of much of the feedback supports a dialogic perspective. Comments on her papers ranged from conversational exclamations of surprise, interest, and doubt, to lengthy commentary offering suggestions, questions to think about, and personal opinion. Occasionally the comments were direct and didactic in tone, particularly when a paper seemed to violate conventions that students were expected to follow. In one set of papers, this is what happened to Karine.

Karine described herself as an experienced teacher, a lover of language, philosophy, and metaphor, and an emotional thinker and writer. She worried constantly about whether her writing was "academic" enough, and was as fascinated with her professors' feedback as she was with our interview topics on academic writing. From the feedback of three different professors she developed a sense of the overall expectations on her less formal reaction papers and her longer more "professional" papers, and on the conventions of some of the small details of academic writing (the fact that appendices are usually named by letters, that every citation needed to appear in a reference list, and that in APA format the authors' first initials are used). She relished all feedback, particularly from those professors who themselves modeled "high standards" of academic language in their spoken and written language: "John is a model to me, his language is highly academic in everything, in class interaction, and this is what I enjoyed most of all," she said in our third interview.

On the papers that she shared with me from the three professors it was clear from the written feedback that the professors found her ideas to be "very interesting" (with "very" underlined twice, a comment on a long paper in which Karine developed an original test). Other positive comments on Karine's papers included the following from the same test development paper: "clear organization," "good question," "Wow!" and "good point." This same paper included a great deal of advice from the professor about key concepts and methodology in test design. On a lesson plan in the Teaching of Reading taught by John, John wrote: "Effective and thoughtful use of available texts and resources! Very solid!" In a journal entry exercise for the same class on using literature in teaching reading Karine began with the emotional statement "First, I would like to comment on my choice of this exercise although it is not required. I LOVE literature. I use many pieces of prose or verse in my teaching." John responded with this positive comment in the margins: "Terrific! We'll have a chance to explore this option a bit later"; and at the end of this entry: "Exemplary entries, Karine. Thank you for attacking them w/such enthusiasm."

However, Karine was one of the participants who wanted detailed feedback on what was wrong as well as what was right. She knew she wrote emotionally at times and wanted to learn what she called a more professional academic style. Because she was the one case study participant whose academic writing in some of her classes received the strongest criticism of style, form, and logic, I will use the feedback on several of the papers she wrote for her Second Language Acquisition (SLA) professor (a visiting professor) to exemplify how some of the professors in the MA program helped students develop academic literacy skills that fit certain norms in the field. In the SLA class, the students had to write a series of reaction papers on various readings and theories and a final project. Karine's reaction papers were quite informal and emotional in tone. Her final project was a library research paper entitled "An SLA Perspective: Just a Try," a mix of impersonal and very personal assertions.

Some of the harshest of the professor's comments concerned technical conventions, specifically Karine's unacceptable style of citing and referencing in her final SLA project paper. Many citations appeared in the paper that were not listed in the reference list, and the list itself violated many conventions of the required APA style. Her professor wrote: "Your uses of references are a mess, totally unacceptable for academically oriented writing, I must say. My advice: LEARN!" On seeing this comment again as we reviewed this paper in an interview, Karine read this comment aloud and said "I like that," indicating how much she appreciated being told clearly what she needed to do. She then admitted that "there are things I will never fully learn to follow in writing, and these are cite and bibliography type things." She noted that she simply had not been able to internalize these "formatting things" to the point where they were automatic. "Knowledge about is not knowledge in practice," she commented with the wisdom of an experienced teacher. The feedback, however, had helped her recognize the "convention problem" with her referencing practices.

This same professor was equally harsh with Karine on a matter concerning her logical presentation of arguments in one of her reaction papers. The second reaction paper, a paper entitled "Why do I Resent the Critique of Krashen's Theory?", was returned to Karine with many comments and questions such as "I don't understand," "What theory," "Why?" Karine had set out (so it seemed) to defend Krashen, but confused her argument with sentences such as the following: "First of all, by trying to explain a most specific human behavior, that is learning or acquiring a second language, Krashen, in my opinion, doubles, if not triples the problems related to the issue." The professor crossed out "in my opinion," and added this question in the margin: "If so, why do you resent criticism of him (if he causes so many problems)?" A stronger criticism comes later in this reaction paper where Karine has written the following about Krashen and his critics. In the example I have included the professor's marginal comments in boldface and brackets at appropriate places in Karine's text, many lines of which he had underlined:

It is here, during this restructuring of information, that in any language the Monitor comes into play with its three (or two) preconditions for use. [**What??**] Now, again for me it is not clear whether what Krashen states and how Gass and Selinker interpret what Krashen states is [**are**] the same or not. Once more, I want to read Krashen to understand it. [**It's irritating to see this! What are you critiquing if you don't even understand what they are debating about?**]

It seems to me that when the critique does not seem to the point, there are two possible explanations. First those who critique have problems in both understanding what they critique and understanding what they want to say. [**This seems to be your problem, too.**] Second, the reader may have problems in understanding both those who critique and those who are critiqued. Actually, this may happen to be the case with me: [**If this is the case, where does your "resentment" come from?**] when I have Krashen read and Gass and Selinker reread, it is quite possible that I will have to admit that is was ME who did not understand any of them—either Krashen or Gass and Selinker. [**You negate your whole argument here**] (Karine, SLA Reaction Paper #2)

The professor wrote a long end comment on this reaction paper reinforcing his criticism of Karine's inconsistent logic in the paper, explained his reasons again, and opened the door to her for personal contact and further discussion with him. He explicitly generalized his comments to "any academic writing":

Karine, I must say this is a messy paper. I respect your opinion, but in any academic paper, you should back up your opinion with clear & convincing arguments & analyses. One thing I don't follow is that how you can resent something you claim you don't yet quite understand. Krashen has his theories, and Gass & Selinker must have read & understood Krashen's theories before they began to critique them. If you don't quite understand either side, how do you know which side you should be on? This is a simple matter of logical reasoning. Talk to me about this. (Professor's response to Karine's SLA Reaction Paper #2)

This is harsh criticism coming from any professor, yet Karine respected this professor and the detailed nature of his feedback. She also knew he respected her and recognized the harshness of his own critiques: At the end of her third reaction paper, entitled "The Impact of the Course on Me As A Teacher," Karine wrote in her typical emotional style, ending the paper with an unfinished thought that looked to the future ("And NOW . . ."). In the following excerpt from this paper, the professor's comments again appear in boldface and brackets:

I must admit, that if I try to apply everything you have tried to make me aware of, my life will turn into a "hell!" Do you want me to THINK! so hard before teaching?! Do you want me, as Sheridan says, "to undergo the fatigue of judg-ing for myself"?! No, you do not mean to make teachers really think and care, do you?!!! [**If you are addressing me, I must say "yes." Teachers should not be brainless teaching machines. They should think; they should care.**]

Yes, I believe, the overall impact of your course on me, whether you like it or not is: THINK BEFORE YOU TEACH!!! [caps Karine's] try to relate the SLA theory to your teaching if you want to at least suspect what in fact your are at-tempting or aspiring to do. Well, really, thank you for making me aware of how hard is the task of a caring and thoughtful teacher. I suspected it, but I was to a degree innocent. And NOW [caps Karine's] . . . [**I have a tendency to push my students to their limits. So accept my apologies if I pushed you too much too hard. (See what I did to your 2nd reaction paper!!)**]

Karine spoke of how her feedback from this professor helped her under-stand that knowing something about teaching academic writing to her own students differed from being able to write an acceptable academic paper herself. I quote her at some length here, since her comments show her re-flecting on several aspects of her growth as an academic writer. The brack-eted areas with three periods indicate ellipses:

[On the final project in Second Language Acquisition] I was trying to show something that I learned, in my writing, my organization of writing. The thing is that SLA papers have some exceptional value to me in the sense that— the— first of all, [. . .] I wrote reactions for him, which were not in a way strictly aca-demic, so it was the first kind of paper where I was to show how I understand what is very kind of rigid academic definition of academic paper and how it was displayed. Although I must say from my previous feedback experience I already had some idea of what it should look like, a kind of really, strictly speaking academic paper, and I knew that in many ways I didn't master just the mechanics. [. . .] I was trying to be clear very— the most clear in a way about the structure of the academic paper first— second I also clearly had in my mind that I had to express very logical way my position, [. . .] and of course what [W] did, he showed to me that I have some certain weaknesses in regard to this, and in regard to- I overuse "this" in my writing, and I tended to forget or not clearly see my audience. [. . .] I often presume that my reader knows what I assume although it should be made quite clear and you have to treat your reader like tabula rasa, [. . .] you don't have to jump some certain kind of logical steps because they are evident to you, they may not be evident to your reader. (Karine, Interview 3)

And indeed, the majority of comments on Karine's SLA papers had to do ei-ther with mechanics or with clarity, support, and logic of her statements. With the feedback from the professor, and from other detailed comments on her work from other professors, she was negotiating an academic iden-tity in which she was trying to preserve in her writing aspects of her effusive and emotional self as well as her sense of self as a complex, if scattered, thinker about linguistic and philosophical matters. She was open in her effusiveness in her reaction papers with John, much less so in her writing for the testing professor and in her final SLA project, and somewhere in between in her presentation of self in her SLA reaction papers. She wrote differently for the different professors and differently according to the type of writing, and managed to generate a great deal of praise, substantive advice, and some harsh criticism, all of which helped her see herself in relation to the values and practices espoused in this program.

From my discussions with the students about the many kinds of writing they did, the different professors they wrote for, and the variations in feedback they got from them, I was not able to identify an overall set of rules or practices for the writing games that these students were learning to play. Only some of the writing practices fit the stereotypes of academic writing that we can find in the literature and in writing textbooks (the writing of research reports, summaries, and critical reviews, for example), and only for some professors and certain writing tasks were students held to strict genre conventions for formatting, citing, and referencing. The students themselves shared some views of academic writing, but also differed in how they characterized some aspects—from writing that is objective and impersonal to writing that includes personal elements. The student who was most concerned about the professional style of her writing, Karine, was the one who interjected the most personal and emotional elements in some of her writing, for only for some of her professors some of the time. The professor described as one of the most demanding about the professional look of papers, John, was also the one who accepted personal and emotion-filled journal entries from students like Karine. If any general rule of practice can be located for the many writing games that students in this program had to learn it might be the requirement that students explain and justify their assertions, whether in personal and reflective journals where they drew on their experience and logical thinking or in reports of research where they added the voices of published authorities to their defenses. The only piece of writing upon which all faculty concurred (at least in public) with a program-wide set of written guidelines was the exit portfolio. The students knew that this final collection of writings had to fit the standards set out in the guidelines even if they had written very differently for particular classes. They also knew, however, that faculty readers differed in their responses to the portfolios, and that an "easier" reader was usually paired with a more critical reader. In the midst of this diversity, students were expected to evolve a sense of professional identity, and to display this new identity in major writing projects and their final portfolios. In the final section of this case study, I turn to the students' views of how they changed during the course of their MA program.

Students' Perceptions of Changes in Writing and Self. In the previous sections, I have described what the students' experiences were like in the MA program for the purpose of culminating my case study in the five women's perceptions of change in their academic literacy practices and identities. In this section, I look in particular at changes in how the students located themselves in relation to their perceptions of the field. I begin with an example from the writings of Kazuko from before and during her MA program. I then describe perceptions of change by all five students, and conclude with examples of Natsuko's pre-MA and final portfolio writings.

When Kazuko and Natsuko learned I was interested in their perceptions of how they had changed since participating in the MA program, both gave me a sample of a piece of writing done the year before they entered the MA program that they now shared with some embarrassment. Kazuko's was a short essay written in Japan for an undergraduate English class (Fig. 3.1). This essay struck me as familiar in that I had seen similar essays written by my own undergraduate students in Japan. It also seemed as though it had been written by a very different person than the one whose MA papers I had looked at, so great was the change in tone, style, and maturity, as can be seen from the sample that follows from an MA paper on test development (Fig. 3.2). The samples of Kazuko's MA writing parallel in some ways

I researched hausing in the Hanshin area with my GBR group members. The purpose of our project was to investigate the situation of the housing market in the Hanshin area and to know what kinds of houses were most sought after. Our research was based on a request from the Canadian consulate inquiring wheter the Hanshin area was a good market for foreign construction companies.

At first, we tried to contact large Japanese construction companies. We made many calls and asked several basic questions. However, most companies did not give us the information we wanted, after telling them that we were students. I belive it is because Japanese society considered students immature and tends to treat us as less important people. I hate that idea and I hope this will change in near future.

[continues for 10 more paragraphs]

[last 2 paragraphs] I was very glad that I joined the GBR project, as I could have many experiences that I would never had if I did not. I learned a lot though these experiences such as how to make appointments or do interviews with executives of companies. I also learned better ways of communicating with foreign students.

I really want to do these kinds of projects again if I have a chance. And I hope that I can still be a good friend to the other members of the group after we have finished the project.

FIG. 3.1. Sample from Kazuko's undergraduate "research" paper, "Introduction to Business Low."

[2nd paragraph of "Rationale"] I have been observing a Japanese class at [the local community college] for the purpose of gaining knowledge in order to teach beginning Japanese at the college level. My goal is to develop a test in which to give a real audience and will enable me to practically adapt what I have learned in the language assessment seminar at Monterey Institute of International Studies. After discussing it with the instructor of the Japanese class, I decided to make a practice midterm, which would give students diagnostic feedback on what they have and have not mastered and what they should study again for the real midterm. I tried as much as possible to make the language used in the test as close to widely used Japanese so that it would match my ideals of designing a test. [. . .]

[subsection on "Descriptive Statistics" from section "Data Analysis"] 'Central tendency' tells us the patterns of how the scores in a date set group together, and it is measured by the means (X), median (middle score in a data set), and mode (most frequently obtained score in a data set. On the other end, the 'measures of dispersion,' which is often indicated by standard deviation (SD) and range of the scores, provides information on the scores are spread out over a given date set. Both of these are very useful in assessing test performance (Bailey, 1998).

Looking at the statistics of central tendency and dispersion (see Table 1 below), we come to notice some interesting factors about the test result. From the SD of each section; we can see that the distribution of scores is much wider in the subjectively scored parts, section IV and V, compared to the objectively scores ones, section I, II, and III. [. . .] [paper continues for 8 more pages of text and tables]

[concluding paragraph] The test had its strengths, though it seems that there were more things wrong than right. The correlation measure by Spearman's rank-order correlation showed that there was a moderately strong relationship between the midterm designed by the teacher and the one I developed. I feel encouraged by this fact because it is good evidence that I developed the test in the way the teacher wanted me to. [. . .] I am glad that I designed the test because, for one, I could help students with their study, and for another, I was able to adapt the skills and knowledge I developed in language assessment seminar this semester. I believe this test is a good starting point for me as a future language teacher.

FIG. 3.2. Sample from a second-semester MA paper report on Kazuko's original test development, "Practice Midterm for MPC [a local community college] Japanese Class" (professor's corrections of language errors not included).

the early essay in that both are samples of "research." The errors are left as they appear in the papers.

We can see that Kazuko began and ended these two very different papers in similar ways, with a first person explanation of the project and a first person conclusion of the benefits of the project to her. Her MA paper, however, is a multivocalic document that uses a more formal, mature style replete with the conventional terminology and phrases from basic statistics that she has learned from the source she sites and from the class itself. Her conclusion speaks to the project results as well as to the benefits to herself, and the MA paper in general shows how careful she was in designing, carrying out, and evaluating her test at a level of sophistication not seen in her Hanshin "research."

In an interview toward the end of her program, Kazuko spoke specifically about how she had changed. She felt she had learned a great deal about research and the "technical skills" involved, but still felt she was not ready to "compete" even with her classmates: "I just feel amazed by reading other people's work," she said. She also told me that it was not until well into the first semester, shortly after she began some tutoring and practice teaching for the first time in her life, the course work started to come together for her. Her writing had improved, she also told me, in the sense that she needed fewer corrections by her boyfriend and that writing in general (much disliked by her all her life) had become less difficult. She also developed more confidence that she could write professionally. In preparing for her portfolio, for example, she noticed that in the Japanese books she was reading that "Japanese people have a similar approach with the American or APA or standard style, they cite references," many authors having studied at the PhD level in the United States. "So in a way," she continued, "that shows that I can write in Japanese professionally, because these kinds of writings are permitted." However, Kazuko knew she had begun the program "behind" everyone else, with no teaching experience and very little experience or confidence with writing. She had gotten over this sense of embarrassment about her perceived deficiencies, but still felt she was on the edge of the field professionally. She talked vaguely about one day going back to school for a PhD when she "knew her goal," and she felt she "should go to a conference once; that would make a lot of difference," in order to "hear directly from those people in the field. Right now they are to me somebody who is not real." Describing how she located herself in relation to the field she said: "Right now TESOL or TFL is just above me, like I'm a person who is a teacher related to the field but not in the field, I think." Though still on the periphery, Kazuko had stepped into the profession by now defining herself as a teacher. She was on the move (Wenger, 1998) and was beginning to see herself as part of a web of social and intellectual relationships.

Other students also spoke about how their perceptions of themselves in relation to the field had changed. Kyla and Natsuko, like Kazuko, had had little teaching experience. Kyla had taught for a year in Japan, and Natsuko had briefly tutored different ages and groups of people. In her interviews, Kyla expressed similar reservations to those expressed by Kazuko about her sense of belonging fully in the field at this point. Like Kazuko, she had become aware of how big the fields of linguistics and applied linguistics were, describing them as some kind of "hodge-podge." She became aware of how much research was required in order to write within the field and how much time was needed to locate some of those resources. "I didn't know that there were all of those journals when I got here," she explained.

Thus, as their knowledge of TESOL writing games expanded, the students became increasingly aware of the size and complexity of the field, characterized as Kyla phrased it "by a whole slew of jargon" as well as specialized ways of "going about" writing and researching. It was the less experienced students like Kyla and to some extent Natsuko who still expressed tentativeness about where they belonged on this shifting playing field. Natsuko talked about TESOL being "a small part of me" when she started the MA program, but having it take over her life: "Sometimes it overwhelms me how much space the TESOL takes over me." She came to see the field as "deep and huge," but at the same time small and narrow, a conflict she described elegantly a month later in her position paper (see Fig. 3.4). "Sometimes I feel like I have so much things to learn from now," she sighed. Natsuko also talked about her realization, a political one, that she needed "allies" in the form of published voices from the literature to bolster her own less authoritative opinions. All the students had talked about the pressure in this program to "cite sources," but Natsuko's images of allies from the literature captured the social and political aspect of this seemingly superficial genre convention. These allies had become more than names from her readings; they were beginning to take shape as a community with which she was forging ties.

Kirsten, more experienced in teaching than Kazuko, Natsuko, and Kyla, expressed her sense of belonging to the professional language teaching field with more assertiveness and confidence than did the less experienced women. Having attended and presented at several conferences during her time in the program, she also located herself firmly within the field by the end of her MA program, having lost some "awe" of the "people at the conferences." She had learned that she "had something to say:"

> I also feel that I have a place now in the professional field, whereas before I was kind of going to JALT [Japan Association for Language Teaching] conferences and going whoa, wow, look at all of these people who have done experiments and have published and have something to say and I didn't feel like I had something to say. Or I didn't feel like I was good enough to say it yet. Now I do feel like I'm good enough to say it. I'm not so in awe of the people at the JALT conferences anymore. I'm still in awe of the professors. The big names in the field. (Kirsten, Interview 6)

This partial loss of awe, combined with the belief that she had something to say, distinguished the changes that Kirsten experienced from those of the Kazuko, Natsuko, and Kyla. The less experienced women had evolved more complex professional identities through their awareness of the enormity of the field; Kirsten developed a firm identity as a professional teacher who had "identified areas of interest" and "basic theoretical beliefs" and who could contribute professionally to the community of professional language teachers and researchers who were interested in Japan. Moreover, Kirsten had rather fortuitously developed an on-campus identity as an expert in computer technology through a graduate assistantship that required she teach herself about Internet technology.

Karine had 26 years of teaching under her belt, but she too claimed to have experienced major changes in her professional identity and her ability to write, both of which stemmed from the increased awareness of conventions and expectations that her academic literacy practices in the MA program encouraged. She spoke passionately of finding some order and system in her previously unanalyzed conceptions of self as a teacher. "I see radical changes," she told me, "and if I mentally open the classroom of when I was teaching first, and I open the classroom in reality now, they're two different teachers ... maybe one thing in common, and that was the drive for doing it as well as you can." She attributed these changes in part to having a language with which to talk about them and to having been forced to reflect on them through the MA program academic literacy practices. She commented as follows:

> I think what the Monterey program did to me, it really made me think about these changes, and that means seeing them or let's say more specifically being able to define the changes, not just abstractly saying, oh, yeah I have changed. [...] Now I know that within my present system of my notion of a professional, what changes I have lived through. If I define a professional as a system, now I know the changes. I can locate exactly where my changes are in that system. (Karine, Interview 6)

She clarified that her present identity was not static, however, but continually in the process of changing. She didn't want to end up as a still-life, she said, noting that "I would like to always be on my way to somewhere."

Karine spoke movingly in one of our last interviews about the moment in which she recognized how profoundly her thinking and language had changed (mentioned in Chap. 1). The day before the interview she had sent e-mail to her American advisor who was coordinating her MA program at her American university in Armenia. In writing him about her ideas for an MA research project, she suddenly "radically felt the difference between the way I thought about it then and now I'm thinking about it." In terms of the game metaphor, she no longer played like a novice for whom everything was new and to whom patterns and regularities were invisible. In her description of this experience, Karine notes that her use of specialized language and related concepts had changed, as well as her sense of identity as a professional, as one who was now able to think ahead to bigger possibilities in her life. In Karine's words:

> When I was writing [the e-mail] I thought how much more professional was my thinking than when I came. In terms of not only terminology that I learned, because I think behind terminology there are concepts that I learned also. [...] I felt that I was thinking about this research and writing to him about this research like a different person. It was like if you try to describe something which you- say you stand in front of a door, and there is a room you have to enter and you know this is a living room. And you start describing a living room according to whatever your experience has kind of shaped the understanding of that concept for you in that particular moment. Now I stand in front of that same door and I have to describe what I may encounter in that room, I think that there is, I don't know what kind of- I say radical to me, a big difference in my possibilities, or abilities, or perceptions of envisioning what I might encounter in that room. It is great. [...] My vision of Karine then, and my vision of Karine today these are different Karines. I'm not a professional probably yet the way I would probably expect a professional to be, but still a closer person to that image than I was before I came. (Karine, Interview 5).

Karine's metaphor of the living room captures vividly the sense Karine and other students had after a year or more in their MA program of being able to see with greater systematicity and awareness than when they began the program and to find the language to talk about previously unimagined details in their worlds of teaching and learning languages. These students had shifted their identities in relation to the language teaching field, all having moved to new locations on the periphery (Lave & Wenger, 1991), where they were beginning to take on the roles of legitimate game players. They were beginning to be able to imagine their professional trajectories (Wenger, 1998) in ways they could not have when they began the MA program.

I conclude this chapter with a second set of writings, those of Natsuko. These samples, both personal statements, show how she represented herself before entering the MA program and in her final MA portfolio position paper (see Figs. 3.3 and 3.4). The key aspect that struck me was the sense of clarity of her vision in the early application essay, and her presentation of herself in the final MA paper as conflicted and confused in the midst of the uncomfortable process of learning to locate herself in a complex professional field.

Natsuko's statements in her position paper about conflict and identity transformation capture elegantly the dilemma that I came to see that all students in this MA program faced. Natsuko's images, and her final acceptance that conflict and change will characterize her professional life and identity, reflect the very themes of this book. Her conclusions confirm the sense I [paragraph 1] A lot of my experiences with other cultures and their people have greatly influenced me. They have awakened my consciousness of the broad world. Many things that I take for granted in Japan are not usual things in other countries: wealth, peace, cleanliness, safety, happiness, and a comfortable life.

[paragraph 4] Although I am not a native speaker of English, I believe my ten years study of English enables me to teach such learners in ways that are different from those of native speakers teaching ESL. I do not think that being a nonnative English speaker is a weakness, but rather a benefit. I may even be better at understanding learners' common mistakes, their frustrations with miscommunication, and find new effective teaching methods which consider learners' points of views. To accomplish this dream, I chose Monterey Institute [. . .]

[final sentence] Flexibility and creativity as well as the constant effort to improve my teaching are my essential qualities; qualities that I will be able to bring into a classroom when I am accepted by your school.

FIG. 3.3. Natsuko's application essay to her MA program (1½ pages double-spaced).

have developed in my own research, reading, and graduate school experiences of how fascinating yet how complex and unresolved the identity-shaping academic writing games are that we and our students play.

I compared myself to the "Asunaro" tree in the previous section (Portfolio Commentary, A1). Sadly, that kind of tree does not grow very tall betraying its strong desire to be as high as the oak: however, as the tree branches out with sunshine and water, its shade pattern changes like a kaleidoscope. The more the tree grows, sunbeams intermingle, twigs and leaves cross each other, creating a more exquisite silhouette as a collaborative art. This is the image that I now associate with "learning" and "growth," not only as a learner but as a teacher.

Before I reached this point, I had naively believed that only if I learned enough, I would have a very clear picture of where I was standing. It was a wrong perception. After a year of struggle in the MATESOL program at Monterey Institute, I realized that the clarity of my vision of myself does not go up in a linear direct proportion with new information and experiences. Rather, despite the massive amount of input, I was getting more confused, and my sight became more blurred. Thrown into such a chaotic condition, I was upset, frustrated and lost: the realization that I have so many options to take, conflicts to deal with, and issues to carry along my career as a teaching professional left me in an uncontrollable sense of disorientation.

FIG. 3.4. First 3 paragraphs of the introduction and several sentences from the conclusion of Natsuko's 40-page position paper, entitled "Beyond Conflicts," for her portfolio.

In order to be positive in the situation, I had to start by accepting my-self as I was, regardless of all the conflicts and dichotomies I felt: a learner and a teacher; a Japanese and a foreigner; a Japanese speaker and a non-native English speaker; a student and an emerging professional in TESOL; a participant in the MIIS community and an observer of the American soci-ety; self-expectation and others' expectations; the use of "I" and avoid-ance of "I" in academic papers; connecting with people in TESOL but dis-connected from people in my personal life; teacher's persona and my real self; an insider and outsider of the class; joy and fear of teaching; expand-ing but narrowing point of view; theory and practice; process and product; voicing and listening; heart and brain; ideals and realities; how I position myself and how I am positioned by others.

Readers may see me drifting in the midst of these conflicts in this posi-tion paper and through this portfolio, but I have to say that these conflicts are what I have learned. In other words, awareness of the existence of conflicts is the sign of potential changes, for that is what triggers deeper thinking and action. [. . .] [39 pages of text]

[conclusion] I still have conflicts and dilemmas in my teaching and edu-cational philosophies, yet my internal chaos enables me to deal with stu-dents, living individuals, whose growth and conflicts cannot always be an-ticipated from research findings. [. . .] Choosing to be a language teacher, I feel grateful that I can share the continuous identity transformation process with my students and have days of discoveries and challenges with a hope that my students will experience the joy of learning for themselves.

FIG. 3.4. *(Continued)*

Agency, Authority, and Authenticity

The games of agency and authority needed to be played particularly sensi-tively in the MA program I studied. Faculty had their areas of expertise, some of which overlapped. Students were expected to develop agency and authority in their writing as part of their professional development, but they needed to continue to play the role of student. Students like Kirsten who had begun participating in the field's professional activities such as conferences developed a sense of agency and authority that allowed them to feel they were legitimate contributors to a professional conversation, but as Kirsten confessed, she was still in awe of her professors by the end of her program. After all, they were not only well-known; they also still had a great deal of power over her in the sense that they determined whether she would graduate and receive letters of recommendation for future jobs. The tensions between students' evolving roles as professionals with a voice and their inescapable roles as students could not be resolved and may consti-tute one of the paradoxes of graduate level and professional training (Freedman & Adam, 1996). As Lave and Wenger (1991) noted in their ap-prenticeship studies and Wenger (1998) in his community-of-practice analy-sis of insurance claims adjustors, the goal of helping newcomers to partici-pate in a community's practices is to ensure that one day the oldtimers will be replaced and the community will thus survive. Although this is what is supposed to happen, the students in this MA program needed to wend their way into the community with great care, learning the skills and appropriating the tools but also learning to survive in a complexly layered network of political and social relationships. Seen in this way, constructing a coherent academic identity that is poised to step into a professional arena seems quite an overwhelming challenge.

Nevertheless, all of the five students who participated in my case study, including those with very little previous teaching experience, moved directly from their MA program into teaching jobs in the second language field. They had indeed stepped into the profession via their MA program and begun a transition of identity from that of student to that of authoritative participant in the diverse community of second language educators. The MA program had provided them not only with a knowledge base (Fradd & Okhee, 1998) and with direct instruction in academic literacy practices, characterized by Freedman and Adam (1996, 2000) as guided participation. It had also provided them with opportunities to participate semi-authentically in the field's authentic practices—research and teaching, lesson and curriculum development, test development and analysis, and the building of a professional portfolio—with guidance and mentoring that was as collaborative in some cases as it was instructional. These practices, because they were used for purposes beyond the program's need for academic evaluation (e.g., community projects and teaching, students' own professional development), can be characterized as examples of attenuated authentic participation (Freedman & Adam, 1996, 2000). They show the potential value of MA programs that are staffed by practicing professionals who can play the roles of mentors and collaborators as well as conventional instructors and who engage students in writing practices that have clear purposes beyond academic evaluation. Such programs can help students develop agency and authority in their new fields and introduce them to the kinds of diverse and authentic literacy practices they are likely to encounter after graduation. They learned games that were neither superficial nor trivial, in other words, and learned to play with increasing skill. A small, intense program such as the one I observed can also increase students' awareness of the social and political complexities that infuse their literacy practices and help them begin constructing a coherent professional identity from multiple sources, demands, and practices.

CHAPTER REFLECTIONS

Students who step into a profession by transitioning into it through a masters degree program seem inevitably to be hovering between two quite different communities of practice, the academic community and the professional community. In the masters program they cannot escape the school community's need to evaluate their work for the purpose of determining whether they are proceeding satisfactorily toward a degree. To achieve this purpose, the academic community does not need to engage students in authentic tasks that serve a professional enterprise; it can engage them in simulated tasks such as case analyses in business programs, in pseudo-research that involves students in their local communities, and in learning and reflective tasks such as reading response journals and language autobiographies in applied linguistics programs. The masters level academic community also requires tasks from students that involve little professional authenticity or little negotiation of meaning, such as tests of knowledge and papers that display knowledge only to one professor. (At the time I drafted this chapter I knew of one MATESOL program that was still using a multiple choice comprehensive examination as one of its exit mechanisms.) In all of these cases, the writing that results is usually read by one person for the purpose of academic evaluation, not of contributing to an aspect of a professional enterprise. Belonging to this kind of academic community means learning the literacy games that characterize school, not professions.

However, in the Monterey MATESOL program, in addition to being required to play to school-centered literacy games (inevitable in a school community), the students were also engaged in some practices that actually contributed to the profession of second language teaching and learning. Some of them designed and evaluated tests that were actually used, did language research or web projects that they presented at conferences, helped teach in local schools or in the Institute's language programs, and prepared portfolios that they would adapt later for job interviews. They also read the field's literature and engaged in substantive discussions, written and oral, with professors and peers about issues in the field. These are all literacy-related activities that characterize the profession of second language education. Through their involvement in the some of the fields' literate activities and their substantive interactions with older generations of experts in the form of professionally active professors, they were able to move from positions as relative outsiders to legitimate positions on the periphery. The students like Kirsten and Karine with previous teaching experience were especially poised to take advantage of the opportunities offered by the Monterey program and spoke most strongly about changes they saw in their identities as professionals. In Wenger's (1998) terms, they were able to combine their experience with their developing competence to reimagine their identities as contributing members of the second language education field. The less experienced students were able to imagine a trajectory into the future, one they had not perceived before completing the MA program. That trajectory (from past, through present, to future) was encapsulated in the portfolio position paper, which required that students construct a discoursal identity (Ivanič, 1998) as a participating member of the profession. As Natsuko's paper shows, this textual journey in the position paper involved reflection on past selves, descriptions of current views and practices, and projections into the future. Still, perhaps with the exception of Natsuko, I sensed that the students were not yet fully aware of how simultaneously broad and narrow their enculturation experiences had been and how deeply political the complex academic literacy games on their campus and elsewhere probably were. There was so much more to be learned and experienced as they moved in and out of different teaching jobs in the future searching for where they belonged.

I conclude this chapter by asking questions about the modes of belonging and the associated identities that might be encouraged in masters degree programs and about what it means to teach academic writing at the masters level. In the first case, Wenger (1998) talks about three modes of belonging to communities of practice: (1) engagement, which he refers to as "active involvement in mutual processes of negotiation of meaning"; (2) imagination, which consists of "creating images of the world and seeing connections through time and space by extrapolating from our own experience"; and (3) alignment, which he describes as "coordinating our energy and activities in order to fit within broader structures and contribute to broader enterprises" (pp. 173–174). Can the work of engagement, imagination, and alignment be pursued in the literacy games of a masters program?

The work of engagement, Wenger explains, requires that participants take part in sustained and meaningful activities and interactions that help achieve a community's goals and transform it over time (p. 184). Looking at a masters program only as a school community, we can claim that a paper or examination designed only to display knowledge does not fit this definition of engagement. The game of transmitting and displaying information does not allow the kinds of negotiations that can prompt changes in community members or in the community itself. However, in the MA program that I observed, there were many examples of meaningful activities and interactions, including some that helped change the community itself. The negotiated portfolio process was one of these, the ongoing practice of having students write reflectively and thus provide not only the writers but also the professors with food for thought was another, and a third was the negotiated nature of some aspects of the classes.

The work of imagination, Wenger (1998) explains, requires that participants step back from their involvement and view their practices through the eyes of an outsider (p. 185). It is the act of imagination, so long as it is connected to lived experience, that helps participants see their trajectories from the past to the present and into the future. In the Monterey MA program, some of the literacy activities asked students to look back to previous teaching and learning experiences, to involve themselves reflectively in current issues and practices, and in the portfolio exit project to look ahead. There is nothing inherent in academic writing games, of course, that triggers this kind of imaginative involvement in academic-professional communities of practice. Such involvement depends in great part on the ability of individual professors to design tasks for students that encourage it and that require cross-generational interactions that will help students visualize their futures.

Finally, the work of alignment requires that participants in a community of practice work together for a common purpose (p. 186). This purpose needs to extend beyond routine local practices and into a broader community. In the Monterey MA program, for instance, the students were learning games skills and strategies that would serve them in the larger second language education field: methods for teaching and doing research, ways of communicating professionally through writing and conference presentation, negotiation strategies for dealing with powerful community members, and standards for evaluating language teaching and learning. Again there is nothing inherent in MA literacy practices that would foster alignments with broader communities. In this same school, Zhang (Schneider & Fujishima, 1995) seemed to be writing to satisfy Writing Workshop requirements, though we know little about his writing in his content classes; Lilah (Prior, 1998) forged multiple alignments with different professors she wrote for, but we don't have a sense of what common community purpose she might have been contributing to.

In stepping into a profession through the guidance of a masters program, students can potentially shift their modes of belonging from ones that are quite narrowly confined to school literacy games to ones that bring them into the peripheries of professional communities of practice. With shifts in modes of belonging come shifts in identity and the need for students to reconcile their expanding views of themselves as members of multiple communities into a coherent whole. As is suggested throughout this book, it is impossible to imagine how such a transformation is possible without complicating the notion of identity, from one that is singular to one that is plural, layered, and in constant flux (Kondo, 1990). People cannot tolerate constant flux, of course, and so create coherent stories that give a sense of wholeness to their identities and practices (Giddens, 1991; Linde, 1993, Polkinghorne, 1991).

My own case study in this chapter in particular has helped me understand that I should not be searching for ways to resolve conflicts and weave fragmented and layered academic identities into seamless wholes. Instead I should look for clues as to how pieces and layers interact and shift over time, influenced by particular settings and demands as well as by genre conventions and an individual's sense of what it means to be a professional.

Even the textual construction of professional identity as in the language autobiographies, research papers, and position papers I read in the MA program in Monterey construct the writers' identities in ways that are rhetorically coherent without conveying the sense that these identities are
singular. There is a sense of wholeness without a sense of singularity.

It is not only MA students who construct identities in their writing. I
also need to continue pondering how the authors' writing of the case
study constructs the selves and the issues that are portrayed (Clifford,
1986; Geertz, 1988; Rosaldo, 1987, 1993; Van Maanen, 1988). My choices of
what aspects of masters level academic enculturation to focus on in the
case studies I review and conduct and what stance to take in reflecting on
these case studies say as much about me as they do about the case study
participants and the authors who tell their stories. My own identity as an
academic writer is thus constructed as a more or less coherent whole
without being singular, as is clear from the several different ways I represent myself in this book.

Questions remain, too, about what it means to teach academic writing at
the masters level in ways that will help students step into their professions.
The published case studies I discussed in this chapter and my own case
studies of five women in an MATESOL program clarify for me how difficult it
is to conceptualize masters level academic enculturation in any kind of generalized way, particularly within the social sciences. Bazerman's (1995)
comment about generalized writing instruction at the undergraduate level
applies as well to these case studies of academic writing at the masters
level: "As we deepen our understanding of situated engagement, pedagogic
practices based on a generalized model of writing skills seems increasingly
thin and pale" (p. 251). A generalized model of writing if applied to the masters level case studies discussed in this chapter will mischaracterize graduate level academic writing by failing to take into account the multiplicity of
genres and subgenres, the social and political aspects of learning to participate in the literate practices of specialized communities in local settings,
and the influence of teacher and student personalities on the demands and
expectations within particular programs. Such a generalized model, if re-
stricted to academic settings alone, also would fail to consider the many
links between writing in academic and workplace settings, the differences
between these settings, and the need to consider many masters programs
as transitional stages into the workplace. Although some scholars may wish
studies like these to take a "more distanced, global view" (see Ramanathan's [2000] critique of Prior [1998], p. 92), I remain committed to the
perhaps less ambitious goal of forging connections between case studies
and the consumers of case studies—people who read books like this one
and wonder how the stories in them apply to their own lives.

ACKNOWLEDGMENTS

I would like to express my deep appreciation to Keio University for granting me a year's Study Abroad, during which time I was able to conduct the research reported in the third section of this chapter. I am also grateful to the Monterey Institute of International Studies and to Ruth Larimer, Dean of the Graduate School of Language and Educational Linguistics, for permission to conduct research in the MATESOL/MATFL program. Special thanks go to the professors who graciously allowed me to visit their classes, the students who put up with my presence, to the case study participants, who were so forthright and so generous with their time, to Hideyuki Kubo, who took care of business from the Japan side, and to Carry Miller, who was charged with the bulk of the onerous clerical and transcribing tasks that a project like this generates.

4

Redefining the Self:
The Unsettling Doctoral
Program Game

FROM CLARITY TO CONFUSION

Getting a PhD in North America involves an enormous commitment of time, money, energy, and patience. The decision to pursue this ultimate example of symbolic capital (Bourdieu, 1977a, 1991) in academe is not to be taken lightly, particularly in an era when the market is glutted with unemployed scholars. A great many people never finish, sometimes for the better, sometimes for the worse. In my own case, I wanted this degree. I was fortunate in a perverse way to have been laid off from my full-time teaching job just at the time when I realized I needed to make a leap forward in my knowledge of my field. I was not young. I was bored. I was craving to associate with people who knew more than I did and I looked forward to studying, having discovered in my masters program that I actually enjoyed it. I also wanted to secure another job in a university setting and knew I would no longer be able to do this without a PhD. The field had changed a lot in the previous 10 years and my MA would no longer let me move into this setting at the level that I wanted.

As I have mentioned elsewhere (Chap. 1, this volume and Casanave, 1997), I entered my PhD program with a clear sense of identity as an ESL specialist and left 6 years later not knowing what to put on my business card. I was still deeply involved in second language education, partly because I had a teaching fellowship in the English program for foreign graduate students for most of my years of study. But my reading and classwork had exposed me to a much broader world of issues and studies in education, language, and literacy through the disciplines of sociology, anthropology, psychology, and linguistics. I guess I became an educator during those years, losing the ability to separate study in language and linguistics from broader issues in education. For this transformation I am eternally grateful to my fragmented and rather loosely structured PhD program and today do not regret the discomforts I experienced.

At the time, I felt comfortable as an older student with many years of teaching behind me so was not overly intimidated by the famous names who instructed me. Why, then, couldn't I understand some of the reading material and some of the language and concepts being used in lectures and class discussions? How could I explain my deep resistance to the language and ways of thinking and researching in one class, my skepticism about a research methodology in another, my incomprehension of readings in another, and my fascination and joyous participation in the literacy activities in others? Why was I having such trouble merging the voices of some of my readings into my own writing? Was it my fault that little of what I was supposed to be learning and practicing felt embodied? (Linda Lonon Blanton's [1999] "unsympathetic look at academic writing" suggests it was not, but of course this potentially comforting piece had not yet been written.) Was there no way to speed up the process of becoming an insider—a "legitimate peripheral participant" (Lave & Wenger, 1991)? As a reader, how would I ever manage to get a feel for who was who, what authors' stances were, and where I might fit? I resisted the whole idea of becoming tightly associated with a disciplinary subgroup in my program, finding that to do so I would have had to concoct for myself arbitrary and unconvincing reasons for committing my allegiances. It is not that I had no stances at all. After taking a sociology class that seemed to be full of happily mentored students I was able to state with confidence, counter to my professor's claim, that some aspects of human behavior couldn't and shouldn't be turned into numbers. Why couldn't people in this class see that the serious game of turning "motivation" into a number didn't make sense to me? Although I had toyed with the idea of asking the professor to be my PhD advisor, I knew then that I would never be able to become part of her research project group.

In spite of a growing sense that some ways of thinking and researching felt wrong and others more comfortable, it became clear to me that I did not and would not fit well into any group of scholars. I therefore opted not to join any research group, a decision that may have contributed to my lingering sense of marginality. So my teaching fellowship funded my way through the program, relieving me from the anxiety of seeking projects to work with each year but perhaps distancing me in some ways from colleagues and faculty, whom I ended up associating with as individuals rather than as project group members. I would have to manage to develop my writing, researching, and thinking outside a mentored group and try to pick up enough of the rules of the game in order to survive. But which game? There seemed to be so many. My sense of marginality, as well as my sense of wonder as to how people found their way into different playing fields and were transformed there in the PhD process, led me to my dissertation research on disciplinary socialization in a PhD program, work that I have revisited numerous times since finishing the degree (see the case study of Virginia below). Since that time I have also discovered over and over again how many people, not just minorities and foreign students, felt unsure as to who they were and where they belonged in their PhD programs. Many felt unsure as well as to how the practices associated with their writing, on which their success or failure in the program depended, contributed to the construction of academic identities. I have also discovered that I am not alone in my sense of knowing less at the end of the doctoral program than I did at the beginning, no doubt because I had become aware of the complexity and partiality of my knowledge.

It is usually the case in educational literature that marginality, confusion, dissonance, and the frustration that attends one's awareness of the incompleteness of one's knowledge are all interpreted with a negative spin. At this point let me clarify that my sense of marginality, skepticism, and partial comprehension did not, do not, oppress me. I cannot say that I have always been comfortable in my confusion, but I felt liberated and exhilarated in my PhD program, being tied to no one and yet marginally connected to many, being full of questions that kept changing and leading me in new directions, being certain only that I was relatively free to study what I wanted without ever reaching a state of certainty in my knowledge and that the pursuit could happily take a lifetime. I see now that my nonparticipation in some practices and frequent partial participation in others (Wenger, 1998) helped me construct the ever-shifting professional identity that began in serious in that program. As Giddens (1991) and Linde (1993) suggested, I will continue reconstructing my own narrative in search of a coherent story, uncomfortably but gratefully armed with the awareness I developed in my PhD program.

This is a long way to say that I no longer expect to resolve my questions about academic literacy (my own or others') with certainty but the pursuit continues to intrigue me. The case studies I discuss in this chapter address some of the questions of how doctoral students, some of whom feel immersed in a chaos of multiple local academic subcommunities just as I did, learn to participate (or not) in the very serious writing games of the academy and thus transform their identities in their search for meaning and coherence.

PUBLISHED STUDIES

Academic and professional socialization has long been a phenomenon of interest to sociologists and educators. Beginning in the mid-1950s some now classic studies of graduate student and professional socialization were con-

ducted by sociologists interested in disciplinary and professional socialization. These were not case studies as such nor were all focused on PhD
students. Nevertheless, they still make fascinating reading for scholars interested in the transitions of identity experienced by students as they proceed through their graduate programs. The authors of these studies did not
concern themselves with issues of academic literacy; later work in rhetoric
and genre studies would take up this aspect of academic enculturation. Instead of case study methodologies they used broader survey and interview
techniques widely used in sociology. Still, the focus on transitions is relevant to any study of academic enculturation so the studies merit mention
here, and for serious scholars of academic and professional enculturation
deserve more detailed reading.

Several studies that were conducted under the guidance of sociologist
Robert Merton explored changes in the professional identities of medical
students over 4 years of graduate education. Fox (1957) discovered how
students became increasingly aware of uncertainties in their field as they
became attuned to the fact that doctors are never able to master completely their knowledge of the field. She noted that students seemed to pass
through a particular sequence during their 4 years: acknowledging uncertainty in the first year, learning to cope with uncertainty in the second, becoming falsely certain in their third year, and facing the reality of uncertainty in the fourth year. Huntington (1957) investigated how medical
students developed a professional self-image, shifting their identities from
that of student to one of doctor. She found that students increasingly
viewed themselves as doctors over the 4 years but that at any particular
moment their self-images depended on the social context and the types of
experiences they had with those around them. Students' self-images were
influenced differently, in other words, by the varying expectations faculty,
nurses, classmates, and patients held for them. In the presence of faculty,
students saw themselves more as students, but in the presence of patients
they felt more like doctors. Another classic ethnographic study of medical
education revealed similar tensions in that the students were pulled in two
directions—their desired goal of studying for professional purposes and the
pragmatic reality of studying to pass classes, with the latter taking precedence (Becker, Geer, Hughes, & Strauss, 1961).

More recently, within the fields of composition and rhetoric some scholars have examined specific aspects of doctoral level students' advanced academic literacy experiences, such as how students learn to participate in
scholarly written conversations in their fields. Connor and Mayberry (1996)
examined how "Timo," a new PhD student in agricultural economics, negotiated a term project with one professor and how his first language (Finnish)
influenced the task process and product. Penrose and Geisler (1994) compared how a freshman student and a doctoral student of philosophy pre-

sented themselves as authorities in an essay they each wrote from eight scholarly articles. The doctoral level student had learned to view his sources as authors with whom he, as another legitimate authoritative voice, was having a conversation and to view his essay as an exercise in the construction of knowledge. The freshman student, on the other hand, saw her task as one of transferring information from her sources to her essay and did not perceive herself as part of the academic discussion. Although the task was identical, the academic writing games differed greatly for the two students according to their experience and expertise.

In another investigation of how difficult it is for graduate students to add their voices to conversations in professional academic communities, Diane Belcher (1995) found that graduate international students in her EAP course were sometimes reluctant to critique existing works in their fields not only because they felt they did not know enough to do so, but also because they felt intimidated by the authoritative scholarly voices in their readings. In the case of some students in science, engineering, and mathematics, there seemed to be a perception that "professionals in their fields never argue" but instead build consensually on each others' work (p. 137). As is no doubt the case with novices in general, these students did not understand the experts' game of using critique to help build knowledge. Believing with Jolliffe and Brier (1988) that students need to practice expert behaviors before actually becoming experts, Belcher helped her students learn to read and write critically by having them analyze the textual features of critical book and article reviews in their own fields. In this way her students developed awareness not only of discipline-specific textual strategies (such as politeness features; Hyland, 1996a; Myers, 1989) for critiquing, but also of the extent to which disciplines are characterized by social interaction, of which critiquing is an essential component. Not all EAP courses provide such scaffolding for graduate students, however. Jette Hansen (2000), in her case study of a PhD math student from Taiwan found that the required ESL writing class contributed nothing to the student's understanding of writing practices in her discipline. Hansen (2000) concluded, unlike Belcher (1995), that the conflict between ESL and content courses is to some extent "irresolvable" (p. 47).

In another study, Belcher (1994) laid out a more explicit apprentice-style framework based on Lave and Wenger's (1991) concept of legitimate peripheral participation in order to study the relationships between three international graduate students and their mentors. Concerned with how graduate students learn to participate in their research communities, Belcher found that two of the three sets of relationships she studied, those between two male Chinese students and two male advisors, did not work smoothly to help students develop an insider's perspective. She speculates that the two mismatches stemmed from a variety of causes, such as differences between the students' and their mentor's views of the academic community, the goals of research writing, and the expectations of readers. The one successful relationship, between a female Korean student and a female advisor, was characterized by close collaboration on a research project and a compatible and respectful personal relationship. The Korean woman thus participated actively with her mentor in constructing and rationalizing a research project as well as in the rewarding process of writing up their findings. As Lave and Wenger (1991) discovered in their study of apprentice butchers and Wenger (1998) in his study of insurance claims processors, Belcher notes that the apprentice model of community participation does not always play itself out in ideal ways in actual work or school settings: If the collaborative and cross-generational relationships among participants do not work well, novices will not be privy to the knowledge and practices of those with more insider knowledge and expertise.

In another case study of a doctoral student–advisor mentoring relationship, Ann Blakeslee (1997) found that the student, Djamal Bouzida, a sixth-year PhD student in physics, was not able to take on an authoritative role in the writing of his first paper for publication. Bouzida's advisor, although supportive and steady in his interactions with Bouzida over the 22 (!) drafts of the paper, nevertheless became frustrated at the slow pace of revision and at Bouzida's apparent inability to make necessary changes. The advisor eventually used his authoritative role to appropriate the draft and make rhetorical changes in how the argument was positioned and at the same time cut most of the technical detail that Bouzida thought his audience needed to know. Blakeslee describes Bouzida's experiences as a case of situated learning, but one that inhibited in some ways the student's ability to participate more authoritatively in the professional practice of writing journal articles. The constraints resulted from the advisor's lack of explicit guidance, Bouzida's reluctance to let go of familiar writing strategies, his lack of understanding of the rhetorical complexity of writing for publication, and the hierarchical nature of authority in the mentoring relationship.

Like Blakeslee (1997), Hugh Gosden (1995, 1996) also looked at how doctoral students—in this case a small group of novice Japanese scientists—prepared a publishable paper in English as part of their graduate requirements from a Japanese technical university. In particular he studied the strategies they used to draft their papers (Gosden, 1996) and the revisions they made as they interacted with various editors and reviewers (Gosden, 1995). The students' biggest challenge was to learn the "game" of academic writing (Gosden's term), part of which involved learning some textual conventions and much of which involved developing an awareness of the audience of external critics and learning "how to play the game well" with them (p. 120). Although impressive in its detail, Gosden's (1995) meticulously coded textual analysis of students' drafts is less relevant to my own work than is his social constructionist commentary about how research supervisors, co-workers, academics outside his institution, editors, and reviewers help regulate the textual production of particular discourse communities (p. 38; see the case study of Flowerdew's [2000] Oliver in Chap. 5). These social and political aspects of academic literacy constitute some of "the many unwritten 'rules of the game' of academic discourse [that] manifest themselves textually in a multitude of subtle ways" and that need somehow to come to be "appreciated and appropriately imitated by novices" (Gosden, 1995, p. 39).

In some ways Gosden underplays the social nature of graduate level academic writing and overemphasizes the textual and imitative aspects. In contrast, Paul Prior (1994, 1998) paints a socially and textually complex picture of academic enculturation in his work, some of which I discuss below and whose study of masters degree student "Lilah" I summarized in the previous chapter (Prior, 1997, 1998). Prior, a close observer of both students and faculty writers and their texts, not only analyzes students' written texts but also the oral texts that surround the production of written work. In his microhistory of a dissertation prospectus in sociology (Prior, 1994), he analyzed the discourse of a dissertation prospectus hearing and compared the seminar talk to the final text. The seminar talk revealed multiple voices and kinds of discourse, including jokes and storytelling, where participants leaped in and out of topics in a very nonlinear way. The final text, however, a dissertation prospectus written by "Sean," was "a linear discussion that is stated purely in terms of disciplinary developments visible in the literature or possible public import" (p. 520). Local contingencies were removed from this final text, Prior tells us, such that it reflected a coherent sense of disciplinarity in spite of the messiness of the seminar response talk setting, a "social space shot through with multiple discourses, multiple histories, and diverse institutional and personal interests" (p. 522). Like Giddens' (1991) and Linde's (1993) perspectives on people's construction of coherent narrative biographies from fragmented life experiences, these doctoral students needed to create coherent discoursal selves (Ivanič, 1998) from fragments of voices and practices in their academic and personal lives.

Part of the fragmentation results from the very nature of academic writing as a multivocalic and layered practice. It also results from the related fact, as Nedra Reynolds (1994) points out, that graduate students are located in the fuzzy area between novice and professional. They contend with "layers of contradiction" in negotiating their multiple identities from home, school, and work, including mixed messages about academic game rules and practices. Referring to the conflicts faced by graduate students in a teacher education program, she says:

> We ask them to follow institutionalized practices in their own classrooms but to question them in ours; to be open-minded readers but to pick a theoretical camp; to align themselves politically but to protect their chances at scholar-

ships or awards. They are caught between the positions of novice and professional, and this in-between stage is most evident as they write. (p. 202)

In sum, the studies of doctoral students learning to participate authoritatively in their academic communities that I have discussed so far and in the
case studies that follow all seem to point to the messy and unsettling nature of the very serious, identity-transforming academic literacy games in
the enculturation process. Amidst this messiness, issues of authority, Reynolds notes, are at the heart of learning to write and of developing a professional identity in a graduate setting. In that setting, tensions are created between novices' pressure to identify and conform to convention on the one
hand and the desire to assert other less academically conventional identities on the other. Tensions are also created in that the sources of authority-
building knowledge and practice are so diverse and partial, encompassing
the social, political, personal, and textual. As Reynolds (1994) concludes,
"[a]uthoritative discourse grows out of pieces, tidbits, leftovers, and scraps—
just as authoritative writers become agents of change through moments of
struggle, glimpses of conflict, and in-between stages" (p. 209).

The following case studies of doctoral students, two published studies
and one of my own, tap into some of the messiness and continue to raise
questions about academic enculturation in graduate university settings.
The first documents the initial academic enculturation of "Nate" into a composition and rhetoric PhD program (Berkenkotter, Huckin, & Ackerman,
1988). The second traces the transition of a PhD student in sociology,
"Moira," from the role of a data manager in a research project to one of
more active contributor (Prior, 1998). My own study of "Virginia," a first-
year PhD student in sociology explores a case of enculturation gone awry.

Nate

In one of the first articles depicting the academic socialization of a new doctoral student into his program and his chosen field, Carol Berkenkotter,
Tom Huckin, and John Ackerman (1988, 1991) tell of the efforts of "Nate," a
first-year student in a rhetoric PhD program to learn to write and think in
ways compatible with expectations within his field. They asked the question that several researchers had already begun to ask about undergraduate academic enculturation (e.g., Faigley & Hansen, 1985; Herrington, 1985;
McCarthy, 1987), namely, how do students acquire the specialized forms
and functions of literacy that characterize their disciplines and professions
and learn what Bazerman (1985) called the "conversations of the discipline"? By this metaphor, Bazerman referred to the fact that members of
disciplines tend to agree on what problems and issues need to be discussed
and researched and on ways to go about investigating those problems. The
point that Berkenkotter, Huckin, and Ackerman (1988) make is that becom-

ing a member of a disciplinary community (usually a subgroup within the broader discipline) involves learning not only how to use conventional textual forms in ways used by established members of that community (e.g., Gosden, 1998; Lynch & McGrath, 1993; Swales, 1990; Swales & Najjar, 1987). It also involves learning how to participate in the community's written and oral conversations about what knowledge in the field consists of and how it can best be advanced (i.e., how to conduct what Thomas Kuhn (1970) called "normal science" and share findings in public forums).

To investigate their question, Berkenkotter, Huckin, and Ackerman examined closely some of the papers that Nate wrote during his first year in the PhD rhetoric program in the belief that the papers constituted the *"visible index of his initiation into an academic discourse community"* (italics in original; p. 11). The linguistic changes in Nate's texts over time, they argued, would highlight his changing relationship with his disciplinary subspecialty and presumably document his journey from the position of an outsider to that of an accepted and knowledgeable insider. In order to make this claim, the authors needed to presume the existence of a relatively well-defined disciplinary community whose textual conventions could be identified. In making this argument, they note that a community's papers and publications "constitute a research community's communicative forum" where "issues are raised, defined, and debated" (p. 12). The ultimate goal of a graduate student like Nate, they claim, is to contribute to this ongoing knowledge conversation.

The main analyses in the 1988 study were done on five of Nate's papers written for one professor over the year, and for comparison purposes on samples of published writing of nine composition theorists whom Nate was reading and citing (the "experts"). One of the authors (Huckin) counted various linguistic features such as use of "I" (cf. Ivanič, 1994; Tang & John, 1999) and the proportion of definite to indefinite articles in samples of these texts. The presence or absence of such features was taken to reflect certain stylistic norms of the rhetoric subcommunity. The authors were also given weekly written self-report memos by Nate, they had numerous interviews with him and with faculty members, and Berkenkotter observed and took notes in some classes (we have no detailed information on these data sources).

Who was Nate? From the 1988 case study we know something about him as a writer, but little about him as a person. We are not told, for example, if he was rich or poor, Black or White, typical or atypical of other students in the program, or even why he entered the PhD program in the first place. In one of his memos, he mentions that "curiosity and initiative brought me to this campus" (p. 26; as opposed to another campus or as a reason for pursuing a PhD?), but beyond this comment, his motives are unclear. (We get a better sense of him as a person from a later piece, to be discussed below.)

We know that he was hardly a beginning writer even though he was labeled in this article a "skilled novice" (p. 11). He had received a BA in English and a masters degree in Education. He had done several years of college level teaching of writing, had written some conference papers, and had participated in a summer writing seminar on a "humanistic perspective" of the writing process before beginning the PhD program. By the end of that seminar, the authors tell us, Nate had developed a strong sense of self as a writer.

However, Nate apparently had numerous problems with his writing at the conclusion of the summer seminar and at the beginning of his program such as mixed metaphors and mixed levels of formality that made it difficult for him to adjust to new expectations in the PhD program. Oddly, one of the "nonacademic" features that the authors point out in a sample paragraph of Nate's seminar writing is the use of sentence parallelism (in one writing he apparently used the same subject-topic in a variety of forms in all five sentences of a paragraph). This feature has been described by others (e.g., Halliday & Hasan, 1976; Lautamatti, 1987) as one way to achieve topical coherence, a characteristic of the writing of skilled writers in that it fulfills the given-new expectations of clear writing. In a less ambiguous case, the authors note that Nate's early writings contained a much higher proportion of the personal pronoun "I" than did his later writings and than did the writing of the composition theorists that he was reading and citing. This change suggested to the authors that Nate was increasing his allegiance to the theorists' conventionally objective stance and distancing himself from a stance that fronted his own persona in his writing. The hyperbole in Nate's early writings also gave way to more measured language, and the percentage of "off-register" words and phrases decreased. The authors summarize their findings about Nate's writing, noting changes in both his use of language and his understanding of what his new field's discipline-specific conversations were all about:

> By the end of his first year in the rhetoric program, Nate had gained increasing control over the language in his texts. His ability to manage information within prescribed conventions is evident in his papers from this period. He had also learned to better accommodate his register to the rhetorical context in which he wrote. But he had learned something else that was to serve him as a writer: he had become familiar with the central concerns and disciplinary issues with which rhetoric program faculty were concerned. (p. 30)

They further suggest that the fact that his writing increasingly took on features of social science expository prose indicated a desire on Nate's part to be considered a member of the group of composition studies scholars he was reading and learning from (p. 40).

Of Nate's own views and developing identity as an academic writer we know little from direct testimony in the 1988 article. We do know from an early self-report memo that Nate had little idea that his writing and thinking would change into a style that could be called "scientific." He expected to learn an accepted "format" but found his professor's suggestion that students' writing would come to reflect a "scientific habit of mind" to be a "Frankensteinian notion" (p. 18). In another memo (no date given) Nate expresses great frustration at the feeling that he was "butting heads finally with ACADEMIC WRITING—and it is monstrous and unfathomable" (p. 21, caps in original). He continues as follows, trying not to but inevitably compelled to compare himself to well-known authors he is reading:

> I know that . . . what I see is only a final product—and that they have much more experience doing all kinds of writing—and that I should not compare myself with people—but I feel that they have access to the code and I do not. (p. 21)

In a later informal memo written to his professor in which he was trying to clarify some ideas for a critical article review, Nate mentions that he was coming to see things in new ways and that he was "just beginning to understand the issues" (p. 23). There are no interview data or other examples of self-report memos.

In a later article, the authors analyzed the introductions to three of Nate's papers over a year and a half, suggesting that Nate showed "increasing mastery of the community's linguistic, rhetorical, and topical conventions" (Berkenkotter, Huckin, & Ackerman, 1991, p. 192). They concluded that the development of academic literacy "involves the ability to adapt one's discourse [to locally preferred conventions] as the situation requires" (p. 211). In spite of this nod to local contingencies, the authors still imply that there is such a thing as a unified discourse community and that social science expository prose can be characterized unambiguously. Moreover, they do not question whether group membership was Nate's desire, or whether he had decided to play a pragmatic game of survival, or some of both. It is only in a later revelation that we learn more about Nate, his identity as coauthor Ackerman, and his emergent identity as a composition scholar in his PhD program (Ackerman, 1995).

I was delighted to find in Ackerman's (1995) brief postscript to the Nate study the autobiographical portrayal of someone who at last felt to me to be a real person struggling with multiple identities and literacies in a real academic setting (Carnegie Mellon) that was "far from monolithic when we were in the middle of our enculturation" (p. 146). Ackerman does not deny transitions in thinking and writing he made during his doctoral program, but points out that the "interpretive leap from textual analysis to intellectual identity" is problematic (p. 145) and that it would be a mistake to infer a single identity from a small selection of the many papers he wrote in graduate school. Other aspects of genre activity and hence the evolution of identity and authority are masked if researchers look simply at textual practices:

> The exterior qualities of the . . . papers that I wrote mask, to some degree, the ongoing epistemological quest of a student who, like all other students in graduate school, simultaneously tries to satisfy the demands and constraints of each professor and class while at the same time seeks a separate scholarly identity. (p. 147)

Ackerman tells us that he sees the three papers analyzed in Berkenkotter, Huckin, and Ackerman (1991) more as "exercises in 'getting by' in the day-to-day expectations of a given class" (p. 148), highlighting the local and circumstantial nature of the development of academic literacies, than as papers that show a clear progression of Nate's assimilation of a research community's literature and lexicon (p. 148). Were he and his two coauthors to write up this study today, he tells us, the report would look different, reflecting a more unconventional hybrid approach that the authors decided at the time not to risk in their very serious game of academic publishing.

In the two original articles, remarkable for being some of the first to explore academic enculturation at the graduate level, identity seems to be the unexplored aspect of Nate's academic enculturation. Not only do we have little sense of Nate's perspective of who he was and how and why he changed in the ways he did, we also have none but the authors' views on most of Nate's writing that is cited (a small portion of what he wrote in his first year), no sense of what a diverse faculty thought of Nate as a writer and thinker, and little information about what kinds of interactions Nate (Ackerman) had with the other two authors during the research process, though we have a better sense of this in Ackerman (1995). This absence of a multifaceted perspective on academic identity highlights a missing link in this study and in many other academic enculturation studies as well. The richness and unconventionality of "Nate's" personal perspective (Ackerman, 1995) fill in some of the gaps and give us added information about Ackerman as a thinker and writer. As Ackerman points out, referring to Rosaldo (1989), the language and interpretations used by scholars as they write up their research need to be examined since these "reveal as much about the genre activities of the authors of that research as the subjects of their writing" (Ackerman, 1995, p. 150). In general, Ackerman's self-reflection points out to me the need for greater multivocality, openness, and complexity in this kind of social science writing, and reminds us that writing for publication involves its own kind of social, political, and textual academic literacy games (Casanave & Vandrick, forthcoming).

Moira

Paul Prior's cases studies of the academic enculturation of masters and doctoral level graduate students in a variety of social science disciplines extend and complexify the work by Berkenkotter et al. (1988, 1991; Berkenkotter & Huckin, 1995) and add a theoretical perspective absent from the studies of Nate (Prior, 1998). Prior's dense and layered studies aim for none of the clarity that comes from abstraction and quantification in the 1988 Berkenkotter, Huckin, and Ackerman study. Rather, Prior confronts head-on the complex array of social, personal, historical, cultural, and linguistic factors that together help make the practice of academic writing into what he calls a situated, laminated activity. Prior does not presume, for example, that an academic discourse community can be unambiguously defined or identified or that linguistic features of genre conventions in the social sciences can be typified in ways that can be used productively for linguistic analyses and comparisons. Prior finds too much diversity for such bold assertions, and instead uses the diversity he finds to his advantage to showcase the multiple influences on students' production of particular pieces of writing in particular settings for particular professors and purposes. In ways only hinted at by Berkenkotter, Huckin, and Ackerman, Prior shows how a graduate student writer's textual identity (Ivanič, 1998; Kramsch & Lam, 1999) is constructed from a blend of voices and practices, the origins of which are rarely evident in the final product.

I chose to focus on Prior's case study of Moira in this chapter because it is one that he has written about at length and because the disciplinary context is that of sociology—the domain for my own case study in the next section. Even though we do not learn very much about Moira herself as a writer and as a participant in the writing practices of a very small research community in sociology, Prior's study is rich with contextual details that influenced Moira's textual production and that reveal some of the transitional activities and stages in the game of authorship at the PhD level.

Prior's (1998) setting for this case study was a sociology research team in a research seminar in which all participants were research assistants on the same project. His original purpose for studying the process of authorship in a graduate seminar was to show how writing tasks were constructed around "literate sequences of initiations, replies, and evaluations" (p. 160). The principal investigator on this team was Professor Elaine West. Two co-investigators sometimes joined the seminar. The students were all preparing texts from the project's data set on adolescent behavior. These texts included papers for journals and conferences, reports to the grantors, and dissertation proposals. In the seminar, the main activity was to be a discussion of each student's work, drafts of which had already been distributed to all the participants. Seven students attended this seminar, five of whom (including Moira) were Professor West's advisees. Four of the advisees were planning to use this project for their dissertation work. Further complicating Prior's goal of exploring the game of authorship was the fact that several papers had already been coauthored by the three faculty investigators and three of the students. The "histories of production" of such papers were both "complex and uncertain" (p. 161).

At the time of Prior's study, Moira was not a first-year PhD student, but was 4 years into her program. We presume but do not know for certain that she was a White native speaker of English. We learn from a side remark that she was a "new parent" (p. 234) and that her interest in adolescent risk may have stemmed from what she referred to in an interview as "a lot of interesting personal history" that was close to her heart (p. 230). In this same interview, she explained without referring to herself directly that in cases of adolescent maladjustment, "they're so quick to blame the family," suggesting that other people and contexts can help the child "overcome some of the deficits of the family" (p. 230). Some of these personal issues seemed to come through in Moira's development of her own work in the sociology research seminar and explain some of her dissatisfaction with some of the literature on adolescent risk that lacked psychological emphases. They also come through in some of her responses to feedback from Professor West.

When Prior began his study, Moira had been involved in West's research seminar project for 2 years as manager of data collection, a job involving distributing and collecting thousands of questionnaires but not coauthoring any of the team's papers. Prior's case study covers a period in which Moira was working on two single-authored papers, one for a graduate student conference and one for a preliminary PhD examination. These documents were produced over time with repeated and detailed responses on Moira's many drafts by Professor West. However, before switching to West as advisor Moira apparently had experienced great difficulty in finding a "home" in her graduate program. She needed a mentor who shared her interest in adolescence and who was already involved in a research project. Until she met West and began working with her, Moira had received no feedback on her writing from peers or professors and had little sense of "what's wrong, what's right" in her writing (p. 220). Moira found West's extensive commentary on and editing of her drafts surprising and welcomed it with little resistance.

Prior's goal in his case study of Moira and West was to examine closely the textual exchanges between them as Moira's two papers developed and to trace how and which of West's words from written feedback became part of Moira's later drafts. The documenting of these surface blendings of voices was only one aspect of the study, however. Prior also wished to learn "what Moira made of those response-initiated revisions, how she understood and felt about them, and what she was appropriating from this literate activity" (p. 216). To analyze the textual interactions between Moira and West, Prior used several constructs from Bakhtin (1981), such as those of centrifugal and centripetal forces in discourse communities, of authoritative discourse (the words of people and institutions with authority, such as teachers, that are not integrated with the self), and of internally persuasive discourse (the words that are in a sense owned by us, developed multivocally through our interactions with others). He illustrates how Moira both appropriated the authoritative discourses and practices of the sociology seminar with West as enculturated expert in the lead, and simultaneously exerted her own influence on the research project through a kind of "centripetal force as [her] ideologies [were] dialogically received and accommodated to as well as altered" (p. 243). Using discourse-based interviews, Prior also learned that some of the changes made in the content if not the actual language of Moira's texts were also internally persuasive to her—that the ideas had begun to constitute part of her identity as a novice sociologist.

When we examine the many examples of Moira's texts and West's responses, it is tempting at first to say that West basically rewrote many of Moira's sentences and phrases and that Moira passively incorporated them into her drafts. In another chapter of his book, Prior tells us that Moira did incorporate the majority of West's revisions into her own work without resistance, creating a kind of "tacit co-authorship" (p. 170) on Moira's single-authored papers. West did not have this kind of relationship with all of her students, but told Prior that she felt confident about Moira's abilities and progress. Mediated authorship, however, went beyond the surface representations in the texts in the sense that the activities, research techniques, and goals of the larger research project that West conducted found their way into Moira's work, contributing to Moira's disciplinary enculturation. Similarly, Moira's resistance, minimal as it was, to some of West's feedback and ways of analyzing data and her insistence on following her particular interest in adolescent risk influenced the project itself.

The changes that Moira experienced, from one of functioning as an outsider (a data manager with no public voice) to one who was actively participating in the literate activities of a specialized group happened gradually and not without discomfort on Moira's part. Early in her participation on West's project, during a year in which she had been trying to develop a dissertation topic, Moira commented that she hadn't read enough, "still [felt] like a real dummy in the area"—not at all like an expert, and that this lack of a sense of authority affected her confidence in her writing (p. 219). She acquiesced to most of West's revisions, trusting in West's expertise, then commented once to Prior that sometimes when she read her papers some months later she would ask herself, "Did I write this? This doesn't sound like me" (p. 221). Moira's textual voice, in other words, seemed to represent poorly what she felt to be her identity, and until the blendings of other voices and practices had become more thoroughly integrated in her work over time—more embodied—she could not escape her sense of being a student in need of guidance. Over the year, and after many drafts of her two single authored yet tacitly coauthored papers, Prior tells us that "Moira moves from being an employee engaged in logistical support of the research (with no authorship credit) to one of two students West thinks of as 'on the verge of entering their academic careers,' as actively engaged in the communicative forums of the discipline (major conferences and refereed journals)" (p. 243). This change did not come about as a result of writing alone, but as a result of Moira's changing functional relation to her disciplinary subcommunity. Similar to Blakeslee's (1997) doctoral student Bouzida in physics, Moira began in a limited way by participating in the technical activities of data management, and concluded the year by participating in the activities of coconstructing authoritative knowledge within West's research project and within the broader discipline of sociology.

Berkenkotter, Huckin, and Ackerman's Nate and Prior's Moira both succeeded in transforming their identities and practices sufficiently so that they developed a sense of belonging to a specialized disciplinary group (even if it was only the size of a small research project group). Their writing practices and their understanding of the layered complexities of the game changed such that both Nate and Moira began participating in local literate conversations in new ways, including in ways that influenced the communities within which they were writing. Their locations within the local academic community shifted, in other words, resulting in altered relationships with key players—authors, faculty, project group members. We have the sense that both of these PhD students probably finished their programs to eventually become mentors of others. Many students who begin PhD programs, however, never finish. The story of Virginia that I recount below differs greatly from those of Nate and Moira in that her tentative game playing on a PhD playing field in sociology ended just a year after it had begun. The games of language, knowledge, and power that she encountered were not ones she wanted to participate in.

CASE STUDY: VIRGINIA: NOT HER KIND OF GAME[1]

The story of Virginia is a story of a clash of cultures. I do not refer here to ethnic culture alone, but to concepts of disciplinary or academic cultures (there are many) and home cultures (also a multiple construct) and to Vir-

---

[1]An earlier version of this study appeared as Casanave, C. P. (1992a), Cultural Diversity and Socialization: A Case Study of a Hispanic Woman in a Doctoral Program in Sociology. Copyright © 1992. From D. E. Murray (Ed.), *Diversity as Resource: Redefining Cultural Literacy* (pp. 148–182). Alexandria, VA: TESOL. Adapted with permission. The story of Virginia also appeared in Casanave (1995b).

ginia's positioning of herself in relation to the numerous cultural communities of practice in her life and to the serious games played in them (cf. Wenger's [1998] notion of multimembership in communities of practice). I will look at three aspects of the tensions among cultures that Virginia was in contact with in the first and only year of her PhD program in sociology: the language of the game players in her local academic community; the epistemological game rules for how knowledge was thought to be constructed; and her perceptions of the power relationships among the key players. I begin the story, however, with the epilogue.

In the spring of 1999 and again in the fall of 2000 I walked across Central Park in New York City to Mt. Sinai Hospital to meet with a woman who had participated in my dissertation research project on disciplinary socialization over a decade before (Casanave, 1990). We had kept in touch over the years so I had been able to follow the changes that had occurred in her life since she left the sociology PhD program where I had first met her. In the vast lobby, designed by architect I. M. Pei, I was met by a tall, handsome woman in her mid-30s, looking professional with her clipboard and beeper in hand. This was Virginia (not her real name), now a social work counselor in one of the divisions of the hospital. Like Prior's Moira, she had been a student of sociology; unlike Moira, she did not complete her doctoral studies. Not bad, I thought, for someone who had, in the eyes of the small disciplinary community of sociologists at her former university, dropped out. In her year in the program, she had seen the game, decided she did not want to play, and had thus moved on.

In the fall of 1987, I was seeking a social science program in which I could collect dissertation data on the topic of writing and disciplinary socialization in the social sciences. I had been a PhD student myself for about 4 years, had read several social studies of science that had fascinated me (e.g., Fleck, 1935/1979; Gilbert & Mulkay, 1984; Knorr-Cetina, 1981; Kuhn, 1970; Latour & Woolgar, 1979), and was becoming increasingly curious about the transformations in identity and outlook that took place in me and my colleagues as we engaged in nonstop text-based practices in our own programs in a school of education. Academic enculturation in a social science field, it seemed to me, was a messy and interesting affair and less studied than enculturation into hard science fields. After querying several different graduate social science programs, I located a sociology department whose key faculty were willing to let me visit classes and talk to students, some of whom volunteered to meet with me over an academic year. I was, thus, a PhD student (older than most, it is true) investigating PhD students partly out of curiosity as to what was happening to me and my doctoral student friends. Virginia was one of the first case study informants that I met in my data collection experience.

Virginia had just entered a PhD program in sociology at a prestigious West Coast research university. A native speaker of English and Spanish from a Puerto Rican family in New York, she was just 22 at the time, and had entered the PhD program immediately after completing a BA degree in sociology at a good East Coast university not too far from her home in the Bronx. She came from a close-knit family where her father had been a bus driver, then a supervisor, for many years. Quiet, shy, and pretty, Virginia volunteered to work with me over the academic year as one of three case study participants in my dissertation research project. She and her 11 classmates formed a culturally diverse group, referred to as a "cohort" in the department: Eight of the 12 students were international students from countries such as Canada, mainland China, Korea, Puerto Rico, and Japan, two were native English speaking Hispanic minorities from the United States (including Virginia), and two were middle-class Whites. Their ages ranged from 22 to 40. One of the old guard professors told me that this kind of diversity was becoming increasingly common in the program. As one way to help develop a group identity in this diverse cohort as was done with past cohorts, all 12 students were given office space in the same room, a large room divided into study carrels.

During this first year of doctoral work, all students had to take a demanding series of required core courses in sociological theory (two courses) and statistical methods (two courses, with a third in the fall of the second year). For a study of socialization in graduate school contexts, such courses are ideal to track, since they presumably are designed to acquaint students with the knowledge and skills that a department considers fundamental in the field. In fact, one of the core course professors described these courses as bringing a disparate incoming group of first-year students to "more or less the same place." He mentioned that the program in some ways preferred students who did not have previous graduate degrees in sociology, since it did not then have to "unteach" them so much.

In order to learn what values and practices this program considered essential for novice sociologists to learn, and to learn the role of language and writing in this training, I sat in on all the sessions of the two theory classes, taping and taking notes, and on selected sessions of one of the two first year methods classes. From the two core theory classes I also collected handouts, drafts of student papers, final copies of written work, and all written feedback on this work. I interviewed three key student participants including Virginia up to eight times and other participants, such as professors and other students, up to four times. From the class sessions, documents, and interviews, I not only became familiar with the key issues, goals, and terminology of this particular disciplinary subcommunity, but I also developed a sense of the 12 first year students as a group. This group came to be known as an unusually close cohort compared to those in previous years. But as is the case with most groups in a classroom situation, my class visits documented that roughly a third participated actively and regularly, a third occasionally, and a third was silent.

Virginia was among the silent third. I got to know her slowly over the first few months through regular interviews we had set up for the purpose of discussing her responses to the core courses and to the several writing assignments she had to complete in each one. We talked briefly at first as she completed the first short writing assignments in her first theory class, then at greater length as we got to know each other better and as she struggled with the longer papers that came later.

For Virginia, it was her experiences in the theory classes more than in the rather straightforward, skill-based methods (i.e., statistics) classes that pushed her to decide to leave the PhD program after 1 year. Let me portray these theory classes in some detail, since the detail will help convey a clear picture of the "culture" into which Virginia and the other first year students were being socialized.

The Core Theory Classes

The first year core courses in sociological theory had been instituted nearly 30 years before by two of the program's original founders, both of whom were still active at the time of my study and very influential in the department. The first theory course, which I will call Theory Analysis, was offered in the first quarter in the fall. It was designed by "Dr. Adams," who was still teaching it. In spite of some changes made over time, Theory Analysis had one main objective—to teach students how to "read" or analyze theories. A second objective was to acquaint students with "seven of the eight major schools of sociological thought in America today."

To these ends, and to help students use their analytical skills later in the course to write a literature review, Adams had them write three short analytical exercises, following step by step instructions provided in handouts (see Appendix D). In these papers, students analyzed several old but influential theories, where "analyze" meant discovering the theory's "basic assumptions," its "empirical generalizations," the definitions of key concepts used in it, as well as writing a precis. The third of these exercises asked the students to use their new analytical skills to compare two theories. The three exercises were written in the first month of the course and were read and commented on by a third year teaching assistant, who consulted with Adams in preparing his responses. The major "culture shock" experienced by nearly all the first year students occurred in this first month as the students struggled to understand and apply the abstract concepts used in the three exercises to talk and write about theories they were to read. These specific readings were themselves dense and jargon-filled. A second shock for students was the requirement to read a 400-page course reading packet consisting of articles from sociological journals. The articles were not discussed in class lectures, however, and not a single student I spoke with claimed to have read all of these articles. It is therefore not clear what role the readings played in helping students learn to analyze and write about theory.

The second theory class, "Theory Construction," was a course in how to construct sociological theory. It was offered in the winter quarter by another of the old guard faculty who had helped establish the department, "Dr. Bernstein." He had taken over the Theory Construction course 6 years before from its originator. He had altered it in the year I conducted my study in a team effort with Dr. Adams in order to solve some of the problems he had encountered in previous years in which graduate students had complained about the course's narrow approach. The course remained controversial, but (as was reported to me) less so than before. Part of the problem lay in the fact that Dr. Bernstein believed there was a right way to do sociology if one wished to "do science," the presumption being that a scientific sociology was better in some ways than other approaches.

As a way to head off student protests during the semester in which I was observer, the Theory Construction course was team taught by both Adams and Bernstein, although most of the teamwork had taken place earlier as the course was being designed. Bernstein told me that, among other changes, he was also trying to be less of a "bull in a china shop" (i.e., to be more accepting of students' work when it deviated from his own prescriptive view of what good sociology consisted of). As for the writing assignments, for the first time since he had taught Theory Construction, they included four short "working papers" on a research topic of students' own choosing, building up to a final research proposal rather than a final exam as in the past (see Appendix D). As in Theory Analysis, these writing assignments were designed to train students in skills they would need to complete dissertations and to contribute later to scholarly work in the field. In four working papers students had to pose researchable questions, formulate a plan for conducting their research, and test competing hypotheses through formal logical analysis. The approach was "empirical" and "scientific."

Sociology as Science in the Core Courses

The intellectual tradition espoused in the core courses (both in theory and statistical methods), I am calling "scientific." Issues, values, and practices from the natural sciences and from the philosophy and sociology of science dominated the instruction. As described by the more senior graduate students, the program's sociology had a "positivistic, empirical, and formal" flavor, where theory, quantification, and (for professors like Bernstein) experiment played important roles in the work that the faculty did.

The message that science was valued highly was couched in a number of different ways, some overt and some covert. In class lectures and discussions in the theory classes and in interviews with me, the professors expressed the following views:

- Sociology isn't a science in the mature sense yet, but it can be if sociologists would just be trained to follow certain standards of language and practice;
- We had a very good, well-liked qualitative researcher here, but she didn't get tenure;
- Sociology is many things, but one of its most prestigious traditions is grounded in practices and values modeled on the natural sciences; if you want to compete as a professional, you should learn this model.

In addition to these views expressed by the professors, a "scientific" sociology was promoted by the ways in which knowledge was represented in handouts, required readings, and boardwork, and by the ways in which the students were expected to represent and treat knowledge in their writing assignments. In this scientific tradition, much of the key information was carried in specialized code words, in certain kinds of verbal and symbolic statements, and in images depicting relations and processes (see examples of the verbal code words below, Figs. 4.1 and 4.2). All of these ways of representing knowledge functioned to distance the phenomena under study from the bias of human influence—to present an objectified world view—and to foster a kind of analytical thinking that fit loosely within the scientific tradition of positivism.[2] In this tradition, students were being trained to conceptualize sociological knowledge not just in discursive prose forms, but also in forms that pushed them to think "scientifically" (i.e., objectively, abstractly, symbolically, logically, and analytically).

Although the program did not discourage students from exploring other ways of investigating the sociological world, its own resources were limited because it was such a small department. Moreover, the covert message seemed to be that—if the socialization process worked as it should—the students from this program would adopt the foundational skills and values they were being taught in the core courses as they moved through the program and into the professional world. The old guard professors in particular seemed to have a well-defined view of what sociology was and should be in this department and to expect that students would come to situate themselves with the boundaries of this playing field.

---

[2] I use this term rather loosely, as did the students in the program, in spite of the fact that arguments as to its various meanings were presented to students early in the year.

Language Games, Knowledge Games, and Power Games

Virginia was one of many in the first year group who experienced varying degrees of discomfort, resistance, and alienation as they proceeded through their first year core courses, in particular the courses in theory analysis and construction. This discomfort can be viewed in an admittedly oversimplified way as stemming from a clash of cultures—that of the local disciplinary community and those of Virginia's world outside the local academic context. (Of course these cultures were themselves constructed from multiple cultural influences.) To help make her decision to leave the program comprehensible (for many decided to stay in the program despite doubts), I examine three perspectives from which we can view this clash of cultures. The first concerns language, the second concerns ways of knowing, and the third concerns power and prestige. Within the game metaphor, these themes can be conceptualized as reflecting their own rules for practice, role relationships, and conventionalized ways of constructing and sharing knowledge.

The Language Game: Sociology as Science

One aspect of acquiring the culture of a disciplinary community involves learning that community's specialized language, that is, the ways it represents knowledge in conventional ways to make it accessible to other community members, usually through written documents. Part of what the core course provided for the first year students was what they referred to as a "jargon" that united them as a group in at least two ways. In the first place, native- and nonnative English speakers alike were joined in the struggle to learn what I came to refer to as "sociology as a second language." Second, the language (especially that of the theory courses) identified the students as a group that was being brought into the fold, so to speak, as members who could eventually play the sociology game by the same rules. All the graduate students had experienced what it was like to suddenly "begin to understand what they're talking about," as one of the first year students put it. For most of the students in the first year cohort this understanding began to emerge after about a month into the fall quarter. Along with this understanding came the skepticism-producing recognition that the specialized language of the theory courses was not necessarily shared by all other faculty in the department. In other words, subcommunities existed within the small department itself that may have shared the broad commitment to science but not the language used to talk about theory.

The specialized language of the theory courses consisted of code words (terminology), acronyms, symbols, and certain constrained sentence types. I focus here on the code words since these represented concepts that the students began to struggle with from the first day of class. On that first day in Theory Analysis, Dr. Adams used more than 50 discipline-specific terms in his 2-hour lecture, most of them nouns. Many of these terms were used throughout the two theory courses as a metalanguage for talking about theory. Other terms were introduced as central to the writing assignments in both theory courses and were thus quite central to the students' lives in the sense that it was difficult to complete the writing assignments without having some sense of what the terms in the assignment prompts meant. Figures 4.1 and 4.2 display the key code words from the handouts in the two theory courses that described the step-by-step instructions for all the writing assignments. Many of these terms also appeared in Adams' first lecture.

These code words of the writing assignments in the theory classes suggest a scientific sociology, with the values of science embedded in the terms themselves. In the ideal enculturation process, the students would learn the words and their concepts and adopt the values embedded in them. However, many of the students were skeptical about the values of theoretical and empirical science reflected in this specialized language. When I looked more closely at Virginia's responses to the writing assignments and to the specialized language used to talk and write about theory, I saw how the conflict of disciplinary and personal values materialized for her over the academic year. In particular, I saw that her home languages (everyday English and Spanish) came to be less useful to her over time as tools for communicating her ideas about her work with friends and family in that they were not valued as resources for communication within the department. At a certain point, in other words, Virginia no longer had everyday language for what she was learning.

domain (of a theory)
basic assumption (underived premise)
scope (of a theory)
unsolved problem
theoretical research program (TRP)
initial theoretical formulation (ITF)
current theoretical formulation (CTF)
elaboration (of a theory)
degeneration (of a theory)
proliferants
competitors
structure (of a theory)
metatheoretical presuppositions
logical implications
empirical implications

FIG. 4.1. Terms from Theory Analysis assignments.

analytical problem
empirical inquiry
trivial question or problem
a "good question"
empirical studies
association between variables
argument
observation statement
knowledge claim
proposition
scope statement/condition
conceptual definition
"system" of concepts
operationalization
indicator
explanatory generality
empirical implication/consequence
heuristic explanation
hypothesis
competing explanation
logical analysis
empirical test
intersubjective understanding

FIG. 4.2. Terms from Theory Construction assignments.

Virginia's Responses to the Language of a Scientific Sociology. For many of the students in the first year cohort, not just those from non-Western and nonmainstream cultures, the main difficulty in completing the first writing assignments in Theory Analysis stemmed from the code words used to talk about theory and their application to a very discursive and jargon-laden piece of theorizing by Robert Merton. The answers, in other words, were not unambiguously obvious in the text. Virginia and others struggled over definitions of terms, then tried to find (as the assignment instructed) example sentences embodying those concepts. Although I was not writing up these assignments along with the students, I myself could not figure out how to do this. Virginia's first concern was just to get the task done and to fix the definitions of the key code words and their synonyms in her mind.

Having finished the first analytical exercise in Theory Analysis at the end of the second week of school, Virginia talked about the process she went through in writing the assignment. The level at which she was engaged with this first task was that of language and definitions (rather than content) as she struggled to link terms with their concepts, then to identify examples of them in the Merton article:

I wrote down all the empirical statements and all the lawlike statements. Um ... from the empirical statements we were supposed to ... um get— no from the lawlike statements we were supposed to have premises. So I I um ... I selected out the premises from the lawlike statements and— once I got the two lists of lawlike statements and empirical statements, everything else was easy. For me. Assuming I got the right [laugh] empirical and lawlike statements. And if I got that wrong, then you know I'll just learn. For the next time. How to do it.

Here Virginia was trying to use code words that, in Week 2 of the program, she had not yet internalized and that had little connection with the world she had just left on the East coast. But she pushed ahead, and described the value of the writing assignment, again in terms of language, as "reinforcing the definitions:"

I think [the exercise] helped reinforce the definitions in my head. So that now I can tell you what a lawlike statement is supposed to look like. And now I can tell you what an empirical generalization is supposed to be. Whereas before, I was very much confused about the differences.

Virginia also used a dittoed glossary of terms made available in the first week of class to help her remember definitions. But the written feedback that she received from the teaching assistant on her first exercise indicated that she (along with many others) had not linked terms and their concepts to examples in the text in appropriate ways. Note the specialized language of the course in the following example of written feedback from the third year teaching assistant:

Your list of basic assumptions are not lawlike statements: A and B are categoricals. C is an empirical generalization.

Given this kind of feedback on the first exercise, we can understand the frustration that some students felt. But the specialized language of the writing assignments was not Virginia's only concern. She also felt intimidated in this first theory class by the discussion carried on between the professor and the vocal third of the class. She judged her own competence and that of others, in other words, according to the way they were able to use language in a spontaneous situation. In the comment that follows, she groups herself with the foreign students, most of whom spoke rarely in class:

I feel like the others have a— aside from the foreign students, um the Americans in the group have an upper hand in terms of um the way they speak and um the kinds of questions they ask in class. I feel they have a better grasp of the material than I do.

By the end of her first month in the program, having completed three of these short writing assignments and having sat in on all of the dense and authoritatively delivered lectures by Dr. Adams, Virginia began to express her misgivings about the way language was used in the Theory Analysis course. She claimed, for example, that the directions for Exercise 3 could have been stated much more simply. "The language sort of covers up the main idea," she said, expressing frustration that the professor had not "gotten to the point" in a way that made the directions clear. Virginia also began to express her discomfort with the abstractness of the specialized language and concepts and to long for discussion that was more down to earth:

> I wish somehow that there wasn't such a big mystery . . . you know a mysterious air surrounding theory, and what theory is, you know? I wish it could be more concrete.

By the time she returned from Christmas vacation, Virginia was more openly voicing her dissatisfaction with the first theory course. The abstract language, she suggested, held little meaning for her in everyday life:

> I felt the whole course was um . . . was based on these— abstract language, you know, and I wish they could have been more simpler, and more um applicable to everyday things. But I guess theory— you know, that's antithetical to theory. Theory isn't particular.

Her gauge of whether she was using language in the clear straightforward way she'd been taught in a college writing class was whether she could explain her ideas to her mother. By the end of her first quarter, she was no longer able to do this. She was "learning the concepts in Dr. Adams' language," she said, and could therefore find no everyday terms for what she was doing. In other words, new concepts had been created for her out of the specialized language, making it impossible to "translate" into language that her family could understand. "You know," she said, "there's no way that I could explain to [my mother] what I was spending my last 2 weeks before Christmas doing. Just sitting at the computer, Mom."

In the second theory class, Theory Construction, given during the winter term, Virginia's concern for language continued. In this class, the students wrote four working papers that led to a final paper in which they were to systematically identify and propose a solution for a research problem. As part of the class requirements, the students shared their four working papers with each other and critiqued them publicly in class, according to guidelines established by Dr. Bernstein. This system of public critiquing allowed the students to see everyone's writing, which Virginia found in some cases to be "awful" because she could not understand what her classmates had written. She lamented the fact that the students were getting no feedback on their writing and claimed, "If you can't understand the writing, how can you understand the concepts?"

A month later after having completed three of the four working papers, she admitted to the value of writing in helping her complete the working papers. They could not have been done orally, she said, "off the top of our heads," without being written first. The reason for this, Virginia explained, was that "they expect us to use that strict language—which isn't normal everyday language." Using this language meant "writing for Dr. Bernstein" rather than for the wider audience she wished to communicate with. It meant, as Virginia phrased it, "using Bernstein's language and the stuff from his lectures."

By the end of Theory Construction, although not happy with the specialized language, Virginia expressed more confidence than before at comprehending it. But after a spring break, she began her third quarter facing an incomplete on her final paper on the topic of repression and collective action in Latin America in this class because of a flaw in the formal logical analysis of her hypotheses (this paper and feedback on it are discussed further in the next section). Over the break, some of the meanings of the key code words had already begun to slip away. In the following quote, Virginia is rereading Bernstein's guidelines for completing the paper:

> It says demonstrate by logical analysis that the two observation statements or two hypotheses are the consequences of the two *explanans*. [small pause, small chuckle] I just feel like I'm gonna have to go over some of these words, definitions. [laugh]

Later in the third quarter, Virginia was still convinced that good writing in sociology should be written in terms that are accessible to nonsociologists:

> Although I use quote proper terms, I still use simple sentences, and um simple phrases, um . . . I try to be as clear and to the point as possible, . . . uh . . . so in some respects I use words which I feel nonsociologists have an idea about. Even though they don't define the term as a sociologist. Something like the word theory.

Virginia was also ready to label many of the terms used in Theory Construction as "useless" ("all of the Latin ones, 'instantiation', . . ."). Yet she now saw the value of learning something about these words, not just in terms of surviving a class assignment, but in more political terms:

I think it's valuable to me (. . .) to know more or less what theoretical sociologists are talking about. Trying to sort of you know learning how to speak their language. In case they try and pull one over on me. [small laugh]

In sum, by the end of the academic year, Virginia recognized the extent to which the theoretical sociologists in the program used language that was different from the language she used in everyday life, including their use of "common" terms in technical or quasi-technical ways. Nevertheless, in her own writing she continued searching for a way to express her new knowledge in language that was accessible to her friends and family, although she found this increasingly difficult to do. Her desire to maintain ties with nonsociologists by means of language rather than to use her new language to move onto the periphery as a "legitimate participant" (Lave & Wenger, 1991) reflects her growing sense of alienation from the sociologists from whom she was receiving her training. Language in some ways lay at the heart of her self-identity by helping define who she was and which reference group she would align herself with. By "using Dr. Bernstein's language" she was aligning herself with scientists, not with the populations she wished to communicate with at home and in future work: women, ethnic minorities, educators in racially and culturally mixed neighborhoods. She rejected this alignment with theoretical sociologists but had no convenient linguistic substitute since so many of the new concepts seemed to be created out of the specialized language itself. As a resource for communicating her new knowledge to her home community, Virginia's "everyday" language had become ineffective. Hence, although Virginia began developing a shorthand for communicating with a small group of sociologists, the sociology program missed an opportunity to help Virginia eventually become a pipeline for communicating its knowledge to the broader community of sociologists and to add her perspective to that knowledge. The knowledge produced by this particular subgroup within the program would probably remain relevant only to a fairly small circle of specialists.

Hand in hand with Virginia's growing awareness of the role of language in shaping the professional identities of people who use it came a greater sense of the different world views, or ways of knowing, that are reflected in language and a realization that she was learning only one of the many ways a sociologist might understand the world.

The Knowledge Game: Where Language and Knowledge Interact

The idea that knowledge and reality are linguistic and social constructions was inspired in part by the now classic work by Peter Berger and Thomas Luckmann (1966). Thomas S. Kuhn (1970) wrote a similarly classic work about the construction of knowledge in the scientific world. He himself was inspired by the work of Ludwig Fleck (1935/1979), whose early book on the socially negotiated development of a scientific fact Kuhn had read in the original German. Following Fleck (who used the term "thought collectives"), Kuhn (1970) described the scientific community as a group of practitioners of a scientific specialty who share language, beliefs, and practices. Language lies at the core of the community in that a group's "knowledge of nature [is] embedded in the language" (p. 272). When novices learn a group's way of knowing nature by learning how to solve a field's classic problems ("exemplars"), they are acquiring a "language-correlated way of seeing the world," says Kuhn, without which "we do not see a world at all" (p. 274).

The notion that a field's specialized language shapes how group members see their worlds has been explored post-Kuhn by rhetorician Charles Bazerman (1981, 1984, 1988, 1994a). Bazerman focuses on the ways in which field-specific written texts embody a group's knowledge and its conception of what knowledge is and does in that field. Hansen (1988) used this idea as the core of a study in which she demonstrated how the different rhetorical conventions in two social science texts on the same theme reflect very different epistemological assumptions. One text was a qualitative study in social anthropology that Hansen refers to as a "particularized representation" of a small number of kinship networks among several Black families. These families appear, along with the author, as real people in the document. The other was a quantitative empirical study within the sociological tradition of survey and experimental research. In this study, the author represented several hundred Black families abstractly, as numbers and objects. The author himself did not appear as a persona in this "objective" portrayal, hence the frequent use of passives and agentless nominalizations. Nature, in this portrayal, revealed itself to the author, who played the role of nature's messenger (Gilbert, 1976). Each type of text, in other words, reflected different assumptions of what can be known, what is worth knowing, and how we can come to know it. As I suggested earlier, the texts written and read in Virginia's sociology program fit the latter tradition.

Virginia and the other students in her cohort came to recognize that they were being indoctrinated (their term) into one way of knowing the sociological world. As she put it, she felt she was "learning not to view certain types of works as sociological." Her first theory class, she said after just 1 month in the program, made her realize that

> there are going to be certain types of works that [we] are not going to be reading about in this course, descriptive sort of works you know. Um . . . comparisons, just you know comparisons between maybe two ethnic groups.

Rightly or wrongly, by the end of the first month, Virginia had gotten the idea that descriptive works were atheoretical and nonscientific, and that whereas such works might be considered sociology in one sense by practitioners working in other paradigms, they would not be valued highly in this program.

It is at this point, early in her first year, that Virginia began to express a sense of discomfort in the program. Her first real clue about the exclusive nature of the department's instruction in theory came early in the first quarter, during a guest lecture that Dr. Bernstein was giving in Adams's Theory Analysis class. In this lecture, Dr. Bernstein had highlighted one of Dr. Adams's messages to students—that there were many ways to approach the study of sociology, even though other ways were not discussed in depth or practiced in the core courses. Virginia expressed the frustration that resulted from this discovery:

> I think the Bernstein lecture also made me realize a couple of comments that Adams had said throughout his lecture about the way other sociologists view sociology. You know um the question just kept coming up more frequently, well what do they—how do they view, you know, and what kind of arguments do THEY use to support their own view of sociology.

In response to her frustration, her bright and assertive Hispanic classmate, Laura, reminded her that any department will enculturate its students into its preferred way of viewing the world. As retold by Virginia, Laura said, "WELL, Virginia, if you go to a department that's very heavily into Marxism, you're just gonna hear about Marxism!" Understanding this helped Virginia realize that there was a very pragmatic side to her enculturation into this department. This involved learning to play the game according to this department's rules—learning to do the work in the ways that were expected in order to get through the program, and somehow separating this pragmatic aspect from the personal epistemological one. In fact, by the time she returned from the Christmas break, she saw that the highly structured writing tasks in Theory Analysis had helped her know what Dr. Adams expected in class and what the department expected on a dissertation literature review. But she also noted that the way she expressed herself in these writing tasks was constrained, as was her thinking: "I'm really not knowledgeable," she said in January, "about the way other sociologists think. So I'm just learning one type of sociology. I'm just learning how to think a certain way."

Later in the winter quarter when she had finished three of the four working papers for Theory Construction, Virginia could express more clearly than before some of the values she saw being promulgated through writing assignments and class lectures: Good sociology is theoretically based—it deals in abstractions as well as in particulars; it is not enough to critique a theory—one must also improve it; empirical research is highly valued when it is exact and precise (numbers are needed); a good question is one that is nontrivial and one for which there are logical and scientific explanations as well as empirical evidence. Moreover, as she was taught in Theory Construction, formal logic is valued by some social scientists as a way to test the consistency and logicality of sets of hypotheses. Of all the valued ways of knowing in the core courses, this one met with the most resistance from Virginia and numerous other students, who found Bernstein's requirement that they learn formal logic to be a waste of time and effort. As Virginia phrased it, "converting knowledge to ps and qs" was not her idea of a fruitful way to understand the world.

By way of example, I present a sample of Virginia's work in her Theory Construction class, the class in which she received an incomplete because of a faulty logical analysis in her final paper. She received ongoing feedback on her four Working Papers (two critiques from Adams and two from Bernstein as well as peer critiques), and a written critique from Bernstein on the problems with her final draft. The sample of writing from her paper and in particular from the professors' feedback exemplifies the ways of knowing that were being promulgated in the theory classes.

Virginia's paper on which she received an incomplete was entitled "Repression and Collective Action." This paper began with the question: "Under what conditions do officials of the Catholic church contribute to the collective action of their laity in Latin America?" The paper was eight pages long, had the two required references, and combined her four working papers in the manner described in the assignment: to pose a researchable question, formulate a research plan, and test competing hypotheses (see Appendix D). The paper introduced some background from the literature on page one, presented competing knowledge claims on page two, logic-based truth tables on pages three and four, definitions on page five, lists of empirical consequences of her knowledge claims on page six, and her criteria for eliminating and preserving knowledge claims on pages seven and eight. Virginia's original knowledge claims are presented as follows:

1. If a repressive institution is divided into opposing factions, then the collective action of people increases as repression by the repressive alliance increases.
2. If a repressive institution is not divided into opposing factions, then the collective action of people increases as repression by the repressive alliance increases.
3. If the source of repression is concentrated in one institution, repression has a negative effect on collective action.

On the next page, she developed hypotheses and constructed a truth table:

The following hypotheses are developed from knowledge claims 1 and 2:

1. In nation A, if the dominant religious institution is divided into opposing factions, collective action of people will increase as repression by the repressive alliance increases.

2. In nation A, if the dominant religious institution is not divided into opposing factions, collective action of people will increase as repression by the repressive alliance increases.

The following table shows how the two hypotheses are consequences of the two knowledge claims.

TRUTH TABLE FOR HYPOTHESIS 1

1. $p \to q$ T   1. If a repressive institution is divided into opposing factions, then the collective action of people increases as repression by the repressive alliance increases

2. p (wp)   T   2. A repressive institution in nation A is divided into opposing factions.

3. q (aa)   T   3. The collective action of people in nation A will increase as repression by the repressive alliance increases.

where p = a repressive institution is divided into opposing factions
q = collection [sic] action of people increases as repression by the repressive alliance increases
wp = working premise
aa = antecedent affirmation

The original paper also concluded with the following paragraph, the language of which seems taken directly from handouts with little evidence of Virginia's other identities and ways of knowing present at all. The ways of knowing social and political events in Latin America are limited to a formal logical construction of a plan to "test" hypotheses:

> If the research does not allow choosing one knowledge claim over the other, then reformulation of the knowledge claims is necessary. One reformulation may specify more clearly the concept of "opposing factions" in order to further distinguish one knowledge claim from the other. Another option is to reformulate the system of explanation to include the statement that the unity or disunity of repressive institutions has no effect on collective action. We may then test whether the extent of unity or disunity of repressive institutions is a factor associated with collective action.

Dr. Bernstein's feedback on this term paper shows clearly what he believed to be important in theory construction in language that represents his small subfield within the discipline of sociology. Six numbered sentences are typed out on a separate sheet of paper, followed by a general comment:

Comments on Term Paper for Virginia

1. You make a serious logical error in KC1 & 2 that makes your paper unsatisfactory. They are not competing; taken together, they assert that collective action increases whether or not a repressive institution is divided into factions. What you have is:

    1. A—→B
    2. Not A—→B

Truth table analysis shows that both can be true so that they are not competing. A—→B and A——not B cannot both be true so that is <u>one</u> form of competing knowledge claims.

2. You need to consider your scope conditions further.

3. Your hypotheses are simple restatements of KCs adding "in nation A;" they are not hypotheses (empirical implications) because terms are not observables.

4. Your truth tables do not address the proof that the hypothesis follows from the KC.

5. How are your indicators related to "collective action"? You need to spell this out.

6. Repression should be defined independently of collective action.
General: You seem to understand the important ideas of the course, but this formulation of your knowledge claims is a major flaw. In addition, you need to make your arguments fully explicit; you have a tendency to present things without a thorough development of your ideas and, as a result, some necessary elements are [sic] linkages are missing.

Having been given a grade of incomplete in Theory Construction at the end of the winter quarter, Virginia chose not to go to Bernstein or Adams to clarify her confusion. Instead, she enlisted help outside the theory courses from an African-American professor, "Dr. Johnson," to help her complete the paper since the guidelines in Dr. Bernstein's feedback provided little in the way of specific changes to make. Virginia had gotten to know and trust Dr. Johnson in another class, and rather than seek help from Adams or Bernstein, she went to him. In Dr. Johnson's class that same quarter, Virginia had received an A– on a data base analysis paper on factors that influenced whether Hispanic students attended college, a topic clearly close to her heart. Dr. Johnson wrote at the end of that paper that the work was "theoretically and methodologically sophisticated." In an extraordinary display of mentorship, he read and commented on all of Virginia's working papers and the final paper from Adams's and Bernstein's Theory Construction class, then drafted a detailed six-page single spaced "memorandum" to Virginia full of questions and suggestions that enabled her to revise her paper. The feedback from Bernstein can be contrasted with the feedback on this same paper from Dr. Johnson, who resided outside the core theory sequence and whose own sociological language and ways of knowing felt less distant to Virginia. Some of this professor's language, especially his rephrasings of hypotheses and knowledge claims, worked their way into the revised draft much in the way that the voices of advisor and student blended in Prior's (1998) study of Moira and Blakeslee's (1997) study of Bouzida. In the following selection from this long memorandum, Dr. Johnson comments on how she can rephrase her knowledge claims and express them in ways that deal with different arguments about real actors in the political environment: State, Church, and People. The tone is that of a friendly human being talking to someone he knows quite well:

> Now we are back to the more subtle (and potentially more interesting argument). You just simply need to move back one level in abstraction. The appropriate unit of analysis is probably the political environment. You are now (again?) concerned with competing political actors—State, Church, People.
>
> KC #1 becomes "in the absence of competition ... the more repressive the actions of a superordinate political organization the less collective action."
>
> KC #2 becomes "when there is competition among political organizations ... the more repressive the actions of a superordinate political organization the more collective action."
>
> The problem is that these are essentially the same argument. [...] What you need to do is to develop counter-arguments. For example, one argument which suggests that collective action increases with repression. Another might argue that collective action declines with the level of repression. [...]

Virginia did revise in these ways, including the following two revised knowledge claims, much more detailed hypotheses from her knowledge claims, and definitions of her symbols in her logic truth table (the truth table itself was redone):

> Knowledge Claim 1: If repressive acts by repressive institutions increase, then the collection [sic] action of people increases.
>
> Knowledge Claim 2: If repressive acts by repressive institutions increase, then the collective action of people does not increase. (revised draft p. 2)
>
> Hypothesis 1: As the number of arrests increases, the number of meetings of community-based political organizations attended by Church officials increases.

Hypothesis 2: As the number of arrests increases, the number of meetings of community-based political organizations attended by Church officials does not increase. (revised draft pp. 3–4)

Truth table terms: P = increase in repressive acts
                    Q = increase in collective action
                    p = increase in number of arrests
                    q = increase in number of meetings (revised draft p. 4)

Virginia also doubled the length of her concluding paragraph, the most notable change being her suggestion that the empirical test approach that she had learned in the Theory Construction class might not work. If the empirical tests do not "allow choosing one knowledge claim over the other," she states in her final sentence, "then one possible solution would be qualitative data collection: i.e., the use of such research methods as interviews, surveys, or participant observation. . . ." This final assertion was hers alone, and did not appear in Dr. Johnson's feedback to her.

Virginia finally received a passing grade on this paper and strong support from a professor who looked like a potential mentor. Nevertheless, she believed that the way of knowing that was promoted in the department's core theory courses pushed students to distance themselves (their biases, personal values) from their objects of study, in essence to remove themselves to the extent possible as sentient human beings from the research process. Knowledge could then be represented abstractly and quantitatively so that it could be compared, tested, publicly critiqued, and perhaps added to the discipline's body of knowledge. Perhaps because of their sparse backgrounds in sociology, some students like Virginia felt constrained, even trapped, by the core course emphasis on what they felt was a dehumanized way of knowing a very human sociological world. They missed the engagement with issues involving real people: women, minorities, immigrant cultures, and families. They witnessed their thinking being shaped by the language and practices they were exposed to, yet felt somewhat helpless to explore other ways of knowing for reasons of time (of which there was none), pragmatics (the need to get through the coursework), and resources (the absence of other kinds of researchers in the department). The department, for its part, was small, and admitted having limited resources. It had opted to specialize in some types of sociological research and not in others in order to graduate PhDs who were competitive in a job market that held scientific ways of knowing in high regard. Given these restrictions to this very serious game, it might still have been possible for the department to demonstrate from early in the core course sequence how issues of gender and ethnicity could be encompassed in a more human way within some kind of scientific framework. A move away from the strict hard science model of knowledge, on the other hand, would have allowed the department to draw more easily on the cultural and ethnic resources within its own graduate student population. As it was, these resources were overlooked.

Students' decisions to stay in the program or to leave thus hinged on a complex array of personal and pragmatic factors. In Virginia's case, many layers of conflicts having to do with language, mentoring, and ways of knowing contributed to her decision to leave. Dr. Johnson, for example, left the university at the end of that year. That fact, plus Virginia's new more assertive role in assessing the ways of knowing in sociology as evidenced in the conclusion to her Theory Construction paper helped her realize by the end of the year that the sociology at this university was not her kind of game. A third factor that fed into her decision was her recognition of who the powerful and prestigious game players were in this broad community of "scientists" and her increasing sense of discomfort at imagining herself playing a contributing role (Ivanič, 1998) on this team. In the final section of this case study, I discuss Virginia's perceptions about who the powerful players were.

The Power Game: Who's in Charge and Who Contributes?

When phrases like "knowledge produced by the academy" (e.g., Bazerman, 1987) are used, we are led to ask what the composition might be of this prestigious group that has the privilege of shaping a discipline in quite fundamental ways. As recognized some time ago by Bazerman (1981), Popper (1979), and Olson (1980), among others, this group consists of a discipline's writers and researchers—those who are published and whose publications are incorporated into a field's "archives." If we view writing as a "social and collaborative act" (Bruffee, 1983) and genre as a social as well as textual phenomenon (Kress, 1993; Miller, 1984; Winsor, 1999), then a field's publications can be thought of as joint productions of writers and the colleagues who exchange ideas with them. The academy of knowledge producers, then, would consist of the community of people whose publications influence the field or subfield and the colleagues who contribute to the knowledge that finds its way into print.

Clifford Geertz (1983) described most effective academic communities as "not that much larger than most peasant villages and just about as ingrown" (p. 157). He claims that the relations among the individuals in these "intellectual villages" are not only intellectual, but also political, moral, and personal. Students in doctoral programs will eventually be obligated as part of the dissertation process to align themselves with one or more of the power groups in their settings, both for the short-term pragmatic purpose of completing the program and for the longer term purpose of forging professional alliances. However, the nature of this developing relationship with the profession is not fully understood.

Some scholars, inspired by the work of Paolo Freire, have described the relation between an academic community and the students it serves as that of the oppressor and the oppressed. In one argument that results from this view, politically oppressed students need to master the discourse of the academy in order to be able to understand critically, and thus resist, its oppression in the academy's own terms (Bizzell, 1982, p. 196). A different argument on the same problem says that minority students need to be educated in their own languages—to "use their own reality as a basis for literacy" (Macedo, 2000, p. 21). Although both these arguments may seem too extreme for some, it is still the case that part of the enculturation process in a PhD program involves learning to recognize who's who in the field, learning to speak with them in their language (as Virginia put it), and eventually making decisions about which intellectual village one wishes to pay taxes in. Once the decision is made, students then need eventually to shift their role relationships from that of student to those of contributor and participant—roles that include resistance—and to participate in the community's practices with increasing authority (Blakeslee, 1997; Ivanič, 1998; Penrose & Geisler, 1994). In the social sciences, novices making such decisions need to achieve enough political awareness to have a sense of which subcommunities are the most influential or interesting or intellectually and ethically compatible with their own developing beliefs and values and which ones they may actively wish to help change (Benesch, 1996, 2001). This is not an easy task when numerous intellectual traditions exist and when the novice has little background or experience in the field, as was the case with most of the minority and foreign students in the sociology program in this study.

Many new graduate students will probably not recognize their own potential as a resource for the academic community. Blakeslee (1997) found in her study of Bouzida that even students at the end of their PhD programs may find it difficult to take on an authoritative role as contributor. Rather, they will attempt as did many of the students in Virginia's cohort to develop a relationship with the profession on the community's terms and to learn to play by its rules as a survival strategy for completing an academic program. In some cases, this means shifting the goals they have on entering a program. Like a number of other students, Virginia had decided to pursue a PhD in sociology so that she could gain the knowledge, skills, and prestige to be able to return to neighborhoods and schools she was familiar with and make a difference in people's lives. She felt particularly committed to the plights of women and ethnic minorities and wished to find ways to better understand and alleviate their difficult lots in life. She needed an authoritative voice to be able to do this. It was thus understandably problematic for her to see the relevance of learning how to identify basic assumptions in a theory, to "convert knowledge to ps and qs," and how to trace the development of a theory over time.

But added to this difficulty was Virginia's gradual recognition that the people she was most interested in were grossly underrepresented in all aspects of the sociology she was learning: in the faculty in the department, in the theories they read, in the field's best journals, and in the issues that were discussed (cf. Margolis & Romero, 1998, discussed below). In the third week of the program she said only, "I have some reservations, but I don't know where it's coming from." By the middle of the academic year, she had gotten the sense that theoreticians constituted a powerful group within the field and that there was something unbalanced about the gender, ethnicity, and focus of this group:

> I'm more skeptical [than last quarter] about the place of theory in sociology, um ... who determines what a theory is, who writes theory and what is the theory about, um [long pause] I think I'm looking at it in terms of a race issue. Most—I guess almost all of the theorists we heard about were White males.

One particular example left Virginia quite puzzled. In Dr. Adam's class, she had chosen a topic for her Theory Analysis literature review (a paper and an oral presentation) on collective violence—a topic that had been approved by Dr. Adams from a choice he had provided on a handout and that she assumed would deal to some extent with populations in the third world, particularly Latin America. But to her surprise, there was nothing in the bibliography that she had been assigned to read that was either written by a Latin American scholar or that was on the topic of Latin America:

> One thing that struck me as I was reading all the literature that was assigned to me for this presentation was that there was no mention of Latin America at all. And this was a theoretical program on collective violence. And there was no mention of Latin America.

She thus took this to be a good starting place for her next writing assignments (a paper in Theory Analysis and her project in Theory Construction) since this seemed to be a fruitful arena for research. Indeed, she received positive feedback from both professors on her choice of topic, and was pleased to be investigating a topic that interested her, in spite of the paucity of studies listed in the bibliography handout.

Nevertheless, Virginia found herself questioning the way she was required to treat her topic in both theory courses—analytically, abstractly, and logically, according to guidelines prepared by two White male professors who had been trained more than 30 years before in the Talcott Parsons school of thought. Both professors, for example, commented to Virginia in written feedback about her needing to "press harder in the future for more analytical power in conceptualizing the problem," but did not appear to take an interest in her personally, as had Dr. Johnson in helping her revise her Theory Construction paper. When she eventually did complete the assignment on which she had received an incomplete, she confessed to me that she believed that grades were based less on hard work and creativity than on students' ability to complete the assignments according to the recipes of the professors. These recipes, Virginia came to believe, were the products of a sociological world run by White middle-class European and American males, "theorists," as she called them.

When Virginia began the program, she had been somewhat skeptical about the people she labeled "the theorists"—who they were and what they were doing, but was "willing to give them a chance." By this she meant she was willing to "be open to their message," and to learn how theory was constructed. But by the middle of her first year, she was fairly certain that this group did not speak to her concerns:

> Well, um ... I found that through the long process of how theories develop that it's very elitist, it focuses on just a few theorists who get published, who come from certain schools of sociology, so ah ... My views have changed. I've become a little bit more closed minded.

This view of who controls what work gets done, how it gets done, and what gets published, and her perception of who was left out of the process, contributed greatly to Virginia's decision to leave the program with just an MA (granted to departing students if they completed the first year of required work in the PhD program) and persisted after she left the program and returned to New York. After having had 8 months away from the program during which to reflect on her experiences, she said with assertiveness and confidence in a taped response to a questionnaire that I sent her in New York that:

> [t]his university's sociology is scientific and formal. My opinion about doing sociology in this way is that I think that it's an elitist way of doing sociology. It's um, especially when you don't combine the scientific and the formal with the informal, the normal, everyday language that is needed to communicate with people outside of sociology. So I find it elitist, um, very exclusive way of doing sociology.

Some months after returning home to New York, Virginia took a job as a research assistant in a small nonprofit Puerto Rican educational organization in Brooklyn. Her experiences there put her in touch with the people she wished to work with and help. Yet she felt a great deal of frustration at not being able to use some of the skills she had acquired the year before. From the inside, this time, rather than from the outside, she felt the need for something more—for further training that would give her a more influential and authoritative voice in what was being done. Having stepped into a world where being "elitist" gave one a voice, she agonized over where she might fit in. In a letter written a year after she left the program, she commented, "I understand why I felt alienated, (. . .) but I have not figured out whether the experience means I should do (study) sociology, or I should do sociology at that university."

In correspondence with me over the ensuing years, Virginia continued to struggle with how to define herself professionally, with what further education she might pursue that would be more relevant to her interests in culturally diverse and underprivileged populations yet that would still give her an influential voice, and with what discipline-specific language, practices, and values she felt comfortable with. Of one thing she was certain: "Having a masters in sociology is not enough to get people to listen to the ideas of a young Puerto Rican woman."

Hence, wishing to add an authoritative voice at a more practical level within the power structure in the world of social science, she decided 2 years after leaving her PhD program with a masters degree to accept the offer of a scholarship for a second masters in social work at an East coast university. Just 25 at the time, with many years ahead of her in which to educate herself even further if she one day chose to, Virginia had opted to leave the theorists to their work and to move ahead with her own more concrete, here-and-now agenda. She completed that degree and moved into work in women's and family counseling. By the time I saw her in New York in 1999, she had moved to Manhattan and begun her new job as a counselor at Mt. Sinai. I overheard part of a telephone call she made in response to her beeper, which had gone off as we drank coffee and chatted in the staff cafeteria. From the wall phone in the cafeteria I listened to a confident and competent young woman participating in an important conversation about the health and well-being of a real person. She seemed to be very good at this new and serious game and to have finally found a professional home.

Uncomfortable Games and Partial Enculturation

In her first and only year in the doctoral program in the sociology program, Virginia was not participating in the practices of professional sociologists. Had she stayed, she probably would have joined one or more research projects, as did Prior's (1998) Moira, and associated with students who were beginning to publish and present papers at conferences. She might also have continued to develop alignments with one or more faculty within or outside the sociology department with whom she felt more comfortable than she did with the two theory professors, such as Dr. Johnson, had he himself stayed in the program. She did in fact feel a bond with her statistics professor, a young untenured man who had confessed to me in an interview that the language and thinking of the old guard theory professors were at times beyond his comprehension. He himself had not yet published in the field's most prestigious journals, and students I spoke with guessed he would not get tenure in spite of his popularity as a teacher.

But Virginia's academic life was split from her personal life to a degree that could not be bridged without more mentoring like that she received from Dr. Johnson. Her own decision to leave the program, however, and to rethink and reshape her academic and professional identities indicated that her sense of agency and intentionality were strong. The act of leaving itself was one that helped her regain a sense of coherence and purpose in her life, enabling her to begin constructing a new biographical narrative (Giddens, 1991; Linde, 1993; Polkinghorne, 1991) for herself in a new setting. She learned that games of language, knowledge, and power can be played in many different ways and that some of them could comfortably suit her.

Ten years after Virginia left her sociology PhD program I came across an article on the experiences of "women of color graduate students in sociology" by Margolis and Romero (1998). Virginia's experiences at the uncomfortable game of disciplinary enculturation resembled those of the women in this study. The authors titled their paper from a quote by one of their 26 questionnaire and phone interview informants: "The Department Is Very Male, Very White, Very Old, and Very Conservative." Their paper does not focus on literacy practices per se but on the "hidden curriculum" in the graduate sociology departments from across the United States that they claim works to reproduce inequalities of race, gender, and class in addition to producing professional sociologists. However, literacy practices, as can be inferred from the case study of Virginia, cannot be separated from other practices, such as who gets funding and which students get mentored, since literacy practices are implicated in these other activities. All these aspects are part of the larger academic literacy game. Minority women, as Margolis and Romero learned, may find themselves struggling on a hostile academic playing field where their literacy practices, as a result of a hidden curriculum, are not nurtured.

Briefly, the women informants in the Margolis and Romero study (Native Americans, African Americans, Asian Americans, and Latinas) told the authors about overly competitive and discriminatory practices among students in their departments. They spoke of systems of ranking, lack of mentoring for some students, stereotyping and stigmatizing of the women in various ways such as assuming they were affirmative action students, students' tendency to blame themselves for the problems they were having, the lack of interest in their programs in research interests that were practical and political rather than theoretical, and loneliness and isolation. As did Virginia, they also noted the paucity of courses and readings that dealt with gender and race. The voice in the quote that follows could have been Virginia's in its reflection on the "silences" in the graduate curriculum:

> The message is that U.S. sociology (that is sociology from a White, male, middle-class, and heterosexual perspective) is the legitimate form of sociology—others are either illegitimate or less valuable forms of knowledge. As one student concludes:
>
> > I mean it was like saying that all the thinking in the world comes from Europe. People in other parts of the world don't have ideas. Your experience as a person of color isn't really reflected in what you study and what you learn.
>
> (Margolis & Romero, 1998, p. 21)

Margolis and Romero learned from the women they interviewed some of the ways they resisted the hidden curriculum of their programs, and as Ortner (1996) noted, found "slippages" in the game rules that enable their resistance. Like Virginia, they worked hard to maintain strong links to their home communities. They also challenged research that had been done on their own communities, finding contradictions between theory and practice. They brought in guest speakers, took classes outside the department (as did the students in Virginia's cohort) and fought to have departmental resources allocated fairly (p. 25). Like Virginia, many of these women were from working-class backgrounds. Unlike Virginia, they were not fresh out of undergraduate school, so perhaps had more mature senses of identity and direction. They were committed to surviving in and helping to transform their graduate environments. They were not helpless, nor were they victims, in spite of the inequalities and their dissatisfactions. Past sociology students in the program I studied likewise helped transform Bernstein's core theory course through their insistence on a less narrow approach to doing sociology, hence the changes in the course in the semester I observed it. In contrast, at the time she left her program, Virginia did not perceive herself as someone who could contribute to change in her program or as someone who could approach the more powerful players in the department to ask for more substantive mentoring of the kind she received from Dr. Johnson. What she did do, however, was to express in her final paper to Bernstein the need for more qualitative studies in sociology. Her voice was small, but it was a voice.

To the extent that academic literacy games are defined by powerful players who are not in touch with the diversity within their own departments and fields, by language and tactics of exclusion rather than inclusion, and by ways of knowing that define narrowly what the games consist of, players like Virginia and those studied by Margolis and Romero will find it uncomfortable to become team players. In the case of Virginia, at least, it was the university team's loss and the Mt. Sinai team's gain.

CHAPTER REFLECTIONS

In this chapter I have explored but not resolved questions about what happens in doctoral programs as students go through the unsettling and sometimes exhilarating process of learning new academic literacy games. These involve unfamiliar language, ways of knowing, and roles and relationships of power among players, and often require that students paradoxically both adhere to convention and pursue complexity, skills of critiquing, and originality.

In the published studies that I reviewed and in my own case study, doctoral students were constructing identities in the face of such unfamiliarity and paradox, often being portrayed as immersed in practices that would ultimately transform them into legitimate participants in their communities of academic practice. However, as Margolis and Romero (1998) point out, graduate programs require that students construct new professional identities but they provide little in the way of concrete assistance in helping students make the leap from other-directed student practices such as taking courses and qualifying exams to self-directed research practices needed by professional members of a discipline (p. 7). Identity transformation takes place over time as students build portfolios of "real" work (Reynolds, 1994) and find their way into research projects and teaching assistantships and engage in informal associations with classmates and professors. But this transformation remains partial in the school setting, as Blakeslee (1997) found with the student she observed in physics, Dannels (2000) with students in mechanical engineering, and Freedman and Adam (1996) with students in public administration.

As the case studies in this chapter show, academic literacy practices, interwoven as they are with other social practices in graduate departments, play important roles in shaping new identities of students, many of whom eventually figure out often with much attendant discomfort how to play and survive the game and how to resist being absorbed by academic cultures and subcultures that at first seem intimidating and impenetrable. Some students like Virginia figure out through their literacy experiences when to quit playing one kind of game and move on to another. However, the game of redefining the self is no zero-sum matter. If the doctoral students in the Margolis and Romero (1998) study can be taken as in any way typical (other studies on academic identity such as that by Ivanič, 1998, suggest that they were), students probably never lose the identities they bring with them to programs in spite of periods in which they may flounder and take on the voices of others. Their multimembership in different communities of practice in ways that are more or less central or peripheral (Wenger, 1998) probably ensures that students at times feel fragmented, pulled in different directions, resistant at times and compliant at others. From this perspective, identities are always in the process of being constructed—a "constant becoming" as Wenger (1998) phrased it. Donna Haraway (1988) suggests that "the knowing self is partial in all its guises, never finished . . . ; it is always constructed and stitched together imperfectly . . ." (p. 586). The search for identity (personal, academic, professional) is thus a search for coherence, not completeness (Giddens, 1991; Linde, 1993; Polkinghorne, 1991; see the discussion in Chap. 7).

Using Ortner's (1996) framing (see Chap. 1), the doctoral students I discussed in this chapter were all learning to redefine their identities by playing or resisting the serious academic games demanded by their graduate school settings. As Ortner (1996) notes, game players, even subalterns, are both construed by the game and influential in changing the game, even in small ways (p. 20). Moreover, as is the case in social life in general, games players exist in webs of power relationships that continually get renegotiated within the loopholes of local power games. In the graduate school setting, the traditionally defined literacy practices of reading and writing could not be disentangled from concrete and local relationships and contests of power, from competition with self and others, and from multiple personal influences. However, in the studies I reviewed in this chapter, success and failure could not easily be distinguished since growth and change happened uncomfortably through bungled as well as successful attempts at participation in literate practices and in Virginia's case, through her eventual realization that she did not need to be trapped into one kind of game. Ortner's game construct within her theory of practice, grounded as it is in the concreteness of particular events, privileges the agency of the players, the subaltern in particular (unlike the theories of practice of Bourdieu and Giddens; see Chap. 1), and helps us see Virginia's case as something other than a case of failure to be enculturated. It also helps us see that Virginia, Nate, Moira, and the women of color in the Margolis and Romero (1998) study were involved in multiple identity-shaping games involving gender, class, and race in interaction with text-based genre games. As Ortner would no doubt concur, learning to identify the multiplicity of games expands game players' choices and thus their agency, including the decision not to play.

ACKNOWLEDGMENT

I am grateful to "Virginia" for her involvement in the third section of this chapter and, as always, for her continued friendship.

5

Juggling and Balancing
Games of Bilingual Faculty

PERSONAL REFLECTIONS ON MULTILINGUALISM

It is very easy to say that anyone teaching language (first, second, foreign, ...) should have experienced what it is like to study a language in addition to one's mother tongue. This advice probably comes across as humorous to a European audience, which routinely not only studies but uses more than one language. In the United States, people understand much less readily the normality of the rest of the world's multilingualism. In the United States, we have to argue repeatedly and persuasively why it is in our interest to know more than one language. This argument becomes increasingly difficult when we limit the discussion to academic contexts, where the language of most journals, international conferences, and electronic communication is English (Swales, 1997).

But in my case, and I think I am not unique, learning a language other than my mother tongue (Spanish well, French less well, survival Japanese), and then having to teach my mother tongue to speakers of other languages, more than anything else in my life have helped me understand my own language and culture more deeply than had I remained monolingual. What I don't know is what "studying another language" means to others, or what level of proficiency a person needs to reach in order to begin to see oneself in expanded ways—ways that help prevent ethnocentrism, for example, or that expose for awe and appreciation the mysteries and miracles of language. I am guessing that one needs more than a year or two of high school French, but I don't think one has to become fully bilingual, whatever that hotly contested political and linguistic term means. I do think that one needs to study enough of another language to be able to perceive that language (and hence one's own) as a whole system, remarkable in its own ways for how it solves the problems of communication and expression for its users.

I also think that it is useful to learn enough about another language to be able to perceive the differences between eloquent and uninspiring uses of that language, a perception that, to me as a non-English major who never studied literature, has helped me see English with new eyes. It is how speakers and writers use language, not the language itself, that is beautiful or clumsy. For both first and second language users, this is optimistic news. Monolingual or multilingual, we can all become competent and even extraordinarily effective users of at least one language. Bilingual and multilingual language users can appreciate this miracle concretely. I for one am astounded at how many people become competent academic users of a second language at such a high level of academic and technical expertise that they can read, write, present, and publish in that language. How many mother tongue English speakers who teach writing, literacy skills, and language teacher education can do this? I know even some second language educators who are competent in no language but their own native English. And how many of us disregard or are unaware of the challenges our diverse populations of students face in our language and content classes, and the related sociopolitical dimensions that some of them encounter later as they move on to higher levels of schooling or return to home countries to teach or work using more than one language?

I recall with some discomfort a time many years ago when I thought I wanted to become a teacher of high school Spanish. I had studied Spanish in high school and college, and a couple of years later found myself in an MA program in Spanish. I had nearly finished the program when I moved to an education department in the same school that allowed me to focus on linguistics and second language education. Fortunately, I was in the Spanish program long enough to experience what it was like to study at the graduate level in a language not my own. Most of my classmates in the small program were native speakers of Spanish, and as such they comfortably dominated class discussions during which I sat attentive but silent. I read the texts slowly (all Spanish literature) with the aid of a large Cassell's dictionary, and had to satisfy myself most of the time with good but partial comprehension. I wrote papers even more slowly, without any sense beyond what I knew of writing academic papers in English (not much at that time) of what was expected. I passed with As and Bs, not sure why, and not sure of how to improve. Although I had been introduced to the rich literature from Latin America by Argentinean Sra Cambas in my intermediate Spanish course at the same school, I had little connection with it in my graduate program, where all that we studied in the major sequence of courses focused on different eras of Spanish (not Hispanic) literature, beginning with the Middle Ages. Our only professor was a Spaniard trained in religion and Spanish literature, passionate about the vast cultural knowledge he wished to share of his beloved country. He lectured nonstop, my attention distracted from *El Cid* by the small white flecks of spittle that formed in the corners of his mouth. Still, my comprehension of spoken and written Spanish soared. In spite of these successes, it was not until long after I left the graduate Spanish program that I discovered Gabriel Garcia Márquez, Jorge Luis Borges, and Isabel Allende in the original and that I was able to hold my own in philosophical arguments with Sra Cambas, now Profesora Emerita, in her mid-80s, and still dancing the tango.

When I consider what it took to get me to the point where I could pass graduate classes in Spanish (3 years in high school, 2 years in college, 1 year of intensive intermediate-advanced), I am awed by what my undergraduates, graduate students, and colleagues are trying to do in their second languages. I need to reflect back more often than I tend to on how I felt as a foreign language user in a class full of native speakers. I wonder now, had I finished an MA in Spanish, whether I could have survived a PhD program in a Spanish-medium setting. Could I have learned to write and publish academic articles in Spanish, as many of my nonnative English speaking colleagues do in English? In spite of my advanced proficiency in Spanish, I cannot conceive of being able to do this. My hat is off to all who try, not only to all who succeed.

I imagine there might be a few English mother tongue readers of this chapter who have not studied a second language in much depth and who are not involved with issues of multilingualism, multidialectism, or multiculturalism in their current teaching or learning. I cannot predict whether the issues and stories from this chapter will resonate with them (Conle, 1996). But the stories should resonate if such readers have any colleagues, classmates, or students in their academic settings whose mother tongue is not English. Some of those teachers and learners may plan to stay in an English-medium setting or to establish academic careers in host or home countries where they will be using English. The stories in this chapter—literacy autobiographies and case studies—may affect monolingual readers' understanding of the challenges facing colleagues, classmates, and students as they develop and practice their evolving academic literacies in languages other than their mother tongues. I wonder, too, if taking the perspective of outsider on occasion helps insiders perceive some of the complex linguistic, social, and political nature of their "insideness," and so see their colleagues, classmates, and students in a new light. I believe this happened with me and culminated with my experiences in Japan, where as an illiterate outsider I was privileged to get to know several Japanese colleagues who published far more than I did *in English* (see the third section of this chapter). I saw myself and them in new lights and found truth in neither perspective. I hope that all readers, monolingual or multilingual, will take courage from these stories for themselves as well as be reminded of the problematic notions of insider and outsider in the discoursal construction of academic identities and the playing of academic literacy games.

PUBLISHED STUDIES

In the mid to late 1990s and into the 21st century, interest and curiosity has begun to grow about how professional language education scholars deal with issues they faced in learning to write for publication (Casanave & Vandrick, forthcoming), and how bi- or multilingual scholars in particular manage to live and work using languages other than or in addition to their mother tongues (Belcher & Connor, 2001; Braine, 1999a, 1999b; Canagarajah, 1996). The challenges are daunting. For example, sociolinguistic studies of published research articles are beginning to reveal the extraordinary rhetorical and linguistic resources that effective academic writers employ. Effective writers know how to position their work within a field in their article introductions (Swales, 1990; Swales & Najjar, 1987); they know how to guide readers' interpretations of a text through strategic uses of metadiscourse (Hyland, 1998); they can employ politeness strategies that work to promote their own ideas without threatening readers (Hyland, 1996a, 1996b; Myers, 1989); they are able to cite the work of others in ways that help them forge alliances and promote harmony with some and distance them from others (Hyland, 1999; Paul, 2000); and in general they are able to use language to position themselves strategically in relation to their fields and their readers in ways that represent their community's values (Hyland, 1997, 2000). They also understand the social and political nature of responding to reviewers, editors, and coauthors and of the need to negotiate, compromise, and revise multiple times in order to bring a piece of writing to print (Berkenkotter & Huckin, 1995; Flowerdew, 2000; Myers, 1985; Ochs & Jacoby, 1997; Sullivan, 1996). They wrestle with power-infused and entrenched academic cultures, where marginalized faculty that include women, part-timers, and untenured teachers risk being excluded if they don't play their academic games in a savvy way (Cayton, 1991; Fontaine & Hunter, 1993; Geisler, 1992; Kirsch, 1993; Thompkins, 1987), yet some find ways to break with convention and still participate in academic conversations (Bishop, 1997a; Bridwell-Bowles, 1997; Villanueva, 1997).

In the case of bilingual academics, all of these linguistic, social, and political practices must be enacted in writers' second languages. Hugh Gosden (1996), for one, has shown how difficult it is for novice Japanese researchers to write an article for publication in English. Even bilingual scholars

who have spent many years in English-medium settings may not comprehend or be able to use to their advantage the many interwoven layers of social, linguistic, and political aspects of writing for publication (Flowerdew,
2000, discussed further below). Moreover, bilingual and multilingual scholars from Third World countries may also be constrained by material short-
ages (books, paper; Canagarajah, 1996) to say nothing of reliable access to
Internet resources. In spite of these challenges facing scholars from around
the world, and in spite of the unfair dominance of English as the primary
language for international publication (Pennycook, 1994; Phillipson, 1992;
Swales, 1997), many nonnative-English speaking authors are finding their
way into print in English-medium outlets.

As trends in scholarly writing have increasingly opened to more reflective and personal styles, bilingual authors are beginning to enlighten English-speaking audiences with insights into their bilingual backgrounds and
experiences (Belcher & Connor, 2001; Braine, 1999a; Connor, 1999; Kubota,
1999; Li, 1999; Liu, 1999; Lu, 1987; Shen, 1989). Questions abound about professional identities, cultural affinities and alignments, and culturally influenced game rules that are adapted, changed, and resisted by practicing
professional academics. I discuss three published stories here, one case
study of a novice academic writer, "Oliver," in Hong Kong (Flowerdew,
2000), and two literacy autobiographies published in George Braine's
(1999b) collection of essays by nonnative-English speaking language educators, those of Xiao-Ming Li (1999) and Ulla Connor (1999).

Oliver

John Flowerdew has explored the experiences of Cantonese academics in
Hong Kong who publish in international English language refereed journals
(Flowerdew, 1999a, 1999b). In his case study of Oliver, a bilingual scholar
just starting a career as an assistant professor at a Hong Kong university,
he takes a closer look at the problems, strategies, and perceptions of a
young academic as he struggled to bring one article to print in his major
field of communication (Flowerdew, 2000). Using a framework from Lave
and Wenger (1991) of legitimate peripheral participation, Flowerdew examined the roles of a local editor, a journal editor, an in-house journal editor and reviewer, and Oliver himself over several months of negotiating,
editing, and revising. Through analyses of interviews and e-mail communications with Oliver and the local editor, communications from the journal
editors, and drafts of Oliver's papers, Flowerdew documented Oliver's fence-
riding journey as a competent but rhetorically naive and not quite native-
like academic writer from the initial accept-with-revisions letter from the
journal to the appearance of the article in print.

Flowerdew tells us that Oliver had a great deal of exposure to English from childhood on, including studying at English-medium elementary and second schools, a bilingual education in English and Chinese at a Hong Kong university, and all graduate work (MA and PhD) in the United States. During his graduate study in the United States he was thoroughly immersed in an English-language environment both in and out of the university. Oliver himself told Flowerdew that both Chinese and English were his native languages, although in some interviews he referred to himself as a nonnative speaker of English. In his PhD program in mass communications, Oliver worked closely with small groups of colleagues and a faculty mentor who provided both academic and personal support and who commented on all drafts of papers written by Oliver and other students. Oliver had published several single and coauthored papers with people from his PhD program, some of whom he was still working with from his new academic home in Hong Kong.

At the time of Flowerdew's study, Oliver was under a great deal of pressure to publish an article in a refereed international journal in time for it to be considered in the review for his contract renewal. Flowerdew (2000) notes that—unlike the case for the bilingual scholars I worked with in Japan (see the third section of this chapter)—"tenure and promotion in Hong Kong are dependent upon publication in international refereed journals" (p. 34). Because most journals in Chinese are not refereed, publication in English is essential. At the same time Oliver was also preparing for his dissertation defense, teaching and preparing a teaching portfolio for his review, and working on several other articles.

Like the two young bilingual scholars in my own case study, Oliver found it easier to write academic material in English than in his native language. He attributed this fact to his graduate education in the United States, which included not only a great deal of writing but also research methods courses. Still, his academic English did not seem to be fully native-like. Oliver knew that journal editors reacted negatively to manuscripts that had a nonnative flavor. He himself had gotten such comments, and given his bilingual status resented somewhat having this label applied to his writing. Oliver, however, was less concerned with language problems than with what he saw as a problem of being isolated from the mainstream academic and research community he wished to participate in. Being in Hong Kong, distanced from the centers of hot intellectual debate in his field, he felt he was losing touch. E-mail, he claimed, was no substitute for "direct conversation" (p. 136).

Oliver worked on the article used in Flowerdew's case study for about a year and a half. On his third try, after a rejection and a luke-warm response from a journal that could not publish in time for his review, Oliver received a positive response from a journal somewhat outside his field. What followed were 8 months of negotiations and revisions that involved some-times difficult communications with Oliver from journal editors and the lo-cal editor. The local editor, for example, believed that Oliver wanted him to edit the drafts independently, but soon realized that the paper needed more than superficial attention. Oliver, however, was not able or willing to consult at length with the local editor at early stages of revision. The pri-mary substantive revisions, then, were prompted by major structural and thematic changes demanded by reviewers and editors of the journal. Noting "that an immense editing job had to be done" (p. 139) the journal ed-itor several times gave Oliver a chance to (hinted that he should?) bail out and submit the article elsewhere, but Oliver persisted. In the ensuing months, the in-house journal editor changed nearly every aspect of the pa-per—its focus, its organization, its length, the language and phrasing of nearly every sentence, and even aspects of the content.

Flowerdew views these negotiations as part of Oliver's legitimate periph-eral participation in communities of scholars who publish and whose arti-cles inevitably blend voices, content, and language from multiple sources. The extremes to which the journal editors went to help Oliver shape his ar-ticle to fit the journal's style and purpose seem unusual, but perhaps under-standable given the editor's early commitment to publish. In spite of the dif-ficulty of the process, Oliver became more aware of the rhetorical nature of writing for publication through this experience, noting that in future writing he would need to pay more attention to the focus and style demanded by particular journals and less to his own attachment to particular content (p. 143). Flowerdew notes too that as a nonnnative speaker living far from dis-course communities that could have afforded him face to face interaction with scholars in his field, Oliver could not be considered a full member of his target discourse community (p. 146). However, many aspects of the pub-lishing "game" (p. 145) played by Oliver will probably resonate with anyone who tries to write for publication (Casanave & Vandrick, forthcoming).

Not fully explored in Flowerdew's (2000) study is the rich multicultural and political nature of Oliver's case. For instance, we have the impression from the case study that a rather well-defined "target discourse commu-nity" (p. 146) existed that Oliver needed to accommodate to—a questionable assumption. Further, Flowerdew's suggestions for how to help bilingual scholars like Oliver publish in international journals imply that it is the non-native speakers who need to do all the learning and accommodating—that "editors, reviewers, and the academic community at large . . . have a duty to facilitate and optimise such learning" (p. 147). Teachers of academic writ-ing, too, can assist nonnative speaking scholars by "bringing together ap-prentice professionals to share their experiences and reflect together on their ongoing legitimate peripheral participation" (p. 147). Certainly Oliver and other novice scholars must understand the rhetorical nature of professional academic writing games, and assistance from journal editors and reflective colleagues plays an invaluable role in this enculturation process. But novice scholars, no matter what their mother tongues, also need to understand that one of the purposes for publishing is to add their own voices to authoritative conversations in a field, and thus help change the field and its practices. I wanted more reflection in this article by both Flowerdew as researcher–author and Oliver as participant on Oliver's evolving identity as a scholar with a potential for authority and agency but as one caught in a political game with gatekeepers at his university and with the journal(s) to which he was submitting his articles.

Xiao-Ming Li

Xiao-Ming Li is herself a bilingual academic, as familiar with the rules of good writing in Chinese as in English, as her study of the responses to student writing of two Chinese and two American teachers shows (Li, 1996). Written up as a book that tries to unravel what "good writing" means in Chinese and American cultural contexts, the study familiarizes us with the perspectives of two Chinese and two American teachers through their written commentary on personal narratives written by Chinese and American students and through additional interview data. The book itself, she tells us, will also be published in Chinese, presumably translated by her. We learn something about her in this book too, partly through her own narrative history brief as it is, and partly through the stance she takes in her analysis. We also learn about her in a later publication in which she traces her journey from her role as a shy mentee of Donald Murray, who taught her about voice and risk and encouraged her first publication, to a battle for tenure at a university with her book, *Good Writing*, at the center of the playing field (Li, 1999).

Li tells us that she was from a family with "an impeccable revolutionary past" that then fell victim to the abuses of the Cultural Revolution from 1966 to 1976 (Li, 1996, p. ix). Later, when the country had stabilized under the leadership of Deng Xiaoping, she received a scholarship to study in the United States. Li described herself as a good writer in the Chinese context. As a teenager, she was encouraged by the praise her writing received from her teachers and often had her writing read aloud to the class, an honor given to the best students. She eagerly looked forward to her teachers' written comments, which regularly noted her essays' good structure and fluency of language (p. xi). Readings were used as models of ideal texts, and students' essays were analyzed in terms of those models: "We were told that without the form, the content would have no body, and without the content, the form would have no soul" (p. xi).

Li (1996) found later that in her American university she was confused about how to write, what to write, and how to improve. She reports in *Good Writing* about getting mixed messages about being specific but subtle, being both too vague and redundant, and being told to write whatever she wanted yet knowing some topics were valued more than others (p. xii). When she herself became a writing instructor as part of her graduate work, she was not sure of how to respond to students' writing, finding the criteria for good writing "elusive" (p. xii). She came to see the standards for good writing in American English as "hidden rather than displayed" unlike in China where her teachers were "more willing to openly admit their power over students" (p. xii).

In spite of these differences in the transparency of criteria in her experiences in China and America, Li asserts that

> all parties share the conviction that the standards of good writing, which are meted out through grades and comments, are entirely objective; a good piece of writing is a good piece of writing—pure and simple. My experience in two cultures, however, shows me a different picture: what is "good writing" is a messy and complex issue, anything but pure and simple. (p. xiii)

Her study explores some of this messiness from the rare perspectives of both insider and outsider in both countries. On her return to China to conduct her dissertation interviews, she was treated with the respect of a foreign visitor. In the United States she was always considered Chinese. When interviewing her two Chinese informants, she questioned them from a base of knowledge and values that she had acquired in her studies in the United States. When interviewing her two U.S. informants, she constructed her questions with the practices and values in mind that she had learned in China. By the end of the study, she was not sure who she was, since she was able to view herself as both "us and them" and as neither "us or them" (Li, 1996, p. xiii).

As a writer in graduate school, Li blossomed under the tutelage of Donald Murray within the safety of the classroom–home setting (Li, 1999). Fascinated by English idioms, she wrote a class paper on this topic, turning it in to Murray for "correction," which he doggedly resisted doing: "What makes the piece interesting, he insisted, is your unique accent, a different perspective, and a different style and voice. And he asked why I should want to sound like an U.S. writer" (p. 49). She explained that Murray helped her understand the concept of voice, which enabled her to view writing as more than emulation ("ventriloquism"—how she characterized her past activity as a writer for Party propaganda in communist China; p. 49). This paper became Li's first publication, a newspaper item in *The Boston Globe*.

Other mentors urged Li to conduct dissertation research that drew on her unusual position as both insider and outsider to two very different cultures, and later to revise and publish this dissertation, which she did. In describing this process, Li refers to her "dual identity" (p. 52) that allowed her to play one set of values and conventions off against another regardless of the setting she was in (cf. the cases of Fan Shen, 1989, and Min-Zhan Lu, 1987).

After graduating, securing a position at a university in New York, and publishing her book, Li continued struggling with issues of identity. "As a non-native speaker of English who teaches English in an English speaking environment to ESL and native students alike," she tells us, "my cultural and linguistic identity is questionable, and so is my professional credibility" (Li, 1999, p. 43). Much to her surprise, the one piece of evidence that should have provided Li with the professional credibility she needed for promotion from assistant to associate professor "created a crisis that almost destroyed [her career]" (p. 52): Her book on *Good Writing* was rejected by the review committee as unscholarly, impressionistic, and unscientific, even though it was an ethnography that should never have been judged according to "positivist standards" (p. 53). With the help of well-known people in the writing community, strong reviews of her book by people who understood ethnography, as well as the nomination of her book for a prestigious award, a faculty review committee and the dean reversed the rejection and awarded her both promotion and tenure.

As a bilingual academic now working in the United States as an English professor, Li continues to struggle with notions of identity and with questions about how to represent herself in her published writing (Li, 1999, personal communication at the Conference on College Composition and Communication). She cannot answer most of her questions since doing so would require clarity and simplicity of vision and absence of dissonance and political interests. She found that academic writing games, and the positioning of self as an academic writer within one, to say nothing of two, cultures, are characterized by none of these.

Ulla Connor

Ulla Connor's journey from Finland to the life of an academic in the United States, like Xiao Ming Li's, took place over many years with the help of several key mentors and colleagues (Connor, 1999). As portrayed in Connor (1999), with the exception of one very low point after failing PhD qualifying exams in comparative literature, her rise to the position of a prominent English language voice in the second language education field seems less anguished than Li's development as a bilingual academic writer even though her literacy autobiography is filled with reflections on differences between Finnish and American English academic writing.

Connor talks of getting a great deal of detailed assistance with her writing in English from the earliest stages of her masters thesis from a Finnish linguist-mentor such that the strong voice that resonates in that document was not her own, but his (p. 31). Later, in a PhD program in comparative literature, she had no mentor in a program that seemed also to have few guidelines and resources to support students' learning. Devastated after failing her oral exams in that program, she left the school and taught as an ESL K–12 instructor and as a teacher of Swedish for 3 years, abandoning academic pursuits altogether. However, she eventually found herself in a PhD program in Education and English linguistics that suited her need for explicitness and precision. This program, she relates,

> taught me new skills in statistics and research design and the orderly, coherent writing of research. An empirical research orientation with a strong education foundation gave me explicit models of good research and good writing for the first time. I adapted them with zeal. (Connor, 1999, p. 32)

She also married a supportive American husband who was himself a good academic writer and regularly sought editorial help on all her academic writing from him and others. In this regard she embraced writing as an openly social practice. Her confidence in herself as a writer of academic English grew along with her increased proficiency in general English and her experience writing papers for her classes. Her first publication was a coauthored paper with one of her professors.

Later, as an assistant professor at Georgetown, Connor worked toward promotion and tenure. This process is often wretchedly difficult for people who are working in their mother tongues as well as in second languages but we do not get a sense of anguish in this part of Connor's journey from her published story. Rather, she speaks of learning from Deborah Tannen how enjoyable writing could be, and how indeed she gradually learned to find writing rewarding (see the case of Yasuko, Chap. 2). She also relates the fact that she received many rejections of her applied linguistics papers when she submitted them for publication, and that some reviews mentioned her "nonnativeness" (p. 33), a comment that Flowerdew's (2000) Oliver also made. However, we do not learn the details of what she experienced or felt in response to these rejections. We can only guess that either Connor bounced back quickly or that there are more personal aspects of the development of her academic identity that she did not include in the public document (see the story of Judy in Chap. 6). We do learn that the most rewarding researching and writing experiences happened in interaction with trusted colleagues who themselves were researching and writing. She explains that now she publishes more than most of her English-speaking colleagues, noting that "[p]erhaps that is because I have never been shy to ask others to read my drafts and comment on them" (Connor, 1999, p. 36).

Connor's confident sense of self as a U.S. academic writer was solidified during her sabbatical in Finland where she was assisting some Finnish researchers in the preparation of a grant proposal for a project that itself culminated in a booklet in Finnish on how to write grant proposals in English. Connor wanted the booklet not only to explain about conventional rhetorical organization in English but to demonstrate it in the writing style of the booklet itself. She found the first draft written by her Finnish colleagues incoherent:

> My point was that the book described how U.S. English writing differs from Finnish writing; therefore it was important to show how to state the main thesis at the beginning, giving examples and providing transitions, and repeating the main points. The Finnish researcher assistants disagreed. (Connor, 1999, p. 35)

In spite of her suggestions, the final version did not reflect any of the major changes that Connor had suggested. Moreover, the Finns found her oral presentation style to be typical of what they believed was the norm in the United States. Rather than calm and measured, Connor appeared to them to be "hyper, out of control, an amusing curiosity" in her dramatic use of gestures, tone, and facial expression (p. 36). After this experience, Connor saw herself in a new light, with a transformed identity as someone thoroughly immersed in and comfortable with U.S. academic culture. Still a Finn by birth and upbringing, she was not part of the Finnish academic writing culture, which "let[s] the reader create order" (p. 35).

Oliver, Ulla Connor, and Xiao-Ming Li, all bilingual, all educated at the graduate level in the United States, differ greatly in their enculturation experiences and in their senses of identity and comfort within their academic settings. They seem to have been participating in very different communities of practice, communities that were constructed not just by external disciplinary norms but also by the personalities that participated in them and their varying modes of participation (Wenger, 1998). Their differences highlight the impossibility of referring to "bilingual academics" or "multiliterate academics" as a coherent singular group (Belcher & Connor, 2001; Braine, 1999b). Their stories also testify to the importance of locally situated enculturation experiences in shaping the discoursal self. Oliver happened to have an article accepted in a field somewhat outside his primary community, interacted in depth with several editors, and as a result was obligated to recognize the importance of professional academic literacy as a rhetorical and social practice. Xiao-Ming Li happened to find her herself in a small community of scholars that included Donald Murray. Ulla Connor found herself the second time around in a PhD program that provided exactly the structure, guidance, and assortment of colleagues she needed to establish an academic home. In each of these local communities the game rules and advice from coaches differed.

But personality, too, no doubt affects a writer's predilection for preferring one kind of playing field over another. We don't know much about Oliver's personality, but do know that he received some good mentoring in his U.S. PhD program and that he was also somewhat unprepared for the vagaries of the publishing game as a young bilingual faculty member. We can glean a bit more from the literacy autobiographies of Connor and Li. Connor seems attracted to the orderliness of much of the research in contrastive rhetoric and relies on contrastive rhetoric to help explain the differences she observed in Finnish and English academic writing (Connor, 1996). The fact that as a new graduate student Connor found the doing and writing of research to be "orderly and coherent" and that she continues be comfortable with a "direct Anglo-American" style as opposed to the less "reader-friendly" style of the Finns (p. 34) might reflect an aspect of her personality that thrives on system, precision, and explicitness as a means of solidifying her identity. In fact, much research in language education is not as tidy as the paradigms that Connor learned from, as she knows from several forays into more qualitative playing fields. It seems that she found a way (or ways) to locate herself in a subcommunity within a very diverse academic culture that did not force her to confront so much of the uncertainty and tension faced by many other academic writers who write in both their first and second languages such as Li (1996, 1999). She made this survival strategy work to her benefit and found a secure community of like-minded scholars who could work together to further each other's contributions to a knowledge pool in second language education.

This systematic approach sets her apart from scholars such as Li, who had far fewer explicit guidelines and models to follow in her enculturation experiences such as those provided by quantitative research. I get the sense from Li (1996, 1999) that the most influential experiences took place in a much more open and free-wheeling playing field in the presence of Donald Murray and others who encouraged experimentation and resisted intervening. Although Li is at an earlier stage of her career than is Connor, I have trouble imagining Li being on a journey that has a clear and attainable destination. Connor, in contrast, portrays herself at the "end of a journey" after her sabbatical writing experience in Finland that helped clarify her identity as a "U.S. writer." Xiao Ming Li is less certain of her identity and will no doubt spend many more years trying to figure out where she is positioned and how she will label herself. Like another bilingual scholar who publishes mainly in English, Ryuko Kubota, Li may use her writing and teaching experiences in the future to try to interrogate her identities, her beliefs, and the cultural and linguistic assumptions in a field that is susceptible to stereotyping (Kubota, 1999).

In short, the rules of the game seem much clearer to Connor than they do to Li, while Oliver's understanding is located somewhere in between.

There is truth to be found in all their stories and in none of them. Each young academic writer faced a challenge unimaginable to monolinguals, that of becoming scholars in communities where their main work of written communication and knowledge production was conducted in a second language. Each dealt with the confusions and conflicts they encountered in different ways, constructing for themselves different identities as bilingual academics and telling different narratives. Oliver's is a story of dislocation, Li's is an in-process story within her community, and Connor's is an arrival story. Li's is a narrative of uncertainty; Connor's is one of system and security. Excerpts from Oliver's much more sparsely told and more event-focused story convey a sense of growing rhetorical awareness. Li and Connor, by publishing their literacy autobiographies, achieved a kind of coherence in the construction of their academic identities that is not evident in the case study format used by Flowerdew (2000) to tell Oliver's story. In all three cases, however, the discoursal selves that are portrayed are partial, including only what the authors choose to reveal and only in the ways that they choose to interpret the raw data of their lives (Li and Connor) or of someone else's life (Flowerdew's Oliver). From the autobiographies we can gather that Li and Connor have played their academic literacy games according to different rules in interactions with different kinds of team players even though both reside in university communities of language and composition educators. What would Connor have made of Li's academic enculturation experiences, and what would Li have made of Connor's? What would a more complexly layered look at Oliver's literacy history have told us about how his academic identities shifted from those associated with student roles to those associated with professional roles? In all three cases, what would more interweavings of social and political aspects of the writing games they were learning have revealed about their evolving identities? In the next section, I address some of these questions by looking at some transitional academic practices, attitudes, and identities of bilingual academics at a university in Japan.

CASE STUDY: THE JUGGLING GAMES OF BILINGUAL FACULTY[1]

When I moved to Japan in 1990 to teach undergraduate English at a new branch campus of a Japanese university, I had already been interested for some time in how graduate students acquire academic literacy and develop an identity within a community of scholars. It was not clear to me at first what aspects of this interest I could pursue in my particular undergraduate

---

[1]Adapted from Casanave, C. (1998). Transitions: The Balancing Act of Bilingual Academics. *Journal of Second Language Writing, 7*(2), 175–203.

setting, until I realized on perusing our faculty profile book that a rather large number of faculty had been educated at the graduate level in the United States or Canada, and that some of them were continuing to publish and present papers in English. I learned from native English speaking colleagues at other universities that they too knew a number of bilingual faculty and that some of my native English-speaking colleagues knew Japanese well enough to be able to write and publish in Japanese. I began to wonder how bilingual faculty managed the transition from the writing life of a graduate student in one country to the writing life of a university faculty member in another country, and how they established identities as scholars in two different linguistic and cultural environments. What were their writing lives like, and how did they manage what I imagined to be a dual existence? How was it possible for a Japanese member of the faculty, with teaching, committee, and project work at the Japanese university, to participate in both Japanese and English worlds of academic writing? These are some of the questions that motivated a long-term interview project with several Japanese university faculty members in which I examined the roles that writing plays in the lives of the informants. As is the case in the rest of the this book, I view writing broadly as a socially and politically negotiated game-like practice, situated within complex environments where interpersonal relationships, identities, specific practices, and local contingencies—as well as artifacts that include actual pieces of writing—interact (Lave & Wenger, 1991; Prior, 1996, 1998; Wenger, 1998).

In this study, I am interested in learning about what kinds of transitional writing experiences, in English and Japanese, several bilingual Japanese scholars had after they returned to work in a Japanese university with a graduate degree from a North American university, and about their perceptions of the role of writing in their lives. I do not intend to frame this study as a cross-cultural comparison. The ideas that the four people in this project shared with me and that I retell are in no way intended to represent generalizations about either Japanese or North American culture or even about the lives of academics. The portrayals are primarily my reconstructions of the stories of two key informants, and less centrally of two other individuals, who are working at one Japanese university. As is the case with all qualitative research, I urge the readers of this chapter to reflect on the issues in light of their own experiences in different sociocultural academic contexts and to make connections and comparisons where appropriate.

Setting

All of the participants in this project worked on the same campus—a new branch of an old and well-known private Japanese university from which all of them had also graduated with masters degrees or, in one case, a PhD. Just over 50% of the faculty on this campus had also graduated from one of the university campuses. About one fourth of the faculty on this campus had done graduate work outside Japan, primarily in the United States. At the time of writing, all but about 8% of the 100 or so faculty members were men, and all but three of the tenured faculty were Japanese. (A PhD was not required for tenure, which was granted as part of a full-time position.) According to faculty annual reports, many faculty published in English (about 25%) as well as in Japanese (about 75%), and about one third attended several conferences per year. The foreign-educated faculty in particular attended many international conferences. My own position within this setting at the time the research was conducted was that of tenured Associate Professor, a post I had held since 1990. I was teaching undergraduate English content courses, writing, and applied linguistics seminars. I had picked up survival level Japanese and could consult minimally with students who could not speak English. I could read some basic *kanji* in addition to the two syllabic *kana* systems of writing, but was functionally illiterate. The following case study was conducted in English.

Participants

To locate participants, I first sent a letter of invitation in English to all faculty on our campus who had received graduate degrees in North America (approximately 25 people), information that was available in a Faculty Profile booklet. Five people responded positively to the letter and agreed to a series of interviews and to share some of their writing with me. One of the five later dropped out of the study. My primary informants were two of the younger faculty members, Mr. Fumihiko Kubo and Dr. Minami Sasaki,[2] both at the university on 3-year research associate contracts that involved minimal teaching duties. They were still finishing up dissertations or joint papers with dissertation advisors in the United States. At the same time, they were also starting to get involved in one or more projects in the Japanese setting and were looking ahead to finding a permanent job either on this campus or elsewhere. It was this transitional period that I was interested in learning about. We met over a period of about 2 years.

Mr. Kubo was in his mid-30s when we first met. We agreed to use first names with each other.[3] He had a warm round face, and a gentle, enthusiastic manner that people around him found quite engaging, and expressed

---

[2]All names are pseudonyms. Certain other background information has been altered in the interest of confidentiality. Samples of their published writing, much of which was coauthored and which could potentially compromise confidentiality, are not included in my account.

[3]I refer to all four of the people who participated in this project by title and last name, even though I was on a first-name basis with three of them. I hope to recognize their status at the university, where Japanese faculty often refer to each other by last name + *san* (or + *sensei*, for older well-respected faculty).

himself easily in native-like English. His father was also an educator. His family had spent some time abroad while his father did research—in Hawaii when Mr. Kubo was an infant, and a full year in Iowa when he was 10. For many years he had written a great deal in Japanese—journals, diaries, essay-type letters to friends. In his MA program in Japan, he had read economics articles in English. He also had attended an MA program in the United States in the field of communication before transferring to his PhD program at Rutgers, where he was currently still enrolled and trying to finish up a thesis in Communications from his base in Japan. He mentioned after our first several interviews how difficult it was to allocate time to his dissertation, particularly given how much he was enjoying his interactions with students and in helping them learn to write and in making inroads into a specialized academic community in simulation and gaming. He also noted that he appreciated our interviews in that they gave him the chance to clarify his thinking about his research topic, his problems with his dissertation committee, and his identity, which he saw as in transition. His personal involvement in the interviews, as well as his interest in writing, contributed to his willingness to spend time talking on a regular basis. We met seven times, for about an hour each time, usually in my office (his choice).

Dr. Sasaki, a rather tall, lanky, high-energy young woman, was also in her mid-30s when I began this project. She wore tiny glasses that either slipped nearly to the end of her small nose or hung from her neck on on a chain necklace-style. On days when she was not teaching she dressed casually and wore her long hair pulled back and fixed with a big plastic clip. When I met her in her office she usually had several computers going and at least one student research assistant hovering about, all paid for with research grants she had been awarded. Her English was fluent and clear, but accented. She had developed an interest in English very early, and in high school it was her favorite subject. As an undergraduate, she had an American female friend in Japan from whom she learned a great deal of English. She spent one summer in the United States, but had no other early travel experiences. Her grandfather had been an English teacher, so there were many English books in her environment as she grew up. She also helped her father, a university professor of medicine, translate some of his articles into English, editing them with the help of her American friend. In her MA program in Japan, she had done a great deal of reading in English in anthropology. When we began our interviews, she had just finished a PhD in anthropology at a good university in the United States where she had transferred from another U.S. university, and was still connected with her advisor and with a colleague with whom she was writing papers.

She radiated an intensity that distinguished her from the more easy-going Mr. Kubo. She was involved in many different research projects at the same time, with both Japanese and U.S. colleagues, and often referred to how much pressure she was feeling to finish them and get working on new ones. She rarely mentioned her teaching. Like Mr. Kubo, Dr. Sasaki also seemed to thrive on the opportunity to discuss her work and her work-related problems with an eager listener, and I looked forward to our talks as well, finding solace in intellectually interesting and in-depth conversations with one of the few women on our campus. In addition to our substantive talks, she occasionally requested my help in proofreading her English when she was getting ready to submit something for publication. Her persona did not fit the stereotype of the meek and modest Japanese woman. She had a strong personality and was an incisive and critical thinker. We met nine times, usually in her office, and were on a first-name basis from the beginning.

Two other faculty members, both male and more well established, participated in this project somewhat less centrally. Dr. Mitsuhiro Matsuyama was in his late 30s when we began our interviews. He was one of the first Japanese faculty members I had met when I first arrived at the university and had been helpful in getting me settled in. We were on a first-name basis from that time. A graduate of a Japanese university at the masters level, he had been hired in his present job as a tenured associate professor, although he indicated that his career was still in transition. His PhD in Industrial and Labor Relations was from the a midwestern U.S. university and he had taught in North America for several years before returning to Japan. Short and round-faced, always ready with a smile, he radiated a cheerfulness even when he discussed problem areas. He had spent many years in the United States, beginning as an exchange student in high school, seemed fully bilingual in English and Japanese, and was married at the time to an American. We met once on campus before he left for a 1-year teaching position in the United States. From his post there, we conducted two e-mail "interviews." Dr. Yuji Ishii, a tenured full professor, was a tall, quiet man who, judging from his calm demeanor and apparent enjoyment of his professional and personal activities, seemed more settled into life at the university than did the other three informants. He was in his early 50s, had a PhD from our university in Japan, but two masters degrees from two different universities in the United States, one in Communications Research, and another in Law. His interests included not only culture and communication, but journalism (an early career pursuit) and piano. His English was very fluent, but he claimed not to be fully confident in his writing, so often enlisted the help of a paid editor to help polish his publications. We met four times in my office. I referred to him as Ishii-san and he called me Chris.

Data Collection and Analysis

The primary data for this project come from taped interviews over a 2-year period (1994–1996) during which I took detailed notes, filling the notes in later with selected quotations from the tapes. Most of the tapes were later transcribed in full with the help of research assistants. I prepared three interview guides, which I used for the first three semistructured interviews with all participants (see Appendix E). The first interview covered the informants' general academic and language backgrounds, their writing backgrounds in Japanese and English, and their current writing habits and activities. The second interview focused on the contexts for writing, and on the participants' attitudes toward writing and publishing. The third interview dealt with more detailed views of writing and publishing processes. In all subsequent interviews (one with Dr. Ishii and several with the central figures, Mr. Kubo and Dr. Sasaki) I asked the informants to update me on their ongoing writing projects and to discuss any relevant issues that they had been dealing with. All interviews lasted 45 minutes to 1 hour. As I got to know Mr. Kubo and Dr. Sasaki better, side discussions on other personal and professional issues helped build collegiality and trust. All material within paragraphs in quotes is taken directly from the interviews.

I met with the two key informants at least twice a semester over a 2-year period, and once a semester (or by e-mail) in the cases of Dr. Ishii and Dr. Matsuyama. I hoped to capture a sense of their writing activities over time, and given that it takes many months, even years, to complete a major piece of writing, this timing of the interviews seemed appropriate. I also collected copies of some of the written work in English and Japanese by all the participants, but did not analyze their writing, this kind of analysis not being directly related to my inquiry. Also, as I mentioned in a footnote, analyzing coauthored work presented a problem of confidentiality. However, the interviews were sequentially linked in many cases by references to ongoing pieces of writing.

Later, as I reviewed my notes and relistened to tapes, relating what I was learning to my own experiences and my current understandings of life in the Japanese university we all worked in, I began to construct the themes that I discuss in this chapter. The themes are not mutually exclusive; unavoidably, they overlap and intertwine with each other, and aspects in one reappear in others. I then shared an early draft of the paper with the three informants with whom I had met most frequently and who were on campus at the time (Mr. Kubo, Dr. Sasaki, Dr. Ishii) as a way to check my interpretations of these issues. However, as with all qualitative data of this type, other issues and themes could no doubt be identified and highlighted. I therefore do not consider my interpretations definitive, but in-progress.

Finally, as is the case with other research of mine in this book, I recognize that what I present here is really my own story about the stories of the people I spoke with. As such, the discussion represents to some extent my own issues, interests, and interpretations, no matter how faithfully I have tried to put myself in the shoes of others.

Balancing and Juggling Games in Japanese and English Academic Writing Practices

In what follows, I look at the academic communities and practices of the informants, in particular the two younger scholars, as best I can from their perspectives, knowing that my reconstructions of their narratives are imperfect and incomplete. They told me something about how they had learned to write in Japan and in the United States, discussed their attitudes toward writing with me, talked about their experiences learning to write for publication, described some of the connections they had made in their fields and how these connections worked, and reflected on their changing identities.

Learning to Write in Japan and the United States. One of the similarities among all of the participants in this project was that none of the four had taken a single writing course either in Japan or in the United States (Leki [1992] noted that the United States is one of the few countries of the world where people take classes in how to write.) Mr. Kubo described himself as self-taught, and both he and Dr. Sasaki claimed that what they learned early on about academic writing in Japanese and English was gleaned from the reading and translating they had done. Both had written papers in their Japanese undergraduate and Japanese MA programs, but had not received feedback on them. They commented that papers were sometimes not even returned, and Mr. Kubo wondered if professors had even read them.

As a graduate student in economics in Japan, Mr. Kubo read many articles on economics in English, as well as in Japanese. He quickly became aware of the specialized technical jargon of economics, and felt determined to "translate" some of the difficult technical concepts into easier language in his own writing in Japanese. As a result, his Japanese writing style in his MA thesis was criticized as being appropriate for a general audience, but not for a specialized one. Later, Mr. Kubo found in his U.S. doctoral program that the field of communications was less "rigid" than that of economics in the sense that there was less specialized vocabulary and more flexibility of style and presentation in writing. He commented that the writing he did in his PhD program in the United States was "freer" than that in his Japanese economics MA, more related to his own interests, and based on a looser model than that in economics.

Still, his first experience writing in the U.S. graduate school context—an MA program in communications before he transferred to the more flexible program at Rutgers—was both "awful" and "memorable." Having little idea at first what was involved in writing just a five-page paper, he described waiting until the last minute to do his reading and writing, and finally writing first in Japanese, then translating to English. Although there was a consultant to help students with writing, Mr. Kubo had no time to see him. He received a "C" on that first paper, but also a great deal of feedback from his professor on what he had said and how he had said it. This feedback, he claimed, was invaluable in helping him learn what was expected on academic papers. He began writing directly in English in his second semester, but also increased the number of statistics courses he took as a way to lessen the burden of writing. The only experience that Mr. Kubo had that might be considered instruction in academic writing was in his pre-Rutgers U.S. MA program, where he had taken an influential proseminar course that was designed to help students "get used to the discipline" of communication. In this course, students were required to look to journals as models for audience and format for their own papers in the class. The professor also was explicit about formal conventions ("because he used to be an English teacher," Mr. Kubo explained):

> He was very strict in how many inches we should have in margins and what to underline, and what not to underline. I think that was helpful because I had never done that during my first two years in the U.S. In the communication field, we follow APA style and right now I'm quite aware that many of the publication manual or guidelines mention the APA manual guidelines, particularly for the references. [...] In that particular course, he was very strict and every paper we submit, he'd check the small details, and the styles, put the right marks on it. So, I began to be aware of that style. (Mr. Kubo, Interview 2)

One of the most valuable experiences for Mr. Kubo was to coauthor a paper for publication with an advisor in his U.S. MA program. He generated his ideas in a first draft, and his advisor, by restructuring the draft, provided him with a template that helped him understand "how parts go together and what parts get elaborated." Commenting about the writing he had to do later in his PhD program, Mr. Kubo said that the PhD program encouraged "free form" writing, not writing based on formalities and models, as was the case in his U.S. MA program. He also attributed his increased comfort with this less structured writing to continual practice, his growing maturity, a greater sense of belonging to his department and graduate school, experience in the U.S. culture, and his contacts with other people in his immediate environment, all of which he believed changed his writing and thinking in both English and Japanese.

As for Dr. Sasaki, she claimed that two powerful early influences on her graduate level writing in English were the models supplied by her reading, and the work she did translating and editing (with help from her American friend) her father's medical articles. This latter work helped her learn how to express nuances of meaning in English. By the time she started her PhD program in the United States, she was told by professors at both universities she attended that she was a good writer—one who got the structure right and who made only small language errors. She attributed this to having captured an acceptable genre style as a result of imitating published papers. But as was the case with Mr. Kubo, perhaps the most influential learning experience for Dr. Sasaki was coauthoring a number of papers with her advisor related to the research projects that her advisor was doing, parts of which formed the basis for her thesis. In fact, her advisor pushed her to publish in conjunction with her thesis work. Typically, Dr. Sasaki would write the first draft, and receive extensive feedback from her advisor. This process, she claimed, taught her a great deal about academic writing. Moreover, she wrote continuously in graduate school, doing almost nothing else, and, from her third year on, had begun doing conference publications and publishing coauthored papers in established English language journals in anthropology. Such experiences familiarized her with the critical review process common to these journals. She claimed that her writing in Japanese, however, now influenced heavily by the expertise she had developed in English, had developed an inappropriate clarity and directness that resulted in part from lessons she had learned about making all referents clear in English academic writing. Her Japanese writing, she observed, was thus far too redundant even for the academic reader in Japan, and she "suffered" when she had to write in Japanese. She stated that she preferred writing in English.

In fact, in early interviews not long after they had returned to Japan from the United States both Mr. Kubo and Dr. Sasaki both claimed to find writing in Japanese more difficult than writing in English. They said that the difficulties writing in Japanese stemmed from their awareness of nuances, subtleties, and ambiguities of meaning in Japanese. Mr. Kubo also commented on how difficult it was to balance the Chinese *kanji* with the syllabic *kana* for the proper stylistic effect. They both mentioned further that the structure, style, and audience are much more clearly specified in English academic writing than in Japanese, and that the patterns and rules made the writing easier.

As I gleaned from their descriptions, these young scholars learned to write academic English in the context of coursework and mentoring in their fields of study, not through instruction in ESL or EAP classes or through the help of writing consultants at the university. The work they were producing did not consist of practice pieces or simulations for the purpose of learning to write but graduate term papers and coauthored papers for conferences and publications. The extensive substantive feedback that they received on course papers and papers for publication contributed to their perception that their academic writing had quite clearly defined purposes, including:

to persuade (professors, and sometimes peers), to fit into a body of existing literature, to add to an advisor's research project, and eventually to add to an existing body of knowledge.

Attitudes Toward Writing. Once back in Japan, having "been raised on academic English" in U.S. graduate study, as Mr. Kubo put it, it was again a shock for the younger scholars to find that although there was pressure to write in Japanese, there was little clear sense of purpose to writing as they had come to understand it from their U.S. graduate studies. Mr. Kubo, Dr. Sasaki, and Dr. Matsuyama all mentioned how important it was to "write a book" in order to be recognized within the Japanese community (see the following section on Writing for Publication), but that the particular content did not matter. The participants did not suggest that they were expected to add to a disciplinary knowledge base, or even to write for an audience of specialized scholars. "Avoid too much jargon," Dr. Sasaki was told as she was preparing a book requested by her Japanese superiors, since the audience would be "general" as well as academic. Most often published by commercial presses via connections with individuals in professional associations, rather than by what are considered to be academic presses like those in North America, such works were side projects for the young scholars recently returned from the United States. Mr. Kubo and Dr. Sasaki noted little concern on the part of senior editors (usually senior faculty members at the same university) for dovetailing major research projects that the young scholars might be doing in English with particular research or writing projects being done in Japanese.

Mr. Kubo and Dr. Sasaki in particular, both of whom were still actively involved in writing activities with U.S. dissertation committees or colleagues, conceptualized their writing in English as a way to contribute to a disciplinary knowledge base. Recognizing that many outlets for writing existed in the English context, they felt the ideal kind of writing meant write-ups of research that would be critically reviewed and then selectively admitted to academic journals. These young scholars were discovering what young scholars in North America discover, that this process was not only highly competitive, but that it was also long and tedious, requiring a tenacity, and a commitment to international scholarship that sapped time and energy. Describing what they felt to be a different attitude toward writing in their Japanese context, they spoke less of scholarship in Japan or of contributing to a disciplinary area than of recognizing the need to align themselves with more senior colleagues who wished to involve them in their own projects, to write something quickly under their auspices, and to get it into print as part of the social and political expectations at the Japanese university. Making decisions about how to fulfill these expectations did not come easily. Mr. Kubo, who enjoyed writing in Japanese, said he often wrote personal journals and student newsletters, writings that would not really help him professionally in either Japan or the United States. He lamented not having sufficient time or self-discipline to fulfill more of the expectations he sensed around him.

The two young bilingual academics in this project, then, seemed to view their scholarly writing in Japanese, particularly at the early stages of their careers, as contributing to allegiance to groups at the university, and their English language academic writing as contributing to international disciplinary scholarship, two very different writing games indeed. Nevertheless, in spite of the strong commitment of Mr. Kubo and especially of Dr. Sasaki to contributing to international scholarship, they recognized that no matter how scholarly and original the work their publications in English did not count as much at this early stage of their careers as would Japanese contributions within the local context of their academic life in Japan.

Writing for Publication. As evidence of how important writing for publication was in the lives of the four participants in this project, they claimed to spend from 20% to 80% of their time in writing-related activities (e.g., preparing conference papers, pursuing grants, conducting research, writing reports, articles, and book chapters, mulling over ideas, and consulting with colleagues in person and by e-mail or fax about issues that arose while writing). These activities all were intended eventually to lead to publications. From graduate school days in the United States and from working on research projects and papers for publication with advisors there they learned the importance of the serious game of publishing in the lives of the people around them.

During the first year of interviews Mr. Kubo, Dr. Sasaki, and Dr. Matsuyama all expressed uncertainty about whether they intended to stay in Japan permanently or to one day seek a position in a U.S. university. All three therefore believed that they needed to develop a publications list in English. Mr. Kubo and Dr. Sasaki expressed more anxiety about this than did Dr. Matsuyama, who already had published a number of papers in English. Both used the expression "publish or perish" to describe their sense of the pressure and competition in the United States, where they saw their career success tied inextricably to the number and quality of papers they would be able to produce in the coming years. Dr. Sasaki in particular spoke of the "enormous pressure to write" in the U.S. context where she worked and studied, taking some consolation in what she saw as the strong support for academic publishing. Familiar with and committed to the critical review process, she felt determined to continue publishing in "first rate journals" even if she stayed in Japan. Like the others, she believed that innovative work that contributed to a field needed to be published in English in order to reach audiences of international scholars. As a recent PhD graduate and a relative newcomer to the Japanese community of scholarship, she described her sense of what writing for publication meant to her in the two settings:

> Dr. S: For me writing in English is particularly important, because in my field most of researchers— If you want your paper read, you have to write in English. . . . other nonnative speakers also write in English. And those journals, like most well read journals in our field [gives examples] are published in English even though it's published in Europe.
>
> C: What about in the Japanese context?
>
> Dr. S: I've heard different views, so since I've just come back it's kind of difficult for me to decide. [. . .] It's sort . . . Japanese academics in my field, it's sort of a closed society. They are not very international. I mean some of them are, but I think the associations, like [gives examples] they invite foreign speakers but usually they don't accept English written manuscripts. [My senior] doesn't discourage me to write English papers, but he told me I should write Japanese as well, for my promotion. (Dr. Sasaki, Interview 2)

Dr. Matsuyama, several years into his tenured job at the Japanese university but still very involved with U.S. connections, noted that he felt obligated to publish in English for two reasons. One was "to play the game" of tenure and promotion—since he was not yet sure whether his career would take him back to the United States and he thus needed to prepare himself to be competitive. The other was a sense of duty he felt to "help Japan," by "contributing to the scant research on Japanese in English." During a 1-year visiting position at a U.S. university, Dr. Matsuyama sent me e-mail to report that he was working on a paper and a book in Japanese, and six conference papers in English. "As you can tell," he says, "my 'writing life' has changed dramatically since I came to Illinois. I can devote 80% of my time to writing and writing-related activities. A BIG CHANGE FROM WHEN I WAS IN JAPAN" (caps Matsuyama's; e-mail, Feb. 1995). The communications professor, Dr. Ishii, well established in his Japanese university, likewise presented and published the majority (he guessed about 70%) of his work in English. English, he claimed, was "the language of international symposiums" that connected Japanese and non-Japanese participants.

But as Dr. Ishii noted, a bilingual scholar runs the risk of "weakening his reputation in Japan by too much international activity" and of "losing a strong foundation in Japan." He himself had struggled for many years to balance his domestic and international publishing, finding at this stage of his career that he was more sought after internationally than within Japan for contributions to conferences and books. Dr. Sasaki, particularly in the second year of our interviews, spoke often about pressure from her "boss" (a senior faculty member who was sponsoring her temporary post) to "publish in Japanese in order to become known in Japan." This man helped set up some opportunities for her to work with him on research projects and to publish, as a way for her to get her name into print alongside those of other senior faculty members. "I can't say no" to these requests, the two younger scholars told me, referring here to the political realities of the Japanese workplace (see the following section on Multiple Connections). As for local publications such as *kiyou* (university journals put together by a group of faculty members), student newsletters such as one that Mr. Kubo edited, and university news bulletins, these helped make an individual visible on the university campus (as did the regular TV appearances on news shows made by some professors). But these outlets were not held in high esteem by several of the people I spoke with, who believed that this kind of visibility—as is the case in the United States—would contribute little to their status within Japan. As Dr. Sasaki put it:

> I really haven't been here long [but] I think a lot of universities just care about numbers. I mean a lot of people write their own technical report published by their own school. And there'll be no review and you'll never have a risk of a paper being rejected. A lot of people do that. They just write it and publish it from their own school journal. [. . .] I wouldn't do it. (Dr. Sasaki, Interview 2)

To the younger informants, "real" publishing in Japanese meant publishing under the auspices of a mentor and an academic association (see the section on Multiple Connections). It also meant publishing a book, in the opinion of Dr. Sasaki and Mr. Kubo. As Mr. Kubo phrased it, the pressures to write for publication in Japan and the United States differ in emphasis. In Japan,

> They would think it's better to have more emphasis on writing a thick book, for example, rather than 10 papers. If you had the same amount of pages or spending the same amount of time, my impression is that publishing a real nice book and spending 10 years is worth writing a hundred papers in 10 years. I do think writing books are regarded as better, or more prestigious (Mr. Kubo, Interview 2).

However, writing in Japanese, whether papers for a Japanese conference or academic association or later a book, tended to distract the three younger scholars from their own research, most of which would be published first in English. This work had begun in the U.S. context and would perhaps later be transformed into Japanese. All four participants talked of time constraints in this regard, because preparing work for publication in English demanded much more time, with no guarantee of acceptance, except in the case of invited publications, than did preparing work for publication in Japanese. In the "no review no risk" publishing environment in Japan, as a young trilingual research associate (not part of this project) described it, it was possible to get things into print quickly, particularly if one was willing to publish in the wide variety of acceptable formats and genres available to

Japanese university academics, many by invitation (e.g., invited book chapters, newspaper and magazine articles, translations of books, project-sponsored monographs). Hence, in choosing what to write and publish in Japanese, the people I spoke with usually selected something that could be written up rather quickly and gotten to press without much revision, such as aspects of their work in English that could be summarized and translated into Japanese. This strategy allowed them to share internationally oriented work with the Japanese audience without having to do totally separate research projects and write-ups. Dr. Sasaki did this 2 years into her 3-year appointment, getting a book out in Japanese in time for it to be considered in her application for a tenured position at the university. Once it was done, she saw the value of this project in personal terms as well in that it helped her develop a vision of her overall purpose, which writing many shorter papers did not do:

> I did write the book, which was really helpful, but it isn't a research book. It's sort of an integration of— it really helped. Like I've done several papers, and when I write the papers the paper is very focused. And of course those different papers different projects are connected for one big purpose. But when you write only research paper it's kind of tough to get at that. So this book gave me a very good opportunity. To do that. To think about what my ultimate goal is. (Dr. Sasaki, Interview 7)

Several years after our project had ended, confirming what Mr. Kubo had told me early in our work, Dr. Sasaki mentioned to me that this book had been well received and that she now saw the publication of a book rather than articles in Japanese as the key to her securing a tenured position.

In short, a dilemma expressed by the participants was that publications in one language were not accepted by the audiences of the other. International publications in English added little to their prestige in the Japanese context, and publications in Japanese never left Japan. There was no time for these scholars to do parallel sets of projects and publications, yet they did not wish to forego publishing either in English or in Japanese. Letting go of the publications in English meant giving up any possibility of working in North America and of infusing international scholarship with what the participants felt strongly was a needed Japanese perspective. Letting go of the writing projects in Japanese meant possible loss of local reputation (or inaccessibility to a reputation), and subsequent isolation within the Japanese academic community. A solution in part seemed to be to write and publish in English, then to translate and synthesize selectively into Japanese.

Multiple Connections. Establishing effective networks of professional relationships was a central feature of the writing games played by the participants in this project. Well-connected scholars, they noted, had better opportunities to establish themselves through their writing than did those without those connections in both the Japanese and U.S. contexts, but they saw the connections as working rather differently. To oversimplify from the participants' experiences, in the United States, they felt that they would become known through their writing, and that connections to other scholars, writing opportunities, and jobs would build from this base. In Japan, academic writing happened most often through invitation. Hence, a rich network of connections had to be established first. For those young scholars who had not worked in a Japanese university and who had "been raised on academic English" in a PhD program in the United States, this came as a bit of a shock, or at least a concern, that required a major reshuffling of how they prioritized their time and activities.

Mr. Kubo, for one, who was working on his PhD dissertation on and off during the 2 years of our interviews, described the need for Japanese scholars to find their way into one of the many "academic associations" in Japan (e.g., in "societies" in fields such as communications, cognitive psychology, economics, and linguistics):

> I guess this applies to Japan, I'm not sure about the U.S. There's some key conferences or key associations that you should be in touch with. So whether or not you're accepted, there are some subcommunities within those associations, subdivisions, or interest groups, so I guess once you're accepted or you feel like you belong to that community, that kind of moves you to another stage of your academic career. (Mr. Kubo, Interview 2)

Within the association, he explained, there might be a clique of professors from the same university, so an initial invitation by someone inside the clique could assist with entry. Once inside an association, a younger member might be assigned some routine duties as a way to demonstrate allegiance, and eventually would be given a chance to present a paper at a meeting. A publication might then result if the senior members approved of the work. Because he was interested in establishing himself in a relevant association, Mr. Kubo had joined several Japanese and international subgroups in his field that were connected by e-mail, as well as a "New Books" group. Keeping track through e-mail and electronic discussion groups of association-related events and issues including dates and deadlines for conferences occupied much of Mr. Kubo's online time. Association membership within Japan played important connecting roles in the lives of the other faculty as well. Dr. Matsuyama was working on a paper at the invitation of an academic association he belonged to, one that was accepted at the time of invitation, before having been written. Revisions (not major, in the experience of Dr. Sasaki, another participant who had written for an academic association in her field) might later be requested by the association member who was editing a particular series.

Because of the key role of such initial local connections via senior faculty members in helping young scholars establish "visibility" (as Mr. Kubo put it) through association membership and find secure employment in the future, the two nontenured scholars I spoke with felt both obligated and torn by requests to participate in projects not related to their own work. Refusing might damage membership possibilities and job prospects, either at their present university or elsewhere in Japan should they decide to stay, in that jobs themselves were often secured through invitation and negotiation by key individuals in the organization rather than through open searches. Mr. Kubo and Dr. Sasaki thus needed to spend a great deal of time "networking" and complying with requests from senior faculty to participate in group projects set up by those faculty and to undertake committee work of various kinds in order to build a cadre of supporters that could open doors for them.

The participants' connections with people in the English-speaking academic context primarily centered around writing and conference projects with advisors and colleagues in the United States. In addition to coauthoring with her advisor, Dr. Sasaki, for one, was working closely with a small number of graduate school colleagues and faculty with whom she was collaborating on specific grants and research projects, all of which were intended to lead to conference papers and publications. The work had to be good, Dr. Sasaki stressed, and so required great care in preparation. Regular connections by e-mail, and often phone and fax, kept work in a constant state of revision as she and collaborators pushed projects forward. Once or twice a year, moreover, she met her coauthors and copresenters at conferences in the United States, thus renewing her face-to-face connections regularly. Mr. Kubo, too, traveled to the United States at least once a year to consult with his dissertation advisor. From his base in Japan, he worked by e-mail with his advisor and committee members, and found these connections essential to moving his work toward completion. He also belonged to an e-mail list that kept him in touch with his PhD program in the United States, including information on their brown bag lunches. During a difficult period when certain ties with his dissertation committee became contentious, he stopped work on his thesis until he was able to form a new committee, which he was able to do on a trip back to the United States. While not working on his thesis, Mr. Kubo spent many hours a week in e-mail discussion and news groups in English as well as Japanese, keeping current with ideas being circulated and with international conferences being advertised. Some of these discussions led to ideas that would then be written up for conference proposals. In one project, one of Mr. Kubo's professors from Rutgers had requested help starting an electronic journal, plans that involved ongoing e-mail discussions. However, as was the case for Dr. Sasaki (and for Flowerdew's [2000] Oliver, discussed earlier), e-mail was not a fully satisfactory way of staying connected. As Mr. Kubo put it:

> It's pretty interesting that some people would say only e-mail is sufficient. But to me, it's important and useful, and I do use it a lot, but still personally, I need to know that person's face, or how he or she talks, or what that person looks like. (Mr. Kubo, Interview 5)

The more established scholars also maintained a network of connections from their Japanese base (e-mail, fax, phone) with people who helped them in various ways to get work in English into print. Dr. Matsuyama, who was just establishing a professional reputation during the 2 years of our interviews, spoke of working relatively alone on his writing, in the sense that most of his work was single authored. However, he said he sent his English conference papers "to colleagues in the U.S., Canada, and Japan" to get suggestions for revisions and subsequent publication. He also noted that he had "submitted an NSF grant proposal with two researchers in the U.S., and worked quite intensively with researchers at the Japan Institute of Labor in Tokyo" (Dr. Matsuyama, e-mail, Feb., 1995). At that time, Dr. Matsuyama told me, e-mail was "not an essential part of my research work, unfortunately," and kept him connected with only about "half of my researchers." In the mid-1990s, his colleagues in Japan "do not use e-mail or are not equipped to," so he communicated with them by fax and international phone calls. Dr. Ishii, too, was well connected with people outside Japan. He routinely asked "American colleagues" to read his papers in English before he submitted them for publication, and, furthermore, paid a native English speaking editor to help him prepare the final versions. Dr. Ishii described how tedious and difficult, yet how important, it was to work closely with an English language editor in order to ensure that his ideas were communicated accurately in his English language publications. Dr. Ishii also had requests from people in Europe to contribute to publications there. Unlike in Japan, the participants had few personal connections to the editors of journals (other than knowing some of them "by reputation," as Dr. Sasaki noted), so the careful preparations before submitting papers to English language journals could not be avoided.

As described to me by all the participants, the writing contacts they had with English-speaking colleagues revolved primarily around the substance and processes of researching and writing. Even the advisor–advisee relationship (always political) that Mr. Kubo and Dr. Sasaki were still enmeshed in concerned issues in writing. Dr Sasaki, for example, was in the uncomfortable position of shifting her relationship with her dissertation advisor from one of student–professor to one of coauthor. She often expressed how difficult and frustrating it was deciding how to handle issues such as who would be listed as first author, who would draft and revise, and generally how to balance the work of preparing an article for publication. Although her credentials in one sense minimized their status differences, power inequities remained quite visceral for Dr. Sasaki, making her negotiations problematic.

The two younger scholars, however, did not describe many writing relationships with Japanese colleagues. Dr. Sasaki had just one ongoing and important relationship with a coresearcher and coauthor in Japan, but this colleague made her academic home on a different campus. Their descriptions of connections with their local colleagues concerned requests from senior faculty to do specific tasks on project and committee work. They saw completing these obligations to the satisfaction of the senior faculty as a type of political maneuvering that would help them gain entry into groups and build a support network, which would then provide opportunities later for writing. Regardless of how they worked, connections with specific people within and outside of Japan allowed writing and publishing to happen, and they all took a great deal of time. The people in this case study project thus needed to decide how to make connections of different kinds work for them, given their limited time, not whether to establish and use connections.

Writing and Identity. Part of the professional academic writing game involves establishing an identity as a member of a community of scholars or as is the case sometimes in Japan as a representative of a particular university. The process of constructing this professional identity begins in graduate school, starting with the identity of "graduate student" and gradually moving toward one of "novice sociologist" or other specialist (Casanave, 1990). Part of the process involves novice scholars' recognizing changes in how others perceive them and in how they perceive themselves.

Dr. Matsuyama wrote me in an e-mail interview from his year-long stay at a university in the U.S. that "my reputation seems to be clearly defined by what I publish":

> I now get calls from other universities in the U.S. to give colloquium talks. In most cases those who invited me have been exposed to what I publish. My writing (or publishing in general) has given me a strong international reputation which seems to be expanding. (Dr. Matsuyama, e-mail, Feb. 1995)

This perspective on identity is external in the sense that it reflects what others perceive. Dr. Ishii, too, claimed to have established an early reputation in a certain area as a result of an influential article published in English in 1980. Dr. Sasaki, by committing to writing only for "first rate journals" when she wrote in English, expressed the desire to develop a "focused international identity" as a scholar within her area of expertise. In Japan, however, she sensed that the identities sought by some academics resulted from their visibility as representatives of their universities in the popular media:

> To a large extent publicity is favored. It's more valued than in the United States. I mean a lot of professors are famous for that reason. You see a lot of them on TV or in newspapers more than on campus. I want to be respected in my field, and I want to my work applied to education, you know, so I don't want to write papers just for the sake of accumulating numbers. (Dr. Sasaki, Interview 2)

Mr. Kubo often mentioned the related phenomena of "visibility" and "fame" in his discussions of identity in Japan as being tied to who one knows and what university and organizations one belongs to, and in the United States as being tied more closely to the number and quality of one's journal publications within particular fields. He commented that in Japan he had observed how a scholar's identity shifted as that person climbed the "ladder" within an academic organization. Beginning as a novice member, the person is gradually given more responsibility within the organization, such as organizing conferences and helping editors with proceedings:

> So gradually you would become a member, or chief member, to support that association. I can see that's happening, even if I can't tell you about it as my experience, I can see their names like shifting, like first appearing in conferences and then appearing in the journal as an editor, or a key person who is organizing an assembly for the university, then become more of a chief member of that association. (Mr. Kubo, Interview 2)

In her Japanese setting, Dr. Sasaki found herself nearing the end of her 3-year contract "without an identity as a Japanese scholar" in the eyes of others and without the promise of a job for the next year. Not heeding fully her faculty sponsor's early advice to "get better known in Japan," she chose instead to immerse herself in the many long-term, grueling research and writing projects in English that she had already started and that were in various stages of completion. "Maybe I should have listened to him," she said, "but I didn't." Disliking intensely the political games required to make connections and become an insider in the correct Japanese circles, and complying only partially with the spoken and unspoken expectations, she continued to seek ways to gain identity as a Japanese scholar without compromising her goal of establishing an international identity through her work in English. One solution for her was to work with a small number of very good Japanese scholars both on and off campus, doing joint research and writing in both Japanese and English. Another solution toward the end of her 3-year contract was, at the request of a senior faculty member, to write a book in

Japanese for a series he was editing for the academic association that he belonged to as prominent member (see the earlier section on Writing for Publication). Dr. Sasaki was rather easily able to summarize various aspects of the work she had done in English, and submit the Japanese draft within a year. Her only revision involved making her Japanese less technical and more accessible to general readers. This publication, along with much political maneuvering and a strong record of international publishing and conference papers, helped Dr. Sasaki secure a tenured contract from the university just as her 3 years there drew to a close.

But identity is also a matter of self-perception, no doubt influenced in part by external labels and events. Dr. Sasaki, for example, viewed herself as a specialist in the U.S. context, and as more of a generalist in the Japanese context, personal academic identities that reflected the kinds of work and writing she was doing in each context. However, in our last interview, unwilling to identify herself either as a Japanese or an "American-based scholar" she said, "You know basically I'm kind of determined to choose what I write. I don't want to be a researcher who is always sort of running after somebody" (Dr. Sasaki, Interview 7). Most important for Dr. Sasaki was "being one of the current" people in her field.

Mr. Kubo's sense of identity changed greatly in the 2 years of our interviews, through a combination of events involving writing and political connections in both the Japanese and U.S. contexts. When we began our interviews, he still saw himself very much as a graduate student. He once spoke wistfully of the simpler graduate school days, saying that he welcomed academic breaks from his work at the Japanese university so that he could "recover his identity" as a graduate student by surrounding himself for days on end with books and papers. But over time, as he began having conflicts with his American advisor and as the dissertation work slowed down, he was becoming more involved with influential people and projects on the Japanese campus. He also became part of a specialized Japanese academic association that he believed he could contribute something new to, given his particular interests, and thus gain a reputation in his field. In one of our last interviews, he informed me that he had changed his dissertation committee, seen his first major writings in print, one in English (a coauthored book chapter with his advisor) and one in Japanese through his connections at the university, and—through personal connections—had landed a full-time job for the next year at another Japanese university. Although he still had to finish his dissertation, he now viewed this work as more connected to his evolving identity as a scholar than to his identity as a graduate student, and indeed, claimed no longer to see himself just as a graduate student. For instance, because he had been hired unconditionally for his new job, the dissertation no longer represented to him just a required research project in his role as student:

So it was quite interesting that all of a sudden I was trying to give different meaning, or a different position to writing a dissertation. Because it wasn't a conditional offer or something, they just gave me a position. So in a way I was relieved because the dissertation was no longer something that I have to do to get a license or something like that. It has to be something that I really want to write, or something that I really want to solve as my problem. (Mr. Kubo, Interview 9)

In sum, the game of shaping a professional identity seemed to involve weaving together internal and external representations of the self and reinterpreting and thus redefining one's relationship with what look to be, on the surface, stable aspects of an academic community (e.g., a dissertation already in progress, key players in an environment, an existing "stable" academic association). In the process of identity construction local connections as opposed to broad disciplinary concerns were central in both the U.S. and Japanese settings. However, in the Japanese setting, the social and political connections apparently needed to be built first, as a way to open doors for professional participation in general and writing in particular. In the United States, to the extent that the faculty I got to know were still actively writing, consulting, and visiting with colleagues there, connections in actual research and writing activities (admittedly social and political practices themselves) helped the participants develop work that then appeared at conferences and in publications. That work led in turn to a "reputation" that influenced how they saw themselves.

Conflicting Loyalties or Flexible Juggling?

Holding visions of academic worlds where writing practices and purposes required different kinds of "legitimate peripheral participation" (Lave & Wenger, 1991; Wenger, 1998), the people I spoke with in this project were trying to establish or maintain bifurcated loyalties. The younger and established scholars alike devised ways to juggle time, connections, and projects so as to be able to write in both Japanese and English from their base in the Japanese university. Let me now summarize some of the "loyalty" and "juggling" games practiced by the people in this project in their academic literacy practices, as I understood them from the stories they told.

1. Although the participants in the project made it clear that not all academic scholars in Japan do research and write, or do either one well (there being many different kinds of academic institutions, expectations, and outlets for writing in Japan), all claimed that in their cases, writing and writing-related activities were central in their lives, and helped define their lives as professionals. All wanted more time to devote to their writing projects.

2. For the nontenured scholars, the process of developing identities as professional academics who write in both English and Japanese involved moving from a relatively simple writing life as graduate student (consisting of a small number of people, tasks, and institutional constraints) to a complex writing life as a university teacher and researcher. In this more complex life, multiple institutional responsibilities competed for their time and energy on personal writing projects. The relationship between them and the people in the Japanese institution could influence their careers, and nurturing that relationship could take precedence over writing projects. Learning to weave one's personal writing projects into or construct them out of this complex environment required a major readjustment in both time and stress management, knowledge of clever ways to focus and dovetail work, and the development of political savvy for dealing with people in positions of power.

3. All four bilingual academics in this project seemed to feel that writing professionally in the Japanese and U.S. contexts differed. In the United States they felt it involved understanding how to present one's writing in the best possible light to critical readers with the goal of communicating effectively to an international audience. To this end, the bilingual academics in this project worked with collaborators, editors, and non-Japanese colleagues to produce pieces of writing that would be accepted by a critical audience, often working at a distance through e-mail and fax, and in person at conferences and during trips back to the United States. In Japan, it involved belonging to the right institution or association and knowing the right people, at which point opportunities became available to present and publish without severe criticism. The people in this project thus cultivated, to greater or lesser degrees, networks of contacts that helped them find their way into projects and environments that both supported writing and fulfilled institutional expectations. Communicating with an international audience in Japanese was not a consideration.

Once established in one setting or the other, whether in Japan or in some other country, if their commitments remain firm to continue writing professionally in two languages, the academic writers I spoke with are facing a lifetime of juggling and balancing the particulars of time, project work, and connections in the local contexts of their specific work environments, and of their specific professional environments outside Japan.

Lingering Questions

At the conclusion of this project, I found myself asking why the people in this project burdened themselves with the enormously complex and time-consuming task of writing academically in both Japanese and English. I do not have a definitive answer, but I believe that all four of them recognized that it was bilingual Japanese scholars such as themselves who would be able to communicate most persuasively to international audiences about Japan. It must have been extremely gratifying for them to be able to help educate the world about Japan from this insider's perspective. Moreover, I sensed that they all truly liked English, respected the scholarly traditions they had learned, and enjoyed greatly their international travels to the United States, Europe, and other countries.

I never learned, however, where the younger scholars in particular felt they truly belonged during their first couple of years as full-time faculty members. I was struck by how complex it was for them to find their way not just into one academic "home," but into several different kinds of homes, all of which involved writing-related activities. This kind of multimembership in different communities of practice (Wenger, 1998) is normal in monolingual settings so I probably should not have been surprised, because many aspects of this search felt familiar to me. Some of my colleagues and I, whether in Japan or the United States, traveled or are still traveling similar tortuous paths, characterized by competing interests for our time, competing or coexisting loyalties to different institutions or associations, decisions about writing that affect our careers, and layers of personal and political connections that help determine what we write and where we and that writing end up. How much more confusing this must be when one is involved in two different kinds of academic writing games by writing professionally in two languages for a variety of different audiences and purposes in each language.

From a disciplinary community perspective, as suggested by Lave and Wenger (1991), I could not recognize a center toward which the four participants were gravitating in their respective fields, nor did any of them appear to be seeking a disciplinary center. It is easy to postulate that this was because their respective social science fields might be viewed as too fuzzy to have a center or that they had chosen to join ranks with one of multiple subfields, and to leave it at that. But the complexities are far more interesting than this. Studies like this one demonstrate that the broad disciplinary community metaphor, with its implied center and notion of insider–outsider participation, simply does not reflect the fragmented and evolving nature of all fields, even in the so-called hard sciences (Geertz, 1983). Dr. Sasaki, for example, had developed some insider expertise in one subfield in her discipline. She knew its games rules well and followed carefully its literature and research traditions only to have one of her major articles rejected (after our official research project had ended), even after positive reviews, by a journal editor from a slightly different camp. In her revisions, with personal advice from a previous editor of the same journal, she made the political and rhetorical decision to angle the paper a bit more toward this editor's camp and eventually the paper was accepted. Likewise, the broad disciplinary community metaphor does not reflect the realities of the local and I believe necessarily peripheral nature of academic writers' participation in their fields' scholarly activities.

Not only was it difficult to identify where my informants were transitioning to in a disciplinary sense, it was also difficult to locate them unambiguously in one cultural context. For example, even though all four faculty members were working at the same Japanese university, I could not in all fairness identify them solely by this one institutional connection. This university, it is true, paid their salaries, provided them with a physical home, and was the locus of much of the work of writing, teaching, and committee activities they engaged in on a daily basis. But ties with other institutions outside Japan remained strong, particularly through continued collegial relationships (electronic, paper, and face-to-face) involving projects, or additionally, as in the case of Dr. Matsuyama, through a sabbatical teaching experience in the United States. Likewise, perhaps only Dr. Ishii, the most senior of the four people I came to know, radiated a degree of certainty and security about his position at the university. Indeed, as I was finishing revisions for the article version of this chapter (Casanave, 1998), Dr. Matsuyama informed me that he would be leaving this campus—where he had been feeling "somewhat isolated"—for the main campus of this Japanese university, a very different environment from this one. Extremely busy with research, writing, and conference presentations in English, he was still not even certain whether he would stay in Japan. Several years later, he wrote that he had left this university altogether for a post in another Japanese university that suited more appropriately his specific interests (Dr. Matsuyama, personal communication, February, 2001).

A more accurate portrayal of the bilingual academic writers in this project might be one of people struggling within a multicontextual and multicultural world to develop several interrelated identities that could be juggled and balanced as needed to their best advantage. Viewed this way, the transition to the life of a professional bilingual academic does not mean choosing Life A or Life B; rather, it means recognizing and then accepting the heterogeneity of their writing lives (Prior, 1996, 1998), and learning techniques of flexible perspective-taking. Specifically, it means coming to understand how to manage the competing and sometimes conflicting demands of writing in two languages within a variety of institutional and disciplinary contexts, most of them very local and contingent indeed.

I have long felt that the realities of academic writing games become enacted for people and comprehensible to researchers only in the very local contexts in which writers are immersed (Casanave, 1995b). However, I realized as a result of this project that the concept of "local interactions" needs to cover far more than interactions within close physical proximity. All four people in this project had what I now consider to be local interactions with people half way around the globe, by means of electronic mail, fax, phone, and the sharing of hard copies of jointly written papers. These interactions were with specific people, concerning specific writing projects, and they influenced the time allocation and stress levels of the participants on a daily basis.

I was also struck in this project by the extent to which the process of developing expertise in writing in a variety of academic institutional contexts involved the kinds of situated practices described by Lave and Wenger (1991) and Wenger (1998) and the kinds of construction of meaning through reflection and storytelling as described by Bruner (1990, 1991), Clandinin and Connelly (1991, 2000; Connelly & Clandinin, 1990), and others (Conle, 1997, 1999; Giddens, 1991; Linde, 1993, Polkinghorne, 1991). As suggested by the stories told to me during interviews, the most powerful learning experiences resulted from hands-on reading, writing, and conference preparation activities, in interaction with specific individuals in the roles of professors, advisors, and colleagues. As was the case with the successful mentoring relationships between faculty and graduate students described by Belcher (1994) and editors and the young faculty member, Oliver, as discussed by Flowerdew (2000), the two younger scholars in particular benefitted from these truly collaborative practices in their graduate writing experiences in the United States, and recognized the need to build a supportive network of colleagues in Japan within whose realms they could practice locally appropriate writing-related activities.

The act of storytelling, particularly when young scholars are making the transition from the life of a graduate student to that of a practicing academic, seemed to me to help the storytellers clarify and re-view complex and contentious issues concerning what it means to write professionally and to help them express and understand their own transitioning identities. The research process we shared figured centrally in constructing the stories that then became material for us to reflect on together. I wondered, at the conclusion of this project, whether a more regular and concerted effort at constructing the stories of my own professional life would help me locate my place in a fuzzy and chaotic academic world where I often seem to feel out of place. I agree with Lave and Wenger (1991) that what they call "peripheral participation" is absolutely normal—that the periphery, with all its complexity, is where many of us reside. They did not suggest that the periphery was a comfortable place to live. They also did not explore the concepts later elaborated by Wenger (1998) of nonparticipation and marginality. Those on the margins, as defined by Wenger, not only do not participate fully, but they are not moving toward fuller participation, by choice or by circumstance whereas those on the periphery are on an inward trajectory.

Finally, as discussed incisively by Spack (1997c), scholars conducting research within multicultural settings risk stereotyping and stigmatizing the people and cultures they study partly as a result of the labels they use. The primary danger comes, I believe, when researchers, educators, and administrators carelessly use generalizations and labels, and proceed as if reality consists of little more. In this study, I found I could not avoid generalizing and labeling to some extent, nor could my participants, whose own generalizations are reflected throughout this discussion. What I have tried to do instead is to situate my views and experiences and those of my participants within a complex array of perspectives and identities that make up our realities. I found that as I discovered and articulated the complexities and layerings, the generalizations did not disappear. Rather, they took their place as one of the many layers making up my current understanding of the people I was getting to know. As the one who is writing their story, I am in a very real sense constructing them rhetorically, as Spack and others suggest (Clifford, 1986; Geertz, 1988; Rosaldo, 1987). My duty is not only to clarify that the portrayals are my constructions, even when checked with informants, but also to honor the complexity of their views and my own, and both inevitably include generalizations. By highlighting this latter fact I hope I can avoid the stigmatizing that often accompanies unexamined generalizations.

CHAPTER REFLECTIONS

As is often the case at the conclusion of an open-ended and exploratory qualitative inquiry such as this one, I am left with more questions than answers about how bilingual scholars learn to write in different academic settings and about how the writing games they play in their professional lives can be characterized. The literacy autobiographies by Li (1999) and Connor (1999) contribute to the richness of the questions but do not resolve them; Flowerdew's (2000) study of Oliver adds to our understanding by examining in some depth just one writing experience by a young bilingual academic but tells us little about how this experience or how Oliver himself was located in the academic communities he was involved with. In my own case study I was afforded a glimpse of what happens to academy-bound students from Japan when they finish their graduate studies in the United States and return home. I developed a sense of the diversity of game-like skills and strategies they develop in a wide variety of contexts on their way to becoming scholarly academic writers and how difficult it is to construct a coherent identity if one opens the doors to all the complexities of ways of knowing and researching within social science disciplines. I felt, too, that I understood some of the different perceptions they had of the forms and functions of their academic writing and writing-related activities in English and in Japanese. But I have no idea if the experiences of the people in this project were in any way typical of those of bilingual writers making a transition from North American graduate schools to universities in their home countries. Nor do I have any clear sense of how the Japanese gatekeepers (e.g., the mentors, academic associations, project leaders, journal and book editors) view the role of writing in scholarly life or in the development of a writer's professional persona.

When I consider that some of my own students may themselves become bilingual academics one day, I am also left with many questions, aspects of which have already been raised by others (e.g., Belcher, 1994; Hansen, 2000; Leki & Carson, 1997; Prior, 1996; Reynolds, 1994), about my role as a university writing instructor interested in helping prepare students to write successfully in graduate school and beyond. If it is the case that activities in EAP (English for Academic Purposes) writing classes bear little resemblance to the far more complex textual, sociopolitical, and locally negotiated nature of writing in graduate courses and later in professional academic settings, then I have a lot more reflecting to do as I continue the ongoing process of constructing my own professional persona. As Belcher (1994) and Prior (1996, 1998) suggest, and as my own research leads me to believe, I should be paying as much attention to helping both first and second language graduate students in my classes develop skills for dealing with the wide range of social and political interpersonal relationships that interact with locally situated writing activities as I do to helping them learn the language and style of formal academic papers (Casanave, 2001).

One of my main goals, perhaps, should be to help raise students' awareness of the extent to which they will be learning the forms and functions of academic writing by being immersed in local practices of writing rather than by learning textbook rules, and that those practices change from one institutional and cultural setting to another. The experiences of Li and Connor show just how different the institutional experiences of academic enculturation can be and the extent to which the personalities of key players influence how bilingual academics, indeed all academics, enact and interpret their literacy practices. In other words, it seems clear from these studies and other studies of community enculturation (Wenger, 1998) that participants do not just absorb community practices through a transfer process, but, as they do in any serious game, contribute to the construction of the contexts in which they are immersed by interpreting them according to their own goals, personalities, and inevitably partial understandings. It is in the interstices of these interactions, where slippages and loopholes occur (Ortner, 1996) that change of identity happens. Although I can help students become aware that learning to write academically in two or more languages requires the flexibility to perform a balancing act that is at once political, interpersonal, and textual (as it is for monolinguals), I am not sure how to help them develop an embodied sense of the "consequential transitions" (Beach, 1999) they will experience if they begin writing professionally, and in particular of the cultural aspects about which I may know little. I believe this embodied learning can happen only in situ as academic writers change their relationships with their communities.

As Beach (1999) notes, the metaphor of "consequential transitions" is an activity-based metaphor that highlights people's changing relations with social activities within organizations that themselves are subject to change, a view compatible with the game metaphor that I use throughout this book. Transitions are consequential, he says, "when they are consciously reflected on, often struggled with, and the eventual outcome changes one's sense of self and social positioning" (p. 114). Like Lave (1996, 1997), Lave and Wenger (1991), Wenger (1998), and Ivanič (1998), Beach is interested in getting rid of the notion that learning and the construction of (professional) identity involve mainly transfer. With a focus on relationships among individuals, activities, and organizations, he suggests moreover that schools cannot be responsible for all the consequential transitions that students undergo. Following Wenger (1998) he claims that schools need to find ways to extend their boundaries into society so that "identity-making ... can become an institutionally sanctioned part of acquiring knowledge and skills in classrooms" (Beach, 1999, p. 132). In the case of bilingual academics who may be practicing professionally in a society unlike and distant from the one they were schooled in, graduate schools can "extend their boundaries" by helping students develop the reflective skills they need in order to recognize the game-like social and political nature of their literacy practices. Such awareness may then help young scholars understand their struggles later and make informed choices in their new academic environments. The two young Japanese faculty I worked with hinted that the long-term reflective interview process helped them see their balancing and juggling games in new ways and to comprehend the transitions they were going through. Equally important, as Wenger (1998) advises, students need to engage in genuine practices with experts in a field, not just with classroom teachers. Mr. Kubo and Dr. Sasaki both described numerous experiences in their graduate programs in which they participated actively and authentically in the scholarship activities being undertaken in their programs by advisors and colleagues. These practices stood out as the ones that prepared them for research and writing activities as young faculty members. They rarely mentioned classwork.

Finally, I believe there is an enormous gap in our knowledge about what happens after academy-bound students whose mother tongue is not English complete their graduate education in the medium of English and return to their home countries and begin writing professionally in two languages, or what it is like for them, as second language speakers, to remain as scholars in an English-medium university setting. We are beginning to close this gap with publications like those of Li (1996, 1999), Connor (1999) and others in the edited volumes by George Braine (1999b), by Diane Belcher and Ulla Connor (2001), by Lucila Vargas (2001), and by Stephanie Vandrick and me (Casanave & Vandrick, forthcoming), with more personal testimonials in mainstream journals by bilingual scholars such as Kubota (1999) and Spack (1997b), and with case study research like the present one. I am hoping in particular that some of those bilingual scholars who make the transition from Japan and other countries to English-medium university settings and back home again will share their stories in published form about the role that writing plays in their professional lives. How are they managing the transitions, the juggling games, and the balancing acts? What is the nature of their memberships in multiple academic writing communities? How are they going about constructing a coherent academic identity for themselves? There is much for those who are interested in multicultural academic identities to learn from such stories of struggle and change, stories that are increasingly relevant in the growing number of multicultural, multilingual academic settings that characterize international scholarship.

ACKNOWLEDGMENTS

I would like to express my warm and heartfelt thanks to the four Japanese faculty who shared their time, ideas, and writings with me as part of the case study described in the third section of this chapter.

6

Bending the Rules

CONFORMING AND RESISTING

It was during my once-in-a-lifetime year-long sabbatical in 1998–1999 that I realized with great clarity that I was on the other side of a long career in second language education. There had been signs of this before, that I no longer considered myself moving, or needing to move, "up" in my career even though there was room to do so, and that I was exploring ways to move in other directions (sideways? in circles? zigzag? out?). But it was during this year that I renewed my late life commitment to bending some rules by conceptualizing a book (this one) that fit some of the conventions but not others. The construction of this book, and my reflection on the author–editor relationship in the construction of an edited book of personal narratives (discussed in the third section of this chapter) both brought me face to face with my own publishing history and the conflicted motivations behind it. I begin this chapter with some of those reflections as a way to introduce the theme of this chapter—the tensions between adhering to and bending the perceived rules of academic writing games. The reflections have helped explain why I both like and dislike writing, why I tolerate the ups and downs in my mood as I write, and why I resist convention and tradition yet submit to them more often than I am comfortable admitting.

I began writing for publication in about 1980, after finishing a masters degree but before beginning my PhD program. Early on I knew I wanted to work in a university and that teaching alone would probably not bring me enough satisfaction, but only later realized with clarity the extent to which my place as a legitimate conversation partner in my academic field was tied to what I wrote. But let me state up front that I don't publish that often. By "that often" I confess that I mean the conventional three articles a year in refereed journals plus the occasional book. I am shocked at how I am still burdened by guilt at not living up to this arbitrary convention, established who knows when by patriarchically structured research universities. I have never had a workload typical of those at research universities (mine is usually 8 to 10 preparations a year), so it makes little sense for someone like me (most of us in academe) to compare myself to those who have half the load. Nevertheless, the guilt continues to waft about me like an unpleasant vapor, even when I can rationalize it away. The pull of convention and tradition in the academic games I learned is strong even though I recognize that one set of standards cannot not be applied to everyone.

There is another reason why this guilt continues to puzzle me, and that is an aspect of my character that should make it easy for me to dismiss standards that don't necessarily apply to me: my resistant nature that balks at being told what to do. It should long ago have helped rid me of the nagging sense of duty that I ought to be publishing X-number of traditional pieces per year. But I have not been able to escape fully the insidious power that the Academic World holds over me. Part of me still accepts as normal the authoritative male voices in the literature and in the power structure at the university, listens with awe as well as skepticism to the heroic male educators and researchers at conferences, and shrinks with intimidation as well as with anger at some of the marginally comprehensible feminist writings that paradoxically might be considered by some as having made inroads into the male-dominated High Theory conversations. Why do I continue to compare myself to game players whose turf I don't wholeheartedly wish to inhabit and whose games I find inimical? Perhaps because as gatekeepers they continue to have power over me. I continue to some extent to be judged by their standards.

I think it is not only the pull of powerful tradition on academic playing fields that prevents me from devoting all of my energies to teaching or from getting out of the game altogether. It is also my desire, since childhood, to produce something that could be held, contemplated in its wholeness, considered finished in some sense, and then recognized by others. My earliest childhood drawings filled this desire, as did later artwork in school and college, but teaching, for all its rewards, is productless and the activity of teaching itself goes on endlessly, without a visible conclusion in spite of occasional students who later achieve goals we both worked on together. There has never been a point at which I could say that "Now student X is taught and can be considered the product of my teaching," nor has such a goal or view ever suited my pedagogical philosophy. Writing for publication gives me the sense that I am creating something that I can behold in a concrete way, that others can recognize. I can't explain where this urge came from, but it is probably fed by my desire as a perpetually low-confidence person for recognition. But knowing that the empty places inside me can never be filled by producing a briefly recognized drawing or piece of writing has not dampened my urge to produce something; it only helps me realize how misguided the effort is. I would therefore like to think that part of this urge also comes from some innate creativity on my part and the sheer satisfaction of working hard at something and seeing the results, even if the need for recognition and the fear of its absence play a part too.

I am not unique in being partly motivated by the need for recognition, the need to somehow prove myself. It seems to be quite common among academic women, who tend to suffer from low confidence even when they are well established in their careers. On reading Gesa Kirsch's (1993) study of how academic women experience their writing lives in the academy and how they struggle to develop an authoritative voice, I found myself nodding at the familiarity of it all. I felt similar connections to Jane Thompkins (1990), who noted that she spent 30 years with a bias against teaching because she was driven by "fear"—the need to perform in a way that caused colleagues and instructors to think highly of her. Teaching, she reminded me, does not engender the praise of the powerful voices in the academy. Praise comes from performing according to the expectation that one is an expert who says the right things. She is refreshingly honest in her characterization of this fear of seeming incompetent and how it drives teachers and scholars in the academy to play the very serious conventional games of writing and performing in front of students according to standards that reward what people say, not what they do:

> Fear is the driving form behind the performance mode. Fear of being shown up for what you are: a fraud, stupid, ignorant, a clod, a dolt, a sap, a weakling, someone who can't cut the mustard. (p. 654)

I related to her descriptions of this fear. If I write with authority that is recognized by gatekeepers and teach by passing on my knowledge in an authoritative way to students, I fit the performance model. If I include my own persona in my writing or teaching or if I step back from an authoritative stance in either activity, I do not fit that model and thus risk being marginalized in the conventional academic circles that judge me. Women academics and part-time and temporary academics (many of whom are women) are particularly vulnerable here (Cayton, 1991) and it is difficult to escape the feeling that we really don't belong, that we are frauds (McIntosh, 1989). The fear of not being recognized by the Powers That Be, in short, prevents many of us from bending rules. Lillian Bridwell-Bowles (1992, 1995) admitted that in spite of her strong support of experimental writing in the academy by both students and teachers, many young or insecure students and scholars don't dare take the risk. As a well-known tenured faculty member, she acknowledges that she takes little risk in calling for or practicing more experimental writing within the academy. When as a young scholar Cheryl Geisler (1992) wrote an account of her own research in an unconventional way that included personal reflection, she expressed the problem this way:

> As a consequence of academic conventions, whenever we venture to account for our research and place this account in print, we run the risk of being taken as less than serious, of having our claims assessed as less than valid, and of being accused of methodological impurity. This will happen to some extent no matter how good our intentions are, and it is particularly likely to happen when the person giving the account has not "earned" the right of personal reflection through a long and distinguished career, as I certainly have not. (p. 41)

Bridwell-Bowles (1992) wants to "use the security [of tenure] I have to open doors for others, to consider new possibilities" (p. 366). Elliot Eisner (1997), too, notes that "opening up new ways of seeing and saying" can be both exciting and treacherous. Edges, he says, "are not a bad location if one is a university professor—especially one with tenure!" (p. 4). Geisler (1992), on the other hand, wants all scholars, including young ones, to question the "myth of rhetorical repression." Even though we feel pressure to conform, she says, "[w]e should ask ourselves why, and—occasionally—do our best to do something different" (p. 52).

What is it that for some years now I have wanted to do differently in my writing? I think that if I had to sum up my urge in a sentence, it would be that I want academic writers, including myself, to become more visible in their writings, as authors, agents, and as human beings who have a life. Wendy Bishop (1999) expressed my own desires in her call for more transparency in our accounts of writing and more discussion of authorial personas and actual authorship (p. 29). My reading in the fields of education, composition and rhetoric, and English (less so in the field of second language education) convinces me that I am in good company, and not just the company of women (e.g., Bleich, 1995, 1998).

My sense, in other words, is that many researchers, teachers, and teacher-educators are calling for more visibility of the people who write and who are written about (I talk more about this in the next section). This is not to say that critics of expressivist pedagogies, interpretive and narrative inquiry, and experimentation in academic discourse have retired to the sidelines (e.g., Bartholomae, 1995; Moore & Muller, 1999; Gardner's views in Saks, 1996). It is to say, rather, that the strong and persuasive voices making these pleas are alive and well and gaining strength as the idea that there are many ways to know something becomes more accepted in professional educational circles. The pleas are expressed and resonate particularly well with women and men who are seeking ways to legitimize new academic literacy games that link their personal and professional lives and who hope to help their students do the same (e.g., Bleich, 1995, 1998; Brannon, 1993; Bridwell-Bowles, 1995; Carter, 1993; Cayton, 1991; Clandinin & Connelly, 1991; Conle, 1996, 1999; Elbow, 1991, 1995, 1999a; Fishman & McCarthy, 1992; Grumet, 1988; Kilbourn, 1999; Spack, 1997b; Thompkins, 1990; Trimmer, 1997). This list strikes me as evidence of the growing numbers of scholars whom I can relate to and converse with. I find comfort in these voices and find they give me the courage to continue finding ways to bend some rules myself and to help my students understand that they have choices.

In this chapter, however, I am less interested in how to help students go about the bending rules of conventional academic literacy games than in how teachers and researchers long steeped in traditional academic practices might themselves bend some of the rules, although the connection with students underlies all the issues I discuss. Teachers and researchers are the people, after all, who model and mentor and whose adherence or resistance to tradition affects their students' lives as much as it does theirs. In my own teaching and writing, I am faced daily with the inconsistencies and contradictions in my beliefs and practices. I wonder how they affect my students and if resolving them would remove the energizing dissonance in my life, leaving me an untroubled but naïve idealist who has Answers. There is no risk without dissonance, I suppose, so I guess I should not wish away the contradictions too hastily.

It is the effort that teachers and researchers make at taking risks in academic writing by constructing unconventional textual identities that I consider in this chapter. I do this by first reviewing several published studies by scholars who have mustered the courage to break some of the rules of the academic writing game, and who have talked about their risk-taking in print. I look in some depth at one of these authors, Victor Villanueva, whose autobiographical book *Bootstraps* (Villanueva, 1993) is itself an example of multivocalic and courageously risky academic discourse: The author himself uses multiple voices, all his own and all reflecting different aspects of his identity, to tell his story of enculturation into communities of academic practice.

In the third section of the chapter, I look closely at an experience I had as coeditor and contributing author of a book I had originally conceptualized as a rule-breaker. In this book we wanted well-known and newer people across subfields of language education to write about themselves and their careers in ways that challenged the conventions of academic discourse—to narrate stories that had a literary flair and that went beyond the I-did-this-and-that-in-my-life-and-finally-got-there type of personal essay. We wanted authors instead to look at key issues and transitions in their careers in complex ways that put themselves at the center of their discourse. With the participation of my coeditor, Sandra Schecter, we gave birth to this book, but it took 5 years (Casanave & Schecter, 1997). The stories are those of the editor–author relationship I had with several of the authors who wrote essays for that book and how we struggled in this relationship to bend a few rules by crafting selves that did not fit the conventional distanced academic persona.

PUBLISHED STUDIES

Two perspectives on identity help me frame the discussion of the construction of unconventional textual identities in this section. One is the postmodern view that "the problem of identity is a problem of language, and thus a problem of fabrication" (Britzman, 1993, p. 54). The second is that "viewing the self as a narrative or story, rather than as a substance" (Polkinghorne, 1991, p. 135) helps bring to light one's identity (Bruner, 1991; Giddens, 1991; Linde, 1993). From these two perspectives it is possible to conclude that narrative and reflective writing deserve a central place in scholarly fields that purport to deal with people and their use of language, including how authors themselves use and select language. Even if I am portraying others as in case study research (Newkirk, 1992), the narratives I choose to listen to and interpret say as much about me as they do about my participants. All writing is therefore in some sense autobiographical (Murray, 1991), and I am heartened to discover increasing numbers of calls for authors in first and second language education to write more transparently about their own identities, agendas, and processes (Belcher & Connor, 2001; Bishop, 1999; Braine, 1999a; Bridwell-Bowles, 1995, 1996, 1997; Geisler, 1992; Kirsch & Ritchie, 1995). These calls for more transparency of author identity accompany the push for more acceptance of qualitative and unconventional research methods in education and composition research in the face of continued resistance (Eisner, 1997; Kilbourn, 1999; Miller, Nelson, & Moore, 1998; Peshkin, 1993; Eisner in Saks, 1996) and in particular for writing that is more narrative and reflective, more multivocalic and layered (Barone, 1992; Cintron, 1993; Conle, 1997, 1999; Kirsch & Ritchie, 1995; Neumann & Peterson, 1997; Trimmer, 1997). Nevertheless, no mode of writing is innocent or neutral, as Renato Rosaldo (1993) notes, and none should be granted sole legitimacy. In this regard I understand the calls for more innovative writing in education to be calls for expanding and redefining what is considered "legitimate," not replacing traditional academic discourse.

In the field of education, Patricia Burdell and Beth Swadener (1999) discussed explicitly their support of texts that "allow us to enter the world of others in ways that have us more present in their experience, while better understanding our own" and that "broaden the 'acceptable' or give voice to the intellectual contradictions and tensions in everyday lives of scholar-teachers and researchers" (p. 21). They describe what they see as an emerging genre in education: critical personal narrative and autoethnography. In fulfilling such a goal, authors cannot escape the need to construct and expose to the public aspects of their own identities that traditionally are hidden behind objectivist and third-person discourse. The risk, as many authors have mentioned, is great for young and unknown scholars who need, or believe they need, to become skilled players at traditional academic literacy games in order to be recognized as legitimate participants in their scholarly communities. But I believe the risk also causes established scholars to think twice before constructing a personal textual identity for others to see. What will be the purpose of personal disclosure and where should authors draw the line between that and confession, which Bleich (1995, 1998) reminds us is a private matter? If authors have or yearn for an authoritative public persona, to what extent will their construction of personal identities in their writing add to or detract from their authority? How can the bending of the rules of academic literacy games in ways that construct more visible personal identities benefit both readers and authors?

In short, even though narrative and reflective writing continues to gain popularity and legitimacy in first and second language education publications (Connelly & Clandinin, 1990; Freeman & Richards, 1996; Schön, 1987; Witherell, 1991), and even though I often see lengthy passages quoted from the narratives of others (e.g., McLaughlin & Tierney, 1993; Witherell & Noddings, 1991), academic scholars less often publish their own narratives. Most of us have never considered the stuff of our personal and academic histories appropriate for the public to scrutinize. It is much safer for the narratives of others to be put forward. Some established scholars, however, are beginning to tell us about themselves.

For instance, Linda Brodkey's (1996) beautifully written story of her background transported me into her world, just as did accounts such as those of Mike Rose (1989, 1995) in the popular press and portions of Madeleine Grumet's work (1988, 1991). William Tierney's (1993) personal touch in his life story of native American teacher Robert Sunchild's battle with AIDS brought his issues vividly to the forefront for me. Cheryl Geisler's (1994) and Paul Prior's (1998) personal reflections at the end of their books on academic literacy connected me with their messages in more memorable ways than did their thoroughly researched volumes. Stephanie Vandrick (1999) wrote courageously about the colonial attitudes she absorbed as a child of missionary parents in India and their continuing influence on her ESL teaching. Ruth Spack (1997b) includes reflection about personal and ethical issues of identity, authority, and voice in her essay on teaching in culturally diverse classrooms. The collections in composition studies and education (Fontaine & Hunter, 1993; Roen, Brown, & Enos, 1999; Trimmer, 1997; Vargas, 2001), in several subfields of language education by my coeditor and me (Casanave & Schecter, 1997), and in the second language education field (Belcher & Connor, 2001; Braine, 1999b) provide evidence of the power of first-person narratives to communicate identities and issues to readers in accessible, jargon-free prose.

In composition studies, for example, I found Lillian Bridwell-Bowles's (1995) references to her Southern White background refreshingly honest. The details of her personal background and gradual political awakening, however, came out first in an orally delivered conference paper (Bridwell-Bowles, 1996), then later in written form (Bridwell-Bowles, 1997). She portrays herself as a well-meaning educator who moved from an early stance of naïve idealism to one in which she is more realistically aware of unresolvable dilemmas in her positioning of herself within a culturally and ethnically complex field. In a bolder example of bending writing game rules, Wendy Bishop (1995, 1997b, 1999) writes nontraditionally structured, mixed-genre pieces that reflect her background in creative writing and her interest in a personal presence in her writing. In the 1999 essay, among other things, she traces the changes she experienced over the years as a participant on the playing fields of composition studies. One of her key concepts—that of writer-teacher-writer—is represented by a symbol rather than word, and she includes a poem she wrote in order to explore the idea of "othering." Her argument for justifying the role of the creative writer in composition studies, in other words, is practiced in this piece of creative and personal yet scholarly writing.

Outside the field of language education, qualitative research in anthropology and education occasionally gives us riveting first person accounts that demonstrate the power and theoretical and analytical potential of narratives that include the authors as central figures. Harry Wolcott's (1990) story of how his informant and lover Brad attacked him and burned his house down kept me glued to the page, causing me to reflect on the meaning of validity in qualitative research and on the nature and purpose of the researcher–informant relationship. This reflection was precisely Wolcott's purpose in telling this personal story. Carolyn Ellis and Arthur Bochner's (1996) collection of experimental ethnographic writings shows graphically the variety of discourse styles authors can use to construct first person narratives, ones that are both fascinating and substantive as well as ones that work less well. (In the introduction to this volume [Bochner & Ellis, 1996], the editors experimented with a dialogue format that I feel succeeded only marginally; the dialogue has an artificial ring to it in its attempt not to sound didactic. See the case of John later in this chapter.) Likewise, Anna Neumann and Penelope Peterson (1997) brought together a collection of autobiographical writings by women researchers in education who vividly connected their personal and professional lives. Some academics, in other words, are pushing at the gatekeepers' fences, bending rules and changing the playing fields. Like all good writing, the narratives written by these risk-takers are generally compelling, thought-provoking, and absorbing to read. And like all good writing, they appear to have been constructed effortlessly.

Appearances are deceiving. Perhaps constructing a personal textual identity for a public forum is easy for some people. My own experiences and those of some of the authors that I worked with in my guise as editor more closely reflect the following comment by Jo Anne Pagano (1991). Her anecdote in a published essay expresses what I and several other authors went through as we searched for appropriate and accurate representations of our professional identities:

> I recently reread an autobiographical essay that I submitted as part of my tenure dossier. My assignment was to talk about the way I think about teaching, to develop a "philosophy" of teaching, and to evaluate my performance as a teacher, scholar, and citizen of the university community. I was terrified. Nothing I've ever written, including my PhD dissertation, was ever as difficult for me as that autobiographical essay. Never had I felt more vulnerable. (pp. 195–196)

She continues by describing how the ways she presented herself for public scrutiny in this tenure review document hid her fear of inferiority. Constructing a self that did not seem vulnerable was a challenge she had not faced in conventional academic writing, where her self was not central. As I read Victor Villanueva's (1993) literacy autobiography, *Bootstraps*, I saw how one courageous author handled the challenge and the vulnerability.

Victor Villanueva

I write about Victor Villanueva's autobiographical journey into academia, *Bootstraps* (1993), in this chapter on bending rules for several reasons. One is that he is a writing teacher and scholar writing about his own academic enculturation. Another is that his long and painful journey onto the playing fields of academia is so different from mine and from that of many other "colorless" middle-class people that contemplating it serves as a vivid reminder to me of how much I don't know and have not experienced about people's academic identities and transitions. At the same time, sensations of familiarity pursued me throughout my reading of his story. Third, I include a discussion of Villanueva's book because the book itself stands as a courageous experiment in the blending of voices and genres. Part adventure story, part poetry, part academic and philosophical treatise, all the voices, and none, belong to Villanueva. None represents him completely, yet none is inimical to the different facets of his personality and experience. And as much as he may wish to unburden himself of the conventional academic discourse he has learned to manipulate, he cannot go back. That voice is also now his.

As a White Middle-Class Woman of Fluctuating Confidence (a WMCWFC—one is compelled in academia to create ridiculous acronyms), I feel I have nothing to say after reading *Bootstraps* and am weighed down by a modicum of guilt that I might think I have something to complain about in my own academic enculturation. I have never struggled with the issues of race, color, class, poverty, and family responsibility that Villanueva has. Any hardships I can point to in my own life come across as sounding trite, and make me sound whiny and ignorant of the harsh realities of others. I can never comprehend fully Villanueva's climb (as I drafted early versions of this chapter, he was chair of the College Composition and Communication organization, and later became the chair of a department at his university). But some of his experiences resonate with me, because they have to do with understanding that choices to follow traditional conventions in academic writing practices or to take risks and try for something different are in part political decisions that can affect one's career.

Villanueva arrived in academia the hard way. A life of poverty, beginning in New York's Bedford-Stuyvesant district and continuing even after he finally received his PhD in composition and rhetoric made it difficult for him to identify himself either as middle class or as an academic. For one thing, academics are supposed to travel to conferences—a financial hardship on many. "He has made it by the bootstraps," he says in third person of himself, from "GED" to "Ph.D." (p. xiv), which on the surface looks like an "American success story" (p. xiv). The "portorican" kid who didn't even finish high school gets a doctoral degree and finds himself teaching writing to all kinds of students, including those much like himself. Not only does he find himself teaching writing. He also realizes that a life in academia includes pressures to write and publish. His lifelong love of language helped him achieve the goal he could never have imagined reaching as a youth, a PhD. But university politics, pressure to publish, and continued poverty gnawed away at his developing sense of identity as a scholar and at his confidence that an "academic of color" could survive on a very serious academic playing field.

Villanueva did not always lack confidence or see himself in political terms as a person of color in the working class. As a youth, he seems to have developed a great deal of strength from a close family and his love of language, but his confidence included his firm belief that he was not college material. The transitions in his academic identity began for him in serious in college, after a stint in the army in Vietnam and Korea, "as I attempted to move within the class system, and as more of America's cultural heritage, seen through literature and rhetoric, became clear" (p. xii). From that time, continuing to the writing of *Bootstraps* and beyond (his keynote address at the Conference on College Composition and Communication in Atlanta, Georgia, Thursday March 25, 1999 was "The Tree and the Woods: Racism in Multiculturalism"), Villanueva has seen tokenism at work in the halls of academia, and "the liberal's fear of being honest with people of color about their abilities" (p. 13). He wonders about his own achievements and whether perhaps "he isn't as smart as people say he is" (p. 13).

Villanueva narrates with passion the ups and downs in his college career. We get to know some of his teachers and classes, and share with him the shock of his move from community college to university, and then on to graduate school. We meet the handful of people (Walter Myles, Bracy, "Floyd") and authors (Freire, Gramsci) who helped him develop a "critical consciousness" (*Bootstraps*, Chapter 4). We learn of his successes at the community college (3.8 GPA), frustrations and failures in university and graduate courses, and the mixed responses from professors that his writing generated ("too formulaic," "too novel," "nonsense," "I never saw that before"). Yet Villanueva was driven to continue pursuing a degree. "I couldn't get enough," he tells us, "despite the pain and the insecurity" (p. 71). The language, the reading, the ideas were magic.

In order to successfully bend the rules of academic discourse, as Villanueva did with *Bootstraps*, he had to learn the rules first and gain the stature that would persuade mentors and publishers to take a chance with him. From what I could glean from his story of how he learned to play the games, he, like many novices, learned how to write according to accepted conventions well before he began to take on the identity of a "legitimate" (his word) member of an academic community in composition and rhetoric (Bartholomae, 1985). His story sounds like a detailed version of what I heard from many of the people I talked to in my own case study research. Villanueva calls his strategy of learning how to write in the university "Professorial Discourse Analysis":

> Professorial Discourse Analysis became a standard practice: go to the library; see what the course's professor had published; try to discern a pattern to her writing; try to mimic the pattern. Some would begin with anecdotes. Some would have no personal pronouns. Some would cite others' research. Some would cite different literary works to make assertions about one literary work. Whatever they did, I would do too. (p. 71)

In the university, in other words, Villanueva did not purposely bend the rules, but did his utmost to discover the patterns in his own professors' writings and to mimic the patterns. It was a strategy that worked for the most part, got him his BA, and helped him get into the university's graduate program, with the additional help of faculty references and his "minority status." His pride was wounded at being labeled minority, in that he had earned his 3.67 GPA.

In graduate school, more insecure than ever, Villanueva discovered that "there are no more overnight papers" (p. 33). He labored over papers for days and weeks, literally cutting and pasting, trying to figure out what the repeated comments in his papers ("Logic?") referred to. Until graduate school, Villanueva observes, he had never fully comprehended written discourse "of the academic variety," where logic rather than imagination or patterned plays of language were the focus. "When I didn't understand what was being argued in my Professorial Discourse Analysis," he explains, "I did not attempt to puzzle out the logic; my concerns were with *patterns*, the sounds" (p. 87). As an undergraduate, he wrote papers that satisfied his sense of pattern and sound, a strategy that did not work in graduate school. "That I was able to get through undergraduate school in this way," he says, "tells me that teachers have different expectations of undergraduates than of graduates" (p. 87). In graduate school, he surmises, "style must have taken a back seat to concept for many" (p. 87).

Then, as is the case so often in life, a major changed happened in Villanueva's life fortuitously: He happened to hear a tape of Robert Kaplan speaking on contrastive rhetoric, and once again referring to himself in third person tells us that he "stumbles into his first rhetoric course" with Anne Ruggles Gere (p. 73). Bit by bit, by studying classical rhetoric, Villanueva became aware of aspects of his own writing and learned something about the teaching of writing that he had not known before. Although Villanueva did not phrase it this way, I sense that this was the point at which he began identifying with past and present scholars of rhetoric and at which, in his own musings and writings as well as at conferences that he was beginning to attend, he began to "converse" with these authors and scholars.

With time, practice, and reflection, and with his growing experience as a graduate assistant reader and teacher of writing, Villanueva learned to use his writing as a vehicle for his thinking and to craft it in ways that fit the expectations of different audiences, a task that never became easy:

> If I am to discover my thinking in the writing, I must give vent to my sophistic tendencies. This is not Peter Elbow's freewriting. I agonize over words choices or sentence constructions. I deliberate over opening sentences to paragraphs, over transitions. I backtrack and redirect. I correct. But I also know that I will have to go back when I am done to reconsider the logical pre-

dispositions of my audience, make connections explicit, relegate some things to footnotes, delete others, even if they are significant to me. (pp. 87–88)

And when it comes to what Villanueva calls the "scientific discourse" expected in academic circles, a discourse "never quite in my grasp to this day," he, as many academics do, coconstructs writing such as grants and journal articles with the help of others, receiving from them "long 'advice' on how I might revise." "My writing," Villanueva confesses, "is always subject to rhetorical 'translation' " (p. 88).

Villanueva bent the rules when he wrote *Bootstraps*, from the position of an employed academic and with encouragement of colleagues and publishers who were familiar with some of his "mixed genre" writing. It came together after a long journey, from New York to California to Washington to Arizona and back to Washington, but also after a long journey into himself and his changing identities and literacies. Villanueva was an army enlistee in Vietnam and Korea; recipient of food stamps as an impoverished college student, husband, and father, player with language, manual laborer, "reader" in graduate school, teaching assistant, head of a basic writing program, "legitimate" holder of a PhD, much sobered learner of the game of university politics, researcher, insecure outsider, symbol to others of racial stereotypes. He cannot identify himself unambiguously as "Latino" or Puerto Rican, or as a member of the dominant White academic culture, or as working class, or as middle class. Aspects of all of these identities both fit and don't fit. But by the time *Bootstraps* was published, Villanueva was identifying himself as "an academic of color," as the subtitle of his book tells us.

The genre of *Bootstraps* cannot be labeled, beyond calling it a "mixed-genre" piece, even though it was published by an academic press and received two awards for distinguished research and scholarship. The mix allows us to see Villanueva in many of his guises. We see him in first person, more often in third person. We read punchy and poetic sentence fragments and conversational discourse, followed on the same page by more conventional academic prose. A great deal of what Villanueva does in *Bootstraps* is storytelling, where woven into the powerful narrative are the denser documented sections culled from other more traditional pieces he has written. The mix for me was moving, jarring, engaging, irritating, curious, sometimes an effective blending and other times less so. Villanueva kept me with him on his journey, however, with threads of reflection, compassion, and confession that exposed the games and the transitions that culminated in the courageous publication of this unconventional literacy autobiography.

In the next section I discuss another kind of courageous and unconventional writing and the author–editor relationships that prompted, intruded into, and sustained it. In this writing experience, three well-established professionals in second language education and I struggled to construct our own unconventional textual identities through personal narrative essays.

CASE STUDY: AUTHOR–EDITOR GAMES IN THE CONSTRUCTION OF UNCONVENTIONAL TEXTUAL IDENTITIES

In the reflective writing project from which I draw the stories in this section, undertaken by a diverse group of 17 first and second language educators between 1992 and 1997 for an edited collection (Casanave & Schecter, 1997), my coeditor, Sandra Schecter, and I wished to turn the spotlight on ourselves. We asked authors to submit narrative essays that dealt with an important career issue or event in their professional development as language educators in the fields of first and second language and bilingual education. In composing their narratives (written, reconstructed retellings of and reflections on temporal events), the authors were faced with the task of constructing textual identities (Ivanič, 1994, 1998; Kramsch & Lam, 1999; Mckay & Wong, 1996; Peirce, 1995). We hoped that these identities would differ from the traditional public persona that academics put forward—the third-person, distanced and falsely objective self that is sanctioned as legitimate by many of the gatekeepers in the academic world. Instead, we hoped that authors would construct selves that reflected the centrality of personal histories in their career paths. As I discussed in Chapter 1, I consider identity to be best construed in plural terms, the implication being that any representation of self whether in oral storytelling or written narrative reconstruction must be considered partial and one of many possible identities that could be crafted in writing (Kondo, 1990).

The reflections I present here are those of the editor–author relationship I had with three of the authors who had great difficulty writing first person narrative essays for the book, as I did myself. These editor–author relationships should not be considered typical of those Sandra and I had; rather, they represent particular relationships and personal negotiations that a small number of contributors had with us and with me in particular as the personal contact person for these three people. Sandra and I took turns signing our names as the main author of written communications with the authors. My personal contacts with them, however, in face-to-face meetings or through informal e-mail, reflect the playing out of our project goals within my particular way of framing issues and the interactions of my personality with those of the authors.

We contacted potential contributors before we had completed an initial prospectus to be sent to publishers, but in our initial letter, we described the project as follows:

[In these essays] [W]e want to help bridge gaps between researcher and teacher, between seasoned professionals and those new to the field, and between first and second language educators. In particular, we want contributors to talk about themselves—about an issue in their own professional development that would potentially provide insights for readers in language education.

Later, once we had commitments from a core of interested authors and had received several drafts, we sent everyone a copy of our initial prospectus to help guide them toward a common goal as they drafted their essays. Here is an excerpt from that initial prospectus:

On Becoming A Language Educator concerns the professional development of language educators. It consists of personal essays by first and second language researchers and practitioners in which the writers reflect on issues, events, and people in their lives that helped them carve out their career paths or clarify an important dimension of their missions as educators. It is intended to provide students, teachers, and researchers in the area of language education with insights into the different struggles that characterize the professional development of language educators. Our primary goals are that both readers and authors use the stories told here to view their own professional lives from fresh perspectives—that they are inspired to reflect in new ways on the ideological, ethical, and philosophical underpinnings of their professional personae, and that they forge links between the concreteness and commonality of the narratives and the potentially profound meanings to be found in human experience. We believe that this kind of reflection leads us as language educators not only to find meaning in the narrative episodes of our professional lives, but also to enhance our respect for the nonstatic "ongoingness" of professional development, as reflected in the progressive mood of our title. This we hope will happen as readers question and explore the mission, substance, and activity of language educating across a variety of first language, second language, and bilingual education contexts.

Our primary purpose, in other words, was to connect with an audience in language teacher education, in the belief that sharing stories about professional development can open avenues of understanding and personal growth that may ordinarily remain hidden behind the more conventional academic stances that we require from ourselves and out students. A secondary purpose was to help expand the range of accepted discourse styles and models in academic literature in language education.

In an excerpt from an early memo from Sandra and me to some of the first contributors, sent before we had completed the prospectus, we noted some of the problems that lay on the horizon:

We'd like to touch bases with you as a group, as well as individually before the summer is over. We're starting to get pieces in for the book (thanks to those of you who have sent early drafts!) and hope to finish up the prospectus within a month. We don't need all the pieces by then, but the more drafts we have, the more focused our prospectus can be. The people we've talked to so far are either finding the more literary, personal style quite a bit easier to write, or far more difficult. Some are also finding it difficult to deal with the rich detail of an issue rather than just narrating a superficial story. At any rate, we're all convinced we're going in the right direction.

I, for one, was surprised at the time at the difficulties some people were having. People are inherently interested in themselves, and many of us claim to be committed to "personal growth" of various kinds. Hence, a book project that asked people to reflect on some aspect of their professional development in a comfortable story form, I reasoned naively, should have generated inspired, flowing prose. Indeed, with some of the authors that I had extended conversations with before we all began writing, stories tumbled out as we talked about the project. As for my own story, I felt that whatever I might say was so much a part of me that I would have little difficulty telling it once I could make myself sit down to do it. Perhaps this task was in fact easy for some people. We did get a number of first drafts that fit well with our vision for this book, as our early memo hints. But for others, including myself, this writing task turned into a kind of torture that more conventional efforts at writing could not match.

In asking people to write about themselves, without needing to disguise agency or cite the voices of others, we were bending some rules and eliminating others, on the surface making the task seem easier. But we were also playing new games, games of identity and relational games embedded in discourse, whose rules and outcomes were less clear and whose strategies ran the risk of wounding egos and damaging collegial trust. The stories in this section are my reflections on these new games, not just my perceptions of what the authors were going through, although their voices are also present. They are my perceptions of author–editor relationships, where the struggles of the authors I worked with cannot be separated from my role as editor or from my role as an author who was having equally distressing problems constructing an unconventional public identity.

THE AUTHORS

John

When I began the editing project and my coeditor and I were beginning to make a list of and contact people we thought might be able to write essays that would fit our rather vaguely defined purposes, I immediately thought of John Fanselow. He was a well-established and well-known second language educator who had been active in the field from his base in New York City for many years. I did not know him personally, had never met him, but knew him through his well-attended always entertaining conference presentations and through his less frequent publications. In his conference presentations, he often talked about and demonstrated the importance of changing one's routines, doing things differently, taking risks. One of his books on teaching, in fact, is called *Breaking Rules* (Fanselow, 1987). I reasoned that the writing task my coeditor and I had designed would suit him ideally, that he would probably find it both easy and enjoyable. I saw him at a conference and approached him about the project, wrote him the details later, and he accepted.

We met in New York on one of my trips there, and began to talk about the project and about what issues in his teaching and writing life might make a suitable story. When we met and I got to sit across the table from him at the apartment of a friend of mine in New York, I found him thinner and older than I'd remembered. He had been someone I'd seen mostly from afar at conferences, and mostly many years ago. It was a bit like time traveling. His slightly hunched shoulders, thoughtful blue eyes wandering down and up and sideways as he constructed thoughts, and casual dress were all familiar as was his distinctive voice and straightfaced humor.

John often commuted to Tokyo, where his Japanese wife (a professor at a Yokohama university) and two daughters resided and where he ran the Tokyo branch of Teachers College Columbia University. He had been past president of the TESOL organization, had helped run the Teachers College Columbia University MA TESOL program in New York and Tokyo for many years, and was unflaggingly committed to helping students and teachers dare to take risks in their thinking and teaching practices. As I got to know him better through our project and by signing on to work as a weekend adjunct in the Tokyo MA program, I learned from some of his MA students that he sometimes gave them no guidelines at all about what to do in class on some days, and that on occasion he would even leave the room. They would have to set something in motion themselves. But after a lifetime of trying to get his students to think and act on their own, he was still treated as the expert whose job it was to tell students and conference goers what to do. It was here that I thought lay an interesting paradox that would make a valuable addition to our book of reflective essays.

Denise

Unlike John, Denise Murray was a known entity to me. I had known her for nearly 10 years, through regular if infrequent contact beginning at the time when she left Stanford University and I entered, taking over her teaching fellowship in the ESL support program for graduate students. Denise was one of the busiest people I knew, a fact that I surmised kept her as thin as she always was. Constantly battling the politics at her university and very active in the California and national TESOL organizations, she somehow managed as well to receive rave reviews from her students, to whom she was devoutly committed. In the tiny spaces between all this activity, she wrote a book, attended and spoke at multiple conferences, had dinners and discussions with her husband, cuddled her two cats, and took trips to Australia to visit her aging parents. In her presence, I could feel myself deflating as one frantic story after another poured from her. I often found myself wondering what I had been doing with my own time and whether my own lack of involvement in political activism signified that I was not fully committed to my field. (These insidious comparisons have often been the bane of my professional life.)

At the time our book project was in full swing, Denise was at the pinnacle of her career. She had been elected president of the now enormous TESOL organization, had carved out a real department in her university of which she was chair, and had been promoted to full professor. Who better to take a risk with writing, to reflect on a career issue, than someone like Denise? I had heard a plenary talk she'd given at a conference, and it was filled with intense and passionate discourse about the need for changes in how second language students were viewed particularly by state governments and education systems. Something in her personal history must have contributed to her reformist zeal. She agreed to join us.

Judy

Judy Winn-Bell Olsen was someone that, like John, I had admired from afar for many years in her role as a popular and charismatic conference presenter at TESOL and affiliated conferences. She had always struck me as poised, confident, strikingly good looking, effervescent and enthusiastic, and an exceptionally competent and committed ESL teacher and teacher educator. I gleaned all this from her conference presentations, which were always packed with admiring teachers whom Judy treated with deep respect and good humor. We spoke once many years ago about her thoughts of one day going back to school for her PhD, and she sought some of my reflections on my life in my own PhD program as an "older" student. It was then that I saw the cracks in the public persona that Judy shared with the world, and realized that here was another one of us whose lack of confidence was deeply buried and disguised. At the time she may not have realized that she was looking at someone of the same ilk, but she was. I was able with certainty to tell her that if I could do it, she could too. A reflective and thoughtful person by nature, if my inferences from her public presentations and my few meetings with her could be trusted, she would certainly be able to construct an unconventional textual self that would make a nice addition to our book. In particular, I wondered how she managed a life so packed with teaching and conference presentations without collapsing from burnout. I wondered what was driving her desire to connect with and inspire other teachers and how she managed, or if she managed, to keep a positive outlook in a field known for marginalizing teachers and students.

ISSUES

During the long and difficult writing and revising process, a number of issues emerged for me and for some of the contributors, including John, Denise, and Judy, as we worked at constructing different versions of our selves. The issues I discuss here are:

1. The difficulty of writing in an unfamiliar genre and letting go of familiar conventions of writing.
2. The purpose and ethics of disclosing personal issues in a public forum.
3. The coconstructed nature of textual identities in edited writings.

My observations of my relationships with the three authors need to be understood in the context of the project we were all involved in, a project that had a specific purpose, and whose purpose evolved in increasingly specific terms in my interactions with the contributors. In my discussion of the author–editor relationship in this section, I refer only to my own relationship with the three authors described in this chapter, and do not speak directly for Sandra, who worked with other authors on the project, other than to refer to some written communications by her. We did, however, both read all drafts by all authors carefully, and agreed on all feedback before we separately communicated with each author.

Letting Go of the Conventions

A number of us, all professional language educators, balked and hemmed and hawed (or whatever the written equivalent is of hemming and hawing) at the prospect of writing our own narratives for this book, skirting personal issues by hiding behind the familiar discourse and purposes of the academy. It was difficult to let go of our deeply ingrained training in academic discourse in order to construct an essay around the personal pronoun "I." For example, some authors who hesitated to use first person throughout their essays began with a strong personal anecdote, then switched to passive and third person constructions as they simultaneously shifted the focus away from themselves to an issue they were interested in. Additionally, in early drafts some of the authors decorated their issues with citations, losing themselves in the words and works of others.

I did this too. I remember how I felt about this dilemma: If I write about my feelings about and experiences with academic discourse (the topic of my essay), I want readers to know two things. First, I want them to know some of the background to my thinking, which has been well documented in the literature on academic discourse. At some level, I felt that readers would not fully grasp my dilemma without knowing that aspects of it have been written about already. Equally important was my desire to let readers know that I had done my homework—that I was not writing about a topic without having studied and paid due respect to the work of others, and that my essay would add to existing literature. In short, I did not want to embarrass myself professionally by not playing one of the academic literacy games that I had learned so well—that of situating my writing within existing literature and couching my own voice in the established voices of others.

Another convention that some of us had trouble letting go of was that of using academic writing to explicate and to teach. I found that in early drafts, I and several other authors tended to make a point, then give some evidence to support that point, then explicate the point to death. We were trained to teach, inform, explicate, analyze, and this is what we teach our students to do. We were not trained to show, to demonstrate, then to step back and let the demonstration (in this case, the story) convey the message without the follow up explication and analysis. Many of us believe that writing that does not explicate and analyze is not academic writing, yet this is just the convention that Sandra and I as editors wished to challenge with this collection of essays.

John was a second language educator known for his unconventional teaching style and conference presenting. He easily challenged the conventional academic format in his first draft by writing a 10-page hypothetical dialogue between himself and two imaginary attendees at one of his conference presentations. When I first glanced at his dialogue-essay, I was thrilled. We had none others like this in the collection so far, and a dialogue format would certainly challenge existing conventions of academic discourse. But after reading the first few exchanges in the dialogue, I saw a problem in the question–answer format John had set up: The attendees were asking him why his conference presentations were so unconventional and he was giving them his answers. I realized that the conversation sounded explicating, self-aggrandizing, and preachy, exactly the opposite of what we were seeking in the book. The dialogue also misrepresented this author, I believe, in that most of his colleagues do not describe him as self-aggrandizing and preachy. Thus, as easy as it was for him to break with the conventional format, he found it challenging to let go of the explicative function of academic prose, particularly when he had set up a dialogue between himself as a knower and two hypothetical conference attendees, Jeff and Erica, as learners.

On a trip back to California I talked at length with Sandra about John's contribution, trying to find ways John could make his dialogue technique work. I then met with John in person over a long lunch on my university campus during one of his stays in Japan. I was struck then and continued to be struck with what I saw could be the heart of his piece—the profound paradox I thought he was faced with and did not fully recognize. This paradox was that of not being able to escape his expert persona in order to convey his deeply felt message that he was not as much of an expert as people thought, and to convince his readers that they had to find their own way to their goals. After I had more conversations and e-mail exchanges with Sandra, she drafted a long letter to John that included the following points that we both agreed we needed to communicate to him:

> As you know, we both have concerns about the effect created by the use of the dialogue technique. Perhaps this is because Erica and Jeff are clearly your apprentices/juniors, and their deference to you (which I understand is an artistic ploy for creating a vehicle for your perspective) causes the piece to sound self-serving. This is an impression that Chris and I are determined to avoid—it is important for us that the focus remain on issues or struggles in the development of a professional persona. ... To cut to the chase: My recommendation for reworking the piece in order to most effectively highlight the central thesis is to convert the piece to essay form. ... (letter from Sandra Schecter, July 13, 1994)

As Sandra pointed out in the letter and as I repeatedly stressed in my informal meetings with John, the piece needed to be about him, about an issue in his experience that caused him some conflict (e.g., the paradox that Sandra and I saw), not about Erica and Jeff and their responses to him as an expert though rather iconoclastic second language educator.

In a later taped interview I had with John, transcribed and used as a handout for a conference presentation by several of the authors who were reflecting on the writing process they had gone through ("The Challenge of Writing Our Own Stories," TESOL 1998, Seattle, Washington), he said that one problem was that

> ... you are used to writing in a particular way. I mean certain articles where you don't use the first person and you're not supposed to show your personal kind of feelings, you're just supposed to stand back and have some distance. ... Academic writing means it has a lot of jargon in it, and it's totally incomprehensible to anyone who reads it, including the author three or four

months after the author has written it. (Interview, March, 1998/TESOL 1998 handout)

In the first two versions of his essay, both dialogues, John was certainly using first person, but I felt he was not present even though he was the central character in the dialogues. In spite of what seemed to him to be a personal stance, he had managed to achieve a certain conventional distance, to stand back, and not to show the workings of his mind and heart. Moreover, the majority of his side of the dialogue with the two naive conference goers sounded like the expert teaching the novices. The irony of course is that he is an expert, but one who does not want to play that particular game in front of conference goers and students, and who in fact does not claim to be the expert people take him for. However, the convention of explication by a distanced authoritative persona permeated John's early contributions.

Two drafts later, after our discussions and Sandra's letter, John went back to the drawing board again, drafting a new piece altogether, in a somewhat more conventional essay form but with a distinct literary quality and without the more insidiously conventional overtones of explication and didacticism (Fanselow, 1997). In our conference preparation interview he admitted that he had written "two versions which were very pedantic and direct and unemotional. And then finally I hit upon the third version," he said, "which is not the third version—it is a totally different piece."

In several other instances, in their attempts to conclude with general solutions and suggestions typical of academic genres, some authors shifted from first person to the omniscient "we": "We need to. . . ." "We should . . . ," "It is essential that we . . . ," and so on. Repeatedly, Sandra and I reminded authors that the conventionally structured concluding message did not belong in this essay. This essay, we hoped, unlike those that academics usually write, would end with the *author*, without an answer or a sense that he or she had "arrived," without a suggestion for what anyone else should do, but with the personal story, at its current stage, with hints of continued developments in the future.

Denise, activist, reformer, teacher, was one of the authors who could not let go of her mission to teach her readership about the injustices in the marginalized field of English as a second language and to end with a "we need to" message. She did not see her role as author as one of talking about herself but about her field and her passionate beliefs about how positive change could be brought about. Denise describes the start of our long and difficult author-editor journey like this:

In the fall of 1991, Chris invited me to participate in this book project, after a discussion about a plenary address I'd given at a [conference] in San Diego—

"Ending Marginalization: An Agenda for Change." Because all of the issues I addressed in this paper are dear to my heart, I thought it could be reworked for the book. Chris agreed. In January 1992, I received the formal letter of invitation. Being pressed for time, I merely mailed off the original plenary paper for feedback. (Murray, 1997b, p. 209)

This first draft did in fact use first person, and did incorporate several narratives, but they were anecdotes about other people, composites of teachers she had known who worked way too hard with too little in the way of recognition and compensation. The core issue of professionalism in the ESL field came across as their issue, not hers. In my first letter to her, after discussions with Sandra, I wrote:

[T]he theme of professionalism is great. . . . The substance of the paper is also right on track, such as your descriptions of how ESL does not enjoy the status of a profession. We're particularly interested in how *you* came to be aware of this as a problem, and how *you* have worked and are continuing to work through it as a driving force in your career as a language educator.

As Denise describes it, she "could not get anywhere" with her revision, having "no sense of audience and certainly no sense of what I wanted to tell them, except the pain I felt because our field was so marginalized" (Murray, 1997b, p. 210). Again pressed for time, she dabbled with the original paper, and resubmitted it, but the paper's conventional message remained. Denise was writing about a problem in her field and her ideas of how to solve this problem rather than about herself. My response in a letter in the summer of 1993 included the following suggestions, this time stated much more directly;

Change title: This should not be a "We Need To . . ." piece, but a personal sojourn.

Theme good—The field is devalued because ESL is a marginalized profession and because ESL learning is considered remediation and therefore looked down on.

Some of the anecdotes are colorful and expressive. . . .

Avoid arguments for and against making ESL a discipline. . . .

There's a lot to work with from p. 1 to top of p. 8. After that the paper fits another purpose, another audience. [Add] a very different conclusion, short, punchy, one that brings you back into the picture. . . .

Denise said she felt "devastated" by the letter, still unsure of where to go next but willing to keep working on this difficult piece of writing. In her next try, after we had had a long and personal discussion about her family background, Denise could still not let go of the "here-is-how-to-end-marginalization" tone, even though she was now prepared to see that she had two selves that somehow worked in tandem—a controlling reformer self and a nurturing teacher self. The title of this next draft reflected this duality but in third-person form and still focused on her how-to message: "Negotiating Standards of Professionalism: Reform or Self-Actualization?" (Murray, 1997b, p. 210). I once again asked her to illustrate her issues and her commitment to self-actualization through scenarios from her own life that illustrated the dilemma that she, not just the field, faced. An editor at our publishing house followed up on these suggestions in a detailed letter to Denise. Then, on her sabbatical in Australia, she created a new essay, one about her (Murray, 1997a). "I realized I was telling MY story, MY dilemma, not advocating for change" (Murray, 1997b, p. 211). How difficult this was, to find the self amidst the issues in one's work, to let go of the need to teach, and to bend the rule that says that authors need to stay in the background of their writing.

In short, some of us found it difficult to let go of the conventions of academic discourse that require writers to situate their work in a body of literature, to "objectify" the issues, to explain and analyze a point, to conclude with a message or implication, and to place ourselves as authors into the background. Even though we wanted stories that set readers up to make their own discoveries, extract their own implications, and construct their own conclusions, it was hard to let go.

Disclosing Personal Issues in Public

I had communicated with Judy by e-mail over several years about the evolution of her essay and was surprised that she was having serious problems completing even a first draft for this project. I asked her to join the project because I knew her from conference presentations and brief interactions as a warm and humanistic teacher, and presumed that our efforts to "humanize" academic discourse would suit her well. We exchanged e-mail over many months as she sought a theme, perhaps related to burnout, that was both fresh and current for her and that suited what she thought we wanted—the search for a "me" that could be printed in a book. In May of 1993, Judy e-mailed me about some questions I had asked her about how she dealt with burnout:

> Since your fax when you asked "Where are YOU in your stories of burnout? What happened to you?" etc. I've been struggling with the writing I said I'd do for you. I think I finally understand the level of personalization that you want, and I'm not sure I can give it to you very extensively on a topic that I've already synthesized into publishable prose. . . . I've put it at some distance from me, and after generalizing, I've lost the personal particulars. (Olsen, 1997, p. 214)

Nearly a year later, still trying to figure out what to write, and what we as editors wanted, she e-mailed again, noting for the first time that it might be "tricky" to be both personal and professional in the same piece:

> I'm rather relieved to hear that many other people seem to be having a difficult time of it too. I think it's particularly hard for people who have polished one style and stance to be "up close and personal"—and still professional—in print. Trading stories over drinks is one thing—that's backstage kind of stuff. But anything in print with one's name attached is definitely front-and-center-stage, and it's tricky. (Olsen, 1997, p. 215)

Eventually, Judy sent an early draft that she titled "Focus on the Teacher," in which she had talked about finding what is essential in teaching and letting that knowledge help teachers ride through the bad times. As was the case with Denise, I didn't see Judy in this early draft and urged her to focus more on herself. As she summarized in an e-mail to me in the summer of 1994:

> It seems to me now that all things are cyclical and in the bad times you figure out what's most essential, hold on to that, and wait for the better times which do roll around again. Which was essentially my drift, I believe, in "Focus on the Teacher," which is what I thought would work for you in the first place but which you said didn't have enough "me" in it.

During a conference panel in which several contributors presented early versions of their essays, Judy in fact found more "me" by delving deeply and emotionally into her family background, setting up a theme of dualities in her life. In her e-mail message to me after the conference, she said that her orally told stories that included deeply personal anecdotes about her father and step-father felt "true" but that "somehow it doesn't feel deeply right, doesn't resonate, for the theme and tone of your book" (Judy, e-mail summer, 1994). She continued, struggling to explain that perhaps it wasn't the time to "freeze" her ongoing and changing human relationships in print and that oral stories of disclosure could not easily be turned into written narratives:

> Maybe [my theme] hasn't grown enough yet. Certainly most of the principals in my duality theme are still living growing human beings, as are the relationships with them, and freezing them in a still shot (much less letting them actually READ what I've written!) is difficult. Or maybe it's one of those elusive creatures that will captivate as it swims by in an oral presentation, but if you land it in print, the colors fade as it flops around and dies.

Judy was beginning to express her discomfort at the thought of exposing deeper layers of herself in print for the public to see. Storytelling over drinks was fine, and "immortalizing ourselves" (her words) in print also sometimes motivated our desire to write for publication. But Sandra and I had asked people for honest, gripping stories—ones that would inspire, and that readers could connect with in their own struggles to become (better) language educators. It turned out that the layers that we were asking her to peel back and commit to print may have left her too vulnerable to comply at that particular time.

Later that same year, she wrote again, this time much more directly about her discomfort with disclosure:

> Somehow a "personal story" is not so personal when it's down there in black and white for anyone to read (one can no longer choose the audience, setting, etc., for disclosure, and degree of disclosure) and when anyone can do anything with/to it, you know not what. One loses control of something very central to oneself. . . . The people who do written self-disclosure best, I think, are the poets, playwrights, novelists—though they fashion their own veils and drape them just so to reveal just what they choose to. But many of the rest of us are at a distinct disadvantage here—not only are we not used to diving into our own unconscious murk for pearls, but we may not recognize them when we find them, and when we do, we're at a loss what to do with them. (Olsen, 1997, p. 217)

Judy expressed the dilemma that many academics face—that of not having experience in our particular academic communities of writing about ourselves. As all of us learned in this project, one way we had to bend the rules was to find a way to fashion our own veils and drape them just so. In Judy's case, she did not find a way to do this in an essay. Instead, some of her e-mail reflections, rather than a personal narrative, ended up in our book.

John, too, had to sought a way to honestly portray himself as both expert and nonexpert and to come to terms with the fact that no matter what his philosophy of equality might be, he was perceived as an authority. The questions he asked rhetorically in our interview applied not only to his relationship with his students but to the construction of his identity in his essay:

> How honest can you be? In other words, how much do you want to be a myth with your students and how much do you want to kind of lord it over them that you know something that they don't know and how much to want to kind of come out and say well we're in this together. . . . so to me the challenge was can I be honest and how honest can I be—I mean how much can I reveal about my total inadequacy, about knowing certain things? (Interview, March, 1998)

In another part of our interview, he spoke of the need to find an honest voice in the face of convention:

> So in teaching, in writing, whether you're in a scientific area or a less scientific area, I think the same thing is important—what is the truth as you see it and how can you step back and honestly reveal to other people what you believe and what you think is going on in reality? And not to try to please other people and not to try to say "Oh, I better do this because this is the kind of convention." . . . So my problem with this [essay] was changing the voice from what I was used to doing and also being honest and [figuring out] how honest can you be. (Interview, March, 1998)

John dealt with his search for an honest voice with relish, returning multiple times to the proverbial drawing board before drafting an essay that received a unanimous enthusiastic response by us as editors and by his collegial readers (Fanselow, 1997).

Nevertheless, it turned out that for a number of us (all women) some of the truly honest stories that we might tell of incidents in our career development touched wires that were too live and nerves that were too raw to set down in print, as Judy suggested in her e-mail reflections. I recall my lunch one day with Denise at a favorite Mexican restaurant in California where we sometimes met. We had been talking for more than an hour about her essay, in which I saw her having great difficulty getting at the heart of the main issue in her professional life. The pieces just didn't fit together. She finished her margarita and suddenly burst into tears. What followed then was her unedited story, one of struggle to lift herself out of a family where her parents had worked like dogs all their lives for little reward. Their passivity in the face of injustice spurred her to social and political consciousness of the sort she had always wished her father had been able to muster. Her mixture of guilt, anger, and sadness about her father's life in particular had driven her entire career, but she could not expose this in print for him and others to see. Not yet, at least, and not in this raw form. Denise later did choose to make this story public, in oral form at our panel conference presentation. She eventually revised this oral presentation into a short narrative for a concluding piece for the book in which she talked about the long and difficult process of constructing her essay and about what seemed to be holding her back from looking closely at her own motives and agendas (Murray, 1997b).

In my own case, I wanted to write an essay about my long and conflicted relationship with academic discourse and my sense that people hid behind their prose (Casanave, 1997). The first rambling version was filled not only with broad impersonal and oversimplified references to "academic discourse," but also with remarks designed to express the depth of my lifelong lack of confidence in my intellect. The result seemed self-deprecating, and even dishonest to those who know me and are not convinced that I lack either confidence or intellect. Moreover, the image that emerged from the early essay was not one that I wanted to be known by, even though at some level it felt true. The permanent and public nature of the essay project shaped how I recast the image of myself, and ultimately prevented my confessing my sense of inadequacy in a way that I might have over cocktails. I rewrote my own story several times, over a period of 2 years, with feedback from Sandra, John, and several other colleagues, before I found the personal angle that I could tell in public without undue shame and self-deprecation—the disclosure rather than the confession (Bleich, 1998). Is it an honest story, given that I am still periodically brought low by feelings that I will never match up to some mythical set of standards against which I have measured myself all my professional life? Perhaps it is one of the many inevitably partially true stories (as all stories of self in print must be) that together constitute an honest portrayal of the self.

It may seem at this point as though this project was intended to extract deeply personal and painful confessions of how things really are from authors, not unlike van Maanen's (1988) "confessional tales" designed for the same purpose in ethnographic writing. We did not conceive of the project in these terms, and if we had, I myself would have questioned the ethics of our motives. But the line between disclosure and confession was thin as well as fuzzy since the project did ask people to look closely and self-reflectively at an aspect of their professional development, and to look below the surface of the basic narrative. What was revealing was the extent to which some of our stories reached into the past and stemmed from acute discomforts in childhood or youth. We encouraged authors to pursue such stories because we believed they would resonate well with an audience of language educators, particularly younger ones who may not realize that today's well-established educators had beginnings not unlike their own. Discomfort accompanied this search process, both at the personal level and at the level of text construction as authors worked to find acceptable ways to construct a self for a public audience. Some of the stories were not ready to be recast as narratives for publication and may indeed be appropriate only as oral stories told to trusted confidants. Other stories remain untold.

The Coconstructed Nature of Textual Identities in Edited Writings

All writing is perhaps in some sense coconstructed in that it is impossible to write without the influence of external voices (from readings, from friends, students, and colleagues, from others' and one's own past voices), as Bakhtin told us long ago. What makes an edited project like this so interesting is that some of the influences on the writings that contributors submitted can be traced directly to the editors because we were insisting on certain kinds of texts and not others. In my own case, the authors I worked with closely also helped me articulate my vision and expectations in ways that I had not done so before. When I sensed that the authors had something important to say, based on rambling conversations or e-mail with them, I had to put my finger on what that something was. Carola Conle (1996) talked about this when she said that she "was able to recognize the resonance among elements in [a preservice teacher's] experiential stories," enabling the preservice teacher to reconstruct her stories (p. 317). What was unseen, by both the authors and by me, came into focus. When they were having trouble finding a focus or a theme or a style, I had to negotiate with them about some of the possible directions to take next. I asked a lot of questions, did a lot of listening, and sometimes even then was not able to help. However, without these dissonances that surfaced in some of the contributions, I would not have been forced to peel back some of the layers of what I later came to call my "agenda." In other words, the clarifications I was forced to make not only pushed the authors to continue, but helped me understand more about the project itself and about my own writing. In some instances actual feedback on my own essay drafts, from John and from Sandra in particular, helped me return to the drawing board more than once.

It is probably the case that the editor–author relationship I had with John, Denise, and Judy differed from most editor–author relationships. Certainly in the several cases where I have contributed a chapter to an edited book I have had no ongoing discussions with editors, beyond requests for small and expected editorial changes in length, transitions, and so on. I had not had experience with an editor who made requests and demands on me the way that Sandra and I were making requests and demands on authors. The authors I worked with were established midcareer scholars, some of them with strong publication records and reputations. I am guessing that they had rarely experienced the kinds of intrusions into their writing that we made.

Judy, Denise, and John and I, went around and around over several iterations of their contributions. Judy, as I mentioned, ended up not contributing an essay but a selection of her e-mail musings. As I look over some of those messages, I realize that our e-mail conversations over several years pulled out ideas (and identities?) from Judy that she might not otherwise have recognized and put into words. Judy's sometimes long and rambling musings, likewise, helped me think about the book project and about my own writing in new ways. I thought initially that we were communicating about her contribution to the book, that my role was to help her focus and to find the theme that ran through her messages. But as time passed, and as Judy herself became increasingly involved in the next major stage in her career (pursuit of a PhD), I realized that there would be no essay. Her messages evolved into one about the role of author disclosure in publications in the field of second language education. Her own public and professional identity remained veiled in the printed musings, as did her personal identity and I could do no more than respect her choices and appreciate her contributions to my own thinking.

In the case of Denise, the more she and I talked, the more clearly I saw a dilemma that I think she did not recognize early in the writing process. It seemed to me that she harbored a fundamental conflict in the images she presented to the professional world (the image of a reformer who controls and the image of a nurturer who lets people discover). For this essay, she had to find a way to articulate sets of conflicting truths about her professional behaviors and beliefs. Attempting in early drafts to teach readers about political issues in the field of second language education that she felt very committed to, she moved in later drafts to a more insightful and at times uncomfortable exploration of her political–legislative self and her nurturing self. I think that she discovered something important about herself by being pushed to write this kind of essay and by negotiating the constructing of her public identity over time. This discovery of self did not evolve just through the writing process. Instead, it evolved partly in response to aspects of her character that others saw in her and that were brought to light through her private reflections and through face-to-face and e-mail interactions with me as editor and friend. I wondered aloud to her about what she told me. How did she manage to reconcile her top-down, demanding, legislative persona devoted to rectifying injustices in the ESL world through activist and reformist agendas with her more nurturing persona dedicated to helping students find their own answers? Her original response of "What dilemma?" evolved over time into an awareness that two very different forces drove her professional life and were in some sense incommensurable. As a writing task, this evolution required many hours of talk and reflection, and relatively few hours of actual drafting and revising. The process was difficult for Denise and me, not just because I kept prodding her to look more closely at herself and at a painful past, but also because it put me in the uncomfortable role of trying to shape the work of a more accomplished peer.

I was in a similarly potentially uncomfortable role with John, who was someone well-known in the field but known to me at first only by reputation. We talked at length several times, but I did not know how to interpret our conversations, which were always friendly and interesting but which gave me few clues as to whether I was expressing myself in a way that he understood my messages. I soon learned that John was exceptional in the sense that he seemed to go willingly and pleasurably back to the drawing board not once, but three times. Each new essay (they were new essays, not new drafts) presented different versions of himself and used different techniques for doing so. I do not know if all of the representations of himself I saw in these essays were different selves in his eyes, but they were, in practice different, since each had been constructed by him after our author–editor negotiations and resulted in a different self in printed drafts. At no point did he submit a draft saying "Here's my latest, but it really doesn't feel like me." On the contrary, with each version, he sent notes saying that this was the most interesting and valuable writing he had done in his professional life, and that each version had also been recognized by colleagues as some of his most interesting and personal work.

What selves emerged in the writings that John submitted and what role did our conversations have in constructing those selves? In early versions I saw a teacher–preacher whose verbal message was that he could not teach anything to anyone, but could only work at convincing people to find their own way. This message actually formed the thread that united all his essays. However, his preachy dialogue-essays contradicted his message, confusing me as to the genuineness of the message itself. He was trying to teach us that he couldn't teach us anything. In our conversations, how was I to handle the problem of what seemed to me to be the portrayal of an inappropriately didactic self who was sending contradictory messages? I recall wrestling with a series of questions and of how to pose them to John: Was the problem in his early drafts one of incompatible selves as it had been with Denise, the legislator–nurturer? Or was it problem of writing style or format or genre? Or was it a profound philosophical dilemma? To what extent was John aware of the dilemma and how should I best talk to him about what I thought I saw? After several conversations where I tried to focus on some of these questions, I remained puzzled as to whether we were connecting. I could not read John's responses the way I could Denise's; I could not tell whether he was listening, cogitating, or resisting, nor did I know how he truly had reacted to the long suggestion-filled letter that Sandra had sent. Over time, if his subsequent drafts are an indication, I think we were connecting. Later versions of John's contribution continued to sound preachy to me, but other selves began emerging—the author as storyteller, the author as close observer of nature and people, the author as poet and lover of poetry. These later selves eventually took over, I believe, because, first, they were there waiting to emerge, and second, because his didactic selves had been pushed aside in the author–editor negotiations.

I often worried that both John and Denise, and even Judy, might see me as an editorial bully, so focused on my own agenda that I would smother their voices. It is a tribute to them that these negotiations—this coconstruction of their identities in their final contributions—did not result in strained relationships between them and me, but in stronger collegial bonds that I was also able to benefit from in my own drafting and rewriting. Always oversensitive to criticism, I believed I was less resilient than they in reconstructing my own public identity. I learned from them how important it is to establish a candid yet sensitive relationship with my own peer readers as well as with them. John's comments in two documents, a long letter to me about half-way through his composing process and his conference interview with me for our TESOL panel presentation more than 2 years later, encapsulate the best parts of the author–editor relationship and represent for me an ideal that I know is rare in such relationships. I mention these here because they reflect key issues about the coconstruction of textual identities that bend the rules of conventional academic discourse.

In his 1995 letter and in our 1998 conference interview, John surprised me with a number of comments, the content of which he had only hinted at in our face-to-face conversations. In the interview, he said, curiously, that the feedback from his closest colleagues was not particularly helpful because they knew him too well—they were "too close and couldn't notice" that his early drafts did not seem honest (John's words). The author–editor feedback, on the other hand, including not just conversations with me but written feedback from Sandra, had pushed him in directions he would not otherwise have gone. In our early conversations he had been skeptical about the place of emotion and reflection in his writing. By the time he was working on his third version of his essay, one that was richly reflective and personal, he wrote this to me in a letter, expressing how much he had changed:

> I am grateful to you for the conversations we had which enabled me to produce this piece. As I pointed out to those who have read the piece, it has been in the making for two years and it represents a third totally different version of where I started my journey with you. I hope in your introduction [to the book] you will remind readers of the journeys you made with the authors and how much energy it took for us to free ourselves from the academic, distanced writing we have been "taught" to do. I mentioned the value of and editor who can be candid and of the need to be able to reject what one has written and to start fresh over and over as part of the writing process. (Letter from John, December 18, 1995)

By the 1998 interview, John was using a concept that he had not used before—that of voice. He said that he had finally gotten "his voice" in the final version and that as editor, "you, Chris, were able to get me to speak with a different voice—different from the voice that I've been trained to use and I think it's more my real voice" (Interview, March, 1998). (He may not know that he, too, with his extensive feedback on my own essay, helped me develop a personal voice that I could put into print.) One of his points in this interview was that "everybody is giving some voice that they think should be their voice," not their own voice. He did not use the concept of "game" here, but in these comments he implicitly referred to at least two kinds of games. One was the game of conventional academic discourse practices, as he noted, those we are taught to play. The other was the delicate author–editor relationship in which two or more personalities and agendas interact to achieve one piece of writing, in this case a piece of writing that unconventionally fronted personal aspects of the authors' identities. It is not possible to disentangle the separate contributions of author and editor or of author and other readers who provided feedback, but I think that John, Denise, and Judy and I would agree that our individual contributions to the book would not have happened without our interacting over time and over our respective troubled waters.

Ironies

I would like to conclude this discussion of author–editor construction of textual identities with some observations that I cannot reconcile in a clean way. These have to do with the fact that in trying to dismantle one kind of academic writing game, my coeditor, Sandra, and I were establishing new games with equally constrained rules for play. A second irony has to do with the fact that reflective and personal narratives resulted in some cases from a great deal of intervention by outsiders, in some case outsiders (i.e., editors) who did not share a personal history with the authors.

In the first case, I guess my point here is that selves in this project, my own included, were discovered and shaped in great part through the requisites of a rather tightly defined writing task, one that became more precisely defined as time passed and we were forced to articulate our vision of what we were looking for. Sandra and I realized early in the project that it was not just any sort of personal narrative of professional development that we sought. These narratives had to match our vision for this collection, a vision we had articulated to some extent in our proposals to publishers, but that we discovered much more about along the way as we got submissions that we sensed would fit or knew would not fit. Then, as our vision grew more detailed, we persuaded, coerced, demanded, suggested, and wrangled until authors' representations of their selves fit what we called "the spirit of the book." It was the nature of this particular writing task that imposed the guidelines for how this self could be storied, guidelines that themselves opened dozens of possibilities and angles, while simultaneously excluding others.

As I struggled with my own essay and worked with John, Denise, Judy, and several other authors, I found myself constructing these guidelines and passing them on bit by bit in oral and written feedback: Present yourself as a fully dimensional person, not just as a scholarly academic. Refrain from citing your own works too much so as to avoid coming across as arrogant or self-satisfied. Avoid citing many works at all so that you don't bury your voice in the authoritative voices of others. Emphasize that you are in the middle of a journey, not that you have come a long way and finally gotten there. Don't pretend to have all the answers. Or, if you think you have answers, go back to the drawing board and look for gaps. Recognize that you did not learn all you know or develop all your beliefs in graduate school—we know your professional self began to be crafted long before that. Write in a way that fronts your reflective powers and your survival capabilities rather than in a way that makes you seem like a victim of your hard times. Recognize the inconsistencies in your own beliefs and practices and exploit these mismatches to peel back layers of self and to connect with readers whose professional lives are also characterized by similar mismatches (a normal state of affairs, we presumed). Write with flair and grace.

More broadly, the practice of this new game involved storytelling, but the nature of the project determined that only certain kinds of stories would fulfill our purposes. The stories, written up in their narrative form, had to be multilayered and nontrivial, and they had to resonate with readers. They had to reveal personal but not confessional aspects of the authors' identities that not only resonated with readers but that helped the authors themselves reconceptualize their own identities and see their professional lives in ways they may not have seen them before. They were supposed to exhibit some kind of personal growth. As Jean Clandinin and Michael Connelly (1991) phrased it, "Deliberately storying and restorying one's life . . . is . . . a fundamental method of personal growth: It is a fundamental quality of education" (p. 259; cf. Donald Polkinghorne's [1991] notion of "re-emplotment"). These guidelines would not fill an *APA Manual*, but they worked to delineate some of the rules of the new game we were playing and show the extent to which the author–editor game in this project involved more than guidelines for textual practices. They involved guidelines for how to see and reconceptualize the self in interaction with an Other, an editor in this case, an ironic and potentially intrusive relationship.

The second irony of the edited book project is related to this potential intrusion of the editors into a project whose purpose was to collect deeply personal narratives by individual authors. We did intrude in perhaps half of the narratives, to greater or lesser degrees, using our roles as editors to justify the intrusions. The nature of the editor–author relationship in the project, in other words, was a relationship among peers but one that was characterized by conventional political game rules in academia about who has the ultimate say in shaping a piece of writing. The academic literacy practice of producing an edited book thus permitted the intrusions, even into these very personal narratives, and resulted in the kinds of negotiations I have already described. Although I now find this intrusion ironic, when I consider the alternative of not intervening at all—of accepting all that authors submitted in the first round of drafts—I realize that for this project, at any rate, the intrusions were justified and actually led some authors paradoxically to write essays that were far more personal than were their original drafts. So while we were bending some rules, we were adhering to other more conventional ones and creating some of our own, uncovering in the process many kinds and layers of serious academic literacy games played by established teachers and scholars who write as part of their lives in academia.

CHAPTER REFLECTIONS

After several iterations of this chapter, I am left with many of the original tensions that I began it with. Yes, established scholars can choose to bend some of the conventional rules that structure and guide their academic literacy practices, but other layers and types of guidelines including ones that might be considered innovative help determine what and how they write and how they represent themselves in their prose. Participating in different academic literacy practices requires that authors know aspects of many different writing games. I think it is within those game guidelines that change happens, but in ways that are negotiated, resisted, situated, and not necessarily predictable (see the collection of well-known influential pieces in Zamel & Spack, 1998).

One of the bright sides of my explorations in this chapter has been the reconfirmation of my belief that positive change can happen at any time in a career—that there is no such thing as finally arriving at some Utopian academic goal. I can bend existing guidelines, invent new ones, reinterpret old ones. I can choose dozens of ways to represent myself in my prose, ones that hide or reveal something about me as a person. I can use my writing and the decision processes that necessarily accompany my writing practices to look at my participation and positioning in those practices in new ways and to purposely recraft my different identities within my field. I don't have to see myself as a powerless victim of grand discourses whose game rules are set in stone. In his literacy autobiography, Victor Villanueva (1993) showed how different writing games can be juxtaposed—distancing games against connecting games—such that different layers of self move into different foregrounds and backgrounds, creating a mosaic of academic identity. John, Denise, Judy, and I also constructed a composite of selves in our edited book contributions by bending some rules and discovering and following new ones.

At some level, I think I have been seeking a way to portray the composite of selves honestly and accurately in academic writing much in the way that researchers in narrative and interpretivist traditions conventionally hope to portray their informants. At some level, in other words, I worry about telling lies, about myself and about the informants in my research, simply because the language I use and the brevity, linearity, and structure of my prose force fabrication. At some level I understand Howard Gardner's concern for accuracy and truth in his debate with Elliot Eisner about what a dissertation should consist of (Saks, 1996). But I think that accuracy implies both a kind of completeness and a kind of consistency that we can only strive for in studies of academic literacy practices that portray people—others or selves. Although some stories are clearly deeper and more complete than others, the story of a self is forever unfinished and therefore forever incomplete. Likewise, a self (an informant, an author) is characterized in part by inconsistencies, contradictions, and ongoing change. A detailed, carefully done study can capture some of these characteristics, but as Judy mentioned in her e-mail during the edited book project, it somehow doesn't feel right to freeze the picture in print. The picture represents just one of many possible angles that a camera could take at one of many possible distances. All selves represented in print are thus inaccurate, incomplete, only deceptively consistent, and necessarily partial.

Accepting the necessary partiality of how I represent myself and others in print has helped release me somewhat from the very constraining academic literacy games that have pushed many of us to demand accuracy, completeness, and consistency, as well as distance in our researching and writing. Because people themselves do not behave according to these standards, they are not achievable except through an academic literacy game that professes them to be so. However, whether I choose to play that particular game or ones that involve bending some of the conventional rules, I am still left with a partial representation of my self and the informants in my research, and therefore I still need to search for coherence in my literacy practices and in my construction and positioning of selves. As Giddens (1991) and Linde (1993) point out, people must find ways to make sense of the pieces of their lives, to do the "work of reconciliation" needed to create coherence from people's multimembership in diverse communities of practice (Wenger, 1998). It is to this search for coherence amidst the multiplicity of academic writing games we play that I turn to in the final chapter.

ACKNOWLEDGMENTS

Many thanks to John Fanselow, Denise Murray, and Judy Winn-Bell for participating in the construction of the third section of this chapter. You are and will remain valued colleagues and friends.

7

The Paradoxical Effort After Coherence in Academic Writing Games

This book has been about how academic writing practices that I refer to metaphorically as game-like are carried out by individuals in different academic settings in higher education and how these practices are implicated in the construction of writers' identities and the positioning of those identities within academic communities of practice. An assumption I do not contest is that within academic communities the purposes for writing differ as do the levels of expertise of the many players and that these purposes and levels of expertise are not fixed. A thread cutting across all settings and throughout this book, therefore, is that people's identities as novices or experts and as more or less peripherally or centrally positioned change as their practices change or as they seek new playing fields. As their practices change, in other words, their understandings change (an intellectual or cognitive transition) and their roles change (a social and political transition). The result is that they come to see themselves and be seen in new ways.

All the themes—writing as a game-like practice, more general theories of practice, issues of identity, transition, and enculturation—reflect the idea that people who write in university settings are all trying to create a sense of order in their worlds. Freshman writers need to make sense of the many disciplines they encounter and to learn to figure out the expectations of individual professors and their assignments. Graduate students need to find frameworks for their writing and thinking into which initially puzzling terminology, methods, and concepts fit. In the academic workplace, young faculty need to learn new academic literacy games from their positions as producers not just consumers of knowledge and to learn to play with political savvy, a task begun in graduate school. Established faculty may have a false sense of order in their routinized lives and need to find a way to create some dissonance, particularly because dissonance as well as order characterize academic inquiry. They may search for new games or ways to play old games in ways that stretch the rules. Their need to create some kind of order in their teaching and research, however, remains.

Although this book is about writing, my conceptualization of people striving through their writing practices to create order in their academic understandings and identities applies to far more than the specific task of constructing a written document. It is the latter task with which many writing textbooks and writing classes are primarily concerned. However, my view of this search for order applies additionally to writers' efforts to identify and locate themselves within relatively local academic communities of practice and to understand their locations as situated in broader playing fields. The need to create order applies as well to writers of books such as this one that consist of many different segments that were originally conceived of and researched if not written up at different times and with different populations of people. In each of the projects reported here I was broadly interested in similar themes but was also influenced by the local issues, readings, teaching, and discussions that I was involved in at the moment. Becoming absorbed with local phenomena can make it difficult for researchers like me to see clearly how the small pieces fit together in some meaningful way. The trick is to achieve a sense of wholeness amidst the complexity without succumbing to the lure of essences and singularity and without dismissing that complexity.

Some of the complexities of academic writing games can be seen in my reviews of studies of academic writing and in my own case study research. These studies have shown that academic writing does not happen in isolation, but within multicultural, social, and political networks of relationships for purposes that suit particular locally situated practices in college and university settings. These studies of individual writers and teachers of writing highlight the fact that each writer brings a history and particular sets of purposes and interpretations to each writing task and writing relationship— the relationships among students, teachers, peers, real and imagined readers, and gatekeepers. Writers' and teachers' histories and purposes encounter other forces within academic settings, such as disciplinary, departmental, and institutional influences, with which their personal histories and purposes may blend or clash. In short, the studies reveal some of the complex ways that writing games are played in local communities of practice, making it difficult to generalize about the umbrella term *academic literacy* or *academic writing*. In the face of such complexity, three groups of people need to find ways to make sense of the diverse writing practices they encounter and to construct coherent accounts of their own involvement in these practices and their own identities as practitioners: researchers, teachers, and writers themselves. I label this sense-making endeavor as *effort after coherence* and consider it basic to how people learn to participate in academic writing games. By *effort after coherence* I refer to the idea that people—academic writers, teachers, and researchers in these cases—need to find ways to construct coherent and meaningful accounts of their complex and chaotic worlds even if those accounts themselves are complex. They do this in part by narrating and describing to themselves, colleagues, and researchers who they are and what their practices consist of and mean, and in part by learning to enact routines that reduce uncertainty and that simultaneously reveal openings where change and flexible participation can occur.

However, a paradox in the idea that people in academic communities of practice need to find ways to construct a sense of coherence in their identities and writing practices is that one of the most serious academic literacy games involves trained skepticism, or the intentional search for complexity and uncertainty where none may be obvious on the surface.[1] Although this intentional search for complexity less frequently characterizes undergraduate academic literacy practices, in graduate programs and beyond, students and scholars are expected to question, doubt, and even disrupt routine beliefs and practices.

Graduate students at the MA level for example, are expected to critique what they read, yet paradoxically produce a written commentary that not only follows sometimes rigid academic conventions but that also presents a coherent discoursal identity to reader-evaluators. In the Monterey MA program that I discussed in Chapter 3, Karine tried to critique Krashen, but had trouble presenting a convincing case because her logic in that particular paper was not coherent, her tone was inconsistent, and as a document the critique did not follow coherent conventions of form. Natsuko on the other hand described in her final position paper her sense of increasing confusion as she became aware of the complexities and uncertainties in the TESOL field, but she did so in an elegant and coherent manner. PhD students like Nate, Moira, and Virginia (Chapter 4) are trained to critique, question, and analyze, yet to do so within the boundaries of coherent disciplinary conventions that may exclude what Virginia called "ordinary language." Later, as an established scholar, Ackerman (1995) ("Nate") was able to construct a more personal less conventional piece to reflect on his academic literacy enculturation, yet one that still fit within the boundaries of an academic book. Young scholars such as Xiao-Ming Li, Ulla Connor, and the bilingual academics in Japan that I worked with (Chapter 5) are simultaneously expected to disrupt their fields by contributing something new, yet, as Xiao-Ming Li discovered in her battle for tenure, to play a very conventional game by conducting research and constructing written documents that fit within familiar disciplinary boundaries. Doing unconventional re-

---

[1] I thank Paul Prior for helping me recognize the importance of this paradox.

search or writing the "wrong" kind of text always entails risk. The established scholars that I worked with in the edited book project (Chapter 6) found their coherent academic identities and writing styles disrupted by me and my coeditor because we were seeking, as part of the mandate we set forth for our book, to do something a bit different. We wanted to unsettle some of the more traditional conventions and expectations in academic writing, yet we hoped that this unsettling would itself result in another kind of coherence within individual pieces of writing and across the essays in the book as a whole. The paradox is inevitable in academic writing, and perhaps not resolvable.

Therefore, let me clarify that the case studies that I have reviewed and researched, as well as my own experiences as an academic writer, suggest to me that in the construct of "effort after coherence" the emphasis needs to be placed on the effort, the search and the struggle for meaning and wholeness and not on the elusive goal of truth. Like Karl Popper's mountain top ("truth"), forever hidden in clouds but pursuable nonetheless (Miller, 1985, pp. 185–186; Popper, 1979), I think that coherence of practice and identity can be pursued without ever being fully attained. In spite of real and intellectually desirable complexity in their lives, academic writers from undergraduate to professional levels behave as though coherence exists, seek it, and in the process go about trying to construct it. The search for coherence is an ongoing endeavor, not a static goal and we seek it at the same time as we seek complexity and accept uncertainty.

In this final chapter, then, I consider how these three groups of players in academic writing games—researchers, teachers, and writers—work to construct meaning and a sense of wholeness from the diversity and complexity of academic writing games. I first revisit the themes of game-playing, transitions, and identity that I introduced in Chapter 1, focusing on some of the complexities facing each group. Then as a backdrop to my discussion of the concept of *effort after coherence* I review the views of Giddens (1991), Wenger (1998), and scholars in narrative inquiry on the construction of coherent identities. Following this theoretical introduction, I explore some of the ways that academic writing researchers, teachers, and writers construct order and meaning from the complexities they face. From the researchers' perspective, I comment on various ways that researchers seek coherence, and then consider some of the ways that teachers seek coherence in their practices. I then speculate on ways that writers both reduce the complexity and uncertainty of their writing practices and come to accept them as normal, thus imposing on the practices and on themselves a kind of coherence that allows them to continue playing their serious writing games with a sense of meaning and purpose. I conclude by reflecting on my own efforts to pull together many years of my own research and writing into a book that has a semblance of coherence.

GAMES, TRANSITIONS, AND IDENTITY REVISITED

As I have implied throughout this book, learning to play academic writing games is not a simple matter of learning a generic set of formal features of texts and applying them to writing in different disciplines. It is, rather, a matter of learning to perceive—through the lenses of one's own cultural, intellectual, and personal history—the roles and functions of writing within localized disciplinary groups and, as many studies have shown, within specific courses and research groups led by individual teachers and researchers. Such groups are not only social; they are also political in that relationships of power are reflected in how and what people write whether they are freshmen or faculty, or whether they are mother-tongue speakers of English, Japanese, Chinese, or Armenian. Learning to play academic writing games is, further, a matter of understanding the potential for agency that all writers have to influence the many different games they will encounter during their time in academic settings. Finally, learning academic writing games requires that participants in academic communities reduce complexity and uncertainty and increase a sense of embodied practice in the process of becoming more proficient at some of many of the possible writing games in particular settings. The changes that accompany participants' efforts after coherence help writers reimagine their identities as members of communities of people who are accomplished in varying degrees in academic literacy practices or as people who wish to forge alliances elsewhere.

Games

In different ways the people I learned about from published studies and from my own work were all learning or teaching different facets of academic writing games, such as game terminology, game rules, and conventions selected from a perplexing array of possibilities. They were also learning to participate, more or less strategically and with varying degrees of expertise, in different sets of game practices and with different sets of players. The roles they were learning to take on ranged from those of players on the sidelines who observed and mimicked more senior players and followed directions from coaches to those of rule-benders, whose seniority allowed them to take chances. Many of the graduate students and young faculty I worked with simultaneously played multiple roles, weaving in and out from positions on the sidelines to positions of greater authority and independence. However, in the settings I became familiar with, roles and practices were not explicitly defined. Because there were few explicit and unambiguous rules—ones that could not be bent, stretched, or interpreted in more than one way—all players necessarily (from a theoretical stance at least) contributed to the reconstruction and reinterpretation of the game itself even if they were not aware of their own roles as agents of construction and change.

One consequence of the lack of absolute clarity as to the rules and of the unequal relations of power among the players was that the participants often enacted their literacy practices under conditions of uncertainty, tension, and frustration. Trial and error thus seemed to be an important aspect of the game. Many of the academic writers that I worked with and read about weren't sure what they were expected to do and reacted to various assignments and tasks with anger, confusion, resistance, cynicism, and avoidance. This reaction was evident not only in the novice undergraduate writers but also in the seasoned academics discussed in the previous chapter who were writing first-person essays for an edited book. The challenge of learning new games can be exhilarating as well, but it helps if the participants voluntarily choose to take them up. In academic settings, of course, choice is a tricky concept. People enter such settings by choice knowing there will be new games to learn, but once in may feel trapped by rules they did not choose and uncomfortable with social and political role relationships they cannot easily escape. For instance, the young bilingual faculty I worked with in Japan conformed to certain games rules with their dissertation advisors in the United States and with senior faculty in the Japanese university but not without some tension and frustration in both settings. Their sense of accomplishment came with effort over time, growing awareness of and familiarity with local practices, and achievement of long-term goals. At the same time, the game players' incomplete knowledge and sense of resistance also contributed in some cases to their roles in changing (even if minimally) some of the academic literacy practices in their local communities.

Whether or not the writers that I came to know in person and through my reading understood clearly the rules of the games they were expected to play, they were all required to produce textual evidence that they knew how to play, from inexperienced freshmen to established faculty. The textual evidence, like the trial and error learning process, was an inseparable requirement of all of the academic literacy games I observed and learned about. The visibility and pervasiveness of textual evidence in academic literacy games have understandably caused many writing researchers and materials developers to focus primarily on the characteristics of texts, to the exclusion or neglect of other less obviously textual aspects of writing games, such as the transitional and identity-shaping dimensions.

Transitions

All the people portrayed in the studies that I have discussed in this book were also experiencing change of one kind or another as they participated in the literacy practices in their academic settings. Perhaps the processes, pace, and nature of change are some of the most difficult aspects of academic enculturation to track, particularly in short-term studies. The real changes, I believe, tend to be invisible, so tracking them requires looking at practices and processes that seem small and superficial, such as learning or teaching how to cite a source at undergraduate and MA levels, and then inferring change or probing in interviews for writers' self-reports of change. We can never be certain. These same small changes can be interpreted as mattering in larger ways, such as students' coming to recognize that their citation and referencing practices can help them situate their work in relation to other established game players, thus helping them to be perceived as legitimate participants in conventional academic conversations. Some changes might look superficial and textual in other words but contribute to or reflect profounder changes in how people learn to participate in literacy practices and in how they view themselves and others in their academic communities.

Change can be experienced as exhilarating but the literature tends to report it more often as a source of discomfort and frustration. Discomfort results partly from the fact that players participate in their writing games at first without the sense of embodied knowledge that fully enculturated members of a community of practice possess. Newcomers to the playing field need to play as if they know what to do and partially enculturated players need to play as if they know more than they do. Change comes about as writers engage in repeated efforts at the games in the presence of more qualified players, who may or may not provide the less experienced writers with explicit game guidelines. Asymmetry is inherent to academic writing games, in other words, and contributes to change as newcomers develop embodied knowledge through interactions over time with more expert players. The case studies discussed in this book testify to some of the discomfort and excitement that the participants experienced as they changed how they viewed their tasks and their roles, how they actually participated in specific literacy practices, and how they pushed at and altered in some cases the conventions of style, form, and content.

Identity

One of the most interesting but least studied changes (most studies being too short) experienced by academic writers is the reimagining of their many identities as they learn the different games in their particular settings. Much research remains to be done in this area and we can hope that more studies like those of Roz Ivanič (1998) and Bonny Norton (2000) will appear in coming years. Many of the studies I reviewed, as well as some of my own work, do not focus specifically on changes in writers' identities, but change is apparent or can be inferred nonetheless. Undergraduates like Yuko (Spack, 1997a) learn that they are survivors or that they can speak with some authority, as did Yasuko's and David's students in the EAP class in Japan (Chapter 2). Masters students like those in the Monterey TESOL program learn to see themselves and their fields with awareness of complexity they did not have before and may learn that they have something to contribute to their field in spite of their continued uncertainty (Chapter 3). PhD students like Nate, Moira, and Virginia figure out who they want or do not want to align themselves with professionally, learning to recognize the political as well as textual facets of these alignments (Chapter 4). Young bilingual faculty like Mr. Kubo and Dr. Sasaki learn how to maneuver flexibly among differently positioned groups, to write as needed for each, and to label themselves accordingly (Chapter 5). Established faculty may learn to reimagine the voices they allow themselves to share in a public forum (Chapter 6).

The identities of the participants in the case studies discussed in this book were thus entangled in the game practices they all participated in but not defined exclusively by them. But, as Hirvela and Belcher (2001) point out, it is difficult to talk about the "academic identities" of the students and teachers in this book in a way that separates these identities from other identities (see the later discussion of Wenger's [1998] "work of reconciliation"). Even in the case of Virginia (Chapter 4), whose strong personal identity linked her academic self inextricably to her Puerto Rican background community in New York and who perceived an uncomfortable gulf between her home and academic communities, it is not possible to talk about either one of these identities without calling up the other. Regardless of how out of place she felt in her elitist PhD program, she could not make her profoundly political and social as well as textual experiences there disappear. Even though she dropped out of the program, her identity, personal and professional, would always include the fact that, having finished her first year successfully, she now held a masters degree from this elitist university. David and Yasuko (Chapter 2), similarly, could not undo their six-plus years of doctoral education and subsequent research and writing activities and dismiss the knowledge, values, and practices they had acquired and now wished to introduce to their undergraduate students—they could not separate their teacher-identities from their own graduate student- and researcher-identities. The MATESOL students (Chapter 3) would never see themselves in the same way after they had completed their grueling masters degree with its heavy emphasis on establishing a professional identity, but also a personal one, through their writing practices. In some cases a field they did not conceive of before entering the program came into existence. In other cases they came to see themselves as potential contributors to a field they had known about before but had participated in only from the sidelines.

The bilingual academics in Japan (Chapter 5) would never be able to fully separate their Japanese academic identities from their identities as graduates from MA and PhD programs in the United States or would they be able to envision themselves only as participants in domestic rather than international academic conversations. The experienced faculty in second language education (Chapter 6) could neither dismiss the ingrained conventions that had shaped their writing and thinking throughout their careers nor erase the influence of the profoundly reflective personal writing experiences they had had that disrupted their more conventional scholarly writing practices. We can talk about different facets of these identities or about people's perceptions that they feel like two (or more) different people, but the different facets are inseparable even if they compete or clash. As Wenger (1998) pointed out, the insurance claims processor does not abandon that identity when the office shuts down each day.

The studies that I reviewed and reported on in this book demonstrate that identities, like game-playing strategies, are always in the process of reconstructing themselves, always in the process of transition particularly in settings where people are learning to participate in practices that are not yet routine to them. Above all, even when experienced as whole and coherent, identities are never singular, but blendings of selves from different personal, work, and academic communities. Once again, as people reconstruct and reimagine their multiple selves, envisioning, trying out, and becoming accustomed to unfamiliar practices and roles within academic communities, they experience the unsettling dissonance (the often exhilarating dissonance) of change.

These particular lenses of games, transitions, and the reimagining of identities through which I have looked at academic literacy practices make the practice of academic writing look complex in different ways than do studies that look primarily at textual aspects of academic writing. However, my own work suffers to some extent because it tends to neglect detailed attention to the written texts that my case study informants produce. I find not surprisingly that the social, political, and textual perspectives of academic writing games play off each other and interweave in ways that are difficult to untangle and difficult to focus on in a balanced way in a single piece of research. It is not my goal to try to do everything, to untangle something that cannot be untangled, to put artificial boundaries around fuzzy concepts, or to categorize the uncategorizable. Still, whether they are concerned with texts, people, or practices, scholars, teachers, and academic writers themselves need to make sense of their experiences, and this sense-making activity is always a serious game in its own right.

EFFORT AFTER COHERENCE

In considering how researchers, teachers, and students work to make sense of their academic literacy practices, I am reminded of some of the work I reviewed in Chapter 1 that deals with people's efforts to construct coherent identities in a complex social world. Adapted to the academic setting, in a world where coherence, complexity, and uncertainty are expected to coexist, these ideas can help us interpret the paradoxical game of effort after coherence.

As Giddens (1991) discussed in his work on self-identity, the humanist longing for certainty, stability, and a coherent sense of self may be part of human nature. In my own work, I pursue the idea that a longing for a stable core helps drive people in their attempts to construct identities in academic settings just as it does in broader social life. I find unsatisfying the postmodern views of the fragmented self that do not posit ways, or even hope, for resolving the fragmentation. We do not need an essentialist view of self in order to accept a view of self that is motivated by a *longing* for an essence or a core as a way to reduce the anxiety that we all face in a world that is full of more complexities and options than we can ever control. How then do people construct coherent identities in the face of such complexities and options, and in the academic setting where we face pressure to complicate our thinking and our practices? Some of the strategies include constructing and revising our biographies (Giddens, 1991), constructing and revising narratives and life stories (Clandinin & Connelly, 1991, 2000; Linde, 1993; Polkinghorne, 1991), and doing the "work of reconciliation" needed to connect people's several identities from the different communities of practice that they participate in (Wenger, 1998). These ideas provide a backdrop for the discussion of more specific ways that researchers, teachers, and students seek coherence in academic literacy games.

Giddens's Reflexive Biographies

One of the themes that intrigues Anthony Giddens in *Modernity and Self-Identity* (1991) is how people manage to construct coherent and stable identities in an age of fragmentation, insecurity, and doubt. Giddens feels that in today's setting of "high modernity," we face challenges that make this goal difficult to reach. He notes that "the self, like the broader institutional contexts in which it exists, has to be reflexively made," but that "this task has to be accomplished amid a puzzling diversity of options and possibilities" (p. 3). Hence the important role of routines and patterns in conjunction with leaps of faith made from an ontologically secure core: The routines and patterns help protect people from being overwhelmed by the complexities of daily life.

It is not only social routines and patterns that help people cope with uncertainty and change. Giddens is also interested in the reflexive nature of self-identity, people's construction of their own biographies via processes involving mediated experiences, and the ways that this reflexive process simultaneously helps structure the broader social system. People make choices that feed back into the construction of self, and the structured and patterned choices that people draw from are themselves constructed, perpetuated, and modified in the process of negotiation. Self-identity thus comes about as individuals continually and reflexively construct and reinterpret their biographies (i.e., as a result of practice in an environment of choices):

> In the post-traditional order of modernity, and against the backdrop of new forms of mediated experience, self-identity becomes a reflexively organised endeavour. The reflexive project of the self, which consists in the sustaining of coherent, yet continuously revised, biographical narratives, takes place in the context of multiple choice as filtered through abstract systems. (p. 5)

The "most elemental feature of reflexive conceptions of personhood," said Giddens, is the "capacity to use 'I' in shifting contexts" (p. 53), to create a flexible biography. In this view, people are seen to have control over the construction of their own identities to the extent that they reflexively and continually revise their own biographies.

Giddens (1991), then, stresses the importance of a person's ability to create a feeling of "biographical continuity" that can be apprehended reflexively and communicated to others to a greater or lesser degree. He points out that biographies are fragile, and require active efforts to sustain: "A person's identity is not to be found in behaviour, nor—important though this is—in the reactions of others, but in the capacity *to keep a particular narrative going*" (p. 54, italics Giddens'). The narrative of self thus weaves concrete events from the past, present, and projected events from the future into one of the many possible stories of self that could be created (p. 55).

Narrative and Story in the Construction of Coherent Identities

As the work of Giddens (1991) suggests, narrative and story are fundamental ways that humans have of constructing order in and making sense of their lives (see also Bruner, 1986, 1990, 1991). Polkinghorne (1991) phrased the function of narrative this way:

Narrative structure is used to make meaningful the actions of friends and acquaintances, public individuals and groups, and governments and institutions. It is also used to interpret and give coherence to past episodes in our own lives and to configure future activities that we expect to lead to desired outcomes. In addition, narrative is used to give form and meaning to our lives as a whole. (p. 143)

Paralleling Giddens' notion of the narrative biography of self is the idea that people's identities are constructed through the stories they create to link and explain events and experiences in their lives. Without the order provided by narrative structures, our lives can seem fragmented and devoid of meaning. For instance, Charlotte Linde (1993) found in her interviews with professional people that her interviewees constructed life stories that pulled together potentially disparate events, ignored ones that did not fit, and created explanations for their behaviors and experiences, all of which helped provide them with coherent identities even during times of change.

Narrative inquiry as a research method in educational settings draws on this fundamental notion that people make sense of their lives, that they construct coherent identities, through the stories they tell and retell (Clandinin & Connelly, 1991, 2000; Conle, 1997, 1999; Connelly & Clandinin, 1990). For example, in her autobiographical story of her experience as an adult learner of Chinese, Jill Bell (1997) takes readers through several stages of her learning process in which her stories shifted from herself as a failure at learning Chinese to one in which she recasts the same events in new and more self-confirmatory ways. The events did not change in any objective sense, in other words, but her construction of the stories about herself did. This research points out that the narrative construction of reality and of identity requires that storytellers flexibly adjust their narratives in times of change without losing the biographical continuity that Giddens (1991) referred to. In their work, Clandinin and Connelly refer to this process as restorying; Polkinghorne, drawing on Ricoeur (1984), refers to it as re-emplotment. As was the case for Linde's (1993) informants and for some my own studies in this book, some of this coherence is no doubt constructed as a result of the narratives that are prompted by the interview process itself, which demands ongoing self-reflection as interviewees tell stories to researchers.

Wenger's "Work of Reconciliation"

Another way to view the construction of coherent identities in a changing and complex environment such as an academic setting is to look at identity as the reconciliation of the many different forms and levels of membership that we all have in multiple communities of practice (Wenger, 1998). Multimembership is a normal part of every person's life, and as Wenger points out, an insurance claims processor does not construct her identity only at work, nor does she lose her identity as a claims processor when she goes home at night. To frame Wenger's ideas in a setting appropriate for this book, members of academic communities participate in a variety of sub-communities in their academic settings in their roles as students, teachers, researchers, or administrators (and often combinations of these), but their identities are shaped as well by countless practices outside academia. Wenger asserts that only through the work of reconciliation can people negotiate a coherent identity from their different forms of membership. This is not just a matter of learning which sets of rules apply when, but of constructing an identity that can help people reconcile these different forms into one nexus (not meant to refer to a singular identity in any essentialized sense). Most pertinent for the cases I present in this book are Wenger's points that "[t]he work of reconciliation may be the most significant challenge faced by learners who move from one community of practice to another" and that the tensions and reconciliations may never be fully resolved (p. 160). The work of reconciliation is ongoing, and constitutes the heart of what it means to be a person.

In studies of academic literacy practices, the search for coherence, meaning, and identity through narrative is central to the lives of people we study. It is also central to the researchers who then write up the stories of the people they study, and to authors who write reviews of the studies of others (stories about stories) and in some cases, such as in this book, authors who write stories about themselves. With these thoughts on coherent identities and with the studies I have presented in this book in mind, let me now look at some ways that researchers, teachers, and writers work to develop a sense of coherence in their academic literacy practices. The search involves another kind of writing game, that of creating a look and sense of coherence to the processes and products of our writing games.

Researchers' Search for Coherence

One of the serious games that writing researchers learn to play is that of using a questioning and skeptical attitude to seek complexity where none may be obvious to the layperson, then imposing clarity and coherence on that complexity in the public documents that result from their work. For instance, studies of writers and their writing practices reveal layers of complexities once we look below the surface, a fact that drives qualitative researchers in particular into frenzies of data management. Making order from mountains of intractable data challenges all researchers, novice and expert alike. Researchers themselves no doubt can recall their own experiences of trying to make sense of the researching and writing games they learned as part of their own enculturation in graduate school.

One way that researchers have of constructing a coherent picture of the game-like aspects of academic writing practices is to throw out ("set aside for later use") most of the data they have collected to focus on just a few aspects of the many possible ones. For example, Connor and Kramer (1995) in their study of five business management students looked at how student writers carried out a single reading–writing task. Berkenkotter, Huckin, and Ackerman (1988, 1991) in their study of Nate were concerned mainly with the writing Nate did for just one professor. And in my study of Virginia in Chapter 4 I concentrated on her writing experiences with just two professors. We may not know or acknowledge how many other writing games these students were immersed in or how their involvement in other games affected the games that the researchers were focusing on.

A related researcher game for reducing complexity is to underreport detail. This is inevitable of course, but is more obvious in some cases than in others. Many of the studies I reported on in this book would have benefited from more detail on aspects of writing games that were not reported. These include Schneider and Fujishima's (1995) study of Zhang and my study of David's and Yasuko's EAP classes in Chapter 2 (Who were Zhang's content class teachers and what did they think of him? Who were David's and Yasuko's students and what did they understand about the writing games they were learning? What academic writing games did they play in Japanese?). Other studies that would have benefited from further detail are: Berkenkotter, Huckin, and Ackerman's (1988, 1991) study of Nate (Who was Nate and what were his experiences writing for his many PhD professors?), Connor's (1999) literacy autobiography in Chapter 5 (What were the real life complexities in this tidy story?), my description of the essay-writing of established faculty in Chapter 6 (What was left unsaid in the author–editor negotiations?), and many other published studies that do not include enough detail for us to get a good sense of the complexity of the different games that writers learn to play or of their personal histories and motivations. We do know, however, that researchers observe, record, think about, and analyze far more than they themselves write about for publication. Depending on the kind of study, some researchers incorporate great detail, particularly in lengthy qualitative studies of writing. In Chiseri-Strater's (1991), Sternglass' (1997), and Ivanič's (1998) book length studies of undergraduate writers, Spack's (1997a) long article on Yuko, and my study of the MATESOL students in Chapter 3 I believe we have enough detail to appreciate the complexity of some of the writing games the students were playing in spite of the necessarily incomplete portrayals even in those studies. Prior's (1998) work too includes great detail, but usually within the context of one small playing field, such as one seminar, among many that students were probably involved in.

The problem with detail, of course, is that it distracts from larger potentially coherent representations at the level of theory. This problem has been discussed by Clandinin and Connelly (2000), among others, in their search for ways to conduct and present research as narratives from the closely observed details of lived experience. Grand theory, the master narratives as they are sometimes called in the educational field, may be coherent but they get in the way of the lives and experiences of real people. Narrative, they and others claim, reflects the ways that people live and interpret their lives and so captures in coherent story form both continuities and discontinuities.

Other scholars have attempted to create coherence by constructing models and employing metaphors. For example, looking at the big picture of academic writing games within which details can fit, David Russell (1995, 1997) and Paul Prior (1998) applied versions of activity theory to academic settings. Rather than growing out of sociology and anthropology, as did some of the theoretical perspectives I discussed in the first chapter, activity theory grew out of a social interpretation of psychological development as first set forth by Vygotsky (1978, 1986) and developed by Soviet psychologists Leont'ev and Luria (Wertsch, 1981) and later by Wertsch (1985, 1991) and his colleagues. Literacy scholars such as Scribner and Cole (1981) developed versions of activity theory in their work, as did Lave and Wenger (1991) and Engestrom (1987, 1993) among others in their studies of learning and interaction in work settings. Russell (1995) reviewed activity theory in a way that is accessible and presents a simple three-part model of writing practice represented as a triangle. From Engestrom (1987), he takes the basic three-part structure of an activity system: a subject (person or people), an object or objective (a shared goal or task), and tools that mediate interactions (physical tools, semiotic and verbal signs). Russell goes on to use a game metaphor, as I have, as a device to construct a coherent picture of specific writing practices within the larger framework of activity theory (cf. Freadman, 1994). Wishing to illustrate that there is no generalizable or autonomous skill called "writing," he notes that different ball games, for example, may share a tool (a ball) in the way that activity systems like disciplines share the tool of writing. However, the kind of game changes the kind of ball that is used and the object of the game changes how the ball is used (Russell, 1995, p. 57). Knowing how to play one kind of ball game may make it easier to learn another in the sense that people learn the activity of playing games, just as they may find it easier to learn a new kind of writing game once they have already acquired skills in another. The tool of writing, however, changes from one activity system to another. The Nobel laureate scientist, Russell says by way of example, may have little idea of how to write up an account of a discovery that is suitable for a newspaper (pp. 58–59). Russell's model and his game analogy, in short, impose coherence on the writing researcher's far more complex world of messy data and unpredictable human behavior.

Prior's (1998) five-part pentagonal model imposes coherence on the complex activity of writing as well, but represents more dimensions and interactions than does Russell's model. This five-part model envisions the following media through which a functional system works: persons, artifacts (physical objects and durable symbolic forms such as language and mathematics), practices (ways of interacting with people and artifacts), institutions (relatively stable social groups), and communities (potentials for alignment when people share experiences). Describing the interactions among different pieces of the activity system verbally as well as graphically, Prior is able to characterize some of the complexity of an activity system in academic settings in ways that are less obvious in the simpler three-part model, although his prose demands patience of the reader. These are some of the ways that researchers use models and analogies to impose clarity and coherence on the messy details of lived experience.

The problem with a researcher's search for coherence through models like those of Prior and Russell is that once we are immersed in a particular setting populated by a small group of very diverse people, the unit of analysis becomes smaller and smaller, eventually becoming unique and thus not easily interpretable within an abstract model. Moreover, boundaries among constituents are inevitable in models whereas they disappear in the intricacies and ambiguities of real settings. It is detailed case studies and textual analyses like Prior's that bring to life a layered, multiperspective view of academic writing practices. Case studies, in other words, recover the intricacies but do not lend themselves to the researcher's effort after coherence through the use of models. They look static even if the label says "this model is dynamic." As Clark and Ivanič (1997) said of their resistance to using models in their work on academic literacy, the visual and abstracted models deceive in their simplicity and coherence. Still, if models can help us interpret detail without glossing over or neglecting that detail, they contribute to researchers' effort to make order of the bits and pieces of their research.

Teachers' Search for Coherence

Teachers, too, whether of writing or of content courses, witness the complexity of writing games on a daily basis. As the coaches of the games, they face new teams of players each semester and each year. If we read about a Zhang, a Yuko, a Lilah, a Kirsten, a Natsuko, or a Virginia, we know that the teachers of these students face a class full of people with diverse backgrounds, motivations, problems, and understandings. How do teachers reconstruct the complex disciplinary knowledge of their fields in ways accessible to such diverse groups of newcomers? Ideally, teachers of undergraduates like David and Yasuko (Chapter 2), of masters students like John and Jean (Chapter 3), and of PhD students like Drs. Adams and Bernstein (Chapter 4) need to find ways to reduce the complexity of their professional academic worlds in order to communicate successfully with students and to design tasks that can be completed in a limited time.

Specific writing tasks and projects, as can be seen from some of the case studies discussed in this book, select and pare down what students need to do from limitless possibilities within disciplines and represent a fraction of teachers' own knowledge and skills. The tasks also convey by their form and function what teachers feel to be the important skills and values for particular groups of students. Of the many possible research games that Yasuko and David could have introduced their young Japanese students to, each teacher chose a different game that resulted in a final paper—one experiential and the other textual. The games themselves were vastly simplified versions of the kinds of research practices the two teachers themselves were involved in: Students had to visit one site and learn about one person or one set of practices in Yasuko's class and to read and summarize five academic articles that supported their paper topics in David's class. In Yasuko's class they had to become aware of and use a simple structure for narrating their experiences, and in David's class they had to follow just one of many possible systems of citation and referencing. Each teacher tried not to overwhelm students, in other words, although students inevitably struggled with the newness and complexity of even these simplified tasks. In the MATESOL program and in the sociology PhD program, the professors stipulated to greater and lesser degrees what students were expected to do on their writing assignments, once again attempting to impose a system, clarity, and coherence on practices they themselves knew were inherently complex and fragmented and that they understood in embodied and tacit ways through years of practice. From Ulla Connor's (1999) literacy autobiography (Chapter 5), we can see how the systematic practices she learned from her mentors and practiced with her colleagues helped her construct a coherent understanding of her field and a coherent narrative of professional identity. Mr. Kubo and Dr. Sasaki learned selected ways of writing and researching from their teachers and mentors in the United States and continued developing versions of the practices they learned in their own professional writing, juggling new games they learned on returning to Japan. In the future, students who worked with them would be similarly enculturated, learning from them selected, simplified ways of thinking and writing as represented in teaching materials and learning activities.

The point to be taken from these examples is that the writing tasks that teachers design for students represent a constructed, deceptively coherent picture of academic communities of practice. It can be no other way, perhaps, because the act of teaching involves settings up comprehensible and feasible opportunities for students to try things they have not tried before. But simplified and ostensibly coherent tasks cannot fully mask the underlying ambiguities, tensions, and complexities in academic fields nor do they capture the tacit, embodied knowledge of experienced practitioners (Lea & Street, 1999). Some of the ambiguities and contradictions are obvious in the very different approaches taken by teachers within the same department or program. Even faced with a step-by-step task, as were some of the students in the MATESOL and sociology PhD programs I observed, students struggled with the newness and the unresolved areas of complexity not addressed by individual writing assignments. Over time students become increasingly aware that their goal as academic writers is not to find coherence but to create it, a process that may involve ignoring the pieces that don't fit (Linde, 1993) as well as developing routines and patterns of thinking and writing that expose opportunities for change and growth within the loopholes.

Academic Writers' Search for Coherence

Students and faculty who write are immersed in the complexities of game playing and of changing practices and identities, but perceive and respond to the complexities differently. The case studies of undergraduate students reviewed in this book lead me to believe that undergraduates are immersed in complexity that they do not see or fully understand. None of the practices they engage in are embodied yet. They have not become routinized or typified in ways described by Schutz (1970) for social life more generally or by Miller (1984), Bazerman (1994b), Swales (1990) and others in genre studies. McCarthy's (1987) Dave, Spack's (1997a) Yuko, and in all probability the students in Yasuko's and David's classes (Chapter 2) knew they were involved in literacy practices they had not experienced before, but saw the game as one of surviving the immediate demands of particular classes or of particular teachers. The MA students in the TESOL program (Chapter 3) also recognized that their survival depended on how they responded to the expectations of individual professors. On the other hand, they also developed awareness of the field of second language education as both more integrated and more complex than they had imagined. They were eventually able to make connections among issues and practices that the undergraduate students were not able to make.

The first-year PhD students like Nate and Virginia (Chapter 4) also struggled within individual courses to make sense of the discipline-based language, concepts, and practices of these courses. However, they also felt the need to see their fields more holistically, to integrate their personal identities and goals into their visions of their fields, and to develop a sense of control over their choices. Rather than a sense of awe of professors and their fields (as Kirsten had described her feelings about her MA professors), Virginia, for one, developed a sense of skepticism. Having just finished undergraduate studies, she learned over the year what she was *not* being taught, and so came to see the field of sociology as much larger than was represented in her two theory courses. The young bilingual faculty in Japan (Chapter 5) had moved from focused PhD work in the United States to a complex social and political environment in a Japanese university where they could not rely exclusively on their English academic writing for career advancement. Given their North American graduate level educational backgrounds, their move to the Japanese setting confronted them with multiple demands from culturally different academic playing fields. Making sense out of their multicultural professional environments was crucial for them to advance professionally. In the cases of the established rule-bending faculty I discussed in Chapter 6, story, narrative, and personal reflection helped all the writers construct meaning and coherence from the complexities of their personal and professional lives without getting rid of the any of the complexities.

In thinking about how academic writers try to make sense of a multitude of possible academic literacy practices and find ways to locate themselves within those practices, I now consider several arenas of practice from which they need to construct meaning.

Coherence in Different Guises in Academic Writing Games

Coherence in any guise is in some sense subjective and unmeasurable, building as it does on perceptions and interpretations of wholeness and continuity rather than on identifiable elements. In discussions of linguistic coherence, a distinction is made between cohesion, where specific linguistic elements hold together a piece of discourse, and coherence, where unity may result from shared experiences and understandings (Connor & Johns, 1990; Halliday & Hasan, 1976; Williams, 1997). Certainly academic writers need to find ways to achieve both linguistic coherence and cohesion in the texts they write, but this is not the kind of coherence I am primarily concerned with. More compatible with the stance taken in this book, although still mainly focused on texts, is Greg Myers's (1999) conceptualization of coherence in academic writing as a social relationship between readers and writers who share background knowledge (p. 53). Broader still are my conceptualizations of coherence inspired by Giddens (1991) and Wenger (1998) in that I am concerned with how people struggle to construct a coherent interpretation of their practices ("This practice makes sense to me") and a coherent academic identity ("I am a person who can participate in academic practices"). I want to conclude by returning to the efforts of real people, to the details of their experiences with academic literacy games.

From the case studies in this book, we can see, for example, how writers' routinization of ostensibly superficial tasks can help them achieve a sense of coherence in their practices and how absence of routinization results in confusion or mindless rule-following. Learning a particular citation and referencing format well enough so it can be used automatically or learning a conventional structure for a specific kind of paper, as did some of the masters students in the TESOL program, eliminates other possibilities for novice writers and helps them focus on other matters. In her MA papers, Karine, on the other hand, had trouble routinizing some of these textual practices, and thus found it difficult to perceive the purposes of or consistently practice such conventions. Similarly, when writers become able to use the specialized language (terminology) of an academic community they develop a sense of coherence in their communicative practices. Virginia struggled with specialized language all year in her first year PhD program, only partially achieving the ability (then giving up the desire) to communicate with "the theorists." Her experiment with formal logic, which never became embodied or routinized, left her feeling confused and ostracized. This example shows the extent to which specialized languages and ways of using language are associated with the concepts and values held by particular professors and with a local sense of coherence among people who successfully adjust to particular programs and classes.

Undergraduates, too, have a particularly difficult challenge making connections between the language and concepts in their classes, given the many "strange lands" (McCarthy, 1987) they inhabit during their college years. Yuko (Spack, 1997a) was nearly defeated by her early inability to find her way through the dense language and concepts of her readings, but found a modicum of coherence in her literacy practices by learning to ignore what she could not understand. Even common sense concepts like "telling a good story," "response," and "interaction" take on specialized meanings as they did in Yasuko's and David's academic reading and writing classes. In some cases, expectations of what adequate responses and interactions consist of remain tacit, leaving students on their own to construct meaning (not of language but of practice) from an overwhelming display of input from teachers and from readings. The efforts are not always successful.

Some of the case studies also show how writers work to achieve coherence in their literacy practices by integrating personal and previous knowledge into academic literacy tasks that were otherwise too unfamiliar to carry out successfully. Yuko did this by contributing her own background knowledge to some her writing assignments, and Yasuko's and David's students did so by controlling the topics and source material of their papers. In the MATESOL program, Kirsten and Kyla, both of whom had experience teaching in Japan, incorporated their experiences there as teachers and language learners into various papers and projects. Virginia sought to make her writing projects in her theory courses meaningful by choosing topics related to Latin America and, in a course for her African-American professor, a topic on Hispanic youth. Prior's (1998) PhD student Moira constructed her major project work around issues of adolescent risk that Prior guesses stemmed from her own background.

Attempts at coherence in another guise come from writers' evolving sense of their own role possibilities and the parameters of their roles (duties, obligations, expectations) as well as from an understanding of who the key players are and what it is that identifies them, even loosely, as members of a group. In academic literacy practices this includes knowing people through a literature in addition to knowing individuals personally. David's undergraduate students and all of the MA students that I worked with were gradually shifting their relationships with the authors they were reading, learning that they were people with whom one could disagree, have a "conversation," and from whom they could build their own ideas. Nate (Berkenkotter, Huckin, & Ackerman, 1988) forged collegial relationships with the professor to whom he was writing his "idea" memos and with Berkenkotter and Huckin, with whom he also shared authorship for some of his first publications. Virginia, on the other hand, distanced herself from her two theory professors, choosing to align herself with others instead. Mr. Kubo and Dr. Sasaki were both in the process of shifting their role responsibilities and relationships from their graduate school contexts to the professional academic context, loosening ties with advisors, reconceptualizing ties with former classmates into collegial and coauthor relationships, and forging new social and political alliances with Japanese colleagues on their campus and in academic associations in Japan. John, Denise, Judy, and I took on unfamiliar personal roles in the writing we did for our edited book, and saw ourselves in new relationships with each other as authors, readers and critics, and editor. Part of achieving coherence of identity in academic writing games, in other words, involves coming to understand what one's relationships are with the key players and to know in particular who the allies are (in the literature and in person).

A sense of coherence of identity and practice also begins to evolve as writers develop a sense of authorship—the feeling that one has something to contribute to an academic conversation. This aspect of coherence was not very obvious in the portrayals of undergraduate writers, in spite of the focus on voice and authority in classes like David's. In many of the studies I reviewed, it appeared that the undergraduates lacked time and experience in a field that interested them, and they did not see their purpose as one of contributing to that field. Still, at the undergraduate level, Yasuko's students all taught her something new in that they had fieldwork experiences that Yasuko had known nothing about beforehand, and a number of David's students wrote papers on topics that he knew little about. The MA students, on the other hand, were learning that part of their responsibilities as credentialed MA holders was to contribute to the field of second language education. They also contributed in some cases to their own professors' evolving knowledge. Some of the MATESOL professors indicated their appreciation of new knowledge in the kinds of feedback they provided the students.

The students also learn that they and their teachers contribute to their fields with varying degrees of authority in relation to different audiences. For example, in David's and Yasuko's undergraduate classes, in the MATESOL classes, and in one of the two theory courses in Virginia's PhD program, peers read and commented on each other's work but not in ways that students felt bound by. Still, in each group, students were learning to speak with (mimic?) authoritative voices about their classmates' writing even though the professors evaluated the writing of all students, holding ultimate power over their success or failure. From the MA level and beyond, students and young faculty also became aware that gatekeepers of other kinds, such as journal editors and older more established colleagues, controlled and evaluated the kinds of contributions their own professors made to professional academic conversations. Mr. Kubo and Dr. Sasaki, needing to construct networks of collegial relationships inside and outside Japan, were subject to control by dissertation advisors, senior colleagues, and journal editors, but both were certain they had contributions to make to their fields. In our book editing project, Sandra Schecter and I were in the sometimes uncomfortable position of playing the roles of gatekeepers with faculty who were far more well-established than we were. Our negotiations complicated the issue of authorship and opened new possibilities for established writers to communicate with readers in ways they had not done before.

A final guise of coherence that I end this discussion with comes from the sense of control that writers develop in their own writing. By this I do not mean that writing becomes a straightforward act of recipe-following (although it may seem so to writers who have not yet developed awareness of the complexities of academic literacy practices), but in the sense that writers do not view their writing problems as insurmountable. Instead, they recognize, as Natsuko did at the end of her MA program, that they cannot escape complexity and ambiguity and that they must develop strategies for trying to construct a coherent self and set of practices in spite of the impossibility of finding the One Right Way. As Russell (1995) noted, they learn how to learn the game.

Reflections on My Effort After Coherence in the Construction of This Book

Because this book represents a decade of my thinking, reading, writing, and researching, one might think a coherent tome would automatically emerge from my millions of keystrokes and pen and pencil scratchings. After all, I am one person, with an ongoing interest in academic literacy in university settings. I read new things each year, but without losing interest in past reading. I write or present something each year that draws on these ongoing interests and readings. This sounds to me like a recipe for a coherent intellectual life. Moreover, each chapter of a book like this represents a piece of a jigsaw of this life, whether that piece be a chronological thread, an issue that persists in intriguing me in a variety of settings and time periods, or contextual continuity given that I tend not to move around much. Why then was it so difficult to put all the pieces together?

As an academic writer and researcher, I faced all the difficulties that I have described above multiplied by the chapters in this book. Each chapter required its own sense of coherence, a challenging task in itself given that I wanted to divide each one into three quite distinct parts. The parts then needed to fit together somehow, and connect to a common framework, even though my own case studies were conducted years apart. And as do all academic writers, I had to imagine a variety of readers, to convince a publisher that the readers were actually there, and then to construct a piece of writing that drew on some recognizable (to publishers and readers) academic conventions to demonstrate that it fit into a niche, however imperfectly. I never reached my goal to my satisfaction and even in final stages of revising continued struggling with many different writing game strategies.

One of the most difficult parts however was trying to express my lived experience, which is chronological but nonlinear, in linear terms, one word after another, one paragraph after another, one chapter after another. Sensation, observation, and thought are multidimensional, and writing is difficult because we try to make them linear. Speech is linear too, but more forgiving in its acceptance of false starts, branchings, interruptions, incompletions, and ellipses. Interestingly, it is when I don't write that my intellectual life feels relatively embodied and coherent. When I try to write and to squeeze thoughts through the narrowest of funnels (i.e., written language) I often bog down. I sympathize here with my eccentric colleague at Keio University, Ted Nelson, the originator of the term "hypertext." Ted has spent his life seeking ways to make representations of knowledge and access to it nonlinear. However, unlike Ted, I see value in the labor-intensive task of transforming experience into lines of words, speech or writing, because my own thinking is transformed in the process, often for the better. My lines of words do not represent truth, of course, but neither do Ted's hypertext journeys.

A related difficulty in achieving coherence in this book had to do not with truth, exactly, but with answers and certainty and assertions on the one hand and questions and uncertainty on the other. The stereotypical piece of academic writing contains assertions, backed up by reasoning and evidence. I did not find a way to fully escape the expectation that a book, or a chapter in a book, be filled with well-organized and supported assertions. But I wanted this book to be filled with questions and reflections on the odd mix of clarity, ambiguity, and paradox that characterizes my thinking about and relation to academic writing. I know more and more and less and less simultaneously. Things that seem simple are really complex, but need to be written about in simple and elegant ways. Creative writing and academic writing are often seen as antithetical, but I can't think or write academically without thinking and writing creatively.

THE END AND THE CONTINUATION

It is the struggle after coherence in the game of academic writing and the eventual acceptance of complexity and uncertainty that seem to me to characterize the phenomenon of academic enculturation and practice. The sense of coherence in practice is constructed from fragments of nonlinear, sometimes contradictory and incompletely perceived experiences rather than developed through pursuit of unambiguous goals. The struggle, both debilitating and exhilarating, is inevitable and cannot, I believe, productively be shortened, simplified, or circumvented. The participants in academic literacy games, with greater or lesser intentionality and agency but never without them, must continually reimagine their stories and images of themselves as writers. And as is clear from the approach I take in this book, it is the individual writer that I am interested in rather than an abstracted model of the activity of writing in academic settings. I am left with unresolved complexity and a surfeit of detail with this approach, and without clear answers to the questions I have raised. These questions apply to me as much as they do to the people I study and read about. I continue, therefore, my effort after coherence in my own professional life, part of which involves trying to understand why I am one of those for whom academic writing doesn't seem to get easier with time. I continue as well, as Dorinne Kondo (1990) would say, to craft a self, in spite of the lingering questions.

Appendices

APPENDIX A: UNDERGRADUATE COURSE IN ACADEMIC READING AND WRITING, GENERAL COURSE DESCRIPTION FOR ADVANCED LEVEL (CHAPTER 2)

This course is designed to help students prepare for graduate study in an English-medium university graduate program. It will familiarize students with reading and writing in academic settings, help them develop a critical and analytic understanding of central arguments, and teach them strategies for reading academic texts and for producing an academic paper. These strategies include: searching for resources from libraries and electronic data bases, citing and referencing sources appropriately, revising, and learning to write with clarity and authorial voice. Students will choose an area of interest to them, and carry out a reading and writing project in this area. TOEFL 550 and above. Enrollment limited to 15.

APPENDIX B: TWO UNDERGRADUATE STUDENT QUESTIONNAIRES ON ACADEMIC WRITING 1 (BEGINNING OF THE SEMESTER) AND 2 (END OF THE SEMESTER) (CHAPTER 2)

(All relevant questions are translated from the original Japanese)

Questionnaire 1

I. Background

1. Sex
2. Department
3. Year
4. Experience Living Abroad
5. Plans after Graduation

II. Writing

6. Have you ever been taught how to write papers in Japanese? If so, when?
7. Have you ever been taught how to write papers in English? If so, when?
8. Do you like writing in Japanese? (Likert scale response)
9. Do you like writing in English? (Likert scale response)
10. From Grade 10 on, what kinds of writing have you done in Japanese?
11. From Grade 10 on, what kinds of writing have you done in English?
12. Do you read any books or magazines in Japanese other than class assignments?
13. Do you read any books or magazines in English other than class assignments?

III. This Course

14. Why did you take this course?
15. What is your goal in this course?

Questionnaire 2

1. What is the topic of your final paper?
2. What was the most difficult aspect of this class?
3. What do you think has benefited you most in this class?
4. Was the class similar to the one you expected before the term started?
5. What were the good aspects of this class?
6. What aspects of the class should be changed for the better?
7. If your friends ask you about this class, what will you tell them about the course?

APPENDIX C: MATESOL PROGRAM INFORMANT
INTERVIEW GUIDELINES (CHAPTER 3)

Interview 1

1. Is there anything from the background questionnaire that you want to comment or expand on?
2. What are your memories about how you learned to write acceptable papers in school (e.g., high school, college)? Does any event or experience stand out for you as memorable?
3. What is your understanding of the term *academic writing*?
4. How important do you think writing is in your present MA program? Explain.
5. When you began your MA program, did you receive any instruction, advice or handouts about writing? If so, describe.
6. What do you think that your MA program expects you to learn about academic writing?
7. In addition to any explicit instruction you might have gotten on how to write for your MA program, in what other ways have you been learning to write your papers?
8. Briefly describe your writing routine in your present MA program.
9. What aspects of your writing in the MA program have you found easy? Difficult?

Interview 2

Past Writing in Your MA Program

1. Considering all the writing that you have done so far in your MA program how would you categorize the kinds or genres of writing? (I know, for example, that in the MIIS program, students do "reaction papers.") In your view, what is the point of each of these kinds of writing?

2. What piece(s) of writing from any previous MIIS classes stands out for you as memorable? (Provide copy if possible) Please describe the past assignment, and discuss why it was memorable. Include comments on what kinds of feedback you have gotten on the paper from your professors, and your response to this feedback.

3. If you have other papers from some or all of the categories of writing that you identified from question 1, tell something about them. What kinds of processes did you go through in preparing the paper? What kinds of feedback did you receive? What was your response to that feedback? What was

your goal in each paper? Why was the paper easy or difficult to write? What is your personal opinion about each paper?

Interview 3

Text-based Interview: Written Feedback from Professors on Specific Papers

1. What, in general, is your view of written feedback from professors in your MA program? What do you think they believe the function of written feedback is? What do you believe the purpose should be?

2. Look at the written feedback provided to you by your professors on several different papers that you have given me copies of. Go through several papers one by one with me. Give the title of the paper, and the class it was written for, so I can be sure to match up your comments with any copies I have. Explain the following, as you understand it. (In the course of our conversation, the items below can be combined in any way you wish.)

   a. What different kinds of feedback are there on the paper? Describe these, and explain what you think their purpose is.
   b. Do you think you received enough feedback on the paper? In your view, what is "enough feedback"?
   c. What is your response to the different kinds of feedback? What do you think you learned from the feedback, if anything? How did the feedback help or not help your writing (thinking-research-practice . . .)?
   d. What other kinds of feedback would you have liked to receive on the paper? (Where are the gaps, for you, in the feedback?) What feedback do you feel was unnecessary?

3. In preparing each paper we talk about, what other oral or written feedback did you get from professors, friends, classmates, etc.? What was the purpose of this feedback? Did you actively seek out this feedback?

4. Any other comments about written feedback that we have not covered?

Interview 4

Commentary on Professors' Written Feedback (Cont'd)

Please refer to the items on Interview 3. Select one or more of your papers to continue commenting on, in the style of Interview 3. Be sure to give the title of the paper and the name of the class you wrote it for, and as you talk, refer to the pages of text that you're commenting on by number. Read any written feedback you'd like to comment on clearly enough so that the tape recorder can pick it up. If you're commenting by e-mail, give the page number and type in the comments you're discussing.

Interview 5

Writing for Different Professors: Similarities, Differences, Issues

In this interview, please talk about what it is like to write for different professors in your current MA program. Some of the issues are related to your comments about the feedback you have gotten on your papers, so feel free to use your papers as a starting point for your discussion. Consider the following:

1. Describe the expectations that different professors have for you in your writing.
2. How do different professors communicate their expectations to you?
3. To what do you attribute the differences among professors?
4. How do you feel about these different sets of expectations? What is it like to write for each of these professors?
5. Are there any other issues that seem important to you on this topic?

Interview 6

Perceptions of Change from First Semester to Now

In this interview, I'd like to learn more about changes that you perceive in yourself, in your writing, and in your perception of the profession of TESOL from the first semester you entered the program.

1. Looking back to your first semester in the MA program, describe how you viewed yourself (your professional identity?), and how your view of yourself has changed, if at all. Do you feel you are still in the process of changing how you see yourself in the field of second and foreign language education? Where do you think you would like to end up (how do you eventually want to see yourself)?
2. Looking back to the first semester, what was it like to do your first writing for this program, and what differences do you perceive now in what it is like to write for your classes? Has your attitude toward your writing changed since the first semester? If so, in what ways?
3. Between the first semester and now, do you perceive that your understanding of or attitude toward the TESOL or foreign language education fields has changed? If so, in what ways?

Interview 7

Current Writing Projects: Description and Update

In this interview, I am interested in learning what writing your are working on now (or very recently, or upcoming projects). As usual, you may combine the following questions in any way you wish.

1. What kind of writing is it? For what purpose?
2. What are you thinking about as you prepare this writing? What issues are you dealing with? (e.g., having to do with the topic? With the process of writing? With formal aspects of the paper? Other?)
3. How are you feeling about your writing these days, and about yourself as a writer in your MA program?

APPENDIX D: SAMPLE ASSIGNMENTS FROM VIRGINIA'S PhD THEORY COURSES (1: THEORY ANALYSIS; 2: THEORY CONSTRUCTION) (CHAPTER 4)

1. Theory Analysis Assignment (from Dr. Adams's handouts)

Exercise #1:

1. Analyze Merton's "Social Structure and Anomie," in Merton, R. K., *Social Theory and Social Structure*," (Revised ed) 185–214.
2. In writing up your analysis,
   1. List the statements in the domain of the theory.
   2. List the basic assumptions, i.e. the underived premises, of the theory.
   3. List the defined terms used in these assumptions and their definitions.
   4. List the statements defining the scope of the theory (if there are any given).
   5. Write a brief (i.e. about a paragraph) precis of the theory.

2. Theory Construction Assignments (from Dr. Bernstein's and Dr. Adams' handouts)

Working Papers

The four working papers present a basic set of core tasks confronted by anyone who undertakes sociological theorizing and research (including most PhD dissertation writers, for example). As earlier noted, these papers are preparation for the course term paper; the working papers have a cumulative character, building on previous papers and laying the foundation for later working papers and the final term paper. Class sessions and readings will provide substantial preparation for writing the working papers, and ongoing assistance will be available from the instructors.

Working Paper #1: Isolating a Problem.

Form an analytical problem that could serve as a focus for developing theoretical ideas and for pursuing empirical inquiry. (In simpler words: try to define a good question that interests you, one that you would like to find or create answers for.)

Your problem/question should be clearly and specifically defined—even if the question is a general or ambitious one. And your problem should not, in your judgment, be a trivial one. (Thus you should spend some time thinking about what distinguishes a good question.)

In addition, you must isolate a problem that enables you to draw upon at least two published empirical studies that you find to be relevant.

(Instructions continue with brief descriptions of 5 required elements of Working Paper #1: Description of problem in the form of a "Why" question; One-paragraph clarification of the question; One-paragraph summary of why the question is a good one; One-to-two paragraph sketch of an argument; Citations for the two relevant studies)

Working Paper #2: Propositions and Conditions

1. For the problem that you have specified in Working Paper #1, provide, if you have not already done so, two or three related empirical observations (i.e., observation statements) that represent the problem. (You may draw these from existing literature.)

2. Develop three alternative knowledge claims, each of which is meant to represent a candidate explanation for your problem. (That is, they are competing "answers" to your question.) The three knowledge claims should be nontrivial ones, i.e., proposition not now known to be obviously true or false. At least one of the three should be original.

Theory Construction Guidelines for Term Paper

1. You are required to:
    (a) formulate a sociological problem;
    (b) justify your problem as worthwhile to study;
    (c) relate your problem to existing theoretical and empirical literature;

(d) develop knowledge claims that bear on the problem; delineate the scope of these knowledge claims;

(e) use these knowledge claims to construct at least one heuristic explanation of two different observation statements from previous research OR two different hypotheses that you have created in thinking about the problems; using your knowledge claims or ideas from other sources, construct one alternative *competing* explanation;

(f) demonstrate by logical analysis that the two observation statements or the two hypotheses are consequences of your two explanans;

(g) develop conceptual definitions of the key theoretical concepts in your formulations;

(h) operationalize those key concepts that need to be operationalized, preferably selecting more than one indicator for each;

(i) use your indicators to generate empirical consequences that will allow you provisionally to prefer one of your explanations to the other;

(j) discuss possible next steps in the research process for three possible outcomes of an empirical test of your explanations—1) Explanation 1 is eliminated in favor of Explanation 2, 2) Explanation 2 is eliminated in favor of Explanation 1 and 3) the research does not allow you to choose between the two explanations.

(The instructions continue for another half page, explaining that the working papers provide most of the material for the paper, that a major literature review is not expected, and that this task resembles what students would do to prepare a prospectus. The final piece of advice is: "Finally, we urge you to be as concise as is consistent with clear, intersubjective understanding of your paper.")

3. Formulate statements defining the scope of each of the three knowledge claims. (The different KCs may have different scope conditions.)

APPENDIX E: GUIDELINES FOR INTERVIEWS 1, 2, AND 3 WITH BILINGUAL ACADEMIC SCHOLARS (CHAPTER 5)

Interview 1: Background

Verify and clarify information from faculty handbook.

General Background

- Tenured/3-year contract/other?

- Spouse? Japanese?
- MA/MS degrees? Where, when, subject?
- Length of time living abroad? When? When returned to Japan?
- Permanent in Japan now? Other plans?
- Frequency of university-related travel outside Japan? Purposes?
- Conferences in Japan? How often? Language(s) spoken at conferences (you and other participants)?
- Conferences outside Japan? How often? Languages spoken?

Writing Background

- Background in writing in Japanese and English? Any specific training in college or graduate school? Courses? Tutors? Seminars?
- Anything memorable about experiences learning to writing?
- Describe what it was like for you to write papers in graduate school in the U.S. and/or in Japan.
- Recall whether there was a special way of talking and writing about issues in your field in Japanese/English? Recall how you learned this discourse?
- Aware of feeling like an outsider at first, then at some point as an insider? In Japanese and English contexts? Describe if possible.
- Recall your first publication? Japanese or English? Why did you publish? Describe the experience for first Japanese and English publications.
- Do you like writing in Japanese? In English?
- In your experience, what has made writing easy or difficult in each language?
- What types of publications have you written in last 2-3 years in Japanese? English?
- What proportion of your professional life do you estimate that you spend writing, or doing work related to completing a publication?
- How much time do you spend writing each week? Regular writing schedule? Sporadic? (including activities related to a writing project, such as reading, revising, proofing)
- Are you working on anything now? What? (Would like to talk with you regularly as you work on a project.)
- Are you willing to lend me copies of your recent publications in Japanese and English so we can talk about them later?
- Copy of CV in English? Japanese?

Interview 2: Contexts of Writing; Attitudes Toward Writing and Publishing

- In your field, what expectations are there about writing and publishing? Within Japan and the Japanese university? Outside Japan?
- Is there pressure to write and publish? If so, from where?
- Is there university support for writing and publishing? Japan? Outside Japan? (financial, merit, other)
- What kinds of publications does the Japanese university (or academic community) value? The American university or academic community? (e.g., are there publications that you do not put on your Japanese or English CV because they will not contribute to or may detract from your professional standing in Japan or outside Japan?)
- What kind of collegial network do you have (e.g., people with whom you do research, write, prepare conference presentations, or generally stay in contact with?) in Japan? Outside Japan?
- Mechanism(s) for maintaining network?
- Are you aware of using specialized and nonspecialized registers in your Japanese and English writing? (e.g., a specialized vocab. or insider language?)
- If so, what is your opinion about the value and function of "insider language"?
- Update on writing you are working on now

Interview 3: More on Writing and Publishing Processes

- How did you learn to write for publication? Any transfer of training or experience from the American to the Japanese context? The Japanese to the American context?
- Your purpose for writing and publishing in Japanese? English?
- Your audience for Japanese and English publications?
- Your sources of information for writing projects in Japanese? English? (readings, original research, discussion with others, conferences, etc.) What readings have you done in both Japanese and English? (Japanese for Japanese publications? English for English publications? Or mixed?)
- Notes and drafts? Thinking and planning? When English and when Japanese?
- What is involved in getting a piece of writing published in Japanese? In English? Describe; give details about specific pieces you've had published.

- Review processes? Gatekeepers?
- Update on current work.

Interview 4 (ff.): Updates on Work; Current Writing Issues

References

Ackerman, J. (1995). Postscript: The assimilation and tactics of Nate. In C. Berkenkotter & T. N. Huckin, *Genre knowledge in disciplinary communities: Cognition/culture/power* (pp. 145–150). Mahwah, NJ: Lawrence Erlbaum Associates.

Allison, D. (1996). Pragmatist discourse and English for academic purposes. *English for Specific Purposes, 15*(2), 85–103.

Anson, C. M., & Forsberg, L. L. (1990). Moving beyond the academic community: Transitional stages in professional writing. *Written Communication, 7,* 200–231.

Atkinson, D. (1997). A critical approach to critical thinking in TESOL. *TESOL Quarterly, 31,* 77–94.

Atkinson, D. (1999). TESOL and culture. *TESOL Quarterly, 33,* 625–654.

Austin, J. L. (1967). *How to do things with words.* Cambridge, MA: Harvard University Press.

Bakhtin, M. M. (1981). *The dialogic imagination: Four essays.* (C. Emerson & M. Holquist, Trans.; M. Holquist, Ed.). Austin: University of Texas Press.

Bakhtin, M. M. (1986). *Speech genres and other late essays.* (V. W. McGee, Trans; C. Emerson & M. Holquist, Eds.). Austin: University of Texas Press.

Barone, T. (1992). A narrative of enhanced professionalism: Educational researchers and popular storybooks about schoolpeople. *Educational Researcher, 21*(8), 15–24.

Bartholomae, D. (1985). Inventing the university. In M. Rose (Ed.), *When a writer can't write* (pp. 134–165). New York: Guilford.

Bartholomae, D. (1995). Writing with teachers: A conversation with Peter Elbow. *College Composition and Communication, 46*(1), 62–71.

Barton, D., Hamilton, M., & Ivanič, R. (Eds.). (2000). *Situated literacies: Reading and writing in context.* London: Routledge.

Baynham, M. (1995). *Literacy practices: Investigating literacy in social contexts.* London: Longman.

Bazerman, C. (1981). What written knowledge does: Three examples of academic discourse. *Philosophy of the Social Sciences, 11,* 361–387.

Bazerman, C. (1984). Modern evolution of the experimental report in physics: Spectroscopic articles in *Physical Review,* 1893–1980. *Social Studies of Science, 14,* 163–196.

Bazerman, C. (1985). Physicists reading physics: Schema-laden purposes and purpose-laden schema. *Written Communication, 2,* 3–23.

Bazerman, C. (1987). Codifying the social scientific style: The APA Publication Manual as behaviorist rhetoric. In J. S. Nelson, A. Megill, & D. N. McCloskey (Eds.), *The rhetoric of the human sciences: Language and argument in scholarship and public affairs* (pp. 125–144). Madison: University of Wisconsin Press.

Bazerman, C. (1988). *Shaping written knowledge: The genre and activity of the experimental article in science.* Madison: University of Wisconsin Press.

Bazerman, C. (1994a). *Constructing experience.* Carbondale, IL: Southern Illinois University Press.

Bazerman, C. (1994b). Systems of genres and the enactment of social intentions. In A. Freedman & P. Medway (Eds.), *Genre and the new rhetoric* (pp. 79–101). London: Taylor & Francis, Ltd.

Bazerman, C. (1995). Response: Curricular responsibilities and professional definition. In J. Petraglia (Ed.), *Reconceiving writing, rethinking writing instruction* (pp. 249–259). Mahwah, NJ: Lawrence Erlbaum Associates.

Beach, K. (1999). Consequential transitions: A sociocultural expedition beyond transfer in education. In A. Iran-Nejad & P. D. Pearson (Eds.), *Review of research in education 24* (pp. 101–139). Washington, DC: American Educational Research Association.

Beaufort, A. (1997). Operationalizing the concept of discourse community: A case study of one institutional site of composing. *Research in the Teaching of English, 31*(4), 486–529.

Becker, H., Geer, B., Hughes, E., & Strauss, A. (1961). *Boys in white: Student culture in medical school.* Chicago: University of Chicago Press.

Belcher, D. (1994). The apprenticeship approach to advanced academic literacy: Graduate students and their mentors. *English for Specific Purposes, 13*, 23–34.

Belcher, D. (1995). Writing critically across the curriculum. In D. Belcher & G. Braine (Eds.), *Academic writing in a second language: Essays on research and pedagogy* (pp. 135–154). Norwood, NJ: Ablex.

Belcher, D., & Connor, U. (Eds.). (2001). *Reflections on multiliterate lives.* Clevedon: Multilingual Matters.

Bell, J. (1997). Shifting frames, shifting stories. In C. P. Casanave & S. R. Schecter (Eds.), *On becoming a language educator: Personal essays on professional development* (pp. 133–143). Mahwah, NJ: Lawrence Erlbaum Associates.

Benesch, S. (1993). ESL, ideology, and the politics of pragmatism. *TESOL Quarterly, 27*, 705–717.

Benesch, S. (1996). Needs analysis and curriculum development in EAP: An example of a critical approach. *TESOL Quarterly, 30*, 723–738.

Benesch, S. (2001). *Critical English for academic purposes: Theory, politics, and practice.* Mahwah, NJ: Lawrence Erlbaum Associates.

Berger, P., & Luckmann, T. (1966). *The social construction of reality.* Garden City, NY: Doubleday.

Berkenkotter, C., & Huckin, T. N. (1995). *Genre knowledge in disciplinary communities: Cognition/culture/power.* Mahwah, NJ: Lawrence Erlbaum Associates.

Berkenkotter, C., Huckin, T. N., & Ackerman, J. (1988). Conventions, conversations, and the writer: Case study of a student in a rhetoric Ph.D. program. *Research in the Teaching of English, 22*, 9–45.

Berkenkotter, C., Huckin, T. N., & Ackerman, J. (1991). Social context and socially constructed texts: The initiation of a graduate student into a writing research community. In C. Bazerman & J. Paradis (Eds.), *Textual dynamics of the professions* (pp. 191–215). Madison: University of Wisconsin Press.

Berkenkotter, C., & Ravotas, D. (1997). Genre as tool in the transmission of practice over time and across professional boundaries. *Mind, Culture, and Activity, 4*, 256–274.

Berne, E. (1964). *Games people play: The basic handbook of transactional analysis.* New York: Ballantine Books.

Bhatia, V. K. (1993). *Analysing genre: Language use in professional settings.* London: Longman.

Bishop, W. (1995). Responses to Bartholomae and Elbow: If Winston Weathers would just write me on e-mail. *College Composition and Communication, 46*(1), 97–103.

Bishop, W. (1997a). Preaching what we practice as professionals in writing. In W. Bishop & H. Ostrom (Eds.), *Genre and writing: Issues, arguments, and alternatives* (pp. 3–16). Portsmouth, NH: Boynton/Cook.

Bishop, W. (1997b). What we don't like, don't admit, don't understand can't hurt us. Or can it? On writing, teaching, living. In J. F. Trimmer (Ed.), *Narration as knowledge: Tales of the teaching life* (pp. 191–201). Portsmouth, NH: Boynton/Cook.

Bishop, W. (1999). Places to stand: The reflective writer-teacher-writer in composition. *College Composition and Communication, 51*(1), 9–31.

Bizzell, P. (1982). College composition: Initiation into the academic discourse community. *Curriculum Inquiry, 12,* 191–207.

Blakeslee, A. M. (1997), Activity, context, interaction, and authority: Learning to write scientific papers in situ. *Journal of Business and Technical Communication, 11*(2), 125–169.

Blanton, L. L. (1999). Classroom instruction and language minority students: On teaching to "smarter" readers and writers. In L. Harklau, K. M. Losey, & M. Siegal (Eds.), *Generation 1.5 meets college composition: Issues in the teaching of writing to U.S.-educated learners of ESL* (pp. 119–142). Mahwah, NJ: Lawrence Erlbaum Associates.

Bleich, D. (1995). Collaboration and the pedagogy of disclosure. *College English, 57*(1), 43–61.

Bleich, D. (1998). *Know and tell: A writing pedagogy of disclosure, genre, and membership.* Portsmouth, NH: Boynton/Cook Heinemann.

Bochner, A. P., & Ellis, C. (1996). Talking over ethnography. In C. Ellis & A. P. Bochner (Eds.), *Composing ethnography: Alternative forms of qualitative writing* (pp. 13–45). Walnut Creek, CA: Altamira Press.

Bogdan, R. C., & Biklen, S. K. (1982). *Qualitative research design for education: An introduction to theory and methods.* Boston: Allyn & Bacon.

Bourdieu, P. (1977a). The economics of linguistic exchanges. *Social Science Information, 16*(6), 645–668.

Bourdieu, P. (1977b). *Outline of a theory of practice.* (R. Nice, Trans.). Cambridge, England: Cambridge University Press.

Bourdieu, P. (1991). *Language and symbolic power* (G. Raymond & M. Adamson, Trans.) (J. B. Thompson, Ed.). Cambridge, MA: Harvard University Press.

Braine, G. (1999a). From the periphery to the center: One teacher's journey. In G. Braine (Ed.), *Non-native educators in English language teaching* (pp. 15–27). Mahwah, NJ: Lawrence Erlbaum Associates.

Braine, G. (Ed.), (1999b). *Non-native educators in English language teaching.* Mahwah, NJ: Lawrence Erlbaum Associates.

Brannon, L. (1993). M[other]: Lives on the outside. *Written Communication, 10*(3), 457–465.

Bridwell-Bowles, L. (1992). Discourse and diversity: Experimental writing within the academy. *College Composition and Communication, 43,* 349–368.

Bridwell-Bowles, L. (1995). Freedom, form, function: Varieties of academic discourse. *College Composition and Communication, 46,* 46–61.

Bridwell-Bowles, L. (1996, August). Master's tools. Paper presented at the NCTE Global Conversations on Language and Literacy, Heidelberg, Germany.

Bridwell-Bowles, L. (1997). Filmclips and the master's tools. In J. F. Trimmer (Ed.), *Narration as knowledge: Tales of the teaching life* (pp. 142–151) Portsmouth, NH: Boynton/Cook.

Britzman, D. P. (1993). Is there a problem with knowing thyself? Toward a post-structuralist view of teacher identity. In T. Shanahan (Ed.), *Teachers thinking, teachers knowing: Reflections on literacy and language education* (pp. 53–75). Urbana, IL: National Council of Teachers of English.

Brodkey, L. (1987). Writing ethnographic narratives. *Written Communication, 4,* 25–50.

Brodkey, L. (1996). Writing on the bias. In L. Brodkey, *Writing permitted in designated areas only* (pp. 30–51). Minneapolis: University of Minnesota Press.

Brown, J. S., Collins, A., & Duguid, P. (1989). Situated cognition and the culture of learning. *Educational Researcher, 18*(1), 32–42.

Brown, J. D., & Yamashita, S. O. (1995). English language entrance examinations at Japanese universities: 1993 and 1994. In J. D. Brown & S. O. Yamashita (Eds.), *Language testing in Japan* (pp. 86–100). Tokyo: Japan Association for Language Teaching.

Bruffee, K. A. (1983). Writing and reading as collaborative or social acts. In J. N. Hays, P. A. Roth, J. R. Ramsey, & R. D. Foulke (Eds.), *The writer's mind: Writing as a mode of thinking* (pp. 159–169). Urbana, IL: National Council of Teachers of English.

Bruner, J. (1986). *Actual minds, possible worlds.* Cambridge, MA: Harvard University Press.

Bruner, J. (1990). *Acts of meaning.* Cambridge, MA: Harvard University Press.

Bruner, J. (1991). The narrative construction of reality. *Critical Inquiry, 18,* 1–21.

Burdell, P., & Swadener, B. B. (1999). Critical personal narrative and autoethnography in education: Reflections on a genre. *Educational Researcher, 28*(6), 21–26.

Campbell, C. (1990). Writing with others' words: Using background reading text in academic compositions. In B. Kroll (Ed.), *Second language writing: Research insights for the classroom* (pp. 211–230). Cambridge, England: Cambridge University Press.

Campbell, J. (1997). Alternative genres for graduate student writing. In W. Bishop & H. Ostrom (Eds.), *Genre and writing: Issues, arguments, alternatives* (pp. 265–275). Portsmouth, NH: Boynton/Cook.

Canagarajah, A. S. (1996). "Nondiscursive" requirements in academic publishing, material resources of periphery scholars, and the politics of knowledge production. *Written Communication, 13*(4), 435–472.

Canagarajah, A. S. (1999). *Resisting linguistic imperialism in English teaching.* Oxford, England: Oxford University Press.

Canagarajah, S. (2001). Addressing issues of power and difference in ESL academic writing. In J. Flowerdew & M. Peacock (Eds.), *Research perspectives on English for academic purposes* (pp. 117–131). Cambridge, England: Cambridge University Press.

Carter, K. (1993). The place of story in the study of teaching and teacher education. *Educational Researcher, 22*(1), 5–12.

Casanave, C. P. (1990). *The role of writing in socializing graduate students into an academic discipline in the social sciences.* Unpublished doctoral dissertation, Stanford University.

Casanave, C. P. (1992a). Cultural diversity and socialization: A case study of a Hispanic woman in a doctoral program in sociology. In D. E. Murray (Ed.), *Diversity as resource: Redefining cultural literacy* (pp. 148–182). Alexandria, VA: TESOL.

Casanave, C. P. (1992b). Educational goals in the foreign language class: The role of content-motivated journal writing. *SFC Journal of Language and Communication, 1,* 83–103.

Casanave, C. P. (1995a). Journal writing in college English classes in Japan: Shifting the focus from language to education. *JALT Journal, 17,* 95–111.

Casanave, C. P. (1995b). Local interactions: Constructing contexts for composing in a graduate sociology program. In G. Braine & D. Belcher (Eds.), *Academic writing in a second language: Essays on research and pedagogy* (pp. 83–110). Norwood, NJ: Ablex.

Casanave, C. P. (1997). Body-mergings: Searching for connections with academic discourse. In C. P. Casanave & S. R. Schecter (Eds.), *On becoming a language educator: Personal essays on professional development* (pp. 187–199). Mahwah, NJ: Lawrence Erlbaum Associates.

Casanave, C. P. (1998). Transitions: The balancing act of bilingual academics. *Journal of Second Language Writing, 7,* 175–203.

Casanave, C. P. (2001, March). *The sociopolitical side of EAP writing instruction.* Paper presented at TESOL 2001, St. Louis, MO.

Casanave, C. P., & Kanno, Y. (1998). Entering an academic conversation: Learning to communicate through written texts. *Keio SFC Review, 3,* 141–153.

Casanave, C. P., & Schecter, S. R. (Eds.). (1997). *On becoming a language educator: Personal essays on professional development.* Mahwah, NJ: Lawrence Erlbaum Associates.

Casanave, C. P., & Vandrick, S. (Eds.). (forthcoming). *Writing for scholarly publication: Behind the scenes in language education.* Mahwah, NJ: Lawrence Erlbaum Associates.

Cassell, P. (Ed.). (1993). *The Giddens reader*. Stanford, CA: Stanford University Press.

Cayton, M. K. (1991). Writing as outsiders: Academic discourse and marginalized faculty. *College English, 53*(6), 647–660.

Chiseri-Strater, E. (1991). *Academic literacies: The public and private discourse of university students*. Portsmouth, NH: Boynton/Cook.

Cintron, R. (1993). Wearing a pith helmet at a sly angle: Or, can writing researchers do ethnography in a postmodern era? *Written Communication, 10*(3), 371–412.

Clandinin, D. J., & Connelly, F. M. (1991). Narrative and story in practice and research. In D. A. Schön (Ed.), *The reflective turn: Case studies in and on educational practice* (pp. 258–281). New York: Teachers College Press.

Clandinin, D. J., & Connelly, F. M. (1994). Personal experience methods. In N. K. Denzin & Y. S. Lincoln (Eds.), *Handbook of qualitative research* (pp. 413–427). Thousand Oaks, CA: Sage.

Clandinin, D. J., & Connelly, F. M. (2000). *Narrative inquiry: Experience and story in qualitative research*. San Francisco: Jossey-Bass.

Clark, R., & Ivanič, R. (1997). *The politics of writing*. London: Routledge.

Clifford, J. (1986). Introduction: Partial truths. In J. Clifford & G. E. Marcus (Eds.), *Writing culture: The poetics and politics of ethnography* (pp. 1–26). Berkeley: University of California Press.

Conle, C. (1996). Resonance in preservice teacher inquiry. *American Educational Research Journal, 33*(2), 297–325.

Conle, C. (1997). Images of change in narrative inquiry. *Teachers and Teaching: Theory and Practice, 3*(2), 205–219.

Conle, C. (1999). Why narrative? Which narrative? Struggling with time and place in life and research. *Curriculum Inquiry, 29*(1), 7–31.

Connelly, F. M., & Clandinin, D. J. (1990). Stories of experience and narrative inquiry. *Educational Researcher, 19*(5), 2–14.

Connor, U. (1996). *Contrastive rhetoric: Cross-cultural aspects of second-language writing*. New York: Cambridge University Press.

Connor, U. (1999). Learning to write academic prose in a second language: A literacy autobiography. In G. Braine (Ed.), *Non-native educators in English language teaching* (pp. 29–42). Mahwah, NJ: Lawrence Erlbaum Associates.

Connor, U. (2000). Variation in rhetorical moves in grant proposals of U.S. humanists and scientists. *Text, 20*(1), 1–28.

Connor, U., & Johns, A. M. (Eds.). (1990). *Coherence in writing: Research and pedagogical perspectives*. Alexandria, VA: Teachers of English to Speakers of Other Languages.

Connor, U. M., & Kramer, M. G. (1995). Writing from sources: Case studies of graduate students in business management. In D. Belcher & G. Braine (Eds.), *Academic writing in a second language: Essays on research and pedagogy* (pp. 155–182). Norwood, NJ: Ablex.

Connor, U., & Mayberry, S. (1996). Learning discipline-specific academic writing: A case study of a Finnish graduate student in the United States. In E. Ventola & A. Mauranen (Eds.), *Academic writing: Intercultural and textual issues* (pp. 231–253). Philadelphia: John Benjamins.

Cope, B., & Kalantzis, M. (Eds.). (1993). *The powers of literacy: A genre approach to teaching writing*. London: The Falmer Press.

Cummins, J. (1981). The role of primary language development in promoting educational success for language minority students. In California State Department of Education (Ed.), *Schooling and language minority students: A theoretical framework* (pp. 3–49). Los Angeles, CA: Evaluation, Dissemination and Assessment Center, California State University.

Cummins, J. (1996). *Negotiating identities: Education for empowerment in a diverse society*. Ontario, CA: California Association for Bilingual Education.

Currie, P. (1993). Entering a disciplinary community: Conceptual activities required to write for one introductory university course. *Journal of Second Language Writing, 2*, 101–117.

Currie, P. (1998). Staying out of trouble: Apparent plagiarism and academic survival. *Journal of Second Language Writing, 7*, 1–18.

Currie, P. (1999). Transferable skills: Promoting student research. *English for Specific Purposes, 18*(4), 329–345.

Dannels, D. P. (2000). Learning to be professional: Technical classroom discourse, practice, and professional identity construction. *Journal of Business and Technical Communication, 14*(1), 5–37.

Deckert, G. (1993). Perspectives on plagiarism from ESL students in Hong Kong. *Journal of Second Language Writing, 2,* 131–148.

Doheny-Farina, S. (1989). A case study of one adult writing in academic and nonacademic discourse communities. In C. B. Matalene (Ed.), *Worlds of writing: Teaching and learning in discourse communities of work* (pp. 17–42). New York: Random House.

Donmoyer, R. (1990). Generalizability and the single-case study. In E. W. Eisner & A. Peshkin (Eds.), *Qualitative inquiry in education: The continuing debate* (pp. 175–199). New York: Teachers College Press.

Eckert, P. (2000). *Linguistic variation a social practice: The linguistic construction of identity in Belten High.* Malden, MA: Blackwell.

Edelsky, C. (1997). Working on the margins. In C. P. Casanave & S. R. Schecter (Eds.), *On becoming a language educator: Personal essays on professional development* (pp. 3–17). Mahwah, NJ: Lawrence Erlbaum Associates.

Eisner, E. (1997). The promise and perils of alternative forms of data representation. *Educational Researcher, 26*(6), 4–10.

Eisner, E. W., & Peshkin, A. (Eds.), (1990). *Qualitative inquiry in education: The continuing debate.* New York: Teachers College Press.

Elbow, P. (1973). *Writing without teachers.* New York: Oxford University Press.

Elbow, P. (1991). Reflections on academic discourse. *College English, 53*(2), 135–155.

Elbow, P. (1995). Being a writer vs. being an academic: A conflict in goals. *College Composition and Communication, 46*(1), 72–83.

Elbow, P. (1999a). In defense of private writing: Consequences for theory and research. *Written Communication, 16*(2), 139–170.

Elbow, P. (1999b). Individualism and the teaching of writing: Response to Vai Ramanathan and Dwight Atkinson. *Journal of Second Language Writing, 8*(3), 327–338.

Ellis, C., & Bochner, A. P. (Eds.). (1996). *Composing ethnography: Alternative forms of qualitative writing.* Walnut Creek, CA: Altamira Press.

Engestrom, Y. (1987). *Learning by expanding: An activity-theoretical approach to developmental research.* Helsinki, Finland: Orienta-Konsultit.

Engestrom, Y. (1993). Developmental studies of work as a testbench of activity theory: The case of primary care medical practice. In S. Chaiklin & J. Lave (Eds.), *Understanding practice: Perspectives on activity and context* (pp. 64–103). Cambridge, England: Cambridge University Press.

Faigley, L., & Hansen, K. (1985). Learning to write in the social sciences. *College Composition and Communication, 34,* 140–149.

Fairclough, N. (1992). *Discourse and social change.* Cambridge, England: Polity Press.

Fanselow, J. (1987). *Breaking rules: Generating and exploring alternatives in language teaching.* New York: Longman.

Fanselow, J. (1997). Postcard realities. In C. P. Casanave & S. R. Schecter (Eds.), *On becoming a language educator: Personal essays on professional development* (pp. 157–172). Mahwah, NJ: Lawrence Erlbaum Associates.

Ferris, D. (1999). The case for grammar correction in L2 writing classes: A response to Truscott (1996). *Journal of Second Language Writing, 8,* 1–11.

Fishman, S. M., & McCarthy, L. P. (1992). Is expressivism dead? Reconsidering its romantic roots and its relation to social constructionism. *College English, 54*(6), 647–661.

Fleck, L. (1935/1979). *Genesis and development of a scientific fact* (F. Bradley & T. Trenn, Trans.). Chicago: University of Chicago Press.

Flower, L. (1994). *The construction of meaning: A social cognitive theory of writing*. Carbondale, IL: Southern Illinois University Press.

Flower, L., & Hayes, J. (1981). A cognitive process theory of writing. *College Composition and Communication, 32*, 365–387.

Flowerdew, J. (1999a). Problems in writing for scholarly publication in English: The case of Hong Kong. *Journal of Second Language Writing, 8*, 243–264.

Flowerdew, J. (1999b). Writing for scholarly publication in English: The case of Hong Kong. *Journal of Second Language Writing, 8*, 123–145.

Flowerdew, J. (2000). Discourse community, legitimate peripheral participation, and the nonnative-English-speaking scholar. *TESOL Quarterly, 34*(1), 127–150.

Fontaine, S. I., & Hunter, S. (Eds.). (1993). *Writing ourselves into the story: Unheard voices from composition studies*. Carbondale, IL: Southern Illinois University Press.

Fox, H. (1994). *Listening to the world: Cultural issues in academic writing*. Urbana, IL: National Council of Teachers of English.

Fox, R. C. (1957). Training for uncertainty. In R. K. Merton, G. G. Reader, & P. L. Kendall (Eds.), *The student-physician: Introductory studies in the sociology of medical education* (pp. 207–241). Cambridge, MA: Harvard University Press.

Fradd, S., & Okhee, L. (1998). Development of a knowledge base for ESOL teacher education. *Teaching and Teacher Education, 14*(7), 761–773.

Freadman, A. (1994). Anyone for tennis? In A. Freedman & P. Medway (Eds.), *Genre and the new rhetoric* (pp. 43–66). London: Taylor & Francis.

Freedman, A. (1993a). Show and tell? The role of explicit teaching in the learning of new genres. *Research in the Teaching of English, 27*(3), 222–251.

Freedman, A. (1993b). Situating genre: A rejoinder. *Research in the Teaching of English, 27*(3), 272–281.

Freedman, A., & Adam, C. (1996). Learning to write professionally: "Situated learning" and the transition from university to professional discourse. *Journal of Business and Technical Communication, 10*(4), 395–427.

Freedman, A., & Adam, C. (2000). Write where you are: Situating learning to write in university and workplace settings. In P. Dias & A. Paré (Eds.), *Transitions: Writing in academic and workplace settings* (pp. 31–60). Cresskill, NJ: Hampton Press.

Freedman, A., Adam, C., & Smart, G. (1994). Wearing suits to class: Simulating genres and simulations as genres. *Written Communication, 11*(2), 193–226.

Freedman, A., & Medway, P. (Eds.). (1994). *Teaching and learning genre*. Portsmouth, NH: Boynton/Cook.

Freeman, D., & Richards, J. C. (Eds.). (1996). *Teacher learning in language teaching*. Cambridge, England: Cambridge University Press.

Frost, P. (1991). Examination hell. In E. R. Beauchamp (Ed.), *Windows on Japanese education* (pp. 291–305). New York: Greenwood Press.

Gee, J. (1990). *Social linguistics and literacies: Ideology in discourses*. Brighton, England: Falmer Press.

Geertz, C. (1983). *Local knowledge: Further essays in interpretive anthropology*. New York: Basic Books.

Geertz, C. (1988). *Works and lives: The anthropologist as author*. Stanford, CA: Stanford University Press.

Geertz, C. (1995). *After the fact: Two countries, four decades, one anthropologist*. Cambridge, MA: Harvard University Press.

Geisler, C. (1992). Exploring academic literacy: An experiment in composing. *College Composition and Communication, 43*(1), 39–54.

Geisler, C. (1994). *Academic literacy and the nature of expertise: Reading, writing, and knowing in academic philosophy*. Hillsdale, NJ: Lawrence Erlbaum Associates.

Giddens, A. (1979). *Central problems in social theory*. Berkeley, CA: University of California Press.

Giddens, A. (1991). *Modernity and self-identity: Self and society in the late modern age*. Stanford, CA: Stanford University Press.

Gilbert, G. N. (1976). The transformation of research findings into scientific knowledge. *Social Studies of Science, 6*, 281–306.

Gilbert, G. N., & Mulkay, M. (1984). *Opening Pandora's box: A sociological analysis of scientists' discourse*. Cambridge, England: Cambridge University Press.

Goffman, E. (1959). *The presentation of self in everyday life*. London: Penguin.

Goffman, E. (1974). *Frame analysis: An essay on the organization of experience*. Boston, MA: Northeastern University Press.

Goffman, E. (1981). *Forms of talk*. Philadelphia: University of Pennsylvania Press.

Gosden, H. (1995). Success in research article writing and revision: A social constructionist perspective. *English for Specific Purposes, 14*(1), 37–57.

Gosden, H. (1996). Verbal reports of Japanese novices' research writing practices in English. *Journal of Second Language Writing, 5*, 109–128.

Gosden, H. (1998). An aspect of holistic modeling in academic writing: Propositional clusters as a heuristic for thematic control. *Journal of Second Language Writing, 17*(1), 19–41.

Gosden, H. (2000). A research-based content course in EAP for graduate students. In A. S. Mackenzie (Ed.), *Content in language education: Looking at the future* (pp. 102–106). Proceedings of the JALT CUE Conference 2000, Tokyo: Japan Association for Language Teaching College and University Educators Special Interest Group.

Greene, S. (1995). Making sense of our own ideas: The problems of authorship in a beginning writing classroom. *Written Communication, 12*(2), 186–218.

Grice, H. (1975). Logic and conversation. In P. Cole & J. Morgan (Eds.), *Syntax and semantics* (Vol. 3: *Speech acts*) (pp. 41–58). New York: Academic Press.

Grumet, M. R. (1988). *Bitter milk: Women and teaching*. Amherst: University of Massachusetts Press.

Grumet, M. R. (1991). The politics of personal knowledge. In C. Witherell & N. Noddings (Eds.), *Stories lives tell: Narrative and dialogue in education* (pp. 67–77). New York: Teachers College Press.

Haas, C. (1994). Learning to read biology: One student's rhetorical development in college. *Written Communication, 11*(1), 43–84.

Halliday, M. A. K. (1978). *Language as social semiotic: The social interpretation of language and meaning*. London: Edward Arnold.

Halliday, M. A. K., & Hasan, R. (1976). *Cohesion in English*. London: Longman.

Hansen, J. (2000). Interactional conflicts among audience, purpose, and content knowledge in the acquisition of academic literacy in an EAP course. *Written Communication, 17*(1), 27–52.

Hansen, K. (1988). Rhetoric and epistemology in the social sciences: A contrast of two representative texts. In D. A. Jolliffe (Ed.), *Writing in academic disciplines* (pp. 167–210). Norwood, NJ: Ablex.

Haraway, D. (1988). Situated knowledges: The science question in feminism as a site of discourse on the privilege of partial perspective. *Feminist Studies, 14*, 575–600.

Harding, S. (1986). *The science question in feminism*. Ithaca, NY: Cornell University Press.

Herndl, C. G., & Nahrwold, C. A. (2000). Research as social practice: A case study of research on technical and professional communication. *Written Communication, 17*(2), 258–296.

Herrington, A. (1985). Writing in academic settings: A study of the contexts for writing in two college chemical engineering courses. *Research in the Teaching of English, 19*, 331–361.

Hinds, J. (1987). Reader vs. writer responsibility: A new typology. In U. Connor & R. B. Kaplan (Eds.), *Writing across languages: Analysis of L2 text* (pp. 141–152). Reading, MA: Addison-Wesley.

Hirvela, A. (1997). "Disciplinary portfolios" and EAP writing instruction. *English for Specific Purposes, 16*(2), 83–100.

Hirvela, A., & Belcher, D. (2001). Coming back to voice: The multiple voices and identities of mature multilingual writers. *Journal of Second Language Writing, 10*(1–2), 83–106.

Huntington, M. J. (1957). The development of a professional self-image. In R. K. Merton, G. G. Reader, & P. Kendall (Eds.), *The student-physician: Introductory studies in the sociology of medical education* (pp. 179–187). Cambridge, MA: Harvard University Press.

Hyland, K. (1996a). Writing without conviction? Hedging in science research articles. *Applied Linguistics, 17,* 433–454.

Hyland, K. (1996b). Talking to the academy: Forms of hedging in science research articles. *Written Communication, 13,* 251–281.

Hyland, K. (1997). Scientific claims and community values: Articulating an academic culture. *Language and Communication, 16*(1), 19–32.

Hyland, K. (1998). Persuasion and context: The pragmatics of academic metadiscourse. *Journal of Pragmatics, 30,* 437–455.

Hyland, K. (1999). Academic attribution: Citation and the construction of disciplinary knowledge. *Applied Linguistics, 20*(3), 341–367.

Hyland, K. (2000). *Disciplinary discourses: Social interactions in academic writing.* London: Longman.

Hyon, S. (1996). Genre in three traditions: Implications for ESL. *TESOL Quarterly, 30*(4), 693–722.

Ivanič, R. (1994). I is for interpersonal: Discoursal construction of writer identities and the teaching of writing. *Linguistics and Education, 6,* 3–15.

Ivanič, R. (1998). *Writing and identity: The discoursal construction of identity in academic writing.* Philadelphia: John Benjamins.

Ivanič, R., & Camps, D. (2001). I am how I sound: Voice as self-representation in L2 writing. *Journal of Second Language Writing, 10*(1–2), 3–33.

Johns, A. M. (1988). The discourse community dilemma: Identifying transferable skills for the academic milieu. *English for Specific Purposes, 7,* 55–60.

Johns, A. M. (1990). Coherence as a cultural phenomenon: Employing ethnographic principles in the academic milieu. In U. Connor & A. M. Johns, (Eds.), *Coherence in writing: Research and pedagogical perspectives* (pp. 209–226). Alexandria, VA: Teachers of English to Speakers of Other Languages.

Johns, A. M. (1991). Interpreting an English competency exam: The frustrations of an ESL science student. *Written Communication, 8,* 379–401.

Johns, A. M. (1995). Teaching classroom and authentic genres: Initiating students into academic cultures and discourses. In D. Belcher & G. Braine (Eds.), *Academic writing in a second language: Essays on research and pedagogy* (pp. 277–291). Norwood, NJ: Ablex.

Johns, A. M. (1997). *Text, role, and context: Developing academic literacies.* Cambridge, England: Cambridge University Press.

Jolliffe, D. A., & Brier, E. M. (1988). Studying writers' knowledge in academic disciplines. In D. A. Jolliffe (Ed.), *Advances in writing research, Vol. Two: Writing in academic disciplines* (pp. 35–87). Norwood, NJ: Ablex.

Kilbourn, B. (1999). Fictional theses. *Educational Researcher, 28*(9), 27–32.

Kirsch, G. (1993). *Women writing the academy: Audience, authority, and transformation.* Carbondale, IL: Southern Illinois University Press.

Kirsch, G. E., & Ritchie, J. S. (1995). Beyond the personal: Theorizing a politics of location in composition research. *College Composition and Communication, 46*(1), 7–29.

Knorr-Cetina, K. D. (1981). *The manufacture of knowledge: An essay on the constructed and contextual nature of science.* Oxford, England: Pergamon.

Kondo, D. K. (1990). *Crafting selves: Power, gender, and discourses of identity in a Japanese workplace.* Chicago: University of Chicago Press.

Kramsch, C., & Lam, W. S. E. (1999). Textual identities: The importance of being non-native. In G. Braine (Ed.), (1999), *Non-native educators in English language teaching* (pp. 57–72). Mahwah, NJ: Lawrence Erlbaum Associates.

Kress, G. (1993). Genre as social process. In B. Cope & M. Kalantzis (Eds.), *The powers of literacy: A genre approach to teaching writing* (pp. 22–37). London: The Falmer Press.

Kubota, R. (1997). A reevaluation of the uniqueness of Japanese written discourse. *Written Communication, 14*(4), 460–480.

Kubota, R. (1999). Japanese culture constructed by discourses: Implications for applied linguistics research and ELT. *TESOL Quarterly, 33*(1), 9–35.

Kuhn, T. S. (1970). *The structure of scientific revolutions* (2nd ed.). Chicago: University of Chicago Press.

Lakoff, R. T. (2000). *The language war.* Berkeley: University of California Press.

Langer, J. A., & Applebee, A. N. (1987). *How writing shapes thinking: A study of teaching and learning.* Urbana, IL: National Council of Teachers of English.

Lather, P. (1991). *Getting smart: Feminist research and pedagogy with/in the postmodern.* New York: Routledge.

Latour, B., & Woolgar, S. (1986). *Laboratory life: The social construction of scientific facts.* Princeton, NJ: Princeton University Press.

Lautamatti, L. (1987). Observations on the development of the topic of simplified discourse. In U. Connor & R. B. Kaplan (Eds.), *Writing across languages: Analysis of L2 text* (pp. 87–114). Reading, MA: Addison-Wesley.

Lave, J. (1993). The practice of learning. In S. Chaiklin & J. Lave (Eds.), *Understanding practice: Perspectives on activity and context* (pp. 3–32). Cambridge, England: Cambridge University Press.

Lave, J. (1996). Teaching, as learning, in practice. *Mind, Culture, and Activity, 3*, 149–164.

Lave, J. (1997). The culture of acquisition and the practice of understanding. In D. Kirshner & J. A. Whitson (Eds.), *Situated cognition: Social, semiotic, and psychological perspectives* (pp. 17–35). Mahwah, NJ: Lawrence Erlbaum Associates.

Lave, J., & Wenger, E. (1991). *Situated learning: Legitimate peripheral participation.* Cambridge, England: Cambridge University Press.

Lawrence-Lightfoot, S., & Davis, J. H. (1997). *The art and science of portraiture.* San Francisco: Jossey-Bass.

Lea, M. R., & Street, B. (1999). Writing as academic literacies: Understanding textual practices in higher education. In C. N. Candlin & K. Hyland (Eds.), *Writing: Texts, processes and practices* (pp. 62–81). London: Longman.

Leki, I. (1992). *Understanding ESL writers.* Portsmouth, NH: Boynton/Cook.

Leki, I. (1995a). Coping strategies of ESL students in writing tasks across the curriculum. *TESOL Quarterly, 29*, 235–260.

Leki, I. (1995b). Good writing: I know it when I see it. In D. Belcher & G. Braine (Eds.), *Academic writing in a second language: Essays on research and pedagogy* (pp. 23–46). Norwood, NJ: Ablex.

Leki, I. (1999a, March). *Is writing overrated?* Paper presented at the Conference on College Composition and Communication, Atlanta, GA.

Leki, I. (1999b). "Pretty much I screwed up": Ill-served needs of a permanent resident. In L. Harklau, K. M. Losey, & M. Siegal (Eds.), *Generation 1.5 meets college composition: Issues in the teaching of writing to U.S.-educated learners of ESL* (pp. 17–43). Mahwah, NJ: Lawrence Erlbaum Associates.

Leki, I., & Carson, J. (1997). "Completely different worlds": EAP and the writing experiences of ESL students in university courses. *TESOL Quarterly, 31*, 39–69.

Li, X. M. (1996). *"Good writing" in cross-cultural context.* Albany, NY: SUNY Press.

Li, X. M. (1999). Writing from the vantage point of an insider/outsider. In G. Braine (Ed.), *Nonnative educators in English language teaching* (pp. 43–55). Mahwah, NJ: Lawrence Erlbaum Associates.

Linde, C. (1993). *Life stories: The creation of coherence.* New York: Oxford University Press.

Liu, J. (1999). Nonnative-English speaking professionals in TESOL. *TESOL Quarterly, 33*(1), 85–102.

Lu, M. Z. (1987). From silence to words: Writing as struggle. *College English, 49*(4), 437–448.

Luke, C., de Castell, S., & Luke, A. (1989). Beyond criticism: The authority of the school textbook. In S. de Castell, A. Luke, & C. Luke (Eds.), *Language, authority and criticism: Readings on the school textbook* (pp. 245–260). London: The Falmer Press.

Lynch, T., & McGrath, I. (1993). Teaching bibliographic documentation skills. *English for Specific Purposes, 12*(3), 219–238.

MacDonald, S. P. (1994). *Professional academic writing in the humanities and social sciences.* Carbondale, IL: Southern Illinois University Press.

Macedo, D. (2000). The colonialism of the English only movement. *Educational Researcher, 29*(3), 15–24.

Margolis, E., & Romero, M. (1998). "The department is very male, very White, very old, and very conservative": The functioning of the hidden curriculum in graduate sociology departments. *Harvard Educational Review, 68*(1), 1–32.

Matsuda, P. K. (1998). Situating ESL writing in a cross-disciplinary context. *Written Communication, 15,* 99–121.

McCarthy, L. P. (1987). A stranger in strange lands: A college student writing across the curriculum. *Research in the Teaching of English, 21,* 233–265.

McCarthy, L. P. (1991). A psychiatrist using DSM-III: The influence of a charter document in psychiatry. In C. Bazerman & J. Paradis (Eds.), *Textual dynamics of the professions: Historical and contemporary studies of writing in professional communities* (pp. 358–378). Madison: University of Wisconsin Press.

McCarthy, L. P., & Gerring, J. (1994). Revising psychiatry's charter document, *DSM IV. Written Communication, 11,* 147–192.

McDermott, R. (1993). The acquisition of a child by a learning disability. In S. Chaiklin & J. Lave (Eds.), *Understanding practice: Perspectives on activity and context* (pp. 269–305). Cambridge, England: Cambridge University Press.

McIntosh, P. (1989). *Feeling like a fraud: Part II.* Work in Progress #37, The Stone Center. Wellesley College, Wellesley, MA.

McKay, S. L., & Wong, S. C. (1996). Multiple discourses, multiple identities: Investment and agency in second-language learning among Chinese adolescent immigrant students. *Harvard Educational Review, 66,* 577–608.

McLaughlin, D., & Tierney, W. G. (Eds.). (1993). *Naming silenced lives: Personal narratives and the process of educational change.* New York: Routledge.

Mehan, H. (1993). Beneath the skin and between the ears: A case study in the politics of representation. In S. Chaiklin & J. Lave (Eds.), *Understanding practice: Perspectives on activity and context* (pp. 241–268). Cambridge, England: Cambridge University Press.

Miller, C.R. (1984). Genre as social action. *Quarterly Journal of Speech, 70,* 151–167.

Miller, C. R. (1994a). Genre as social action. In A. Freedman & P. Medway (Eds.), *Genre and the new rhetoric* (pp. 23–42). London: Taylor & Francis.

Miller, C. R. (1994b). Rhetorical community: The cultural basis of genre. In A. Freedman & P. Medway (Eds.), *Genre and the new rhetoric* (pp. 67–78). London: Taylor & Francis.

Miller, D. (Ed.) (1985). *Popper selections.* Princeton, NJ: Princeton University Press.

Miller, S. M., Nelson, M. W., & Moore, M. T. (1998). Caught in the paradigm gap: Qualitative researchers' lived experience and the politics of epistemology. *American Educational Research Journal, 35*(3), 377–416.

Moore, R., & Muller, J. (1999). The discourse of 'voice' and the problem of knowledge and identity in the sociology of education. *British Journal of Sociology of Education, 20*(2), 189–206.

Morita, N. (2000). Discourse socialization through oral classroom activities in a TESL graduate program. *TESOL Quarterly, 34*(2), 279–310.

Murray, D. E. (1997a). Changing the margins: Dilemmas of a reformer in the field. In C. P. Casanave & S. R. Schecter (Eds.), *On becoming a language educator: Personal essays on professional development* (pp. 179–185). Mahwah, NJ: Lawrence Erlbaum Associates.

Murray, D. E. (1997b). On getting there from here. In C. P. Casanave & S. R. Schecter (Eds.), *On becoming a language educator: Personal essays on professional development* (pp. 209–211). Mahwah, NJ: Lawrence Erlbaum Associates.

Murray, D. M. (1991). All writing is autobiographical. *College Composition and Communication, 42*(1), 66–74.

Myers, G. (1985). The social construction of two biologists' proposals. *Written Communication, 2,* 219–245.

Myers, G. (1989). The pragmatics of politeness in scientific articles. *Applied Linguistics, 10*(1), 1–35.

Myers, G. (1999). Interaction in writing: Principles and problems. In C. N. Candlin & K. Hyland (Eds.), *Writing: Texts, processes and practices* (pp. 40–61). London: Longman.

Neumann, A., & Peterson, P. L. (Eds.). (1997). *Learning from our lives: Women, research, and autobiography in education.* New York: Teachers College Press.

Newkirk, T. (1992). The narrative roots of case study. In G. Kirsch & P. A. Sullivan (Eds.), *Methods and methodology in composition research* (pp. 130–152). Carbondale: Southern Illinois University Press.

Norton, B. (1997). Language, identity, and the ownership of English. *TESOL Quarterly, 31,* 409–429.

Norton, B. (2000). *Identity and language learning: Gender, ethnicity, and educational change.* Harlow, England: Pearson Education Ltd.

Nunan, D. (1992). *Research methods in language learning.* Cambridge, England: Cambridge University Press.

Ochs, E., & Jacoby, S. (1997). Down to the wire: The cultural clock of physicists and the discourse of consensus. *Language in Society, 26*(4), 479–505.

Olsen, J. W. B. (1997). Reflections by fax and e-mail. In C. P. Casanave & S. R. Schecter (Eds.), On becoming a language educator: Personal essays on professional development (pp. 213–220). Mahwah, NJ: Lawrence Erlbaum Associates.

Olson, D. R. (1980). On the language and authority of textbooks. *Journal of Communication, 30,* 186–196.

Ortner, S. B. (1996). *Making gender: The politics and erotics of culture.* Boston: Beacon Press.

Pagano, J. A. (1991). Telling our own stories: The reading and writing of journals or diaries. In C. Witherell & N. Noddings (Eds.), *Stories lives tell: Narrative and dialogue in education* (pp. 193–206). New York: Teachers College Press.

Pally, M. (1997). Critical thinking in ESL: An argument for sustained content. *Journal of Second Language Writing, 6*(3), 293–311.

Parkinson, J. (2000). Acquiring scientific literacy through content and genre: A theme-based language course for science students. *English for Specific Purposes, 19*(4), 369–387.

Paul, D. (2000). In citing chaos: A study of the rhetorical use of citations. *Journal of Business and Technical Communication, 14*(2), 185–222.

Peirce, B. N. (1995). Social identity, investment, and language learning. *TESOL Quarterly, 29,* 9–31.

Pennycook, A. (1994). *The cultural politics of English as an international language.* Harlow, UK: Longman.

Pennycook, A. (1996). Borrowing others' words: Text, ownership, memory, and plagiarism. *TESOL Quarterly, 30,* 201–230.

Penrose, A. M., & Geisler, C. (1994). Reading and writing without authority. *College Composition and Communication, 45*(4), 505–520.

Peshkin, A. (1993). The goodness of qualitative research. *Educational Researcher, 22*(2), 23–29.

Petraglia, J. (Ed.). (1995). *Reconceiving writing, rethinking writing instruction.* Mahwah, NJ: Lawrence Erlbaum Associates.

Phillipson, R. (1992). *Linguistic imperialism*. Oxford: Oxford University Press.

Polanyi, M. (1966/1983). *The tacit dimension*. Gloucester, MA: Peter Smith.

Polkinghorne, D. E. (1991). Narrative and self-concept. *Journal of Narrative and Life History, 12*(2 & 3), 135–153.

Popper, K. R. (1979). *Objective knowledge: An evaluatory approach* (rev. ed.). Oxford: Clarendon Press. (Original work published 1972).

Posteguillo, S. (1999). The schematic structure of computer science research articles. *English for Specific Purposes, 18*(2), 139–160.

Prior, P. (1991). Contextualizing writing and response in a graduate seminar. *Written Communication, 8*, 267–310.

Prior, P. (1994). Response, revision, disciplinarity: A microhistory of a dissertation prospectus in sociology. *Written Communication, 11*, 483–533.

Prior, P. (1995). Redefining the task: An ethnographic examination of writing and response in graduate seminars. In D. Belcher & G. Braine (Eds.), *Academic writing in a second language: Essays on research and pedagogy* (pp. 47–82). Norwood, NJ: Ablex.

Prior, P. (1996, June). *Resituating academic needs: A sociohistoric perspective on literate activity in the academy*. Paper presented at the Knowledge and Discourse conference, Hong Kong.

Prior, P. (1997). Literate activity and disciplinarity: The heterogeneous (re)production of American Studies around a graduate seminar. *Mind, Culture, and Activity: An International Journal, 4*(4), 275–295.

Prior, P. A. (1998). *Writing/disciplinarity: A sociohistoric account of literate activity in the academy*. Mahwah, NJ: Lawrence Erlbaum Associates.

Ramanathan, V. (2000). Review of *Writing/Disciplinarity: A sociohistoric account of literate activity in the academy*. Paul Prior, 1998. *English for Specific Purposes, 19*, 90–93.

Ramanathan, V., & Atkinson, D. (1999). Individualism, academic writing, and ESL writers. *Journal of Second Language Writing, 8*, 45–75.

Ravotas, D., & Berkenkotter, C. (1998). Voices in the text: The uses of reported speech in a psychotherapist's Notes and Initial Assessment. *Text, 18*(2), 211–239.

Reddy, M. J. (1979). The conduit metaphor: A case of frame conflict in our language about language. In A. Ortony (Ed.), *Metaphor and thought* (pp. 284–324). Cambridge, England: Cambridge University Press.

Reynolds, N. (1994). Graduate writers and portfolios: Issues of professionalism, authority, and resistance. In L. Black, D. A. Daiker, J. Sommers, & G. Stygall (Eds.), *New directions in portfolio assessment: Reflective practice, critical theory, and large-scale scoring* (pp. 201–209). Portsmouth, NH: Boynton/Cook.

Ricoeur, P. (1984). *Time and narrative* (K. McLaughlin & D. Pellauer, Trans; Vol. 1). Chicago: University of Chicago Press.

Roen, D. H., Brown, S. C., & Enos, T. (Eds.). (1999). *Living rhetoric and composition: Stories of the discipline*. Mahwah, NJ: Lawrence Erlbaum Associates.

Rogoff, B. (1990). *Apprenticeship in thinking: Cognitive development in social context*. New York: Oxford University Press.

Rosaldo, R. (1987). Where objectivity lies: The rhetoric of anthropology. In J. Nelson, A. Megill, & D. McCloskey (Eds.), *The rhetoric of the human sciences* (pp. 87–110). Madison: University of Wisconsin Press.

Rosaldo, R. (1989/1993). *Culture and truth: The remaking of social analysis*. Boston, MA: Beacon Press.

Rose, M. (1989). *Lives on the boundary*. New York: Penguin Books.

Rose, M. (1995). *Possible lives: The promise of public education in America*. New York: Penguin Books.

Russell, D. R. (1995). Activity theory and its implications for writing instruction. In J. Petraglia (Ed.), *Reconceiving writing, rethinking writing instruction* (pp. 51–77). Mahwah, NJ: Lawrence Erlbaum Associates.

Russell, D. R. (1997). Writing and genre in higher education and workplaces: A review of studies that use cultural-historical activity theory. *Mind, Culture, and Activity, 4*(4), 224–237.

Saks, A. L. (Ed.). (1996). *Viewpoints:* Should novels count as dissertations in education? *Research in the Teaching of English, 30,* 403–427.

Santos, T. (1992). Ideology in Composition: L1 and ESL. *Journal of Second Language Writing, 1,* 1–15.

Schneider, M., & Fujishima, N. K. (1995). When practice doesn't make perfect. The case of an ESL graduate student. In D. Belcher & G. Braine (Eds.), *Academic writing in a second language: Essays on research and pedagogy* (pp. 3–22). Norwood, NJ: Ablex.

Schön, D. (1987). *Educating the reflective practioner: Toward a new design for teaching and learning in the professions.* San Francisco: Jossey-Bass.

Schutz, A. (1970). *On phenomenology and social relations* (H. R. Wagner, Ed.). Chicago: University of Chicago Press.

Scollon, R. (1995). Plagiarism and ideology: Identity in intercultural discourse. *Language in Society, 24,* 1–28.

Scribner, S., & Cole, M. (1981). *The psychology of literacy.* Cambridge, MA: Harvard University Press.

Searle, J. (1969/1978). *Speech acts.* Cambridge, England: Cambridge University Press.

Selzer, J., & Crowley, S. (Eds.). (1999). *Rhetorical bodies.* Madison: University of Wisconsin Press.

Shen, F. (1989). The classroom and the wider culture: Identity as a key to learning English composition. *College Composition and Communication, 40,* 459–466.

Silva, T., Leki, I., & Carson, J. (1997). Broadening the perspective of mainstream composition studies. *Written Communication, 14*(3), 398–428.

Spack, R. (1988). Initiating ESL students into the academic discourse community: How far should we go? *TESOL Quarterly, 29,* 29–51.

Spack, R. (1997a). The acquisition of academic literacy in a second language: A longitudinal case study. *Written Communication, 14,* 3–62.

Spack, R. (1997b). The (in)visibility of the person(al) in academe. *College English, 59,* 9–31.

Spack, R. (1997c). The rhetorical construction of multilingual students. *TESOL Quarterly, 31,* 765–774.

Sternglass, M. S. (1997). *Time to know them: A longitudinal study of writing and learning at the college level.* Mahwah, NJ: Lawrence Erlbaum Associates.

Strauss, A. L. (1987). *Qualitative analysis for social scientists.* Cambridge, England: Cambridge University Press.

Strauss, A., & Corbin, J. (1990). *Basics of qualitative research: Grounded theory procedures and techniques.* Newbury Park, CA: Sage.

Street, B. V. (1995). *Social literacies: Critical approaches to literacy in development, ethnography and education.* London: Longman.

Sullivan, D. (1996). Displaying disciplinarity. *Written Communication, 13*(2), 221–250.

Swales, J. M. (1990). *Genre analysis: English in academic and research settings.* New York: Cambridge University Press.

Swales, J. M. (1997). English as *Tyrannosaurus rex. World Englishes, 16*(3), 383–382.

Swales, J. M., & Feak, C. B. (1994). *Academic writing for graduate students: A course for nonnative speakers of English.* Ann Arbor: University of Michigan Press.

Swales, J. M., & Feak, C. B. (2000). *English in today's research world: A guide for writers.* Ann Arbor: University of Michigan Press.

Swales, J. M., & Najjar, H. (1987). The writing of research article introductions. *Written Communication, 4,* 175–191.

Tang, R., & John, S. (1999). The 'I' in identity: Exploring writer identity in student academic writing through the first person pronoun. *English for Specific Purposes, 18,* S23–S39.

Thompkins, J. (1987). Me and my shadow. *New Literary History, 19,* 169–178.

Thompkins, J. (1990). Pedagogy of the distressed. *College English, 52,* 653–660.

Tierney, W. G. (1993). Self and identity in a postmodern world: A life story. In D. McLaughlin & W. G. Tierney (Eds.), *Naming silenced lives: Personal narratives and the process of educational change* (pp. 119–134). New York: Routledge.

Toulmin, S. E. (1972). *Human understanding: The collective use and evolution of concepts.* Princeton, NJ: Princeton University Press.

Trimmer, J. F. (Ed.). (1997). *Narration as knowledge: Tales of the teaching life.* Portsmouth, NH: Boynton/Cook.

Truscott, J. (1996). The case against grammar correction in L2 writing classes. *Language Learning, 46,* 327–369.

Truscott, J. (1998). Noticing in second language acquisition: A critical review. *Second Language Research, 14,* 103–135.

Truscott, J. (1999). The case for "The case against grammar correction in L2 writing classes": A response to Ferris. *Journal of Second Language Writing, 8,* 111–122.

Vandrick, S. (1999). ESL and the colonial legacy: A teacher faces her 'missionary kid' past. In B. Haroian-Guerin (Ed.), *The personal narrative: Writing ourselves as teachers and scholars* (pp. 63–74). Portland, ME: Calendar Island Publishers.

Van Maanen, J. (1988). *Tales of the field: On writing ethnography.* Chicago: University of Chicago Press.

Vargas, L. (Ed.). (2001). *Women of color in the white college classroom.* New York: Peter Lang.

Villanueva, V. (1993). *Bootstraps: From an American of color.* Urbana, IL: National Council of Teachers of English.

Villanueva, V. (1997). Shoot-out at the I'm OK, you're OK corral. In J. F. Trimmer (Ed.), *Narration as knowledge: Tales of the teaching life* (pp. 43–50). Portsmouth, NH: Boynton/Cook.

Vygotsky, L. S. (1978). *Mind in society: The development of higher psychological processes* (M. Cole, V. John-Steiner, S. Scribner, & E. Souberman, Eds.). Cambridge, MA: Harvard University Press.

Vygotsky, L. S. (1986). *Thought and language* (A. Kozulin, Trans. & Ed.). Cambridge, MA: The MIT Press.

Walvoord, B., & McCarthy, L. (1990). *Thinking and writing in college: A naturalistic study of students in four disciplines.* Urbana, IL: National Council of Teachers of English.

Weedon, C. (1997). *Feminist practice and poststructuralist theory* (2nd ed.). London: Basil Blackwell.

Wenger, E. (1998). *Communities of practice: Learning, meaning, and identity.* Cambridge, England: Cambridge University Press.

Wertsch, J. V. (Ed.). (1981). *The concept of activity in Soviet psychology.* Armonk, NY: M. D. Sharpe.

Wertsch, J. V. (1985). *Vygotsky and the social formation of mind.* Cambridge, MA: Harvard University Press.

Wertsch, J. V. (1991). *Voices of the mind: A sociocultural approach to mediated action.* Cambridge, MA: Harvard University Press.

Williams, J. M. (1997). *Style: Ten lessons in clarity and grace* (5th ed.). New York: Addison-Wesley.

Williams, J. M., & Colomb, G. G. (1993). The case for explicit teaching: What you don't know won't help you. *Research in the Teaching of English, 27*(3), 252–271.

Winsor, D. (1996). *Writing like an engineer: A rhetorical education.* Mahwah, NJ: Lawrence Erlbaum Associates.

Winsor, D. (1999). Genre and activity systems: The role of documentation in maintaining and changing engineering activity systems. *Written Communication, 16*(2), 200–224.

Witherell, C. (1991). The self in narrative. In C. Witherell & N. Noddings (Eds.), *Stories lives tell: Narrative and dialogue in education* (pp. 83–95). New York: Teachers College Press.

Witherell, C., & Noddings., N. (Eds.). (1991). *Stories lives tell: Narrative and dialogue in education.* New York: Teachers College Press.

Wittgenstein, L. (1953). *Philosophical investigations* (G. E. M. Anscombe, trans.). Oxford, England: Basil Blackwell.

Wolcott, H. F. (1990). On seeking—and rejecting—validity in qualitative research. In E. W. Eisner & A. Peshkin (Eds.), *Qualitative inquiry in education: The continuing debate* (pp. 121–152). New York: Teachers College Press.

Wolcott, H. F. (1994). *Transforming qualitative data: Description, analysis, and interpretation.* Thousand Oaks, CA: Sage.

Wood, D., Bruner, J. S., & Ross, G. (1976). The role of tutoring in problem solving. *Journal of Child Psychology and Psychiatry, 17,* 89–100.

Zamel, V. (1995). Strangers in academia: The experiences of faculty and ESL students across the curriculum. *College Composition and Communication, 46*(4), 506–521.

Zamel, V. (1996). Transcending boundaries: Complicating the scene of teaching language. *College ESL, 6*(2), 1–11.

Zamel, V., & Spack, R. (Eds.) (1998). *Negotiating academic literacies: Teaching and learning across languages and cultures.* Mahwah, NJ: Lawrence Erlbaum Associates.

Author Index

Subject Index